Sep 1938

TWENTIETH-CENTURY ECONOMIC HISTORY

TWENTIETH-CENTURY ECONOMIC HISTORY

Critical Concepts in Economics

Edited by
Lars Magnusson

Volume III

LONDON AND NEW YORK

First published 2010
by Routledge
2 Park Square, Milton Park, Abingdon, OX14 4RN

Simultaneously published in the USA and Canada
by Routledge
711 Third Avenue, New York, NY 10017

Routledge is an imprint of the Taylor & Francis Group, an informa business

Editorial material and selection © 2010 Lars Magnusson; individual owners retain copyright in their own material

Typeset in 10/12 pt Times NR MT by Graphicraft Limited, Hong Kong

All rights reserved. No part of this book may be reprinted or reproduced or utilised in any form or by any electronic, mechanical, or other means, now known or hereafter invented, including photocopying and recording, or in any information storage or retrieval system, without permission in writing from the publishers.

British Library Cataloguing in Publication Data
A catalogue record for this book is available from the British Library

Library of Congress Cataloging in Publication Data
Twentieth century economic history / edited by Lars Magnusson.
v. cm. – (Critical concepts in economics)
Includes bibliographical references and index.
ISBN 978-0-415-49607-0 (set) – ISBN 978-0-415-49608-7 (1) –
ISBN 978-0-415-49609-4 (2) – ISBN 978-0-415-49610-0 (3)
– ISBN 978-0-415-49611-7 (4) 1. Economic history–20th century.
2. Economic policy–History–20th century. I. Magnusson, Lars, 1952–
HC54.T78 2010
330.9′04–dc22
2009049996

ISBN10: 0-415-49607-1 (Set)
ISBN10: 0-415-49610-1 (Volume III)

ISBN13: 978-0-415-49607-0 (Set)
ISBN13: 978-0-415-49610-0 (Volume III)

Publisher's Note

References within each chapter are as they appear in the original complete work

CONTENTS

Acknowledgements   vii

Introduction   1

PART 5
The feudal and early modern economy   5

30 The general crisis of the European economy in the 17th century   7
ERIC J. HOBSBAWM

31 The crisis of the 17th century II   26
ERIC J. HOBSBAWM

32 American treasure and the rise of capitalism (1500–1700)   46
EARL J. HAMILTON

33 The rise of the gentry, 1558–1640   65
R. H. TAWNEY

34 Mohammed, Charlemagne and Ruric   99
STURE BOLIN

35 The common fields   130
JOAN THIRSK

36 The efficiency and distributional consequences of eighteenth century enclosures   150
ROBERT C. ALLEN

37 The causes of slavery or serfdom: a hypothesis   171
EVSEY D. DOMAR

38 The rise and fall of a theoretical model: the manorial system   185
STEFANO FENOALTEA

CONTENTS

PART 6
Free trade, mercantilism, and imperialism — 207

39 Manpower and the fall of Rome — 209
    M. I. FINLEY

40 Eli Heckscher and the idea of mercantilism — 215
    D. C. COLEMAN

41 'Imperialism': an historiographical revision — 236
    DAVID K. FIELDHOUSE

42 The imperialism of free trade — 262
    JOHN GALLAGHER AND RONALD ROBINSON

43 Imperialism and the rise and decline of the British economy, 1688–1989 — 278
    PATRICK O'BRIEN

PART 7
The Great Depression — 311

44 A new interpretation of the onset of the Great Depression — 313
    ALEXANDER J. FIELD

45 What ended the Great Depression? — 324
    CHRISTINA D. ROMER

ACKNOWLEDGEMENTS

The publishers would like to thank the following for permission to reprint their material:

Oxford University Press for permission to reprint Eric J. Hobsbawm, 'The General Crisis of the European Economy in the 17th Century', *Past & Present*, 5, 1954, 33–53.

Oxford University Press for permission to reprint Eric J. Hobsbawm, 'The Crisis of the 17th Century II', *Past & Present*, 6, 1954, 44–65.

Taylor & Francis Ltd for permission to reprint Earl J. Hamilton, 'American Treasure and the Rise of Capitalism (1500–1700)', *Economica*, 9, 1929, 338–57. www.informaworld.com

John Wiley & Sons for permission to reprint R. H. Tawney, 'The Rise of the Gentry, 1558–1640', *Economic History Review*, 11, 1941, 1–38.

John Wiley & Sons for permission to reprint Sture Bolin, 'Mohammed, Charlemagne and Ruric', *Scandinavian Economic History Review*, 1, 1953, 5–39.

Oxford University Press for permission to reprint Joan Thirsk, 'The Common Fields', *Past & Present*, 29, 1964, 3–25.

John Wiley & Sons for permission to reprint Robert C. Allen, 'The Efficiency and Distributional Consequences of Eighteenth Century Enclosures', *Economic Journal*, 92, 1982, 937–53.

Cambridge University Press for permission to reprint Evsey D. Domar, 'The Causes of Slavery or Serfdom: A Hypothesis', *Journal of Economic History*, 30, 1, 1970, 18–32. © Economic History Association, published by Cambridge University Press.

Cambridge University Press for permission to reprint Stefano Fenoaltea, 'The Rise and Fall of a Theoretical Model: The Manorial System', *Journal of Economic History*, 35, 2, 1975, 386–409. © Economic History Association, published by Cambridge University Press.

ACKNOWLEDGEMENTS

Viking Penguin, a division of Penguin Group (USA) Inc and The Random House Group Ltd for permission to reprint M. I. Finley, 'Manpower and the Fall of Rome', in *Aspects of Antiquity*, copyright © 1960, 1962, 1964, 1965, 1966, 1967, 1968 by M. I. Finley.

Taylor & Francis Ltd for permission to reprint D. C. Coleman, 'Eli Heckscher and the Idea of Mercantilism', *Scandinavian Economic History Review*, 5, 1, 1957, 3–25. www.informaworld.com

John Wiley & Sons for permission to reprint David K. Fieldhouse, ' "Imperialism": An Historiographical Revision', *Economic History Review*, 14, 2, 1961, 187–209.

John Wiley & Sons for permission to reprint John Gallagher and Ronald Robinson, 'The Imperialism of Free Trade', *Economic History Review*, 6, 1, 1953, 1–15.

New Left Review for permission to reprint Patrick K. O'Brien, 'Imperialism and the Rise and Decline of the British Economy, 1688–1989', *New Left Review*, 238, 1999, 48–80.

Cambridge University Press for permission to reprint Alexander J. Field, 'A New Interpretation of the Onset of the Great Depression', *Journal of Economic History*, 44, 2, 1984, 489–98. © Economic History Association, published by Cambridge University Press.

Cambridge University Press for permission to reprint Christina D. Romer, 'What Ended the Great Depression?', *Journal of Economic History*, 52, 4, 1992, 757–84. © Economic History Association, published by Cambridge University Press.

Disclaimer

The publishers have made every effort to contact authors/copyright holders of works reprinted in *Twentieth Century Economic History (Critical Concepts in Economics)*. This has not been possible in every case, however, and we would welcome correspondence from those individuals/companies whom we have been unable to trace.

INTRODUCTION

This volume deals with a number of topics which spread over a vast territory but which have all been intensely debated among economic historians, some of them ever since the subject was established at the end of the nineteenth century. In 1950 the American Marxist Paul Sweezy published a critical review of Maurice Dobb's contribution to economic history: *Studies in the Development of Capitalism*, published in 1946. As the doyen of British intellectual Marxism at the time, Dobb's publication had been a timely one. At the time there was a heated debate between those who doubted the validity of the concept of capitalism (Eli Heckscher among others) and those like Tawney who defended it as an important tool for designating a historically specific socio-economic system which had been born at a time when another such system, feudalism, dominated the scene but would eventually be replaced by capitalism.[1] Dobb's version of the causes of the rise of capitalism was of course heavily influenced by Marx. He saw the rise of capitalism primarily as an inherent process whereby – from the sixteenth century onwards – new relations of production were established within the handicraft and rural sector, creating a class of producer-capitalists on the one hand and a propertyless proletariat on the other. It was the closure of this process which Sweezy called into question. Instead he pointed to the significance of international exchange, the luxury trades, merchant capitalism and colonialism as the birthplace of the capitalist order. Sweezy's intervention was followed by a rejoinder from Dobb which triggered off the so-called 'transition to capitalism' debate, which involved lengthy discussions.[2]

While this discussion of a transition from feudalism to capitalism may have mainly interested Marxist economic historians, many with other inklings have still been ready to agree that the issue of such a transition, as well as the use of concepts like 'feudalism' and 'capitalism', has at least a heuristic value and can also be useful in understanding economic and social change in Europe from the mediaeval period onwards. Hence, while many have remained sceptical about the use of '-isms' – including concepts like 'mercantilism' and 'imperialism' – viewing them mainly as political and ideological catchwords, it seems that economic history has problems doing without them. Discussing whether or not they are relevant as conceptual tools – as well as their actual definitions – has without doubt been a major occupation among economic historians and has helped to establish the subject and its self-identity.

INTRODUCTION

Then what, for example, was 'feudalism'? Basically it can be understood as a socio-economic system based upon the dominance of agricultural production and its potential to produce a surplus above subsistence level. According to a view still dominant among economic historians, and developed most prominently by M. M. Postan, this system relied upon a delicate balance between production and population. Hence Postan used a simple Ricardo–Malthus model of diminishing returns on land to understand the long cycles of the mediaeval period, during which a great rise in production and population up until the middle of the fourteenth century was followed by a decline triggered off by the Black Death. However, feudalism was also a set of social relations that defined the roles of landlords and peasants, and the haggling between them about the agricultural net surplus – as was pointed out, for example, by Robert Brenner in his famous critique of Postan from the 1970s.[3] The gradual emergence of a free peasant class from serfs working on their landlords' demesnes brought about a tremendous change in these relationships during the feudal age. Especially in the western part of Europe, the emancipation of peasants subsequently led to the emergence of an agricultural revolution with the introduction of new technologies and methods of production. The emergence of enclosures – an often-discussed theme, especially among British economic historians – must be seen in the context of this decline of feudal social relations and the emergence of (petty) capitalist agriculture in the countryside. Moreover, mediaeval society was also inhabited by merchants and artisans, who were often organized in guilds and concentrated around trading towns. An important long-distant trade also grew rapidly from the middle of the fifteenth century onwards.

The rise and increase of international trade has always interested economic historians. The early roots of this long-distance trade before the eleventh century were the topic of the Swedish economic historian Sture Bolin (whose main article is included here), and also formed the main argument of the so-called Pirenne thesis put forward in series of articles in the early 1920s by the Belgian economic historian Henri Pirenne. The latter argued – while Bolin contested – that long-distance trade came to a halt with the emergence of Mohammed and only came into force again hundreds of years later. There is no doubt, however, that international trade increased even more with the opening-up of the Atlantic economy from the late fifteenth century onwards. A number of points have been discussed especially with regard to this period. What was the role of Spanish silver and gold, not only in the rise of international trade but also in the development of capitalism? To what extent did the importation of bullion lead to price inflation in Europe, and what effects did this inflation have on the different economies? To what extent can it help to explain the rise of the north-west (Holland and Great Britain) and the relative decline of Spain (and perhaps also the city-states in Italy)? While there are still no definitive answers to such questions, they have undoubtedly brought about much new historical knowledge about this period and about the role of international trade in the development of modern capitalism.

The emergence of European colonialism and imperialism from the early sixteenth century onwards has had a tremendous effect upon world history ever since. That it has changed the shape of societies and their paths of development – both for the colonialists and the colonized – seems without doubt. The extent to which it also brought about modern industrial growth and the start of the Industrial Revolution – as we argued in the previous volume – has been a keenly debated topic. According to Eric Williams, for example, colonialism (as well as slavery) played a pivotal role in the emergence of capitalism, but this view has been energetically opposed for overstating the role of merchant capital as a major source of capital accumulation and investment in early industry. While there seems to be ample evidence for such a critique – formulated by Charles Kindlerberger, for example, when he insisted that merchant capital played only a small part in this process[4] – the role of colonies and empire may have been important in other respects. The argument that colonies played an important role in reducing the pressure on agriculture and in supporting a growing population, both at home and abroad, has more recently been put forward by so-called world economic historians such as Kenneth Pomeranz (see the introduction to Volume IV). It also leads us to focus on an even broader issue: who were the losers and winners with regard to colonialism and imperialism? As Patrick O'Brien and others have argued, the losers – at least during the nineteenth and twentieth centuries – may very well have been the taxpayers. The winners, on the other hand, were various private interests. But once again a clear answer to this question must include a wide variety of factors, some of which are measurable while others are perhaps not.

A topic closely connected with the birth of economic history as a particular field of study is the controversy surrounding the concept of mercantilism. While it was created as something of a straw man by Adam Smith to bolster his own 'system', many scholars over the years have been highly sceptical as to whether 'mercantilism' or 'the mercantile system' ever was a 'true' system as for example physiocracy. To some extent this goes back to many (mainly British) economic historians, with regard to '-isms' in general. But in this case it is not the whole story. There have been almost endless squabbles about the definition of what might have been the kernel of the mercantile system, from Schmoller to Keynes and Heckscher, and to Brits such as Coleman and Charles Wilson. In general a modern consensus may have emerged that especially Heckscher's all-embracing definition of mercantilism, as not merely a stream of economic thought but also a specific (*dirigiste*) economic policy and a world-view, is perhaps a bit too much to swallow. Thus its usefulness as a tool for understanding economic policies and economic thought in the past is called in question. What is clear, however, is that it played an important role when the subject of economic history was formed more than 100 years ago: the conflicting definitions of mercantilism proposed by Adam Smith and Gustav Schmoller find echoes in the late nineteenth-century discussions between, for example, William Cunningham and W. J. Ashley.

Lastly in the present volume, two articles are included about another landmark occurrence in economic history: the Great Depression of the 1930s. Since the 1970s, several economic historians have tried to analyse the causes of this tumultuous event. Among different scholars there is a distinction between those who view the Great Depression mainly as a consequence of monetary disturbances and those who emphasize the role of the so-called 'real' economy. A modern and more balanced view is presented in contributions by Alex Field and Christina Romer, both included here.

Notes

1 R. H. Tawney, *Religion and the Rise of Capitalism*, London, 1948, p. x f.
2 Some of the most important contributions to this debate are included in Rodney Hilton (ed.), *The Transition from Feudalism to Capitalism*, London: Verso Books, 1978.
3 T. H. Aston and C. H. E. Philpin (eds), *The Brenner Debate*, Cambridge: Cambridge University Press, 1985.
4 See, for example, Charles Kindlerberger, *World Economic Primacy, 1550–1990*, Oxford: Oxford University Press, 1996, p. 212f.

Part 5

THE FEUDAL AND EARLY MODERN ECONOMY

30

THE GENERAL CRISIS OF THE EUROPEAN ECONOMY IN THE 17TH CENTURY

Eric J. Hobsbawm

Source: *Past and Present* 5, 1954: 33–53.

In this article I wish to suggest that the European economy passed through a "general crisis" during the 17th century, the last phase of the general transition from a feudal to a capitalist economy. Since 1300 or so, when something clearly began to go seriously wrong with European feudal society[1] there have been several occasions when parts of Europe trembled on the brink of capitalism. There is a taste of "bourgeois" and "industrial" revolution about 14th-century Tuscany and Flanders or early 16th-century Germany. Yet it is only from the middle of the 17th century that this taste becomes more than a seasoning to an essentially medieval or feudal dish. The earlier urban societies never quite succeeded in the revolutions they foreshadowed. From the early 18th century, however, "bourgeois" society advanced without substantial checks. The 17th century crisis thus differs from its predecessors in that it led to as fundamental a solution of the difficulties which had previously stood in the way of the triumph of capitalism, as that system will permit. In this article I propose to marshal some of the evidence for the existence of a general crisis, which is still disputed by some, and to suggest an explanation of it. In a subsequent article I propose to discuss some of the changes it produced, and how it was overcome. It is very probable that a great deal of historical work will be done on this subject and period in the next few years. Indeed, lately historians in various countries have tentatively suggested something like that "general check to economic development" or general crisis with which this paper deals.[2] It may therefore be convenient to take a bird's eye view of the field, and to speculate about some sort of working hypothesis, if only to stimulate better ones, or further work.

Evidence for a general crisis

A good deal of evidence for the "general crisis" is available. We must, however, be careful to avoid the argument that a general crisis equals economic retrogression, which has bedevilled much of the discussion about the "feudal crisis" of the 14th and 15th centuries. It is perfectly clear that there *was* a good deal of retrogression in the 17th century. For the first time in history the Mediterranean ceased to be a major centre of economic and political, and eventually of cultural influence and became an impoverished backwater. The Iberian powers, Italy, Turkey were plainly on the downgrade: Venice was on the way to becoming a tourist centre. With the exception of a few places dependent on the Northwestern states (generally free ports) and the pirate metropolis of Algiers, which also operated in the Atlantic,[3] there was little advance. Further north, the decline of Germany is patent, though not wholly unrelieved. In the Baltic Poland, Denmark and the Hanse were on the way down. Though the power and influence of Habsburg Austria increased (perhaps largely because others declined so dramatically), her resources remained poor, her military and political structure rickety even at the period of her greatest glory in the early 18th century. On the other hand in the Maritime Powers and their dependencies — England, the United Provinces, Sweden, and in Russia and some minor areas like Switzerland, the impression is one of advance rather than stagnation; in England, of decisive advance. France occupied an intermediate position, though even here political triumph was not balanced by great economic advance until the end of the century, and then only intermittently. Indeed an atmosphere of gloom and crisis fills the discussions there after 1680, though conditions in the previous half-century can hardly have been superior. (Possibly the huge catastrophe of 1693–4 accounts for this.[4]) It was in the 16th not the 17th century that invading mercenaries marvelled at how much there was to loot in France, and men in Richelieu's and Colbert's era looked back on Henry IV's as a sort of golden age. It is indeed possible that, for some decades in the middle of the century the gains made in the Atlantic did not replace the losses in the Mediterranean, Central European and Baltic, the total proceeds from both stagnating or perhaps declining. Nevertheless what is important is the decisive advance in the progress of capitalism which resulted.

The scattered figures for European *population* suggest, at worst an actual decline, at best a level or slightly rising plateau between the mounting slopes of the population curve in the later 16th and 18th centuries. Except for the Netherlands, Norway and perhaps Sweden and Switzerland and some local areas no major increases in population appear to be recorded. Spain was a by-word for depopulation, Southern Italy may have suffered, and the ravages of the mid-century in Germany and Eastern France are known. Though Pirenne has argued that Belgian population increased, figures for Brabant do not seem to bear him out. Hungarian population fell; that of Poland even more. English population growth probably slowed down rapidly and may actually have ceased after 1630.[5] In fact it is not easy to see why Clark concludes that "the 17th century in most of Europe saw, like the 16th, a moderate increase in population."[6] Mortality was certainly higher than in either the 16th or 18th. No century since the 14th has a worse record for epidemic disease and recent work has demonstrated that its ravages cannot be dissociated from those of famine.[7] While a handful of court and administrative metropoles or centres of international trade and finance grew to great size the number of great cities, which had risen in the 16th century, remained stable and small and medium towns frequently declined. This appears to apply in part even to the maritime countries.[8]

What happened to *production?* We simply do not know. Some areas were plainly de-industrialized, notably Italy which transformed itself from the most urbanised and industrialized country of Europe into a typical backward peasant area, most of Germany, parts of France and Poland.[9] On the other hand there was fairly rapid industrial development in some places — Switzerland, and in the extractive industries, England and Sweden, and an important growth of rural out-work at the expense of urban or local craft production in many areas which may or may not have meant a net increase in total output. If prices are any guide we should not expect to find a general decline in production, for the deflationary period which followed the great price-rise of the pre-1640 era is more easily explained by a relative or absolute falling-off in demand rather than by a decline in the supply of money. However, in the basic industry of textiles there may have been not only a shift from "old" to "new" draperies, but a decline of total output for part of the century.[10]

The crisis in *commerce* was more general. The two main areas of established international trade, the Mediterranean and the Baltic underwent revolution, and probably temporary decline in the volume of trade. The Baltic — the European colony of the western urbanized countries — changed its staple exports from foodstuffs to products like timber, metals and naval stores, while its traditional imports of western woollens diminished. Trade as measured by the Sound tolls reached its peak in 1590–1620, collapsed in the 1620s, and declined catastrophically after some recovery until the 1650s, remaining in the doldrums until 1680 or so.[11] After 1650, the Mediterranean became like the Baltic an area exchanging locally produced goods, mainly raw materials, for the Atlantic manufactures and the oriental goods now monopolized by the Northwest. By the end of the century the Levant got its spices from the North, not the East. French Levantine trade halved between 1620 and 1635, sank almost to zero by the 1650s and did not really recover from depression levels until after the 1670s. Dutch Levantine trade did poorly from about 1617 to about 1650.[12] Even then the French hardly exceeded pre-depression levels much before 1700. Did the British and Dutch sales drive in the South make up for losses in the Baltic markets? Probably not. It may barely have made up for the decline in previous sales of Italian products. The international trade in foodstuffs — Baltic corn, Dutch herrings and Newfoundland fish — did not maintain its Jacobean levels. The international trade in woollen cloths may have shrunk; nor was it immediately replaced by other textiles, for the great centres of exportable linen, Silesia and Lusatia, seem to have declined somewhat after 1620. In fact it is not unlikely that a general balance of rising and declining trade would produce export figures which did not rise significantly between 1620 and 1660. Outside the maritime states it is unlikely that sales on the home-markets made up for this.

As we know from the 19th century, the malaise of business cannot be measured simply by trade and production figures, whatever these may be. (It is nevertheless significant that the whole tone of economic discussion assumed stable markets and profit opportunities. Colbertian mercantilism, it has often been said, was a policy of economic warfare for large slices of a world trade-cake of fixed size. There is no reason why administrators and traders — for economics was not yet an academic subject — should have adopted views which were greatly at variance with appearances). It is certain that even in countries which did not decline there were secular business difficulties. English East India trade languished until the Restoration.[13] Though that of the Dutch increased handsomely, the average annual dividend of their East India Company fell for each of the ten-year periods from the 1630s to the 1670s (including both), except for a slight rise in the 1660s. Between 1627 and 1687 sixteen years were without dividend; in the rest of the Company's history from 1602 to 1782 none. (The value of its goods remained stable between 1640 and 1660). Similarly the profits of the Amsterdam Wisselbank reached a peak in the 1630s and then declined for a couple of decades.[14] Again, it may not be wholly accidental that the greatest messianic movement of Jewish history occurred at this moment, sweeping the communities of the great trading centres — Smyrna, Leghorn, Venice, Amsterdam, Hamburg — off their feet with special success in the middle 1660s as prices reached almost their lowest point.

It is also clear that the *expansion of Europe* passed through a crisis. Though the foundations of the fabulous colonial system of the 18th century were laid mainly after 1650[15], earlier there may actually have been some contraction of European influence except in the hinterlands of Siberia and America. The Spanish and Portuguese empires of course contracted, and changed character. But it is also worth noting that the Dutch did not maintain the remarkable rate of expansion of 1600 to 1640 and their Empire actually shrank in the next 30 years.[16] The collapse of the Dutch West India company after the 1640s, and the *simultaneous* winding-up of the English Africa Company and the Dutch West India Company in the early 1670s may be mentioned in passing.

It will be generally agreed that the 17th century was one of *social revolt* both in Western and Eastern Europe. This clustering of revolutions, has led some historians to see something like a general social-revolutionary crisis in the middle of the century.[17] France had its Frondes, which were important social movements; Catalan, Neapolitan and Portugese revolutions marked the crisis of the Spanish Empire in the 1640s; the Swiss peasant war of 1653 expressed both the post-war crisis and the increasing exploitation of peasant by town, while in England revolution triumphed with portentous results.[18] Though peasant unrest did not cease in the West — the "stamped paper" rising which combined middle class, maritime and peasant unrest in Bordeaux and Brittany occurred in 1675, the Camisard wars even later[19] — those of Eastern Europe were more significant. In the 16th century there had been few revolts against the growing enserfment of peasants. The Ukrainian revolution of 1648–54 may be regarded as a major servile upheaval. So must the various "Kurucz" movements in Hungary, their very name harking back to Dozsa's peasant rebels of 1514, their memory enshrined in folksongs about Rakoczy as that of the Russian revolt of 1672 is in the song about Stenka Razin. A major Bohemian peasant rising in 1680 opened a period of endemic serf unrest there.[20] It would be easy to lengthen this catalogue of major social upheavals — for instance by including the revolts of the Irish in 1641 and 1689.

Only in one respect did the 17th century as a whole overcome rather than experience difficulties. Outside the maritime powers with their new, and experimental bourgeois régimes most of Europe found an efficient and stable form of government in *absolutism* on the French model. (But the rise of absolutism has been taken as a direct sign of economic weakness.[21] The question is worth exploring further). The great age of *ad hoc* devices in politics, war and administration vanished with the great world empires of the 16th century, the Spanish and Turkish. For the first time large territorial states seemed capable of solving their three fundamental problems: how to have the orders of government obeyed directly over a large area, how to have enough cash for the large lump-sum payments they periodically needed, and — partly in consequence of this — how to run their own armies. The age of the great independent financial and military sub-contractors faded with the Thirty Years' War. States still had to subcontract, as the practice of selling offices and farming taxes bears witness.[22] However, the whole business was now officially controlled by governments, not merely controlled in practice by the fact that, as the Fuggers and Wallenstein had found to their cost, the monopoly buyer can dictate terms as much as the monopoly seller. Perhaps this obvious political success of the absolutist territorial states with their pomp and splendour has in the past distracted attention from the general difficulties of the age.

If only part of this evidence holds water, we are justified in speaking of a "general crisis" in the 17th century; though one of its characteristics was the relative immunity of the states which had undergone "bourgeois revolution." It is probable — though here we venture on the complex territory of price history[23] — that the crisis began about 1620; perhaps with the slump period from 1619 into the early 1620s. It seems certain that, after some distortion of price movements by the Thirty Years' War, it reached its most acute phase between 1640 and the 1670s, though precise dates are out of order in the discussion of long-term economic movements. From then on the evidence is conflicting. Probably the signs of revival outweigh those of crisis not only (obviously) in the Maritime States but elsewhere. However, the wild oscillations of boom and depression, the famines, revolts, epidemics and other signs of profound economic trouble in 1680–1720 should warn us against ante-dating the period of full recovery. If the trend was upwards from, say, the 1680s—or even earlier in *individual* countries — it was still liable to disastrous fluctuations.

It may, however, be argued that what I have described as a "general crisis" was merely the result of 17th century wars, particularly of the Thirty Years' War (1618–1648). In the past historians have in fact tended to take (or rather to imply) this view. But the crisis affected many parts of Europe not ravaged by generals and quartermasters; and conversely, some traditional "cockpits of Europe" (e.g. Saxony and the Low Countries) did notably better than more tranquil regions. Moreover, there has been a persistent tendency to exaggerate the long-term and permanent damage done by 17th century wars. We now know that (other things being equal) the losses of population, production and capital equipment of even 20th century wars, whose destructive capacities are much greater, can be made good within a matter of 20–25 years. If they were not in the 17th century, it was because wars aggravated already existing tendencies of crisis. This is not to deny their importance, though their effects were more complex than appears at first sight. Thus against the ravages of the Thirty Years' War in parts of Central Europe we must set the stimulus it gave to mining and metallurgy in general, and the temporary booms it stimulated in non-combatant countries (to the temporary benefit of Charles I in the 1630s). It is also probable that, but for it, the great "price-rise" would have ended in the 1610s and not the 1640s. The war almost certainly shifted the incidence of the crisis and may, on balance, have aggravated it. Lastly, it is worth considering whether the crisis did not to some extent produce a situation which provoked or prolonged warfare. However, this point, which is not essential to the argument, is perhaps too speculative to be worth pursuing.

The causes of the crisis

In discussing the 17th century crisis we are really asking one of the fundamental questions about the rise of capitalism: why did the expansion of the later 15th and 16th centuries not lead straight into the epoch of the 18th and

19th century Industrial Revolution? What, in other words, were the obstacles in the way of capitalist expansion? The answers, it may be suggested, are both general and particular.

The general argument may be summarized as follows. If capitalism is to triumph, the social structure of feudal or agrarian society must be revolutionized. The social division of labour must be greatly elaborated if productivity is to increase; the social labour force must be radically redistributed from agriculture to industry while this happens. The proportion of production which is exchanged in the supra-local market must rise dramatically. So long as there is no large body of wage-workers; so long as most men supply their needs from their own production or by exchange in the multiplicity of more or less autarchic local markets which exist even in primitive societies, there is a limit to the horizon of capitalist profit and very little incentive to undertake what we may loosely call mass production, the basis of capitalist industrial expansion. Historically, these processes cannot always be separated from one another. We may speak of the "creation of the capitalist home market" or the divorce of the producers from the means of production which Marx called "primitive accumulation"[24]: the creation of a large and expanding market for goods and a large and available free labour force go together, two aspects of the same process.

It is sometimes assumed that the development of a "capitalist class" and of the elements of the capitalist mode of production within feudal society automatically produce these conditions. In the long run, taking the widest view over the centuries from 1000 to 1800 this is no doubt so. In the shorter run it is not. Unless certain conditions are present — it is by no means yet clear what they are — the scope of capitalist expansion will be limited by the general prevalence of the feudal structure of society, i.e. of the predominant rural sector or perhaps by some other structure which "immobilizes" both the potential labour-force, the potential surplus for productive investment, and the potential demand for capitalistically produced goods, such as the prevalence of tribalism or petty commodity production. Under those conditions, as Marx showed in the case of mercantile enterprise[25] business might adapt itself to operating in a generally feudal framework, accepting its limitations and the peculiar demand for its services, and becoming in a sense parasitic on it. That part of it which did so would be unable to overcome the crises of feudal society, and might even aggravate them. For capitalist expansion is blind. The weakness of the old theories which ascribed the triumph of capitalism to the development of the "capitalist spirit" or the "entrepreneurial spirit" is, that the desire to pursue the maximum profit without limit does not automatically produce that social and technical revolution which is required. At the very least there must be mass production (i.e. production for the greatest aggregate profit — large profits, but not necessarily large profits per sale) instead of production for the maximum profit per unit sale. Yet one of the essential difficulties of capitalist development in societies which keep the mass of the population outside its scope (so that they are neither sellers of labour-power nor serious buyers of commodities) is that in the short view the profits of the really "revolutionary" types of capitalist production are almost less, or look less attractive, than those of the other kind; especially when they involve heavy capital investment. Christian Dior then looks a more attractive proposition than Montagu Burton. To corner pepper in the 16th century would seem much sounder than to start sugar-plantations in the Americas; to sell Bologna silks than to sell Ulm fustian. Yet we know that in subsequent centuries far vaster profits were achieved by sugar and cotton than by pepper and silk; and that sugar and cotton contributed far more to the creation of a world capitalist economy than the other two.

Under certain circumstances such trade could, even under feudal conditions, produce large enough aggregate profits to give rise to large-scale production; for instance if it catered for exceptionally large organizations such as kingdoms or the church; if the thinly spread demand of an entire continent were concentrated into the hands of businessmen in a few specialized centres such as the Italian and Flemish textile towns; if a large "lateral extension" of the field of enterprise took place, e.g. by conquest or colonization. A fair amount of social re-division was also possible without disturbing the fundamentally feudal structure of society — for instance the urbanization of the Netherlands and Italy on the basis of food and raw materials imported from semi-colonial territories. Nevertheless the limits of the market were narrow. Medieval and early modern society was a good deal more like "natural economy" than we care to recall. The 16th and 17th century French peasant is said hardly to have used money except for his transactions with the State; retail trade in German towns was unspecialized, like that in village shops, until the late 16th century.[26] Except among a small luxury class (and even there changing fashion in the modern sense probably developed late) the rate of replacement of clothes or household goods was slow. Expansion was possible and took place; but so long as the general structure or rural society had not been revolutionized it was limited, or created its own limits; and when it encountered them, entered a period of crisis.

The expansion of the 15th and 16th centuries was essentially of this sort; and it therefore created its own crisis both within the home market and the overseas market. This crisis the "feudal businessmen" — who were the richest and most powerful just because the best adapted for making big money in a feudal society — were unable to overcome. Their inadaptability intensified it.

Before analysing these things further, it may be worth stressing that the purely *technical* obstacles to capitalist development in the 16th and 17th century were not insuperable. While the 16th century may not have been capable of solving certain fundamental problems of technique, such as that of a compact and mobile source of power which so baffled Leonardo, it was quite capable of at least as much innovation as produced the 18th century revolution. Nef and others have made us familiar with the innovations which actually occurred, though the phrase "Industrial Revolution" seems less apt for the period 1540–1640 than for the Germany of 1450–1520 which evolved the printing press, effective fire-arms, watches, and the remarkable advance in mining and metallurgy summarized in Agricola's *De Re Metallica* (1556). Nor was there a crippling shortage of capital or capitalist enterprise or of labour, at least in the advanced areas. Sizeable blocks of mobile capital anxious for investment and, especially in the period of rising population, quite important reservoirs of free wage-labour of varying skill existed. The point is, that neither were poured into industry of a potentially modern type. Moreover, methods for overcoming such shortages and rigidities of capital and labour supplies might have been utilized as fully as in the 18th and 19th centuries. The 17th century crisis cannot be explained by the inadequacies of the equipment for Industrial Revolution, in any narrowly technical and organizational sense.

Let us now turn to the main causes of the crisis.

The specialization of "feudal capitalists": the case of Italy

The decline of Italy (and the old centres of medieval commerce and manufacture in general) was the most dramatic result of the crisis. It illustrates the weaknesses of "capitalism" parasitic on a feudal world. Thus 16th century Italians probably controlled the greatest agglomerations of capital, but misinvested them flagrantly. They immobilized them in buildings and squandered them in foreign lending during the price-revolution (which naturally favoured debtors) or diverted them from manufacturing activities to various forms of immobile investment. It has been plausibly suggested that the failure of Italian manufacture to maintain itself against Dutch, English and French during the 17th century was due to this diversion of resources.[27] It would be ironic to find that the Medici were Italy's ruin, not only as bankers but as patrons of the expensive arts, and philistine historians are welcome to observe that the only major city state which never produced any art worth mentioning, Genoa, maintained its commerce and finance better than the rest. Yet Italian investors, who had long been aware that too large cathedrals harm business,[28] were acting quite sensibly. The experience of centuries had shown that the highest profits were not to be got in technical progress or even in production. They had adapted themselves to business activities in the comparatively narrow field which remained for them once one left aside the majority of the population of Europe as "economically neutral." If they spent vast amounts of capital non-productively, it may have been simply because there was no more room to invest it progressively on any scale within the limits of this "capitalist sector." (The 17th century Dutch palliated a similar glut of capital by multiplying household goods and works of art[29] though they also discovered the more modern device of a speculative investment boom). Perhaps the Italians would have been shocked into different behaviour by economic adversity; though they had made money for so long by providing the feudal world with its trade and finance that they would not have learned easily. However, the general boom of the later 16th century (like the "Indian summer" of Edwardian Britain) and the suddenly expanded demands of the great absolute monarchies which relied on private contractors, and the unprecedented luxury of their aristocracies, postponed the evil day. When it came, bringing decay to Italian trade and manufacture, it left Italian finance still upright, though no longer dominant. Again, Italian industry might well have maintained some of its old positions by switching more completely from its old high-quality goods to the shoddier and cheaper new draperies of the North. But who, in the great period of luxury buying from 1580–1620 would guess that the future of high-quality textiles was limited? Did not the court of Lorraine, in the first third of the century use more textiles imported from Italy than from all other non-French countries put together?[30] (One would like to reserve judgment on the argument that Italy lost ground because of higher production costs for goods of equal quality, until stronger evidence for it is brought forward or until we have a satisfactory explanation for the failure of Italian production, after promising beginnings, to shift as wholeheartedly from towns to countryside as did the textile industries of other countries.[31])

The case of Italy shows why particular countries went down in the crisis, not necessarily why it occurred. We must therefore consider the contradictions of the very process of 16th century expansion.

The contradictions of expansion: Eastern Europe

The comparative specialization of west-European towns on trade and manufacture was to some extent achieved in the 15th and 16th centuries by the creation of a sizeable surplus of exportable food in Eastern Europe and perhaps by ocean fisheries.[32] But in Eastern Europe this was achieved by the creation of serf agriculture on a large scale; i.e. a local strengthening of feudalism. This, we may suggest, had three effects. It turned the peasant into less of a cash customer than he had been or might have been. (Or else it forced him off good-quality western textiles into cheap locally produced cloth). It diminished the number and wealth of the minor nobility for the benefit of a handful of magnates. In Poland the former controlled 43.8% of ploughs in the mid-15th century, 11.6% in the mid-17th; the share of the latter rose from 13.3 to 30.7 in the same period. Lastly, it sacrificed the livelier market of the towns to the free trade interests of exporting landlords, or else seized much of what trade was going for the benefit of the already bloated lords.[33] The expansion thus had two results. While creating the conditions for the expansion of manufactures in Western Europe, it cut down, for a time at least, the outlets of these manufactures in the Baltic area — perhaps its most important market. The desire to cash in rapidly on the growing demand for corn — the Baltic now began to feed not only Northern Europe but also the Mediterranean — tempted serf-lords into that headlong expansion of their dominions and intensification of exploitation which led to the Ukrainian revolution, and perhaps also to demographic catastrophes.[34]

The contradictions of expansion: overseas and colonial markets

Much of the trade between Europe and the rest of the world had, as we know, been passive throughout the ages, because Orientals did not need European goods to the same extent as Europe needed theirs. It had been balanced by bullion payments, supplemented from time to time by such exports as slaves, furs, amber or other luxuries. Until the Industrial Revolution the sales of European manufactures were not important. (African trade, which was not deficitary, may be an exception because of the staggeringly favourable terms of trade which European goods commanded among the ignorant local buyers and indeed — almost by definition — because the continent was valued chiefly as a source of bullion until late in the 17th century. In 1665 the Royal African Company still estimated its gain from gold at twice its gain from slaves.[35]) The European conquest of the main trade-routes and of America did not change this structure fundamentally, for even the Americas exported more than they imported. It greatly diminished the cost of Eastern goods by cutting out middlemen, lessening transport charges and enabling European merchants and armed bands to rob and cheat with impunity. It also greatly increased bullion supplies, presenting us with American and African Peters to be robbed to pay the Asian Pauls. Unquestionably Europe derived immense windfall gains from this. General business activity was immensely stimulated as well as capital accumulated; but our exports of manufactures were on the whole *not* greatly expanded. Colonial powers — in good medieval business tradition — followed a policy of systematic restriction of output and systematic monopoly. Hence there was no reason why exports of home manufactures should benefit.

The benefit which Europe drew from these initial conquests was thus in the nature of a single bonus rather than a regular dividend. When it was exhausted, crisis was likely to follow. Among the colonial powers costs and overheads rose faster than profits. In both East and West we may distinguish three stages: that of easy profits, that of crisis, and with luck eventually that of a stable and more modest prosperity. In the initial phase conquest or interloping brought temporarily unchallenged profits at low costs. In the East, where profits rested on the monopoly of a restricted output of spices and the like, the crisis was probably brought on by the steep rise in "protection costs" against old and new rivals; rising all the more steeply the more the colonial power tried to screw up the monopoly price. It has been estimated that the Portuguese spice trade barely paid its way for these reasons.[36] In the West, where they rested on the cheap bulk production of bullion and other raw materials, protection costs probably played a smaller part, though they also rose with piracy and competition. However, there the technical limits of the primitive "rat-hole" mining of the Spaniards were soon reached (even allowing for the uses of the mercury process), and very possibly the labour force was virtually worked to death, being treated as an expendable asset.[37] At any rate American silver exports diminished after 1610 or so. Eventually, of course, in the East colonial powers adjusted themselves to the new level of overheads and perhaps found new sources of local taxation to offset them. In the West the familiar structure of quasi-feudal large estates came into being in the 17th century.[38] Since the economic basis of the Spanish colonial system was broader than the Portuguese, the results of crisis would be more far-reaching. Thus the early emigration to the Americas temporarily stimulated the export of goods from the home country; but as, inevitably, many of the colonists' wants came to be supplied locally, the expanded manufactures of Spain had to pay the price. The attempt to tighten the metropolitan monopoly merely made matters worse by discouraging the development, among other things, of the potentially revolutionary plantation economy.[39] The effects of the influx of bullion into Spain are too well-known to need discussion.

It is therefore understandable that the "old colonial system" passed through a profound crisis; and that its effects on the general European economy were far-reaching. A new pattern of colonial exploitation which produced steadily rising exports of manufactures from Europe did indeed replace it. (Acting largely on their own the sugar planters of Northern Brazil had shown the way to it from the end of the 16th century). Yet the lure of the old monopoly profits was irresistible to all those who had a chance of capturing them. Even the Dutch remained resolutely "old-fashioned" in their colonialism until the 18th century, though their entrepôt position in Europe saved them from the consequence of colonial inefficiency. Old colonialism did not grow over into new colonialism; it collapsed and was replaced by it.

The contradictions of the home markets

There can be little doubt that the 16th century came nearer to creating the conditions for a really widespread adoption of the capitalist mode of production than any previous age; perhaps because of the impetus given by overseas loot, perhaps because of the encouragement of rapidly growing population and markets and rising prices. (It is not the object of this article to discuss the reasons which caused this expansion to follow the "feudal crisis" of the 14th and 15th centuries). A powerful combination of forces, including even large feudal interests[40] seriously threatened the resistance of gild-dominated towns. Rural industry, of the "putting-out" type, which had previously been largely confined to textiles, spread in various countries and to new branches of production (e.g. metals), especially towards the end of the period. Yet the expansion bred its own obstacles. We may briefly consider some of them.

Except perhaps in England no "agrarian revolution" of a capitalist type accompanied industrial change, as it was to do in the 18th century; though there was plenty of upheaval in the countryside. Here again we find the generally feudal nature of the social framework distorting and diverting forces which might otherwise have made for a direct advance towards modern capitalism. In the East, where agrarian change took the form of a revival of serfdom by exporting lords, the conditions for such development were inhibited locally, though made possible elsewhere. In other regions the price-rise, the upheavals in landownership, and the growth of demand for agrarian produce might well have led to the emergence of capitalist farming by gentlemen and the kulak-type of peasant on a greater scale than appears to have occurred.[41] Yet what happened? French lords (often "bourgeois" who had bought themselves into feudal status) reversed the trend to peasant independence from the middle of the 16th century, and increasingly recovered lost ground.[42] Towns, merchants and local middlemen invested in the land, partly no doubt because of the security of farm produce in an age of inflation, partly because the surplus was easy to draw from it in a feudal manner, their exploitation being all the more effective for being combined with usury; partly perhaps in direct political rivalry with feudalists.[43] Indeed, the relationship of towns and their inhabitants as a whole to the surrounding peasantry was still, as always in a generally feudal society, that of a special kind of feudal lord. (The peasants in the town-dominated cantons of Switzerland and in inland Netherlands were not actually emancipated until the French Revolution.[44]) The mere existence of urban investment in agriculture or urban influence over the countryside, therefore, did not imply the creation of rural capitalism. Thus the spread of share-cropping in France, though theoretically marking a step towards capitalism, in fact often produced merely a bourgeoisie parasitic on a peasantry increasingly exhausted by it, and by the rising demands of the State; and consequent decline.[45] The old social structure predominated still.

Two results may have followed from this. First, it is improbable that there was much technical innovation, though the first (Italian) handbook on crop rotation appeared in the mid-16th century, and certain that the increase in agrarian output did not keep pace with demand.[46] Hence towards the end of the period there are signs of diminishing returns and foodshortage, of exporting areas using up their crops for local needs etc., preludes to the famines and epidemics of the crisis-period.[47] Second, the rural population, subject to the double pressure of landlords and townsmen (not to mention the State), and in any case much less capable of protecting itself against famine and war than they, suffered.[48] In some regions this short-sighted "squeeze" may actually have led to a declining trend in productivity during the 17th century.[49] The countryside was sacrificed to lord, town and State. Its appalling rate of mortality — if the relatively prosperous Beauvaisis is any guide — was second only to that of the domestic outworkers, also increasingly rural.[50] Expansion under these conditions bred crisis.

What happened in the non-agricultural sectors depended largely on the agricultural. Costs of manufacture may have been unduly raised by the more rapid rise of agrarian than of industrial prices, thus narrowing the profit-margin of manufacturers.[51] (However, manufacturers increasingly used the cheap labour of rural outworkers, who were again exploited to the point of debility.) The market also had its difficulties. The rural market as a whole must have proved disappointing. Many freeholding peasants benefited from the price-rise and the demand for their goods, provided they had enough land to feed themselves even in bad years, a regular surplus for sale, and a good head for business.[52] But if such yeomen bought much more than before, they bought less than townsmen of equal standing, being more self-sufficient.[53] The experience of 19th century France shows that a middle and rich peasantry is about as uninviting a market for mass manufactures as may be found, and does not encourage capitalists to revolutionize production. Its wants are traditional; most of its wealth goes into more land and cattle, or into hoards, or into new building, or even into sheer waste, like those gargantuan weddings, funerals, and other feasts which disturbed continental princes at the turn of the 16th century.[54] The increase in the demand from the non-agricultural sector (towns, luxury market, government demand etc.) may for a time have obscured the fact that it grew less rapidly than productive capacity, and that the persistent decline of the real income of wage-earners in the long inflation may actually, according to Nef, have stopped "the growth of the demand for some industrial products."[55] However, the slumps in the export markets from the late 1610s on brought the fact home.

Once the decline had begun, of course, an additional factor increased the difficulties of manufacture: the rise in labour costs. For there is evidence that — in the towns at least — the bargaining power of labour rose sharply during the crisis, perhaps owing to the fall or stagnation in town populations. At any rate real wages rose in England, Italy, Spain and Germany, and the mid-century saw the formation of effective journeymen's organizations in most western countries.[56] This may not have affected the labour costs of the putting-out industries, as their workers were in a weaker position to benefit from the situation, and their piece-rate wages were more easily cut. However, it is clearly not a negligible factor. Moreover, the slackening of population increase and the stabilization of prices must have depressed manufactures further.

These different aspects of the crisis may be reduced to a single formula: economic expansion took place within a social framework which it was not yet strong enough to burst, and in ways adapted to it rather than to the world of modern capitalism. Specialists in the Jacobean period must determine what actually precipitated the crisis: the decline in American silver, the collapse of the Baltic market or some of many other possible factors. Once the first crack appeared, the whole unstable structure was bound to totter. It did totter, and in the subsequent period of economic crisis and social upheaval the decisive shift from capitalist enterprise adapted to a generally feudal framework to capitalist enterprise transforming the world in its own pattern took place. The Revolution in England was thus the most dramatic incident in the crisis, and its turning-point. "This nation" wrote Samuel Fortrey in 1663 in his "England's Interest and Improvement" "can expect no less than to become the most great and flourishing of all others." It could and it did; and the effects on the world were to be portentous.

A note on price history

Long-term price movements have been deliberately kept outside the main argument, because other discussions of long-term economic development emphasize them so much; perhaps too much. Nevertheless, the course of prices calls for some comment.

The traditional view, as put forward by *Simiand* and accepted by *Labrousse* and others, is that the long price-rise came to an end around 1640 and was followed by a price-fall, or fluctuations round a stable trend until the second quarter of the 18th century. This view seems too simple. There are signs of a change in the price trend between 1605 and 1620; for instance in Spanish wheat prices. *Cipolla* has also noted that Milanese prices cease to rise rapidly after 1605 and continue steady or rising slowly from then until 1630. (*Mouvements monétaires dans l'état de Milan* 1580–1700. 1952). We should expect this, since *Hamilton* shows that the import of American bullion reached its peak in 1590–1610, though it held up quite well until 1620 or so (*American Treasure*, 35). If prices went on rising until 1640 (or 1635, which seems to have been the turning-point in Italy) it was probably due to debasement of coinage, to the demand for scarce goods in the Thirty Years' War, or to a combination of both. Hence it is not unlikely that, but for the war, the period of price-fall or price-stability would have begun in 1610–20. The end of the war intensified the crisis, which undoubtedly reached its most acute phase (and the lowest point of prices) in the 1660s and early 1670s. The effects of drastic post-war deflation may be studied in the typical war-profiteering country of Switzerland, where they led to the peasant war of 1653.

The course of prices differed, of course, according to regions and commodities, and some of the local and sectional phenomena are still very obscure. No attempt can be made here to account for them. In general, however, secular price-movements tally quite well with the periods of the crisis as discussed in the text.

Notes

1 Perroy, Boutruche, Hilton have discussed this in recent years in the *Annales* and elsewhere. See also the discussion among Dobb, Sweezy, Takahashi, Hilton and Hill in *Science and Society* 1950–53, and the general survey by Malowist in *Kwartalnik Historiczny* 1953, I. (I am indebted to the Polish Institute, London for a translation of this).
2 Braudel, *La Mediterranée... au temps de Philippe II*, 1097. R. Romano, Industries textiles et conjoncture à Florence au 17e s. (*Annales* Oct.–Dec. 1952, 510). French historians regard the "phase de contraction du 17e siècle" as "un fait maintenant établi" (*Rev. Hist.* 428 (1953), 379). In what follows I owe a great deal to discussion with J. Meuvret who confirmed many of my non-specialist guesses. However I doubt whether he would agree with much of this paper.
3 C. A. Julien, *Histoire de l'Afrique du Nord*, 538 ff; the "industrial revolution" in piracy, due to the introduction of Northern sails by English and Dutch after 1604 may be noted.
4 J. Meuvret in *Mélanges d'Histoire Sociale* V, 1944, 27–44; in *Population*, 1946, 653–50 and an unpublished paper on the effects of the 1693–4 and 1709–10 famines on French diplomacy.
5 There are, of course, no reliable statistics and not always good indirect indices. This paragraph is based, in particular, on: K. Larsen, *History of Norway*, 1948, 304 (figures only for 1665 and after); Mayer, *The Population of Switzerland* (1952), and Patavino's estimate for 1608 which is as great as M's for 1700 in Nabholz, Muralt, Feller, Bonjour, *Gesch. d Schweiz* II, 5; H. Wopfner, *Gueterteilung u. Uebervoelkerung*, 1938, 202 ff; H. v. z. Muehlen, "Entstehung d. Gutsherrschaft in Oberschlesien", in *Vierteljahrschrift f. Soz. und Wirtsch. Gesch.* XXXVIII, 334–60; Beloch, *Bevoelkerungsgeschichte Italiens* I, 153, 225 ff; Keyser, *Bevoelkerungsgesch. Deutschlands*, 1941, 361 ff, 304 ff; Roupnel, *La vie et la campagne dijonnaises au* 17e s.; P. Goubert, "Problèmes démographiques du Beauvaisis au 17e s." (*Annales*, Oct.–Dec. 1952, 452–468), for an area which seems to have suffered rather less; G. Debien, *En Haut-Poitou; Défricheurs au Travail* (XV–XVIII s.) and for absence of forest-clearing and recovery of forests Bull. Soc. Hist. Mod. Mai-Juillet 1953, 6–9; Pirenne, *Hist. de Belgique* IV, 439–40; A. Cosemans, *Bevolkering v. Brabant en de 17e eeuw* 1939, 220–4; G. N. Clark, *The Seventeenth Century*; Rutkowski, *Hist. Econ. de la Pologne avant les Partages*, 1927, 91–2; Stone in *IX Congrès International des Sciences Historiques* II, 1951, 49–50; Hoskins, "The Rebuilding of Rural England 1570–1640," *Past and Present* 4, 1953.
6 *Op. cit.* 6. The same criticism may be made of the estimates of Urlanis, *Rost nasielenia v. Jewropie* (Moscow 1941) 158 which seem rather optimistic. I am indebted to Mr. A. Jenkin for drawing my attention to these figures.
7 S. Peller, "Studies in mortality since the Renaissance" (*Bull. Inst. Hist. of Medicine*) 1943, 443, 445, 452, and esp. 456; *ibid* 1947, 67, 79. Meuvret and Goubert *op. cit.* and the literature quoted in Habbakuk, English Population in the 18th Century (*Econ. Hist. Rev.* 2dS. VI, 2, 1953). For the epidemiology of the century, in addition to innumerable local studies, Haeser, *Gesch. d. Medizin u. d. epidem. Krankheiten* (Jena 1882), C. Creighton, *Hist. of Epidemics in Britain* (1891, 1894), L. F. Hirst, *The Conquest of Plague* (1953); Prinzing, *Epidemics resulting from wars* (1916); Brownlee, "Epidemiology of Phthisis in Great Britain and Ireland (*Medical Research Council* 1918); Campbell, "The Epidemiology of influenza (*Bull. Inst. Hist. Medicine* 13, 1943); W. J. Simpson, *A Treatise on the Plague* (1905).
8 Sombart, *Luxus u. Kapitalismus*, 26–7; Schmoller, *Deutsches Staedtewesen in aelterer Zeit*, 1922, 60–95; B. Bretholz, *Gesch. Boehmens u. Maehrens* 1924, III, 61–3; Baasch, *Hollaendische Wirtschaftsgeschichte*, 24–5.

9 Cipolla, "The Decline of Italy" (*Econ. Hist. Rev.* 2 S.V., 2, 1952); Roupnel, *op. cit.* for reversion of Burgundy to autarky; Reuss, *Hist. de Strasbourg*, 1922, 280–6; P. Boissonade, "La crise de l'industrie languedocienne 1600–1660" (*Annales du Midi*, 1909); G. Aubin and H. Kunze, *Leinener-zeugung ... im oestl. Mitteldeutschland*, 1940.

10 For figures of the Dutch and Florentine production, N. W. Posthumus, *Gesch. v. d. Leidsche Lakenindustrie* III, 932; Romano in *Annales, loc cit.*

11 Bang and Korst, *Tabeller over Skibsfart*; A. Christensen, *Dutch Trade and the Baltic about* 1600 (Copenhagen 1940).

12 G. Tongas, *Relations entre la France et l'Empire Ottoman durant la premièré moitié du 17e s.*, 1942; P. Masson, *Le Commerce Francais dans le Levant au 17e s.*, 1892, esp. 130–4, App. XV, 236; H. Wätjen, *D. Niederlander im Mittelmeergebiet*, 1909, 145, 149.

13 Bal Krishna, *Commercial Relations between India and England* 1601–1757, caps ii-v; S. A. Khan, *East India Trade in the 17th C.*, 1923, 74, ff.

14 C. de Lannoy and H. Van der Linden, *Hist. de l'Expansion des Peuples Européens: Néerlande et Danemark* (XVII et XVIII ss.), 1911, 334, 344–5, 363. The indebtedness of the Company was also higher than before or after. J. G. Van Dillen, *Bronnen tot d. Geschiedenis d. Wisselbanken*, 1925, II, 971 ff.

15 Barbados began to export sugar in 1646, Jamaica started planting in 1664, Haiti re-established plantation in 1655, Martinique began it in the same year, St. Kitts' sugar exports passed its indigo exports in 1660. (Lippman, *Gesch. d. Zuckers*, 1929).

16 For a comparison of its size in 1641 and 1667, J. Saintoyant, *La Colonisation Européenne*, 1947, 271–3.

17 B. Porshnev in Biryukovitch, Porshnev, Skazkin etc., *Novaya Istoriya* 1640–1789 (Moscow 1951), 444. This follows a suggestion of Marx in 1850 (*Sel. Essays*, ed. Stenning, 1926, 203). The coincidence has often been noted, e.g. Merriman, *Six Contemporaneous Revolutions*, 1938.

18 Merriman, *op. cit.*, Porshnev, *Narodnie vosstaniya vo Frantsii pered Frondoi* 1623–1648 (Moscow 1948); O. Schiff, *D. deutschen Bauernaufstaende* 1525–1789 (*Hist. Ztrschr.* CXXX 189 ff). Feller, *Gesch. Berns* II (1953), cap. iv and v.

19 J. Lemoine, *La revolte du Papier Timbré*, 1898 prints numerous documents.

20 Marczali, *Hungary in the 18th C.*, 1910, p. xxxvii; Bretholz *loc cit.* 57–61.

21 A. Nielsen, *Daenische Wirtschaftsgeschichte*, 1933, 94–5.

22 R. Mousnier, *La venalité des offices sous Henri IV et Louis XIII*, 1945; K. W. Swart, *Sale of offices in the 17 c.*, 1949.

23 See the Note on Price History.

24 V. I. Lenin, *The Development of Capitalism in Russia*, cap. I (conclusions), cap. II (conclusions), cap. VIII (the formation of the Home Market). *Capital* I (1938 ed.) 738, 772–4. That Marx did not think primarily of the actual accumulation of resources is shown, I think, by a preparatory draft to the Critique of Political Economy: "Eigen ist dem Kapital nichts als die Vereinigung von Haenden und Instrumenten, die es vorfindet. Es agglomeriert sie unter seiner Botmaessigkeit. Das ist sein wirkliches Anhaeufen; das Anhaeufen von Arbeitern auf Punkten nebst ihren Instrumenten." (*Formen die der kapitalistichen Produktion vorhergehen*, pp. 49–50, Berlin 1952).

25 *Capital* III pt. IV (Merchant's Capital); and esp. *vol. II*, 63. See also R. H. Hilton, "Capitalism, What's in a Name" (*Past and Present* I, 1952).

26 J. Meuvret, "Circulation monétaire et utilisation économique de la monnaie dans la France du 16e et du 17e s." (*Etudes d'Histoire Moderne et Contemp, tome I*, 1947, 14–29); R. Latouche, *La vie au Bas-Quercy*, 1923; E. Koehler, *Der Einzelhandel im Mittelalter*, 1938, 55–60.

27 A. Fanfani, *Storia del Lavoro in Italia dalla fine del secolo XV agli inizii del* XVIII, 1943, 42–9.
28 R. S. Lopez, "Economie et architecture médievales" (*Annales* Oct.–Dec. 1952, 443–8).
29 G. Renier, *The Dutch Nation*, 1944, 97–9.
30 H. Roy, *La vie, la mode et le costume au 17e s.*, 1924, prints a full list of all the types of textile used at this court.
31 Cipolla, *The decline of Italy* (*loc. cit.*) for the high-cost argument.
32 M. Malowist in Report of *IX Congrès International des Sciences Historiques I*, 1950, 305–22.
33 For the extent of this increasing exploitation, J. Rutkowski, "Le régime agraire en Pologne au 18e s." (*Rev. Hist. Econ. and Soc.* 1926 and 1927, esp. 1927, 92 ff); J. Rutkowski, "Les bases économiques des partages de l'ancienne Pologne" (*Rev. Hist. Moderne* N.S. IV, 1932); J. Rosdolsky, "The distribution of the agrarian product in feudalism" (*Journ. Econ. Hist.* 1951, 247 ff), For unimportance of cash payments, Rutkowski 1927. 71. Rutkowski 1926, 501; Malowist, 317 ff. An example of town improverishment due to this, F. Tremel, Handel d. Stadt Judenburg im 16 Jh. (*Ztschr. d. hist. Vereins fuer Steiermark*, 1947, 103–6).
34 An expansion of the total area of serf exporting agriculture — e.g. in the Black Sea area might have offset this. But this did not take place until the 18th century, possibly owing to Turkish strength and grain policy earlier. D. Ionescu, *Agrarverfassung Rumaeniens*, 1909, 10–19, A. Mehlan, "D. grossen Balkanmessen in der Tuerkenzeit" (*Vierteljahrschrift f. Soz. und Wirtsch. Gesch.* 1938, 2–7).
35 *Cal. St. P. Col.* 1661–8, 266.
36 F. C. Lane, "National Wealth and Protection Costs" (in Clarkson and Cochran ed., *War as a Social Institution*, 1941, 36 ff).
37 C. G. Motten, *Mexican Silver and the Enlightenment*, 1950, caps. 2–3.
38 Thus from the end of the 17th century the Dutch East India Company expanded the income from colonial taxes, previously about 9% of its revenue, much more rapidly than trading profits. Lannoy and Linden op. cit. 266–7. F. Chevalier, *La formation des grands domaines au Mexique. Terres et Société au XVI-XVIIe s.*, 1952. I have only seen the summary of this in *Rev. Hist.* 428, 1953, 376 ff.
39 For the ending of sugar-plantations in the early 17th century, E. O. v. *Lippmann, Gesch. d. Zuckers*, 1929.
40 Cf. the import H. Aubin, "D. Anfaenge d. grossen schlesischen Leineweberei" (*Vierteljahrschr. f. Soz. und Wirtsch. Gesch.* XXXV, 154–73).
41 Raveau: *L'agriculture... en Haut-Poitou au 16 s.*, 127; Marc Bloch, *Caractères Originaux de l'histoire rurale française*, 148–9); but the "gentil-homme campagnard" is not ipso facto a capitalist farmer.
42 Bloch *op. cit.* Braudel 624 ff.
43 Bloch, *op. cit.* 145–6; P. Raveau, *op. cit.*, 249 ff; A. Kraemer, *D. wechselnde... Bedeutung d. Landbesitzes d. Stadt Breslau* (1927) for systematic buying of land 1500 — Thirty Years' War.
44 Baasch, *Hollaend. Wirtschaftsgeschichte*, 50; Roupnel *op. cit.*
45 Marx, *Capital* III, xlvii, sec. v on *métayage*; G. de Falguérolles, Décadence de l'économie agricole à Lempaut (Languedoc) (*Annales du Midi* 53, 1941, 142–) — an important article.
46 Raveau, *op. cit.*, cap. III. For non-innovating character of French agricultural handbooks, G. Lizerand, *Le régime rural de l'ancienne France*, 1941, 79–81. M. J. Elsas, *Umriss einer Geschichte c. Preise u. Loehne in Deutschland*, 1949 for stable agric. productivity.

47 G. Coniglio, *Il regno di Napoli al tempo de Carlo V*, 1951 and Braudel, *op. cit.* V. Barbour, *Capitalism in Amsterdam*, 1949, 26-7; A. Juergens, *Z. schleswig-holsteinschen Handelsgeschichte im 16. u. 17. Jh*, 1914, 10-12 for change from an exporting to an importing area at end of 16th century.
48 Because they relied on local food supplies, while towns imported in any case, often from great distances. Meuvret, "La géographie du prix des céréales," (*Revista de Economia*, Lisbon 1951, 63-9). Falguérolles, *loc cit.* for peasants ceasing to eat wheat, which they have to sell to pay taxes.
49 Falguérolles, *loc cit.* argues so.
50 Goubert, *loc cit.*
51 Elsas, *op. cit.* O. Roehlk, *Hansisch-Norwegische Handeslpolitik im 16. Jh.* 1935, 74-5 for an excellent discussion of this, though relating to the "price-scissors" between corn and fish-prices. Report of Royal Commission on Cloth Industry, 1640 (*E.H.R.* 1942, 485-6).
52 Bloch, *op. cit.* 145 on this important last point.
53 M. Campbell, *The English Yeoman*, 1942, 186-7, cap. vi passim, and Hoskins, *Past and Present* 4, 1953.
54 H. Widmann, *Geschichte Salzburgs*, 1914, III, 354; Feller, *op. cit.* II, 368; H. Schnell, *Mecklenburg im Ztalter d. Reformation* (1900) 201.
55 "Prices and Industrial Capitalism" (*Econ. Hist. Rev.* VII, 184-5).
56 Knoop and Jones, *The Medieval Mason*, 1949, 207-12, Cipolla in *Econ. Hist. Rev.*, *loc cit.* 184,Elsas, *op. cit.*, E. J. Hamilton, *War and Prices in Spain 1650-1800*, 1947, 219. G. Unwin, *Industrial Organisation in the 16th and 17th Centuries*, 1904, cap. VIII; G. Des Marez, *Le Compagnonnage des Chapeliers Bruxellois*, 1909, 17-21; M. St. Léon, *Le Compagnonnage*, 1902; L. Guéneau, *L'organisation de travail à Nevers au 17e s.* 1919, 79 ff; J. Gebauer, *Gesch. d. Stadt Hildesheim*, 1925, 221 ff; etc.

31

THE CRISIS OF THE 17TH CENTURY II

Eric J. Hobsbawn

Source: *Past and Present* 6, 1954: 44–65.

In the last number of *Past and Present* I attempted to outline some of the evidence for the view that there was a "general crisis" of the European economy in the 17th century and to suggest some reasons why it should have occurred. I argued that it was due, in the main, to the failure to surmount certain general obstacles which still stood in the way of the full development of capitalism. The article also suggested that the "crisis" itself created the conditions which were to make industrial revolution possible. In this article I propose to discuss ways in which this may have come about, i.e. the outcome of the crisis.

It is perhaps worth recalling that the period of difficulties lasted for about a century — say from 1620s to the 1720s. Thereafter the general picture is rosier. The financial problems of the age of wars were more or less solved, at the expense of numerous investors, in Britain and France by means of such devices as the South Sea Bubble and Law's System. Plague and pestilence, if not famine, disappeared from Western Europe after the Marseilles epidemic of 1720–1. Wherever the eye turned, it saw growing wealth, trade and industry, growing population and colonial expansion. Slow at first, the pace of economic change became precipitous from sometime between the 1760s and the 1780s. The period of Industrial Revolution had begun. There were indeed, as we shall see, signs of a "crisis of growth" in agriculture, in the colonial economy and elsewhere from the third quarter of the 18th century, but it would be impossible to write the history of the 18th century in terms of a "phase of contraction," as a recent historian has written that of the 17th.[1]

However, if the argument that the fundamental obstacles in the way of capitalist development disappeared sometime in the 17th century is right, we may legitimately ask why industrial revolution did not get into its full stride until the end of the 18th. The problem is a very real one. In England, at any rate, it is hard to escape the impression that the stormy pace of economic development towards the end of the 17th century "ought" to have brought about industrial revolution much sooner. The gap between Newcomen and James Watt, between the time the Darbys of Coalbrookdale discovered how to smelt iron with coal and the time when the method was generally utilized, is really quite long. It is significant that the Royal Society complained in 1701 that "the discouraging neglect of the great, the impetuous contradiction of the ignorant, and the reproaches of the unreasonable, had unhappily thwarted them in their design to perpetuate a succession of useful inventions."[2] Even in some other countries there are signs of economic changes in the 1690s which lead no further, for instance agricultural innovations in Normandy and Southwestern France.[3] Again, a malaise hangs over British farming in the 1720s and 30s and perhaps over some industries.[4] In the intellectual field there is an analogous gap. The present article does not propose to tackle this problem. It must certainly be solved if we are to have a really adequate understanding of the process of modern economic development and the origins of the Industrial Revolution, but space forbids any attempt, however cursory, to discuss it here.

The conditions of economic development

The obstacles in the way of industrial revolution were of two types. *First*, as has been argued, the economy and social structure of precapitalist societies simply did not leave enough scope for it. Something like a preliminary revolutionizing had to take place before they were capable of undergoing the transformations which England underwent between the 1780s and the 1840s. This had of course begun long since. We must consider how far the 17th century crisis advanced it. However, there is a *second* problem, though a more specialized one. Even if we remove the general obstacles in the way of industrial revolution, it does not follow that a society of machines and factories will immediately result. Between 1500 and 1800 many industries evolved methods of expanding output rapidly and without limit, but with fairly primitive organization and technique; for instance the metal goods producers of Birmingham, the gun-makers of Liège, the cutlers of Sheffield or Solingen. These towns produced their characteristic wares in much the same ways in 1860 as in 1750, though in vastly greater quantities and with the use of new sources of power. What we have to explain, therefore, is not merely the rise of *Birmingham* with its subdivided craft industries, but specifically the rise of *Manchester* with its factories, for it was Manchester and its like which revolutionized the world. What conditions in the 17th century helped, not only to sweep away the general obstacles, but to produce the conditions which gave birth to Manchester?

It would be surprising if the conditions for the development of the modern industrial economy were to arise everywhere in 17th and 18th century

Europe. What we must show is that, as the result of 17th century changes, they developed in one or two areas sufficiently large and economically effective enough to serve as a base for revolutionizing the world subsequently. This is very difficult. Perhaps no really conclusive demonstration is possible until we have far more quantitative information about the period than we have at present. It is all the more difficult because in the most vital areas of the economy — agricultural and manufacturing production properly speaking — we not only know very little, but lack the sort of revolutionary landmarks which cheer the historian of the industrial revolution on his way: spinning-mills, power-looms, railways. Hence the economic historian of our period may have the very strong impression that "somewhere about the middle of the 17th century European life was so completely transformed in many of its aspects that we commonly think of this as one of the great watersheds of modern history,"[5] but he cannot prove it conclusively.

The 17th century, an age of economic concentration

The main argument of this article may be summarized as follows. The 17th century crisis resulted in a considerable concentration of economic power. In this it differed, I think, from the 14th century crisis which had — at least for a time — the opposite effect. This may indicate that the old structure of European society had already been considerably undermined, for it is arguable that the normal tendency of a purely feudal society, when in difficulties, is to revert to an economy of small local producers — e.g. peasants — whose mode of production easily survives the collapse of an elaborate superstructure of demesne agriculture and trade.[6] Directly and indirectly this concentration served the ends of future industrialization, though of course nobody intended it to do so. It did so directly, by strengthening "putting-out" industry at the expense of craft production, and the "advanced" economies at the expense of the "backward" and speeding the process of capital accumulation; indirectly by helping to solve the problem of providing a surplus of agricultural products, and in other ways. Of course this was not a Panglossian process, in which everything was for the best in the best of all possible worlds. Many of the results of the crisis were sheer waste, or even regression, when considered from the point of view of an eventual industrial revolution. Nor was it an "inevitable" process in the short run. Had the English Revolution failed, for instance, as so many other revolutions in the 17th century failed, it is entirely possible that economic development might have been long retarded. Nevertheless, its net effect was economically progressive.

Though the generalization may be contested, like all generalizations, there is little doubt that economic concentration took place in various forms, in East and West, under conditions of expansion, contraction or stagnation. Within the countryside large landowners gained at the expense of peasants and smaller owners, in Restoration England as in Eastern Europe. (If we regard towns as special forms of feudal lords the impression of concentration is even stronger on the continent). In non-industrial areas towns gained at the expense of the countryside, whether as a result of their greater immunity to lords, soldiers and hunger or for other reasons.[7] Administrative measures like the Prussian excise might intensify this process, but were not wholly responsible for it. The east-European areas in which towns declined, like small landowners and peasants, before the pressure of magnates, are an exception which merely confirms the general picture of concentration. Within the towns wealth may have concentrated also, at any rate where the lords were not strong enough to capture the old town rights of exploiting the countryside for themselves, as they did in Eastern Europe.[8] In industrial areas we have what Espinas called "the double orientation of production in small and large centres"[9] that is, the substitution of rural out-work controlled by great national or foreign trading groups for the medium-sized town crafts. We also have a certain re-grouping of industries which may sometimes be regarded as concentration, e.g. where specialized manufactures for a national or international market grew up in particular areas instead of more widespread manufactures for regional markets.[10] Everywhere the great metropolitan cities grew at the expense of town, countryside or both. Internationally trade concentrated in the maritime states, and within these in turn capital cities tended to preponderate. The growing power of centralized states also made for some economic concentration.

Agriculture

What were the effects of this process in agriculture? We have seen that there is evidence that towards the end of the 16th and the beginning of the 17th centuries the expansion of the marketable agricultural surplus was lagging behind that of non-agricultural consumption. In the long run the vast surplus essential for the development of a modern industrial society was to be achieved primarily by technical revolution — i.e. by raising productivity and expanding the cultivated area through capitalist farming. Only thus could agriculture produce not merely the necessary food surplus for the towns — not to mention certain industrial raw materials — but also the labour for industry. In the developed countries, notably in the Low Countries and England, signs of agricultural revolution had long been visible, and from the middle of the 17th century they multiply. We also find a marked increase in the cultivation of novel and rare crops such as *maize, potatoes* and *tobacco* which may be regarded as a species of agricultural revolution. Before the mid-17th century maize had only been grown in the Po delta (from 1554); soon afterwards it spread to Lombardy and Piedmont. Rice cultivation in Lombardy covered 5,000 hectares in 1550; by 1710 it covered over 150,000, about as much as today and only 3/8 below the peak acreage of 1870. Maize and cotton cultivation certainly spread in the Balkans. Potatoes appear to have made serious headway in Ireland and perhaps northern England by 1700, though virtually uncultivated elsewhere.[11] Nevertheless, it would be unwise to conclude that technical innovation contributed much to agricultural production before the mid-18th century — again England and the Low Countries may be exceptions, as also the areas of maize cultivation — or that it extended much beyond gardening which, as M. Meuvret has pointed out, lent itself easily to technical experimenting.[12] It is doubtful whether in many areas of Europe the cultivated area in 1700 had extended much beyond what it had been in 1600.

Exactly what happened in Western Europe is by no means clear, though we know that England exported corn increasingly from the end of the 17th century. It would seem, to judge from what we know of France, that the increasing demand from such large food-markets as Paris was met (*a*) by drawing on the reserves of proverbially rich agricultural areas which had not previously been fully tapped in normal times and (*b*) by increasingly "poaching" on the preserves of of other cities.[13] Since there is no obvious evidence of increases in productivity one would expect this to have meant, in the last analysis, either a transfer from food with a lower to food with a higher yield per acre (e.g. from cattle to corn), or a simple transfer from some Peter — probably the miserable peasant — to some Paul. There is some evidence that peasants were forced onto a worse diet, selling their wheat on the market, at any rate in the South, which had never had much of a food-surplus. A decline in the dietary standard in England has also been suggested for the later 17th century.[14]

What happened in Central and Eastern Europe is rather more clear.

The development of an economy of serf-estates was accelerated and accentuated in the 17th century, which may be regarded as marking the decisive victory of the new serfdom, or more precisely of large serf-owners ("magnates") over the lesser nobility and gentry. We need not discuss how much of this revival of feudalism was due to the increasing demand of outside food-markets — at home or abroad, how much to other factors.[15] At all events, a number of factors coincided to increase the economic and political power of the magnates, who were both the most effective and the most wholesale enserfers of the peasantry. With rare and transitory exceptions — the Swedish monarchy's peasant policy in the Baltic towards the end of the century may be one[16] — even the absolutist monarchies were unable and unwilling to interfere with it. Indeed they tended to advance it, because their victory over estates and similar institutions generally meant the weakening of the lesser nobles (whose strongholds they were) and of the towns, and the relative strengthening of the smaller groups of magnates who gathered round the ruler's court, which may often be regarded virtually as a mechanism for distributing the country's taxable income among them in one form or another. In any case, as in Russia and Prussia, the power of the monarch in the state was sometimes bought by renouncing all interference with the power of the lord on his estate. Where royal power was vanishing, as in Poland, or declining, as in Turkey (where non-heritable fiefs for military service gave way to heritable feudal estates), the lord's task was in any case even less complicated.

The decisive victory of the serf-estate did not lead to an increase in productivity, but it was able to create, for a time at least, a large pool of potentially saleable, and as time went on, actually sold agrarian produce. In the *first* place, in the most primitive areas such as the Balkans and the Eastern frontier zones, it could oblige peasants to stay in the economy rather than to escape by migration or nomadism[17] and to cultivate exportable rather than subsistence crops, or to switch from a dairying to a tillage economy. This last change was also encouraged by the Thirty Years' War, in Bohemia and elsewhere.[18] The example of 18th century Ireland shows that a mere transfer from cattle to field-crops can have, for a time, the effect of an agricultural revolution. In the *second* place, the feudal estate could increasingly become a "Gutsherrschaft" drawing profits from the sale of serf-produced farming rather than a "Grund-herrschaft" relying on income in money or kind from dependent peasants. Estates differed in the degree to which they did so; 69% of the income from some Czech estates in 1636–7 came from demesne profits, but only between 40 and 50% of that on some East German estates in the mid-18th century.[19] We may assume, however, that the transfer of estates from smaller to larger owners would increase their profit-exploitation, for at the shockingly low level of serf-agriculture only the really large lord might find that the profits of running his estate as a corn-factory made the trouble of organizing and supervising the huge gangs of reluctant serfs worth while. In the neighbourhood of exporting ports merchants might encourage lords to enter the exporting economy, or force them to do so by lending money against the promise of crop-sales, as in Livonia.[20]

Admittedly this could not permanently solve the problem of capitalist growth. The serf economy was shockingly inefficient. The mere fact of forced labour tied it down to the least efficient utilization of land and manpower. Once an area had been completely "enserfed," and forced labour intensified to its maximum — say 5 or 6 days a week[21] — production stabilized itself, unless new areas could be "enserfed." But difficulties of transport imposed limits. The expulsion of the Turks might open up the hinterland of the Black Sea ports, but — to take an obvious example — Western Siberia was still bound to remain inaccessible. Hence, as soon as the effective limits of serf agriculture had been reached, it entered upon a period of crisis. From the 1760s on this was recognized, and to some extent reflected in the projects of enlightened despotism.[22] The serf-economy was transformed between 1760 and 1861. This transformation takes us beyond the limits of our period and cannot therefore be considered here. The important thing for our purposes is, that the transfer to the serf-estate economy coincided with the 17th century crisis, and perhaps entered its decisive stage after the Thirty Years' War — say about 1660.[23]

The ways in which the crisis hastened this transfer are clear. Under the circumstances obtaining almost any outside event — a war, a famine, the raising of new taxes — weakened the peasant (and with him the traditional agrarian structure) and strengthened his exploiters. The crisis, moreover, encouraged all of them — landlords, provincial middle class, and State in the West, lord and State in the East, to save themselves at his expense. Moreover, it has been argued that the decline in commerce and urban life over parts of the continent would encourage the rich to invest capital on the land, thus encouraging even further exploitation; as did the fall in agricultural prices. It is perhaps worth pointing out that such investment must not be confused with investment for the improvement of agriculture as in the 18th and 19th century. Normally it merely meant investment in the right to turn the screw on the peasant.

Industry and manufactures

The main result of the 17th century crisis on industrial organization was to eliminate the crafts, and with them the craft-dominated towns, from large-scale production and to establish the "putting-out" system, controlled by men with capitalist horizons and operated by easily exploitable rural labour. Signs of more ambitious industrial developments, "manufactories" and the like, are not lacking, especially in the last third of the century, and in industries like mining, metallurgy and shipbuilding which required a fairly largescale of operation, but even without these the industrial changes are striking. "Putting-out" (a protean stage of industrial development) had developed in certain textile industries in the later middle ages, but as a general rule the transformation of crafts into "putting-out" industries began seriously during the boom of the later 16th century.[24] The 17th is clearly the century when such systems established themselves decisively.[25] Once again, its middle years appear to mark some sort of watershed: for instance, the large-scale export of Liège small-arms began after the 1650s.[26] This was only to be expected. Rural industries did not suffer from the high costs of urban ones, and often the small local producer of cheap goods — e.g. "new draperies" — found himself able to expand sales while the high-quality and expensive goods of the old exporting industries — broad-cloth, Italian textiles—lost their markets. "Putting-out" made regional concentration of industry possible, as it was not in the narrow town boundaries, for it made production easy to expand. But the crisis encouraged such regional concentration, for only this — for instance the concentration of European tinplate manufacture in Saxony[27] — could enable large-scale production to survive when home markets were small, and export markets perhaps not expanding.

(The case of countries with a developed market will be considered below). The negative side of this development was, that towns were often left to become little islands of self-sufficiency and technical stagnation under tighter craft domination than before;[28] that is to say, since people do not live by taking in each others' washing, to batten increasingly on the surrounding countryside or on transit trade. This may incidentally have helped sections of the provincial middle class to accumulate capital, but this is not certain. The positive side was, that "putting-out" was a most effective dissolver of the traditional agrarian structure, and provided a means of rapidly increasing industrial production before the adoption of the factory system.

Moreover, the large-scale development of putting-out normally either depends upon, or at least implies, considerable concentration of commercial and financial control. The local smith can expect to rid of his wares on the local market. A specialized community of smiths producing scythes for an export market stretching from Central Europe to Russia — as did the Styrians — depends on export merchants in some, generally a very few, trading centres.[29] (It also depends, of course, on a whole hierarchy of intermediaries). "Putting out", therefore was also likely to increase the accumulation of capital in a few centres of wealth.

The accumulation of capital

Concentration thus helped to increase the accumulation of capital in various ways. However, the problem of capital supply in the periods preceding the industrial revolution was a double one. On the one hand, industrialization probably required much greater preliminary capital accumulation than the 16th century was capable of achieving*. On the other, it required investment in the right places — where it increased productive capacity. Concentration — i.e. an increasingly uneven distribution of wealth within countries — almost automatically increased the capacity to accumulate, though not where the crisis led to general impoverishment. Moreover, as we shall see, concentration in favour of the maritime economies, with their immensely effective new mechanism for capital accumulation (e.g. from foreign and colonial enterprise) laid the basis for accelerated accumulation such as we encounter in the 18th century. It did *not* automatically abolish misinvestment. But as we have seen this, rather than underinvestment was the chief difficulty, and a contributory cause of the 17th century crisis. Nor did it cease. In many parts of Europe the crisis diverted wealth to aristocracies and provincial bourgeoisies who were far from using it productively. Moreover, even the redistribution of capital in favour of the maritime economies might produce misinvestment, though of a different kind: for instance the diversion of capital from industry and agriculture into colonial exploitation, overseas trade and finance. The Netherlands are the standard example of such diversion, but it probably also occurred in Britain in the 18th century.

The crisis therefore produced no *automatic* mechanism for investing capital in the right places. However, it produced two indirect ways of doing so. *First*, in the continental countries, government enterprise in the new absolute monarchies fostered industries, colonies and export drives which would not otherwise have flourished, as in Colbertian France, expanded or saved from collapse mining and metallurgy[30] and laid the foundations of industries in places where the power of the serf-lords and the weakness or parasitism of the middle classes inhibited them. *Second*, the concentration of power in the maritime economies incidentally encouraged much productive investment. Thus the increasing flow of colonial and foreign trade, as we shall see, stimulated the domestic industries and agricultures supplying it. Home exports may, in the eyes of the great Dutch or British trading interests, have been merely a supplement to re-exports of foreign (chiefly colonial) goods, but their development was not negligible. Moreover, it is possible that the virtual Dutch monopoly of international trade may have led rival, but as yet less successful "bourgeois" areas to invest much more of their capital at home than they would have done, had they enjoyed the Dutchmen's opportunities. Thus it seems that there was a very great deal of home investment in Britain between 1660 and 1700, which is reflected in the extremely rapid development of many British industries. In the early 18th century this slackened off. The sluggish period of the 1720s–40s, which we noticed above, may thus be due in part to the diversion of capital overseas following the extraordinary successes of Britain in the wars of 1689–1714. Nevertheless, the basis of future industrial advance had been laid.

The commercial and financial apparatus

Little need be said about the changes in the commercial and financial apparatus which occurred during the period of the crisis. These are most obvious in Northern Europe (where public finance was revolutionized), and particularly in Britain. We need not discuss how far these changes, which were, in effect, the adoption by Northerners of methods and devices long known to people like the Italians, were due to the crisis itself.

Nor need we discuss the effect of the crisis on the growth of what used to be called "the capitalist spirit" and what is now fashionably known as "entrepreneurship." There is no evidence that autonomous vagaries in businessmen's states of mind are as important as the German school used to think and an American school thinks now. Some of the reasons for this were suggested in the previous article.

II

We must now turn to the specific problem of the origin of the industrial revolution. Concentration and redistribution may have laid the foundations for further advance, but in themselves do not explain its precise nature. For if industrialisation was to emerge from it, it had to produce two peculiar forms of expansion. First, it had to encourage manufactures in the countries with the strongest "capitalist" base and on a scale sufficient to revolutionize (by degrees) the rest of the world. *Second*, it had to establish the primacy of production over consumption which is a fundamental prerequisite of capitalist industry.

The case of the Dutch

The first point is simple. Thus the development of manufactures in a country like Russia, though it heralded and prepared the eventual dissolution of feudalism there, was in fact at this period absorbed into the general feudal framework. Ural metalworkers were not proletarians, but special types of serfs. Potentially capitalist entrepreneurs like the Stroganovs, Demidovs or Yakovlevs became special types of serf lords.[31] Russian industry eventually developed not as an extension of such enterprise but on its ruins. But the greatest beneficiary of 17th century concentration, the *Netherlands*, was in many respects a "feudal business" economy[32]; a Florence, Antwerp or Augsburg on a semi-national scale. It survived and flourished by cornering the world's supply of certain scarce goods and much of the world's business as a commercial and financial intermediary. Dutch profits did not depend greatly on capitalist manufacture. Hence the Dutch economy to some extent did a disservice to industrialisation in the short run: to their own, by sacrificing Dutch manufactures (until 1816) to the huge vested interests of trading and finance; to that of the rest of Europe, by encouraging manufactures in feudal and semi-colonial areas where they were not strong enough to break out of the older social framework: Silesia, or West Germany. In Belgium and England the opposite was true. Thus the Belgians compensated for their loss of trade and finance to the Dutch in the late 16th century by developing industrial production and therefore became a major industrialized power before them. Against the free-trade and pacific policy of the Dutch, Britain upheld militant discriminatory and protectionist policies backed by aggressive wars for markets. The industrial future was more likely to be with "modern" states like the British rather than with "old-fashioned" ones like the United Provinces.

Indirectly, of course, the operations of the Dutch helped to advance industrial development. Theirs was an extremely powerful apparatus for dissolving feudal economies and societies, as well as bringing them more effectively into the international economy. Moreover, the mere existence of an immense mechanism for general trading and finance, at everyone's disposal, helped more progressive economies. The fact that the Dutch, the main immediate profiteers of the crisis, succeeded in cornering so much of the world's trade made it easier for rivals and successors to do the same. Thus we can speak not merely of Anglo-Dutch rivalry, but also of Anglo-Dutch symbiosis. The height of Dutch commercial success in fact coincided with the rise of their rivals, 1675–1725,[33] as the period of maximum British prosperity in the 19th century, 1850–73, was also that of the most rapid development of Britain's future competitors. The tendency to monopoly imparted to trade by the Dutch may also have been important in another respect. It may be doubted whether before the 19th century the world market was large enough for the simultaneous industrialization of two or more countries on the modern scale. (In fact we know that British industrialization coincided with the British capture of virtually all the world's markets for certain manufactured goods, and the control of most of the world's colonial areas). Dutch concentration thus proved extremely important, but it should not therefore tempt us to exaggerate the "modernity" of the Dutch. If the only "capitalist" economies available in the 17th century had been like the Dutch, we may doubt whether the subsequent development of industrial capitalism would have been as great or as rapid.

The conditions for industrial revolution

The second point is equally evident. If the cotton industry of 1760 had depended entirely on the actual demand for piece goods then existing, the railways on the actual demand of 1830, the motor industry on that of 1900, none of these industries would have undergone technical revolution. They might instead have developed like the building trade, which fluctuates roughly with the actual demand for building, sometimes running ahead, sometimes lagging, but never — until the present — pushed to the point of wholesale technical upheaval. Capitalist production therefore had to find *ways of creating its own expanding markets*. Except in rare and localized cases this is just what it could not do within a generally feudal framework. In a broad sense it achieved this end by transforming social structure. The very process which reorganized the social division of labour, increased the proportion of non-agricultural workers, differentiated the peasantry and created classes of wageworkers, also created men who depended for their needs on cash purchases — customers for goods. But this is the analyst's way of looking at the matter, not the entrepreneur's, who decided whether or not to revolutionize his production. Moreover it is not at all clear whether in these early stages social transformation was rapid and vast enough to produce an expansion of demand so swift, or a prospect of further expansion so tempting and certain, as to push manufacturers into technical revolution. This is partly so because the "developed areas" in the 17th and early 18th centuries were still relatively small and scattered, partly because the creation of the conditions for capitalist production creates markets for its goods in very different ways. At one extreme we have countries like the U.S.A., which were to develop an intense home market for their manufactures. At the other end — and this was, for various reasons, much more likely in our period — we have countries in which the *per capita* demand for goods was extremely low, at any rate among the mass of peasants and labourers. If there was to be industrial revolution, a number of countries or industries therefore had to operate within a sort of "forced draught," which fanned the entrepreneurs' cupidity to the point of spontaneous combustion.

How was this "forced draught" generated? The following answers may be suggested. First, (as we have seen) the trade of all countries was largely concentrated in the hands of the most industrially advanced, directly or indirectly. Second, these countries — England in particular — generated a large and expanding demand within their home markets. Third, and perhaps most crucial, a new colonial system, based mainly on the slave-plantation economy, produced a special forced draught of its own, which was probably decisive for the British cotton industry, the real industrial pioneer. All three were probably essential. Which of them provided the main incentive may be debated. But if the argument of this article is correct, we expect to find signs of fundamental change and advance in the world's markets in the latter part of the 17th century, though these should be more marked in the markets controlled by "advanced" capitalist economies than in others.

The undeveloped markets

We know very little about home markets (i.e. the demand of the mass of citizens in any country) before the 20th century. We know even less about that characteristic phenomenon of the modern era, the rise of demand for unprecedented goods and services like radio (or, in our period, tobacco, tea, coffee, chocolate), as distinct from the demand for new goods substituting for old needs — nylons for silk stockings (or, in our period, sugar for older sweetening agents). Hence we can only speak about market developments with extreme caution. However, it is most unlikely that demand increased greatly in the bulk of continental countries, even among the comfortable urban middle classes who were the most intensive buyers of standardized manufactures before the 19th century. Tea and coffee remained luxury articles until the 18th century, and sugar production remained sluggish between 1630 and 1670.[34] There was as yet little substitution of glass and pottery for metal even among prosperous middle class families.[35] The Swiss watch-making districts (with the exception of Geneva, which produced luxury articles) did not get into their stride until the 18th century.[36] Retailing remained unspecialized in many German towns and until the mid-17th century even Parisians still drew much of their corn from farmers rather than traders.[37] There may have been a growth of rural retailing in the late 16th century, where towns and lords did not prevent it. However, complaints about the growth of hawking may indicate a weakening of town monopolies rather than an increase in rural cash purchases[38], and in any case rural trade slumped during the crisis. Certainly

Rennes and Dijon in our century were no longer the markets they had once been[39]. Only the demand for some goods, often monopolized by states and lords and farmed out by them, may have increased: tobacco and alcohol[40]. On balance the crisis can therefore hardly have favoured the spontaneous development of capitalist industry for continental home markets. It might favour (a) craft production for a series of local markets, which retarded the progress of industry or (b) the rise of very cheap manufactures, by-products of peasant leisure or oppression.

The most available market in most such countries was also the least suitable for capitalist development — that of states and aristocracies. The fact that aristocrats were the greatest savers did not prevent them from also being great spenders. Thus the Counts Czernin lent the Emperor four million gulden between 1690 and 1724, yet had enough left over for the most sumptuous building and spending[41]. But much of this did not lubricate the wheels of industry half so effectively as middle class purchases. Thus a medium-sized Holstein Junker in 1690 employed 45 lackeys and servants in addition to serfs about the house; more than the regular staff of the Duke of Bedford in the mid-18th century[42]. Yet the future industrialist required not an infinite willingness to keep scores of chefs, stucco artists and perruquiers employed, but mass demand.

Some of this the states and aristocracies did provide, rather inefficiently[43]. *First*, they did so by means of direct orders for standardized army equipment, uniforms — a 17th century innovation — and the like. Probably the effect of this was greatest in the metal-industries for whom, before the Industrial Revolution, war was the chief customer. *Second*, they passed on purchasing power to classes with a higher propensity to buy standardized goods than theirs: to soldiers, and the publicans and shopkeepers who battened on them, to small and medium rentiers, and to the mass of civil and personal servants and minor dependents. Indeed in many areas the prospects of a good market depended largely on the efficiency with which valets robbed their masters. Most of these methods found expression in the "great city," a much more efficient market for goods than the small and medium-size town, let alone the miserable village. In Paris or Vienna a simulacrum of a capitalist home market, with a mass demand for food[44], household goods, middle class textiles, building materials etc, could come into being — encouraged by the concentration of wealth during the crisis period — though perhaps it stimulated semi-craft expansion like that in the building trades more than industry[45].

Absolutist states did, of course, also provide financial, political and military backing for risky commercial undertakings such as wars and new industries, and acted as agents for the transfer of wealth accumulated from the peasantry and others to entrepreneurs. It is possible that this may have led to a more efficient tapping of home demand, though, as we know, the main effort of continental mercantilist states was for exports: or at any rate for a combination of various home markets, the country's own and the captured ones of others. In this task, however, the entrepreneurs of undeveloped states, even with state backing, were at a great disadvantage compared to the developed ones which really did possess a growing home market. Over part of Europe, therefore, the 17th century crisis, unlike that of 1815–48, proved economically sterile; or at any rate, the seeds then sown did not germinate until very much later.

In the maritime areas the home market unquestionably grew greatly. In England at least one is tempted to see the 17th century as the decisive period in the creation of a national market, Here we can claim with some confidence that, by 1700, all sections of the population apart from the most remote were, to some extent, cash customers for goods produced outside their area, and that goods of common consumption were manufactured in specialized areas for national or for wide regional sale. The giant size of London, of course, gave the home market a great advantage. No other country (barring the Dutch) possessed so vast a proportion of its people concentrated in a single urban block. Prof. Fisher has illuminated the effect of this London market on the English economy as a whole. However, if the rise of the Tyneside collieries — to take one example — is almost entirely due to London, that of the other coalfields, which expanded almost as rapidly, is not[47]. By the beginning of the 18th century, if Defoe is to be believed "there are shopkeepers in every village, or at least in every considerable market town"[48] and a nation of shopkeepers implies a nation of customers. Equally important, hawkers were by this time wholesalers or commercial travellers as much as direct retailers of textiles and hardware[49]. The second half of the 17th century saw the rise of some important semi-industrialized cheap consumer goods industries. The sudden growth of specialized areas for making popular pottery began then: no potters are reported from the Bristol apprenticeship lists before 1671. The Midland hardware trades also began their rise about this time.[50] Most significant of all, even the rural population became, to some extent, customers. Earthenware (instead of the more durable pewter) occurs in Essex farms and cottages from the middle of the century.[51] The growth of the home market certainly exceeded that of population at this period. If we take Harper's estimates of the tonnage of coastal shipping as an index, we find that the combined coastwise and collier tonnage increased by an average of less than 1,000 tons per year from 1582 to 1609–15 and by an average of over 1,100 tons per year from then on till 1660; the number of London's coastwise ships trebled between 1628 and 1683.[52] Similarly the rise of imports in this period appears to have been greater than that of exports.[53] At any rate we can see why 17th century English economists congratulated themselves on possessing a large home market for "middling" goods, unlike the chief continental states.

In certain respects, moreover, all the maritime states may be considered as one large, diversified home market, lying as they did close to one another.

Within this area international trade could be, and was, far more intense than trade between each maritime state and its (non-colonial) export markets.[54] Thus English coal was sold almost entirely to the home market, the Dutch and their dependencies, and the colonies. Again, the trade in beer between Hamburg and the United Provinces[55] can count virtually as trade within such an extended "home market."

Three results would follow the development of such home markets. *First*, they would assist the disintegration of the old economy, progressively turn citizens into cash purchasers and cash earners, and encourage the increasing import of food and raw materials, thereby stimulating the growth of exports. (Indeed, the development of an intensive home market was itself a sign that social transformation had gone quite a long way). Moreover, as Marx has shown, the home market demands not only consumer but also capital goods.[56] *Second*, it provided a large and fairly steady reservoir of demand for goods, and hence of productive capacity — a stable foundation for rapid expansion, and a cushion against the chanciness of the export market. Moreover, the maritime home markets with their millions of inhabitants were vastly larger than the medieval city markets at their greatest. *Third*, it might under specially favourable conditions expand so rapidly as to produce within itself the impetus to revolutionize certain industries. The mining industry had clearly by 1700 got to the verge of industrial revolution mainly by such means. Perhaps industries like brewing and soap-making benefited in a similar manner. Nevertheless this was probably not normal. The really headlong and limitless prospects of expansion which encouraged, and indeed compelled, technical revolution were probably most easily achieved in the export markets, though it is doubtful whether any country not possessed of a developed home market could, in the 17th and 18th centuries, have been in a position to seize export opportunities. We must therefore consider export prospects.

Colonial and export markets

The major achievement of the 17th century crisis is the creation of a new form of colonialism. As we have seen under the 16th century colonial system — which, by the way, the Dutch took over virtually unchanged — the colonial market for home manufactures was unimportant, though a large colonial undertaking or the state, considered as an employer of labour and a buyer of capital and consumer goods, stimulated the home economy in addition to bringing in profits for accumulation. Between 1660 and 1681 the East Indies traffic is said to have been only one twelfth of the total Dutch traffic.[57] Traders seemed to show little enthusiasm for the consumer demand in Latin America.[58] However the possibilities of colonial markets were transformed with the foundation of plantation colonies which produced without systematic restriction of output, and of European colonies of settlement.

The middle of the 17th century, here again, marks a turning point.[59] At any rate such quantitative information as we have about the slave-trade demonstrates how incomparably smaller the imports before the Restoration were than in the golden age of the trade in the 18th century. We may, summarising the scattered information,[60] estimate the average annual import of live slaves into the Americas in the 1640s — the peak of Brazilian sugar-production — as of the order of 10,000, between the 1730s and the 1780s as of the order of 50–100,000. By the time the British Africa Company had been reconstituted, and two French Companies, the Senegal and Guinea, had been founded specifically for the slave trade in 1673 and 1685, the stage was set for the great colonial boom.

The new types of colony were to some extent "captive markets" which depended on home supplies. Half of the planter's profit, it was estimated, returned to the West Indies in the form of merchandise:[61] nails and ironware, saddlery, a variety of ordinary textiles, bricks for ballast, pots for molasses, in fact just the sort of merchandise to encourage the future industrialist and perhaps the progressive farmer.[62] The rising supply of slaves set up a rising demand for goods in Africa — always a market for European exports; the growing supply of increasingly cheap plantation goods like sugar and tobacco, a rising demand for European goods in the plantations and elsewhere. Political control by European powers enabled them to cope with any unwelcome competition from the colonies, as well as to rob their unhappy natives with remarkable efficiency. This was very much the kind of expansion which manufacturers needed, though the self-expanding market was bound to fluctuate with the vagaries of war and politics, not to mention economic difficulties. Indeed, as Marx argued that they must, they relied largely upon it in these early stages.[63] By 1700 something like 20% of English exports may have gone to areas which could be described as colonial (including the colonies of other states).[64] In 1759–60 and 1770 over one third went to British colonies alone, not counting direct exports to Spanish and Portuguese colonies. Moreover, if one can judge by the statistics of 1784, when exports first came to be distinguished from re-exports, the colonies were even better customers than these figures imply. Half our exports then went to them (including the recently emancipated USA). The importance of the colonial market for cotton piece-goods exports is even more striking. Until 1770 — that is to say in the crucial period leading up to the industrial revolution — it (including Ireland) never took less than some 90% of them.[65]

However, like the new serf-economies, the new colonial economies were not capable of permanent expansion, and for the same reasons: their use of land and labour was essentially extensive and inefficient. Moreover, the supply of slaves (who rarely reproduced themselves on a sufficient scale) could not be increased fast enough, as is suggested by the rapidly rising trend of slave-prices. Hence exhaustion of the soil, inefficiencies of management and labour difficulties led to something like a "crisis of the colonial economy" from the 1750s.[66] This found various forms of expression — for instance anti-slavery sentiment, and the Home Rule movements of local white settler oligarchies which grew up rapidly in the last third of the 18th century in Latin America, in the West Indies, North America and Ireland, and contributed to the development of revolution in Western Europe. However, we cannot here discuss the difficulties of the new colonialism. It is sufficient to remind ourselves that its adoption gave the "advanced" economies several precious decades of dizzy economic expansion from which they drew inestimable benefits.

None of these developments were wholly new, yet all were greatly advanced by the 17th century crisis. Absolutism and its great capital cities on the continent were strengthened by it. The triumph of the English Revolution hastened the social transformation of England, and thereby the formation of an active home market. Lastly, the new colonialism developed where the old was impossible or no longer profitable, and when the old colonialists had grown too weak to fight off interlopers, though remaining strong enough to stop them from capturing bullion and spices. On the other hand none of them were the result of planning. Brazil had grown up as a plantation colony while Portugal was looking elsewhere, and flourished greatly as a result, resisting Dutch attempts to detach it from Portugal.[67] The Dutch, on the other hand, had all the old fashioned distaste for expanded production and lowered prices, as is shown by their attitude to sugar — and to a lesser extent coffee — production in their empire and to overseas settlement.[68] The Brazilians turned their eyes to gold and diamonds as soon as they discovered them on their territory at the end of the century. In a sense, therefore, the progressive "new" economies established themselves because of the partial ruin of the old, which the 17th century crisis brought about.

III

This article has attempted to show two things, first, that the seventeenth century crisis provided its own solution, and second, that it did so in indirect and roundabout ways. But for the existence of countries capable of wholeheartedly adopting the new — and as it turned out, revolutionary and economically progressive — economic systems, it might well have led to far greater stagnation or regression than it did. But of all the economies the most "modern," the most wholehearted in its subordination of policy to the capitalist entrepreneur was England: the country of the first complete "bourgeois revolution." Hence, in a sense, the economic history of the modern world from the middle of the 17th century hinges on that of England, which began the period of crisis — say in the 1610s — as a dynamic, but a minor power, and ended it in the 1710s as one of the world's masters. The English Revolution, with all its far-reaching results, is therefore in a real sense the most decisive product of the 17th century crisis.

These, then, are some suggestions about the economic development of Europe in a crucial, but still surprisingly obscure period. They may not resist criticism. However, it is to be hoped that they will serve to stimulate further work on the origins of modern capitalism.

Notes

* It is sometimes argued that the cheap and piecemeal character of early industrial plants — e.g. cotton mills — enabled them to be financed with very small initial capital and by ploughing back profits. This example is misleading. We must consider not merely the investment required to start the individual firm, but the total investment required to get an industrial economy off to a flying start — roads, canals, docks, shipping, buildings of all sorts, agricultural investments, mines, etc. Really rapid industrialization needs not only this initial equipment, but continued investment of the same kind. This gives the economy with accumulated reserves — say 18th-century Britain — a vast advantage over the economy without them — say 18th-century Austria. It is too often forgotten that every government in the later 18th century tried to industrialize, but few succeeded.

1 R. Mousnier, *Le XVI et le XVII Siècles* (Paris 1954).
2 S. Mason, *A History of the Sciences* (1953), 223.
3 H. Enjalbert, Le Commerce de Bordeaux et la vie econ. dans le Bassin Aquitain au 17e s. (*Annales du Midi* 62, 1950, 21 ff.); Les études d'histoire normande de 1928 à 1951 (*Annales de Normandie* I, 1951, 178).
4 I owe my knowledge of this to Prof. H. J. Habbakuk, Dr. J. D. Chambers, Mr. D. C. Coleman, Mr. D. Joslin and other students of the period.
5 G. N. Clark, *Seventeenth Century*, p. ix.
6 H. Takahashi, The Transition from Feudalism to Capitalism (*Science and Society* XVI (1952), 334.
7 A. Girard, La repartition de la population en Espagne (*Rev. Hist. Econ. & Soc.* 1929, 350–1, 354); Roupnel, *La vie et la campagne dijonnaises au* 17e s. (1922), 89–91, 150; G. Schmoller, *Deutsches Staedtewesen in aelterer Zeit* (1922), 272–89.
8 A striking example in A. Helbok, *Bevoelkerung d. Stadt Bregenz* (Innsbruck 1912) 148, 150. Karaisl, Z. Gesch. d. Muenchner Patriziats (*Jb. f. National-oekonomie* 152 (1940) 1 ff. But see F. Tremel, Handel d. Stadt Judenburg (*Ztschr. d. hist. Vereins f. Steiermark* 1947) for levelling effect of general impoverishment.
9 *Annales d'Hist. Ec. & Soc.* VII, 186–8.
10 G. N. Clark, *op. cit.* 76.
11 *Encicl. Italiana.* T. Stoyanovitch, Land Tenure etc. of the Balkan Economy (*Journ. Econ. Hist.* XIII, 4, 1953, 398–412). R. N. Salaman, *History & Social Influence of the Potato* (1949).
12 *Essays in honour of L. Febvre*, vol. II (1953).
13 A. P. Usher, *Hist. of the grain trade in France, 1400–1710* (1913), 56, 80–2, 180.
14 Drummond and Wilbraham, *The Englishman's Food* (1939), 119–22.
15 See Doreen Warriner, Some controversial issues in the history of Agrarian Europe (*Slavonic Review* XXXII, 1953, 168 ff:).
16 O. Liiv, *D. wirtschaftl. Lage d. estnischen Gebietes am Ausgang d. 17. Jh.* (Tartu 1935). Review in *Baltic Countries* III, 1, 129–30.
17 Stoyanovith *loc. cit.*
18 W. Stark, Niedergang u. Ende d. landwirtsch. Grossbetriebs in d. boehmischen Laendern (*Jb. f. Nationaloekonomie* 146 (1937), 418, 421–2, O. Klopp, *Geschichte Ostfrieslands 1570–1751* (1856), 412.

19 Heisig, *Die Schaffgotschen Gueterkomplexe* (1884) W. Stark: Abhängigkeitsverhältnisse Boehmens im 17–18. Jh. (*Jb. f. Nationalöken.* 164, 1952 272–3). But in Hungary it was still only 10–15%. E. Szabo, Les grandes domaines (*Rev. Hist. Comparée* 1947, N.S. Vol. 2, p. 188).
20 U. Handrack, *Handel d. Stadt Riga* (Jena 1932). Rev. in *Baltic Countries* II, I.
21 J. Rosdolsky, The distribution of the agrarian product under feudalism (*Journ. Econ. Hist.* 1951, 247 ff.), Stark (1952), 363–4.
22 P. Iwanow, Zur Frage des "aufgeklaerten Absolutismus" der 60er Jahre d. 18. Jh. (*Zur Periodisierung d. Feudalismus u. Kapitalismus in d. USSR*, Berlin 1952, 208ff.); F. Posch, Robotstreiks steirischer Bauern z. Zeit Josefs II (*Blaetter f. Heimatkunde*, 25, 2, Graz 1951), C. Dame, *Entwicklung d. laendl. Wirtschaftslebens in d. Dresden-Meissner Elbtalgegend* (Leipzig 1911), 180–1; Stark 1937, *loc. cit.* A. Agthe, *Ursprung u. Lage d. Landarbeiter in Livland* (Tuebingen 1909), 57, 73 ff.
23 E. Jensen, *Danish Agriculture* (1937) 41 ff.; J. Rutkowski, *Hist. Econ. de Pologne avant les partages* (1927), 119 ff.
24 Kulischer *Allg. Wirtschaftsgesch* II, cap. 9, esp. 117. To the works there quoted add Pirenne, *Hist. de Belgique* IV, 427 ff., Wadsworth & Mann, *Cotton Trade & Industrial Lancashire*, pt. I, G. Unwin, *Studies in Economic History*, W. H. B. Court, *Rise of Midland Industries*, U. Rottstaedt, *Besiedlung d. Thuer-ingerwaldes* (1914), 32, etc.
25 Kulischer, 115; Des Marez, *Le compagnonnage des chapeliers bruxellois* (1909), 13–16.
26 C. A. Swaine, Heimarbeit in d. Gewehrindustrie v. Luettich (*Jb. f. Nationaloekonomie* 3. Folge XII, 177–8.
27 L. Beck, *Gesch. d. Eisens* II, 979–80.
28 E. Coornaert, *Les corporations en France* (1941), cap. V.
29 F. Tremel, Steirische Sensen (*Blaetter f. Heimatkunde* 27, 2, 1953).
30 e.g. L. Beck, *op. cit.* 1039–41.
31 Tugan-Baranowsky, *D. Russische Fabrik*; E. Kutaissoff, The Ural Metal Industry in the 18th century (*Econ. Hist. Rev.* 2d Ser. IV, 1951, 252 ff.); A. M. Pankratova, Die Rolle d. Warenproduktion (*Sowjetwissenschaft* 1954, 3 esp. 439 ff.).
32 For a discussion of this type of business, *Past & Present* V.
33 A. Hyma, *The Dutch in the Far East* (1942) 3–4, 170, 216.
34 Simonsen's estimate, qu. in N. Deerr, *History of Sugar* (1949) I, 112.
35 J. M. Richard, *La vie privèe à Laval aux 17e & 18c ss.* (1922), 59–75.
36 A. Pfleghardt, *D. Schweizerische Uhrenindustrie* (1908).
37 Usher, *op. cit.* 85. For a general bibliography of retail trade, Sombart, *D. moderne Kapitalismus* II, i, 421–35; also E. Koehler, *D. Einzelhandel im Mittelalter* (1938), 55–50.
38 Gebauer, *Gesch. d. Stadt Hildesheim*, 227; R. Scholten, *Z. Gesch. d. Stadt Cleve* 412; E. v. Ranke, Koeln u. d. Rheinland (*Hans. Gesch. Blaetter* XXVII, 1922, 29).
39 H. Sée, *Hist. Econ. de la France* I, 232.
40 For the importance of alcohol in the seignorial economy, Stark (1952), Szabo, *loc. cit.* 185–70.
41 B. Bretholz, *Gesch. Boehmen's u. Maehrens* (1924) III, 52–3.
42 G. Hanssen, *Agrarhistorische Abhandlungen* (1880), 457; G. Scott Thompson, *The Russells of Bloomsbury* (1940), 238.
43 These have been discussed, but their importance exaggerated, by Sombart: *Krieg u. Kapitalismus, Luxus u. Kapitalismus*.
44 For the Viennese meat market, Hassinger, D. erste Wiener orientalische Handelskompanie 1667–83 (*Vierteljahrschr. f. Soz & Wirtsch. Gesch/* XXXV, 1).

45 G. des Marez, La transformation de la ville de Bruxelles au 17e s. (*Etudes Indédiets*, 1936, 129–31).
47 J. U. Nef, *Rise of the British Coal Industry*.
48 *The English Tradesman* (1727), 334.
49 *ibid.* R. B. Westerfield, *Middlemen in British Business*, 313.
50 W. Burton, *English Earthenware and Stoneware* (1904), 7, 28, 30–2, 58; W. Pountney, *Old Bristol Potteries* (1920) Append. I, p. 3. W. H. Court, *op. cit.* H. Hamilton, *The English Brass & Copper Industries to* 1800.
51 F. Steer, *Farm & Cottage Inventories of Mid-Essex* (1950), G. E. Fussell *The English Rural Labourer* (1949).
52 L. A. Harper, *The English Navigation Laws* (1939), 339; T. S. Willan, *The English Coasting Trade* 1600–1750 (1938), esp. cap. vii, pp. 203–5.
53 E. Lipson, *Econ. Hist. of England* II, 189, Harper, *op. cit.* 343.
54 This problem is discussed in League of Nations, *Industrialization & Foreign Trade* (1945), 118.
55 Nef, *op. cit.* Appendix D. W. Vogel, Ueber d. Groesse d. Handelsflotten (*Festschrift f. D. Schaefer*, 1915, 274–5).
56 *Capital* I (1938 ed.), 772.
57 Lannoy & Linden, *Hist. de l'expansion coloniale: Neérland & Danemark* (1911), 334; I. J. Brugmans, D. oost-Ind. Compagnie.... (*Tijdschr. v. Gesch.* LXI, 225–31).
58 Savary, *Le Parfait Négociant* (1675), II, 78.
59 cf. the dates of the beginning of sugar-plantation and exports in the West Indies in *Past & Present* V, note 15, cf. also W. Borah: *New Spain's Century of Depression* (Ibero-Americana 35, 1951), a very suggestive study.
60 This passage is based on the following authorities, and calculations derived from them. There is no space to discuss the methods of arriving at the estimates: v. Lippmann, *op. cit.*; the materials in N. Deerr, *op. cit.* (I, 123–4, 132–3, II, 266, 278–9); U. B. Philips, *American Negro Slavery* (1918), 18, E. Donnan, *The Slave Trade to America* (1920) I, 17 — I cannot accept her estimate —; G. Freyre, *The Masters and the Slaves* (1946), 463 n.; C. R. Boxer, *Salvador de Sa* (1952), 225 n.; Calogeras-Martin, *History of Brazil* (1939), 27; Waetjen, D. Negerhandel in Westindien u. Suedamerika (*Hans. Gesch. Blaetter* 1913, 417 ff.); J. Saintoyant, *Les colonies françaises sous l'ancien régime* I, 252; Macpherson's *Annals of Commerce*; E. Williams, *Capitalism & Slavery* (1945).
61 Oldmixon, *The British Empire in America* (1708), II, 163.
62 Wadsworth & Mann, *op. cit.* 72 n. Enjalbert, *loc. cit.* The demand of settlement colonies like New England would be even better.
63 *Capital* I (1938 ed.), 775, 778–9.
64 From the figures in An Essay Towards Finding the Ballance of our whole Trade, in G. N. Clark, *Guide to English Commercial Statistics* 1696–1782 (1938), L. A. Harper, *op. cit.* 266, Sir C. Davenant, Works II, 17, V, 356, 403.
65 Macpherson, *op. cit.* vol. IV; Wadsworth & Mann, *op. cit.* 146–7.
66 Well discussed in L. Dermigny, Saint Domingue au 17e & 18e ss. (*Rev. Hist.* 1950, No. 204, p. 237–8.)
67 J. L. De Azevedo, *Epocas da Portugal Econômico* (1929). C. R. Boxer, *op. cit.* G. Freyre, *op. cit.* 253, for an interesting argument of 1573 for the superiority of the plantation economy.
68 Lannoy & Linden, *op. cit.* 264 ff., 360; A. N. Coombes, *Evolution of Sugar Cane Culture in Mauritius* (1937).

32

AMERICAN TREASURE AND THE RISE OF CAPITALISM (1500–1700)

Earl J. Hamilton

Source: *Economica* 9, 1929: 338–57.

I

"The discovery of America, and that of a passage to the East Indies by the Cape of Good Hope, are the greatest and most important events recorded in the history of mankind." So wrote Adam Smith in his immortal *Wealth of Nations*.[1] This statement may be—doubtless is—an exaggeration; but had he spoken of the effect of these two events upon the origin of modern capitalism, one of the most important developments of history, his contention would have been incontrovertible.

The present paper purposes to examine the effects of the discovery of an all-water route to the East Indies, the opening of extensive markets in the New World, and above all the heavy European imports of Mexican and Peruvian treasure upon the rise of modern capitalism. For two reasons the study is confined to the sixteenth and seventeenth centuries. First, during this period American gold and silver and the markets of the East and West Indies exerted their greatest influence upon the progress of capitalism. Second, there was a significant development of capitalism in England, France, and the Low Countries. In fact, the progress of capitalism during the sixteenth and seventeenth centuries prepared the way for the Industrial Revolution. Significant experiments with the factory system were carried out in England in the sixteenth century and in France during the seventeenth. There is abundant evidence of a groping toward the factory system before the great inventions of the eighteenth century made such a course inevitable.

Perhaps it is best not to seek too narrow and rigid a definition of *capitalism*, not to formulate a concept upon which there cannot be general agreement. With this desideratum in mind, it may be defined as the system in which wealth other than land is used for the definite purpose of securing an income.

II

Capitalism did not develop out of a void during the early modern period. There were traces of it in the great nations of antiquity, and near the end of the Middle Ages it played an important rôle in the economy of Flanders, the Italian city states, and certain French cities. In these oases, especially in the great industrial, commercial, and financial centres of Italy—Amalfi, Pisa, Genoa, Florence, and Venice—many of the characteristic features of modern capitalism evolved. Arabic notation, destined to supersede cumbersome Roman numerals in accounting, was introduced. Double-entry book-keeping, an indispensable instrument for the rational conduct of business, was developed. The mariner's compass, invaluable to ocean shipping, was introduced into the Western World. Portolan charts, later to be combined with the resuscitated theoretical geography of Ptolemy and Strabo to give birth to modern geography, arose to meet the needs of navigation in the Mediterranean. Important advances were achieved in naval architecture and in the art of navigation. Oriental arts and products were diffused through the trading centres of Italy. In the great seaports and in the fairs arose the law merchant—flexible, expeditious, and fashioned to meet the needs of trade. As a concomitant development, negotiable instruments originated or were popularised. Perhaps the development of organised dealings in foreign exchange and advances in the technique of banking by houses located in Genoa, Venice, and Florence—with agents scattered to the utmost confines of Europe—represented the greatest contribution of the Middle Ages to the rise of modern capitalism. These great banking houses aided materially in the perfection of banking and in the spread of the institution into countries where a fully developed species of capitalism was destined to emerge.[2]

The origin of capitalism cannot be ascribed to the phenomena generated by the discovery of America and of the Good Hope route to the East Indies. The movement already under way was profoundly affected by both these events, especially by the former; but they alone were not responsible for the phenomenal progress of capitalism during the sixteenth and seventeenth centuries. A host of other factors were working in the same direction.

III

The strong national states that arose in the early modern period loosened, but did not entirely remove, medieval fetters on domestic commerce. Princes became interested in the improvement of facilities for land and water transportation. Through the suppression of piracy and robbery, they furnished greater security for private property and better protection to traders. Common customs and institutions, fostered by national unity, increased the demand for standardised products. The widening of the trade area and the standardisation of products afforded an unexampled opportunity for large-scale industry and mass marketing. In other words, they placed a premium upon capitalism. The simplification of public administration and unification of legal systems freed capitalists from the multifarious jurisdictions and erratic, capricious law which hampered their activities in the Middle Ages. The rise of modern states gave a wider scope to the rentier who financed the princes of larger territories than they had hitherto governed. Perennial wars between the incipient national states furnished great investment opportunities. Impecuniosity of the monarchs fighting for the hegemony of Europe and ascendancy in colonisation caused exorbitant interest rates on public obligations, which enabled international bankers shrewd enough to anticipate repudiation to reap fabulous returns on their advances. These gains were important factors in the accumulation of capital, most of which probably sought outlets in industry, commerce, and finance. The sale of shares in public debts prepared the way for the financing of joint-stock enterprises. It should be remembered, however, that Governments competed with business for investment funds and that they diverted capital from productive to destructive uses.[3] Certain efforts on the part of Governments, such as the introduction of new products, subsidies to favourite industries, and public instruction in commercial subjects, played an important rôle in the progress of capitalism.

Undoubtedly the mass demand for standardised products, especially for military uniforms and munitions of war, originating in the perpetual wars of the sixteenth and seventeenth centuries, was favourable to the rise of capitalism. But these wars, on the whole, retarded rather than stimulated this movement. The fruits of years of saving were sacrificed in the support of armies and navies. Capital equipment in the warring nations deteriorated. The production of wealth—which sets an absolute upper limit to saving—and the accumulation of capital were arrested.

According to Max Weber,[4] the inventions basic for the genesis of the factory system in the textile industry in the eighteenth century would not have been possible without the English patent law of 1612. This progressive Act, which limited patent rights to fourteen years, contained the essential features of modern legislation.

IV

In the early modern period farming tended to become more capitalistic. Considerable wealth was devoted to the reclamation of waste land and to the improvement of soil already in use.[5] The great contribution of agriculture to the rise of modern capitalism, however, did not consist of its own development along this line, but rather of the changes which promoted the progress of capitalism in commerce and industry. Better tillage, partially ascribable to the enclosure movement in England, and the introduction of improved plants and animals into England and France from the Low Countries, enabled fewer men to feed and clothe these nations and to supply them with raw material. This, the conversion of arable into pasture in England, and the loss of rights in the soil in the process of enclosure, caused a migration of peasants to the cities, where they supplied the increasing demand for industrial and commercial labour.

V

As Max Weber pointed out,[6] Protestantism probably exerted some influence upon the rise of capitalism. Protestant churches were plainer, and the ritual was simpler than those of the Catholic Church. The probable reduction in the expenses of the Church facilitated saving and capital formation by its members. And the example of the Church in parsimony probably inculcated this quality among the parishioners. Calvin deplored the evils of indiscriminate almsgiving as practised by the Catholic Church in the Middle Ages and inveighed against idleness, which he stigmatised as both a sin against God and a social evil.[7] Max Weber tells us that our word *calling* is known only to the languages influenced by Protestant translations of the Bible. Among the Protestants, honest and assiduous work—one's calling—was supposed to lead to eternal life. This notion permitted the employer to exploit the workman, who expected to receive a supplementary reward in heaven.[8]

On the other hand, there is good reason to believe that Protestantism may have had little to do with the rise of capitalism. That Catholicism and capitalism are not incompatible is demonstrated by the fact that in the late Middle Ages "religious zeal was nowhere so hot and strong as in Florence,"[9] a veritable cradle of capitalism. In fact, the financial practices of the Vatican, such as the collection of money dues from far-flung regions, contributed to the development of international finance. The Florentine and other bankers who served as intermediaries waxed prosperous. It is commonly accepted that Catholic opposition to cupidity, usury, regrating, and to prices fixed by the free play of economic forces seriously hampered the progress of capitalism.[10] But Luther and Calvin substantially agreed with Rome on all these points.[11] According to Sombart,[12] the later Schoolmen, such as Saint Antoine of Florence (1389–1459) and his contemporary, Bernard of Sienna, had more "sympathy for and understanding of capitalism than the seventeenth-century zealot preachers of Puritanism." In the sixteenth and seventeenth centuries Protestantism afforded little relief from the plethora of religious holidays that afflicted most Catholic countries. Puritans prohibited markets on Saturdays, Sundays, and Mondays. Numerous church services were held during the week.[13] Through opposition to "usury," Catholicism and Protestantism alike created an atmosphere that permitted lay princes to pillage money-lenders. Through mysticism both generated a state of mind diametrically opposed to the rational conduct of business enterprise. The multifarious sects into which Protestantism split in its early stages resulted in wasteful multiplication of churches and duplication of effort. May it not be possible that capitalism arose without aid from Protestantism and that the Puritans and other Calvinists finally accepted the inevitable? It has even been argued that Calvinism "was the natural outgrowth of the economic ideas of the age, and can be readily traced to such an origin."[14] It is probable, however, that the Calvinistic doctrine of predestination facilitated acceptance of the changing economic order.

VI

It may not be amiss to examine at this point Sombart's views concerning the capitalist spirit. His thesis, as follows, is strikingly reminiscent of Aristotle[15] and of Karl Marx[16] (who was influenced by Aristotle). "In earlier times, when the needs of the community determined economic activities, these had natural boundaries or limits. There can be no such limits when economic activities are determined by acquisitiveness and by flourishing businesses."[17] This is a typical manifestation of man's ubiquitous tendency—from Confucius and Plato to the present—to idealise the dim past, of which the sordid has been forgotten, and to depreciate the present, of which the glamour is recondite. This tendency to postulate a golden age with subsequent degeneration probably explains the attempts of Sombart and others to show that the development of a capitalistic spirit antedated or roughly synchronised with the early stages of modern capitalism.

Most writers have invested the term *capitalist spirit* (*Geist des Kapitalismus*) with two distinct meanings. Sometimes it is used as the equivalent of economic motive, a sheer desire for gain. Again it is taken to mean a knowledge of the principles of business management. The supposed genesis of an absorbing desire for economic gain cannot be traced to the late Middle Ages or the early modern period. To prove this assertion, one need only point to the writings of ancient and medieval theologians and moral philosophers. That these writings are replete with denunciations of cupidity is a fact too patent to require citations. The widely held opinion that members of medieval guilds were not animated by a desire for gain—that production at their hands was for use rather than for profit—has little foundation in fact. That the economic motive was present throughout the Middle Ages is attested by the constant and persistent efforts of guilds to prevent transverse division of labour and to limit the number of apprentices employed by one master. These regulations were obviously inspired by the fear that capitalistically inclined masters would proletarianise their fellow craftsmen. When used to mean a knowledge of sound principles of business management, the *capitalist spirit* is a complex development that must have synchronised with the rise of capitalism. There doubtless was some interaction between progress in commerce, industry, and finance and the art of business management, but it would be difficult to prove that better business management was the prime mover.

VII

Although, as has been shown, many other forces contributed to the rise of modern capitalism, the phenomena associated with the discoveries of America and of the passage around the Cape of Good Hope to the East Indies were the principal factors in this development. Long distance voyages led to increases in the size of vessels and improvements in the instruments and technique of navigation analogous to the recent advances in aviation stimulated by transatlantic flying. As Adam Smith pointed out,[18] the widening of the market facilitated division of labour and led to technological improvements.[19] The introduction of new agricultural commodities from America and of new agricultural and manufactured goods, especially luxury products, from the East stimulated greater industrial activity to provide the wherewithal to pay for them. Emigration to colonies in the New World and to settlements in the East lessened the pressure of population upon the soil of the mother countries and thus enhanced the surplus—the excess of national production over national subsistence—from which savings could be drawn. The opening of distant markets and sources of supply for raw materials was a significant factor in the transfer of the control of industry and commerce from the guilds to capitalist employers. The old guild organisation—unable to cope with the new problems in purchasing, production, and marketing—commenced to disintegrate and finally gave way to the capitalist employer, a more efficient medium of control.

Let us turn to the greatest influence that the discovery of America had upon the progress of capitalism, to the vast influx of gold and silver from American mines. During the fifteenth century—perhaps in the fourteenth also—expanding industry and commerce in conjunction with stationary production of the precious metals generated a decline in prices which, through its effect on profits, seriously hampered business enterprise. It is probable that even if additional supplies of the precious metals had not been procurable in the New World, its colonisation, though retarded, would ultimately have taken place and that to some extent the markets of the East Indies would have been exploited. The consequent increase in the volume of trade would have had a disastrous effect upon prices, and the progress of capitalism would have been impeded. As the familiar complaints of Buridan and Oresme indicate, the orgies of debasement that swept over Europe in the late Middle Ages and early modern period did not alleviate the price situation. Monetary depreciation, causing increases in prices sufficient to breed chaos, was often followed by sudden restoration of the coinage, resulting in a precipitous decline of prices. Not until El Dorados were discovered in the New World did European business find relief from falling prices.

All the great colonising powers of the early modern period sought gold and silver. Greed for treasure was one of the greatest stimuli to colonisation, but Spain alone was successful in her quest.[20] As early as 1503 Spain commenced to receive gold from Hispaniola with surprising regularity and shortly afterwards from Cuba and Porto Rico as well. Bating the driblets of gold from the region around Panama after 1513, no treasure came from the American continent before November 5th, 1519, when the first Aztec spoils reached Spain. Some fifteen years later the motherland began to enjoy Incan booty sent by Pizarro. Though the conquests of Mexico and Peru, with the resultant robbery, are among the most dramatic episodes in human history, the treasure obtained in this way was—contrary to general opinion—a mere bagatelle in comparison with the receipts from mining at a later date, especially after the discoveries of the renowned silver mines at Potosi, Guanajuato, and Zacatecas and the perfection of the amalgamation process for extracting silver, all of which occurred between 1545 and 1560. From the middle of the sixteenth century to the 'thirties of the seventeenth the treasure of the Indies poured into the motherland at a rate that exceeded the most fantastic dreams of the *conquistadores*. Thereafter the stream of gold and silver lessened considerably, but did not cease entirely.[21]

With minor exceptions, all the treasure, public and private alike, that legally entered Spain from the New World was deposited in the House of Trade (*Casa de la Contratación*) at Seville, where it was delivered to its original owners or to silver merchants who bought it.[22] Through the "Ricardian" specie-flow mechanism[23] and divergent bimetallic ratios,[24] American gold and silver were diffused throughout the world. Satisfactory data concerning the absorption of American treasure are lacking,[25] but there is good reason to suppose that most of it went to the great trading centres of England, France, and the Low Countries. Writing in 1629, Alonso de Carranza, who was thoroughly familiar with the India trade, gives us a list of the cities that first received the gold and silver smuggled into Spain.[26] They were London, Rouen, Antwerp, and Amsterdam. Documents preserved in the Archivo General de Indias at Seville prove that some smuggled treasure reached Lisbon. Though most of the American treasure that came to Europe passed through Spain,[27] interlopers carried some of it directly to other countries. Since the English, French, and Dutch took the lead in this practice, it may be presumed that they received the bulk of the gold and silver. Spanish armies in France during the sixteenth century and in the Low Countries during the seventeenth spent large sums of the precious metals in or near important trading centres.

It is significant that Portugal, Holland, England, and France—the countries that received a large percentage of American gold and silver—

monopolised the East India trade. Was there a causal connection between treasure and trade?

Undoubtedly the discovery of the Good Hope passage to the fabled Spice Islands would have stimulated trade in any event, but the physical barriers to transportation and the political throttling of trade along former routes by the Ottoman Turk were not the only obstacles to be overcome. For some inexplicable reason Orientals have always had a penchant for hoarding treasure.[28] Hence, even in response to a protracted inflow of specie, Oriental prices, unlike those of the Western World, did not rise sufficiently to induce a counter flow. For more than two thousand years the East has proved a necropolis for European gold and silver.[29] The seventeenth-century pamphleteers who in tract after tract denounced the English East India Company for draining away the country's treasure were not mistaken as to the facts. European products were carried to the East, but silver was the commodity that could be exchanged for Oriental goods on the most advantageous terms.[30] So treasure flowed from Portugal, Holland, England, and France to the Orient in exchange for the eagerly sought spices and luxury goods of that region. Notwithstanding the enormous profits obtained in the East India trade, the passage around the Cape of Good Hope might have been rendered nugatory by a dearth of specie but for the vast streams of Mexican and Peruvian silver flowing into Europe.[31] The voyage of Columbus was an imperative supplement to that of da Gama.

For about two thousand years monopoly of the East India trade—a trade that has always enriched the nations able to control it—has been an object of policy and a prize of diplomacy. But in the first two and a half centuries after the voyages of da Gama and Columbus the struggle for hegemony in the East Indies was intensified manyfold. Not only did statesmen precipitate or sanction sanguinary wars, but writers counselled aggression as a means of achieving political and economic ascendancy. Did the profits of the trade justify this rivalry?

From the very beginning of the modern era trade with the East Indies by the Cape route was almost incredibly lucrative. It is difficult to find in the annals of business either greater profits than those obtained on some of the early voyages to the Spice Islands or records of sustained earnings that surpass those of the English and Dutch East India Companies during the seventeenth century. "Da Gama returned to Lisbon in 1499 with a cargo which repaid sixty times the cost of the expedition,"[32] affording a profit of about 6,000 per cent. The *Victoria*, sole survivor of the memorable fleet of Magellan, brought back to Spain 556.72 quintals of spice, of which 501.35 were sold in Seville at 42 ducats[33] per quintal.[34] If we assume that the remaining 55.37 quintals were saleable—and at the same price—, the cargo was worth 23,382.24 ducats, a sum comparable to the value of the specie borne by the average treasure ship at that time. I know of no satisfactory account of the profits Portugal obtained from commerce with the East in the sixteenth century, during most of which she was in the ascendency;[35]

but such figures are not wanting for Holland—the nation upon which the Portuguese mantle fell in the seventeenth century. The Dutch East India Company, organised in 1602, was a highly successful enterprise until the close of the seventeenth century. "For nearly two hundred years it declared dividends ranging from 12 1/2 per cent. to 20, 40, or even 50 per cent.; the average dividend from 1602 to 1796 was over 18 per cent."[36] The earnings of the English East India Company were stupendous. On some of the early voyages profits of 195, 221, 311, 318, and 334 per cent. were realised. During the seventeenth century dividends averaged about 100.21 per cent.[37]

Although the joint-stock company antedates the English and Dutch East India Companies, the fabulous dividends paid by these two concerns fomented its progress and diffusion. "It was these great successful companies which made the device of share capital generally known and popular; from them it was taken over by all the continental states of Europe."[38]

The enormous profits obtained from the East India trade doubtless contributed powerfully to capital formation and thus to the rise of modern capitalism. The bulk of savings at the present time come directly or indirectly from individuals with high incomes,[39] and presumably this has always been true. Therefore the profits of the Dutch and English East India Companies, not to mention those of interlopers engaged in the same trade, must have afforded considerable stimulus to saving. Bating loans to Governments and ecclesiastical organisations, most of the savings were invested in commercial, industrial, or financial enterprises.

Particularly important is the price revolution precipitated by the great influx of American gold and silver.[40] Could a mere upheaval of prices stimulate or retard the progress of capitalism? Obviously a general increase in prices, all rising equally and simultaneously, could disturb the existing order only in so far as it benefited debtors at the expense of creditors. May it not be argued that capitalists[41] as a class could not gain through divergent movements of prices, that at most some might profit to the extent that others lost? If all commodities and services were sold by capitalists, this argument would be tenable. But two important classes of services, those of land and labour, were sold to entrepreneurs by landlords and labourers.

Precise data concerning the course of rents during the sixteenth and seventeenth centuries are lacking, but for England reasonably satisfactory evidence indicates that rents lagged considerably behind prices. The Knight in Hales' *Discourse on the Common Weal of This Realm of England* (1549) repeatedly stated that the lag of rents behind prices had impoverished landlords.[42] He declared that "the most part of the landes of this Realme stand yet at the old Rent" and explained that "sume have takinges therein, as lessees or copies not yet expired, which cannot be enhaunced, thoughe the owners wold."[43] On acquiring new land or upon the expiration of leases the Knight raised rents, but he did not expect a third of his land to come to his "disposition" during his lifetime, nor perchance during the lives of his

Table I Index Numbers of Prices and Wages in England, 1500–1702 (Index for 1451–1500 = 100).

Period	Prices	Wages	Period	Prices	Wages
1501–1510	95	95	1603–1612	251	124.5
1511–1520	101	93	1613–1622	257	134
1521–1530	113	93	1623–1632	282	138.5
1531–1540	105	90	1633–1642	291	152.5
1541–1550	79	57	1643–1652	331	175
1551–1560	132	88	1653–1662	308	187
1561–1570	155	109	1663–1672	324	190
1571–1582	171	113	1673–1682	348	205.5
1583–1592	198	125	1683–1692	319	216
1593–1602	243	124	1693–1702	339	233

sons.[44] We are told by such eminent economic historians as Lipson[45] and Tawney[46] that rents rose less than prices during the sixteenth century. Consequently the landowning class suffered a diminution of income. This tends to support the contention of von Strieder that capital accumulation did not come largely from rent, as Sombart maintained.

A paucity of data concerning wages—unlike the case of rent—does not handicap our investigation of the relations between prices and wages. Utilising the price statistics collected by Thorold Rogers[47] for England and for France by Vicomte d'Avenel,[48] Georg Wiebe[49] has constructed index numbers of prices and wages during the price revolution.

Table I[50] comprises index numbers of prices and wages in England, 1500–1702, and Chart I shows the same data in graphic form. The prices of seventy–nine commodities and the wages of nine classes of labour enter into the index numbers.

Table II and Chart II present index numbers of prices and wages in France, 1500–1700.[51] Twenty–four commodities and nine grades of labour are included in the index numbers.[52] The value of the wage index is impaired by the fact that the pay of three classes of labourers includes subsistence. As might be expected, the money wages of these workmen rose slightly less than those of the labourers who supported themselves.[53]

Since almost all the American treasure that legally entered Europe came to Seville, the relations between prices and wages in Andalusia merit consideration. We do not have data for the period after 1660; but, as has been said, by about 1640 the stream of American gold and silver had dwindled to insignificant proportions.

Chart III shows index numbers of prices and of the wages of landmen and seamen in Andalusia, 1503–1660.[54] For the sake of brevity, the table is omitted. The index numbers include the prices of twenty–four homogeneous commodities and the wages of four classes of landmen and thirteen classes of seamen.[55]

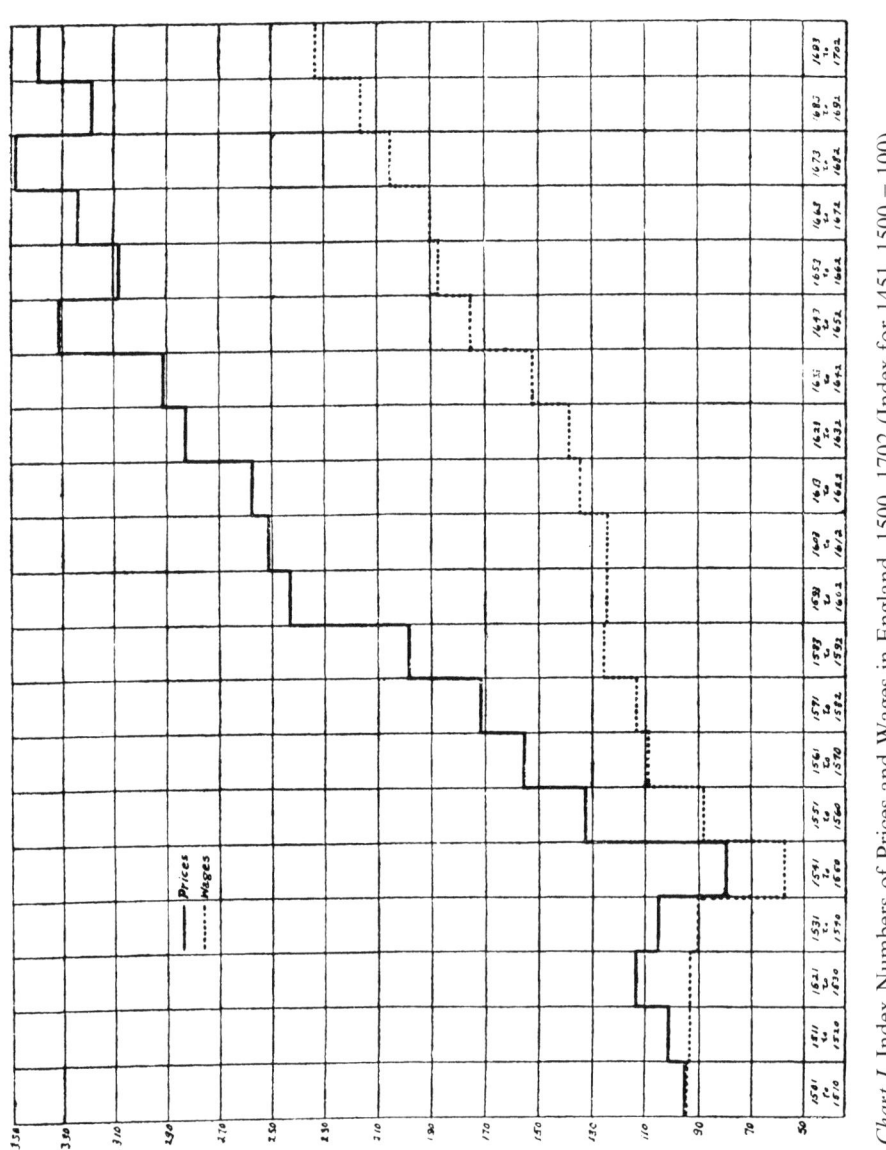

Chart I Index Numbers of Prices and Wages in England, 1500–1702 (Index for 1451–1500 = 100).

Table II Index Numbers of Prices and Wages in France, 1500–1700 (Index for 1451–1500 = 100).

Period	Prices	Wages	Period	Prices	Wages
1501–1525	113	92	1601–1625	189	113
1526–1550	136	104	1626–1650	243	127
1551–1575	174	103	1651–1675	227	127
1576–1600	248	113	1676–1700	229	125

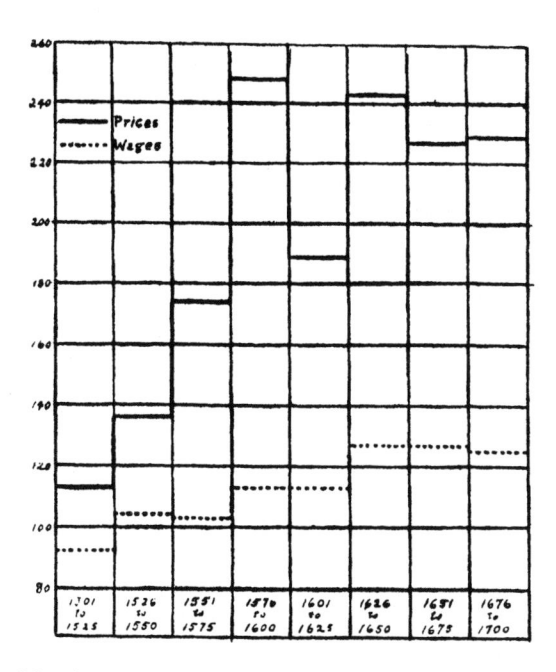

Chart II Index Numbers of Prices and Wages in France, 1500–1700 (Index for 1451–1500 = 100).

VIII

The conclusion is inescapable that the discoveries of America and of the Cape route to the East Indies were highly important factors in the rise of modern capitalism. Changes in trade routes, the widening of markets, contacts with distant lands and strange peoples, and a more perfect knowledge of geography conspired to perturb the minds of men much as does our increasing power over nature to-day. The price revolution set in motion by American gold and silver contributed directly to the progress of capitalism. Textile manufacturing, the leading industry, was dominated by the domestic (putting out) system, and its disintegration caused production to be spread over a considerable interval of time. The price paid for goods in the East

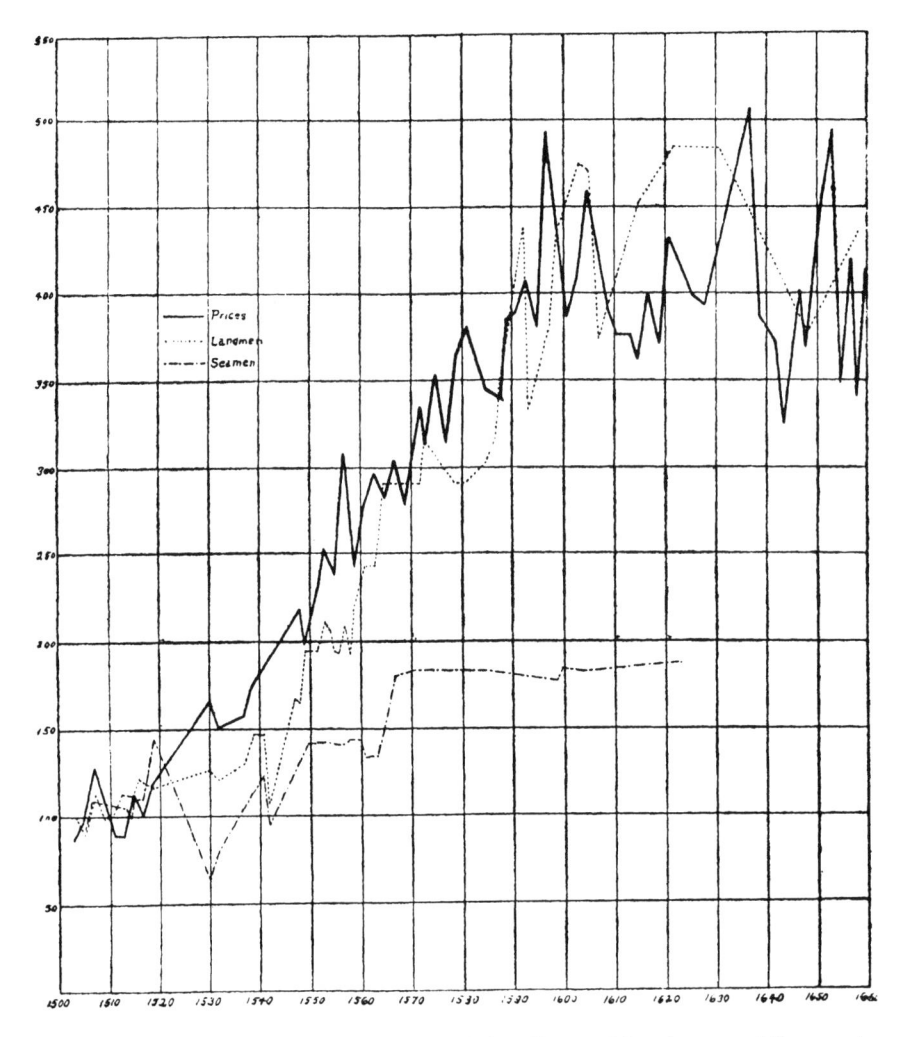

Chart III Index Numbers of Prices and of the Wages of Landmen and Seamen in Andalusia, 1503–1660 (Index for 1503–1511=100).

Indies was largely determined by their value in Europe when the traders sailed, but by the time the ships returned prices had usually risen a great deal. Hence enormous windfalls were thrown in the laps of traders and manufacturers.

In England and France the vast discrepancy between prices and wages, born of the price revolution, deprived labourers of a large part of the incomes they had hitherto enjoyed,[56] and diverted this wealth to the recipients of other distributive shares. As has been shown, rents, as well as wages, lagged behind prices; so landlords gained nothing from labour's loss. For a period of almost two hundred years English and French capitalists—and presumably those of other economically advanced countries—must have enjoyed incomes analogous to those American profiteers reaped from a similar divergence between prices and wages from 1916 to 1919.

Perhaps a hypothetical example will clarify the connection between prices, wages, and profits. Let us assume that of every 100,000 pounds' worth of goods produced by a capitalist in England or France at the beginning of the sixteenth century 60,000 went to wages, 20,000 to rent, and 20,000 to profits. The profits on the turnover amount to 25 per cent. Reference to Tables I and II will prove it not unreasonable to suppose that at the close of the sixteenth century the same product would have been sold for about 250,000 pounds; that wages would not have amounted to more than 75,000; and, making the unreal assumption that rents did not lag behind prices, not more than 50,000 pounds would have gone to rent. Profits amount to 125,000 pounds, or 100 per cent. on the turnover. The lag of wages behind prices has quadrupled profits.

The windfalls thus received, along with gains from the East India trade, furnished the means to build up capital equipment, and the stupendous profits obtainable supplied an incentive for the feverish pursuit of capitalistic enterprise. We find, as might be expected, that during the seventeenth and latter part of the sixteenth centuries England, France, and the Low Countries were seething with such genuinely capitalistic phenomena as systematic mechanical invention, company formation, and speculation in the shares of financial and trading concerns. The developments of this period, accelerated and fructified by the important series of mechanical inventions in the last half of the eighteenth century, were a significant step in the direction of the modern factory system, with the concomitant developments in commerce and finance.

The close connection between the East India trade and American treasure and the rise of modern capitalism has been overlooked or neglected largely because Portugal, the first nation to profit from trade with the Spice Islands by the Cape route, and Spain, the recipient of American gold and silver, showed no significant progress toward capitalism. It is true that well-rounded capitalism did not emerge in Portugal or Spain, but this fact is not incompatible with the thesis of the present paper—namely, that profits from the East India trade and the influx of Mexican and Peruvian silver were the most important, but not the only, factors in the rise of modern capitalism and that American treasure exerted its influence through a lag of wages behind prices during the price revolution. Factors essential to the progress of capitalism were lacking in Portugal. The loss, in colonial enterprise, of the best blood of the nation, which was largely of foreign origin, stripped the country of able and virile leaders, and the inane expulsion of Jews[57] deprived business of much of its best talent. Religious fanaticism, resulting in various persecutions and expulsions of Jews and Moors, precluded or interfered with the conduct of business by two of the most economically capable classes in Spain. An examination of Chart III will reveal that the mechanism through which American treasure operated did not function in Andalusia, nor presumably in the rest of Spain, as it did in England and France. Wages lagged behind prices, but not enough to afford extraordinary profits and thus to give a great impetus to capitalism. Through possession of El Dorados in New Spain and Peru, Spaniards expected to wax prosperous without work.[58] Similar results were engendered in France in the wake of the Great War by the delusion that Germany would be made to pay fantastic reparations and in the South of the United States after the Civil War by the confident expectation of manumitted slaves that the Government would provide every nascent freeman with a mule, farming equipment, and forty acres of fertile soil.

Notes

1. Cannan edition, London, 1904, Vol. II, p. 125. This statement appears to have been taken from Raynal's *Histoire Philosophique* (*ibid.*, p. 125 n.).
2. It has been argued that the system of clearing developed in the fairs at Lyons served as a model for the London Clearing House (M. Vigne, *La Banque à Lyon*, Lyons and Paris, 1903, p. 152).
3. In Spain 70 per cent. and in other countries two-thirds or more of public revenue was spent for war (Max Weber, *General Economic History* [English translation], New York, 1927, p. 308).
4. *Op. cit.*, p. 312.
5. As early as the fourteenth century land was being improved and reclaimed, but there was a significant increase in both of these movements in the sixteenth and seventeenth centuries.
6. "Die Protestantische Ethik und der Geist des Kapitalismus," *Archiv für Sozialwissenschaft und Sozialpolitik*, Vols. XX, XXI. Like most writers who hit upon a new idea, Weber probably exaggerated the influence of Protestantism upon the rise of capitalism.
7. R. H. Tawney, *Religion and the Rise of Capitalism*, London, 1926, pp. 114–115.
8. *General Economic History*, p. 367. Cf. George O'Brien, *An Essay on the Economic Effects of the Reformation*, London, 1923, pp. 68–134.
9. Werner Sombart, *Quintessence of Capitalism* (English translation), London, 1915, p. 229.
10. Upon grounds that do not seem convincing, Sombart (*op. cit.*, pp. 243, 247–250) denied that canonical prohibitions of interest interfered with the progress of capitalism. He argued that partnerships were always considered legitimate and that the illegitimacy of interest forced investors to take risks. In this way a spirit of adventure was developed. Apparently Sombart did not take account of the fact that a fair percentage of the population consisted of the timorous, who would hoard rather than adventure their funds.
11. R. H. Tawney, *op. cit.*, pp. 79–102, 119.
12. *Op. cit.*, p. 244.
13. *Ibid.*, chap. xix.
14. Simon N. Patten, *The Development of English Thought*, New York, 1899, p. 112. Cf. Werner Sombart, *op. cit.*, chap. xxi.
15. *Politics* (Jowett edition), Oxford, 1920, pp. 42–46.
16. *Capital*, Vol. I, pt. ii, chap. iv.

17 Werner Sombart, *op. cit.*, pp. 173-174.
18 *Op. cit.*, Vol. II, pp. 92-93.
19 For an excellent recent discussion of this matter, see A. P. Usher, *Industrial History of England*, New York, 1919, p. 23.
20 Beginning about 1693. Portugal obtained considerable quantities of gold from Brazil (Adolf Soetbeer, *Edelmetall-Produktion und Werthverhältniss zwischen Gold und Silber*, Gotha, 1879, pp. 83-91).
21 A comprehensive account (written from original sources) of the gold and silver Spain received from her colonies in the New World can be found in my article. "Imports of American Gold and Silver into Spain, 1503-1660," *Quarterly Journal of Economics,* May, 1929, pp. 436-472.
22 As is well known, a part of the treasure was sequestered upon arrival in Spain.
23 We may safely assume that at the opening of the sixteenth century a rough equilibrium existed between the price levels of Andalusia, the region first flooded with American gold and silver, and those of England and France. Since Andalusian prices rose a great deal faster than those of England and France during the sixteenth century—rising in that period almost twice as much as those of England and France had increased by the middle of the seventeenth century—there must have been an outflow of specie to settle an adverse trade balance (Earl J. Hamilton, "American Treasure and Andalusian Prices, 1503-1660," *Journal of Economic and Business History,* November, 1928, pp. 31-33).
24 Fabulous profits were obtainable through the shipment of gold or silver from a country in which it was undervalued to one where it was overvalued. For instance, a gross profit of 20.74 per cent. could be had on shipments of silver from Spain to Venice, 1609-1630, and during the next eight years the profit stood at 29.27 per cent. (computed from data in W. A. Shaw's *History of Currency*, London, 1895, pp. 69-70, and some of the unpublished results of my research in Castilian money). But can even so great a gain account for the diffusion of American treasure? Obviously equal profits could have been made by shipping gold from Venice into Spain, and the gold would have had a mint price greater than that of the silver to the extent of the profit on the two transactions. Hence it appears that writers who have listed divergent bimetallic ratios as a cause of the international movement of the precious metals may have erred. Yet it should be remembered that prices were considerably higher in Spain than in Italy at this time—so more than 30 per cent. profit could be made on goods shipped into Spain—and that most dealers in bullion and foreign exchange were then merchants as well. It follows that the undervalued metal moved from Spain into other countries and goods in the reverse direction. Therefore it seems that divergent bimetallic ratios were a significant factor in the scattering of American gold and silver throughout the world.
25 It is possible that material deposited in archives of the Spanish Basque provinces will throw a good deal of light on this subject. I hope to make use of these records in the future.
26 *El Adjustamiento i Proporción de las Monedas de Oro, Plata, i Cobre*, Madrid, p. 377.
27 In the second decade of the eighteenth century the anonymous author of *Comercio de Holanda* said (p. 95) that almost all the specie in Europe had been brought to Spain from Mexico and Peru. According to Manuel Colmerio, Spain received from 83 to 87 per cent. of all the American treasure reaching Europe during the first three centuries after the discovery (*Historia de la Economia Politica en España,* Madrid, 1863, Vol. II, pp. 434-435).

THE FEUDAL AND EARLY MODERN ECONOMY

28 Alonso de Carranza averred (1629) that the Chinese, anticipating a cessation of production at Potosi, were making and burying huge balls of silver (*op. cit.*, pp. 371–375).
29 "Pliny tells us of the immense amount of Indian spices consumed at the funeral of Sabina Poppaea, the favourite of Nero, in A.D. 65, and laments the consequent drain of precious metals to the East." George Unwin, *Studies in Economic History*, London, 1927, p. 229.
30 From January 17th, 1873, to March 3rd, 1887, the United States coined a "trade dollar" of 420 grains for the specific purpose of enabling Mexican traders in the Orient to compete with merchants using Mexican silver dollars (A. B. Hepburn, *History of Coinage and Currency in the United States*, New York, 1903, pp. 278–280, 571).
31 It is significant that bitter complaints against the English East India Company commenced about 1640, thus synchronising with the precipitous decline in the imports of American gold and silver into Europe (see my article on "Imports of American Gold and Silver into Spain," *Quarterly Journal of Economics*, May. 1929, pp. 464–465).
32 Clive Day, *History of Commerce,* New York, 1928, p. 184.
33 The Spanish ducat, a money of account, was equivalent to about 543.75 grains of pure silver.
34 Archivo General de Indias, *Contaduria*, 3–1–1/15.
35 Abundant material in the archives of Portugal probably awaits the investigator who cares to make a study of trade and navigation between Portugal and the East Indies during the sixteenth century.
36 Clive Day, *op. cit.*, p. 196. During the eighteenth century dividends were paid largely with borrowed money, the last being declared in 1782 (Clive Day, *Dutch in Java*, New York, 1904, p. 71).
37 This figure is not to be taken as minutely correct. It has been computed from data in W. R. Scott, *Joint-Stock Companies,* Cambridge, 1910, Vol. II, pp. 123–128, 177–179.

"We learn from Macaulay's History that during the twenty years succeeding the Restoration, the value of the annual imports from Bengal alone rose from £8,000 to £300,000, and that the gains of the Company from their monopoly of the import of East Indian produce were almost incredible" (Lyall, *British Dominion in India*, p, 38).
38 Max Weber, *op. cit.*, p. 282.
39 Cf. A. B. Wolfe, "Savers' Surplus and the Interest Rate," *Quarterly Journal of Economics*, Vol. XXXV, pp. 10–16: David Friday, "Wealth, Income, and Savings," *Annals of the American Academy of Political and Social Science*, Vol. LXXXVII, p. 42.
40 Werner Sombart (*op. cit.*, pp. 317–318), Henri Sée (*Les Origines du Capitalisme Moderne*, Paris, 1926, chap. iii), and Max Weber (*op. cit.*, pp. 311, 352–353) have averred that American specie contributed to the rise of capitalism, but have failed to indicate the mechanism through which its influence was exerted.
41 Following the lead of most economists who wrote before the nineteenth century, I am making no distinction in this paper between *capitalist* and *entrepreneur*. By the end of the eighteenth century investment and management had not become separate functions. As I am using the term, *profits* comprise wages of management, insurance against risk, and interest on capital.
42 Lamond edition, Cambridge, 1893, pp. 19, 38, 39, 41, 81, 86.
43 Pp. 38–39.
44 P. 19.

45 *Economic History of England*, London, 1912, p. 309.
46 *Agrarian Problem*, London, 1912, p. 309.
47 *A History of Agriculture and Prices in England*, Oxford, 1882–1887, Vols. III–VI.
48 *Histoire Economique de la Propriété, des Salaires, des Denrées, et de Tous Prix en Général*, Paris, 1894–1926, Vols. I–VII.
49 *Zur Geschichte der Preisrevolution des XVI und XVII Jahrhunderts*, Leipzig, 1895.
50 Compiled from data in Georg Wiebe, *op. cit.*, pp. 374–377.
51 Compiled from data in Georg Wiebe, *op. cit.*, pp. 378–379.
52 The following table (compiled from figures in Wiebe, *op. cit.*, pp. 372–373) shows that the relative trends of prices and wages in Alsace were similar to those of France:

Index Numbers of Prices and Wages in Alsace, 1500–1700 (Index for 1451–1500 = 100).

Period	Prices	Wages	Period	Prices	Wages
1501–1525	99	89	1601–1625	237	105
1526–1550	114	91	1626–1650	341	138
1551–1575	156	88	1651–1675	220	114
1576–1600	205	103	1676–1700	252	103

53 The following table gives index numbers of wages with subsistence and without subsistence (computed from figures in Georg Wiebe, *op. cit.*, pp. 378–379). Index for 1451–1500 = 100.

Period	Without Subsistence	With Subsistence
1501–1525	92	94
1526–1550	108	97
1551–1575	108.5	91
1576–1600	122	95
1601–1625	116	103.5
1626–1650	126	132
1651–1675	129.5	123
1676–1700	123	128.5

54 For a statement of the commodities used, sources of the statistics, and methods employed in studying Andalusian prices, see my article, "American Treasure and Andalusian Prices, 1503–1660," *Journal of Economic and Business History*, November, 1928, pp. 1–35. For similar information concerning wages, see my forthcoming article (in press), "Wages and Subsistence on Spanish Treasure Ships," in the *Journal of Political Economy*.
55 In addition to money wages, seamen received maintenance.
56 It is noteworthy that almost all writers on wages between 1500 and 1700 held a subsistence theory of wages, a theory that is discredited by Charts I and II. Either real wages were not at the minimum of subsistence during the base period, 1451–1500, or they fell to about one-half this amount by 1700. This goes to show how unsatisfactory is general observation as a means of verifying economic theory. If adequate data had been available and economists had had satisfactory knowledge of statistical methods, one wonders whether the subsistence theory of

wages would not have been thrown overboard. It is significant that Sir William Petty, perhaps the best economic statistician of the seventeenth century, held this theory. It should be remembered, however, that Petty was never satisfied with the statistical sources at his disposal.

57 See Werner Sombart, *The Jews and Modern Capitalism* (English translation), London, 1913, p. 13.

58 Jean Bodin seemed to realise that gold and silver from the New World tended to make indolent the Spaniards of his day (*Réponse aux Paradoxes de Malestroit*, Paris, 1568).

33

THE RISE OF THE GENTRY, 1558–1640[1]

R. H. Tawney

Source: *Economic History Review* 11, 1941: 1–38.

The first French translator[2] of Locke's *Thoughts on Education* introduced it with the remark that foreign readers, in order to appreciate it, must remember the audience to whom it was addressed. It was composed, he explained, for the edification of an element in society to which the Continent offered no exact analogy, but which had become in the last century the dominant force in English life. To M. Coste, in 1695, the triumphant ascent of the English gentry—neither a *noblesse*, nor a bureaucracy, but mere *bons bourgeois*—seemed proof of an insular dynamic of which France, with the aid of his translation, would do well to learn the secret. His compatriots, a century-and-a-half later, hailed the effortless survival of the same class in an age which had seen *seigneurs* in flight from their castles, and even *junkers* cajoled into some semblance of concessions, as an example of social stability as eccentric as it was remarkable, and marvelled at the depth to which the tree had struck its roots. De Tocqueville in the 'forties, de Lavergne in the 'fifties, Taine in the 'sixties and 'seventies, wrote in a mood of reaction; but they had some excuse for opening their eyes.[3] In spite of the influx in the interval of Scots, Nabobs, some merchants, a few bankers, and an occasional industrialist, not less than one in every eight of the members sitting for English and Welsh seats in the last un-reformed House of Commons, and one in five of the House of Lords, belonged to families which, two centuries before, had given representatives to the House of Commons in the Long Parliament.[4] Ten English counties had been blessed in 1640 with some sixty-two leading landowners, masters of six or more manors apiece. Of those in the whole ten one-half, of those in five just under two-thirds, had descendants or kin who owned 3,000 acres or upwards in 1874.[5]

I

The political rôle of this tenacious class has not lacked its eulogists. It has itself, however, a history, which is not only political, but also economic; and the decisive period of that history is the two generations before the civil war. "Could humanity ever attain happiness," wrote Hume of that momentous half-century, "the condition of the English gentry at this period might merit that appellation." Contemporary opinion, if more conscious of the casualties of progress, would have been disposed, nevertheless, to endorse his verdict. Observers became conscious, in the later years of Elizabeth, of an alteration in the balance of social forces, and a stream of comment began which continued to swell, until, towards the close of the next century, a new equilibrium was seen to have been reached. Its theme was the changing composition, at once erosion and reconstruction, of the upper strata of the social pyramid. It was, in particular, since their preponderance was not yet axiomatic, the increase in the wealth and influence of certain intermediate groups, compared with the nobility, the Crown and the mass of small landholders. Of those groups the most important, "situated," as one of its most brilliant members wrote, "neither in the lowest grounds . . . nor in the highest mountains . . . but in the valleys between both,"[6] was the squirearchy and its connections. Holding a position determined, not by legal distinctions, but by common estimation; kept few[7] and tough by the ruthlessness of the English family system, which sacrificed the individual to the institution, and, if it did not drown all the kittens but one, threw all but one into the water; pouring the martyrs of that prudent egotism, their younger sons, not only into the learned professions, but into armies, English and foreign, exploration and colonisation, and every branch of business enterprise; barred themselves by no rule as to *dérogeance* from supplementing their incomes from whatever source they pleased, yet never, as in Holland, wholly severed from their rural roots, the English gentry combined the local and popular attachments essential for a representative rôle with the aristocratic aroma of *nobiles minores*, and played each card in turn with tactful, but remorseless, realism. Satirists[8] made merry with the homely dialect, strong liquor and horse-coping of the provincial squire; but, in spite of the Slenders and Shallows, the mere bumpkins of the class, for whom the French invented a special name, were not too distressingly conspicuous. Its failures, instead of, as on the Continent, hanging round its neck and helping to sink it, discreetly disappeared with the disappearance of their incomes. Its successes supplied the materials for a new nobility. They provided more than one.

Inconsistencies were inevitable in speaking of a class freely recruited from below, in a society where the lines of social stratification were drawn, not, as in most parts of the Continent, by birth and legal privilege, but by gradations of wealth. The elasticity which such peculiarities conferred has often been applauded, but they were not favourable to precise classifications; nor was precision in demand. There were moments, it is true, when it was convenient to stand on an hereditary dignity, authentic or assumed; did not the arch-leveller of the age, free-born John himself, win one of the earliest of his famous collection of judicial scalps by refusing to plead to an indictment drawn against "John Lilburne, yeoman"?[9] There were voices from the past which, when the crash came, hailed the fall of the monarchy as the inevitable nemesis of a general downward slide towards the abyss of social "parity," and reproached the professional custodians of traditional proprieties with opening to fees doors which a prudent rigour would have locked.[10] But agricultural, commercial and industrial interests were, in most parts of the country, inextricably intertwined. Mere caste had few admirers—fewer probably among the gentry militant of the early seventeenth century than among the gentry triumphant of the early eighteenth—and that note was rarely heard. Common sense endorséd the remark that "gentility is nothing but ancient riches,"[11] adding under its breath that they need not be very ancient. Sir Thomas Smith had said that a gentleman is a man who spends his money like a gentleman.[12] Of the theorists rash enough to attempt a definition, few succeeded in improving on that wise tautology.

In spite, nevertheless, of ambiguities, the group concerned was not difficult to identify. Its members varied widely in wealth;[13] but, though ragged at its edges, it had a solid core. That core consisted of the landed proprietors, above the yeomanry, and below the peerage, together with a growing body of well-to-do farmers, sometimes tenants of their relatives, who had succeeded the humble peasants of the past as lessees of demesne farms; professional men, also rapidly increasing in number, such as the more eminent lawyers, divines, and an occasional medical practitioner; and the wealthier merchants, who, if not, as many were, themselves sons of landed families, had received a similar education, moved in the same circles, and in England, unlike France, were commonly recognised to be socially indistinguishable from them. It was this upper layer of commoners, heterogeneous, but compact, whose rapid rise in wealth and power most impressed contemporaries. Literature celebrated its triumphs. Travelled intellectuals sought to polish its crudities. Manuals[14] written for its edification laid the foundations of a flattering legend. Education, the professions, the arts, above all, architecture, reflected its influence. Nor were there wanting observers who discerned in a changing social order the herald of a new state.

Interpretations of the political breakdown of the age, of a kind which to-day would be called sociological, have commonly received short shrift from historians. The tougher breed which experienced it has some right to an opinion. It was disposed to take them seriously. Once thought has been stirred by a crisis, the attempt to pierce behind controversial externals to the hidden springs of the movement is in all periods common form. The influence in the second half of the century of doctrines which sought one of the dynamics of revolution in antecedent economic change is not, therefore, surprising. But the disturbance of the social equilibrium had excited the curiosity of a generation which could only guess at its political repercussions. Theories canvassed in the 'fifties in the Rota Club had faint fragmentary anticipations before Harrington had started on his travels, and when Neville was still a schoolboy.

The facts were plain enough. The ruin of famous families by personal extravagance and political ineptitude; the decline in the position of the yeomanry towards the turn of the century, when long leases fell in; the loss, not only of revenue, but of authority, by the monarchy, as Crown lands melted; the mounting fortunes of the residuary legatee, a gentry whose aggregate income was put even in 1600 at some three times that of peers, bishops, deans and chapters, and richer yeomen together, and who steadily gathered into their hands estates slipping from the grasp of peasant, nobility, Church and Crown alike—such movements and their consequences were visible to all. Not only a precocious economist like Thomas Wilson the younger, the nephew of Elizabeth's Secretary of State, but men of greater eminence; Bacon; Cranfield; Selden; the shifty, but not unintelligent, Goodman; those artists in crying stinking fish, the Venetian embassy in London; Coke, most amiable and most futile of secretaries of state, who begs Buckingham, of all people, to save Crown lands from the spoiler—wrote footnotes on the same theme.[15]

The man who saw deepest into the moral of it all was primarily neither a theorist nor a politician, though he had the gifts of both. He was a great man of action, perhaps the greatest of his age. The doctrine that political stability depends on the maintenance of that Balance of Property, which was later to become a term of art, was not, in essence, novel. It was implicit in the conception of society as an organism, requiring the maintenance of a due proportion between its different members, which was part of the medieval legacy. But it is one thing to repeat a formula, another to apply it. Raleigh's dialogue, composed, it seems, in 1615, just after the central crisis of James' reign, was the first attempt to state the relevance of that conception to the changing circumstances of his day, and to deduce from it the need, not for mere conservatism, but for reform. The argument with which his country gentleman confutes the noble parasite is no abstract disquisition on constitutional formalities. It is a deduction from social history. The centre of social gravity has shifted; political power is shifting with it. The Earl who could once put a thousand horse into the field cannot now put twenty-five; if the greatest lord lifts a finger, he will be locked up by the next constable. The commons to-day command most of the wealth, and all the weapons. It is they, not the heirs of the feudal past, who hold the keys of the future. It is with them; with their natural leaders, the gentry; with the House of Commons, which is their organ, that the monarchy, if it is wise, will hasten to makes its peace.[16]

II

These hints of political deductions from the fact of social change must not now detain us. In considering the character of that change itself, the right point of departure is that which Raleigh suggests. To speak of the transition from a feudal to a bourgeois society is to decline upon a *cliché*. But a process difficult to epitomise in less hackneyed terms has left deep marks on the social systems of most parts of Europe. What a contemporary described in 1600 as the conversion of "a gentry addicted to war" into "good husbands," who "know as well how to improve their lands to the uttermost as the farmer or countryman,"[17] may reasonably be regarded as an insular species of the same genus.

It was a precocious species, which later, when its survival was assured, was to be the admiration of foreigners, but which for long found few imitators; nor was it accomplished without anguish. The movement passed through the three familiar stages of breakdown, reconstruction and stabilisation. If one aspect of the first phase consisted in the political and legal reforms[18] by which the Tudor State consolidated its power, another aspect was economic. Jolted sharply by the great depreciation; then squeezed by its masters to find the means for new styles in fashion and display; then pulled by expanding markets, when expedients adopted to stave off catastrophe were discovered, once systematised, to pay dividends beyond hope, agrarian society was everywhere under strain. The ability of nature to cause confusion with her silver is greatly inferior, we now know, to that of human art; and, in view of the dimensions of the movement, the lamentations provoked by it seem to-day overdone. But, in judging the effects of this most un-revolutionary of monetary revolutions, three truisms must be remembered. It broke on a world which had known within living memory something like a currency famine. The society which experienced it was crossed by lines of petrification, which make modern rigidities seem elastic. Except for brief intervals, the movement was continuous, on the Continent for some three generations, in England for nearly four. The wave of rising prices struck the dyke of customary obligations, static burdens, customary dues; rebounded; struck again; and then either broke it, or carved new channels which turned its flank.

More than one country had known a dreadful interlude, when anarchy was not remote. In most it was discovered, when the worst was over, that the land system which came out of the crisis was not that which had gone into it. The key, as usual, was finance. The items comprising the landowner's revenue change their relative importance. The value of all customary and non-commercial payments tumbles down;[19] that of the more elastic sources of income increases. Some groups can adapt themselves to the new tensions and opportunities; others cannot. The former rise; the latter sink. Examples of both are to be found in every stratum of society. There are grounds, nevertheless, for thinking that what Professor Bloch has called *la crise des fortunes seigneuriales*[20] was felt more acutely, and surmounted with greater difficulty, by the heirs of ancient wealth, with its complex and dispersed interests, and large public responsibilities, than by men of humbler position or more recent eminence. Contemporaries noted the turn of the wheel in their superb prose. "How many noble families have there been whose memory is utterly abolished! How many flourishing houses have we seen which oblivion hath now obfuscated . . . ! Time doth diminish and consume all."[21] But time was not the chief destroyer.

Such a family, inheriting great estates, often inherited trouble. Its standards of expenditure were those of one age, its income that of another. "Port"— the display becoming in a great position—was a point of honour; who would wish to be thought, like Lord Dencourt, to "live like a hog"?[22] "What by reason," wrote a close observer, "of their magnificence and waste in expense, and what by reason of a desire to advance and make great their own families,"[23] the life of a considerable part of the aristocracy was apt to offer an example of what a modern economist has called "conspicuous waste." Other regalities might have gone; what remained, and, indeed, increased, was a regal ostentation. The overheads of the noble landowner—a great establishment, and often more than one; troops of servants and retainers; stables fit for a regiment of cavalry; endless hospitality to neighbours and national notabilities; visits to court, at once ruinous and unavoidable; litigation descending, like an heirloom, from generation to generation— had always been enormous. Now, on the top of these traditional liabilities, came the demands of a new world of luxury and fashion. With the fortunes resulting from inflation and booming trade all standards are rising. London, rapidly advancing in financial and commercial importance, with a court that under James is a lottery of unearned fortunes, exercises a stronger pull. Town houses increase in number; visits to the capital are spun out; residential quarters are developed; to the delight of dress-makers, something like a season begins to emerge. Culture has demands to which homage must be paid. New and more costly styles of building; the maintenance of a troop of needy scholars and poets; collections of pictures; here and there—an extreme case—the avenues of posturing nudities which Bacon saluted at Arundel with ironical dismay—"the resurrection of the dead!"[24]—all have their votaries. Public duties, in some cases, complete what private prodigality has begun. They yielded some pickings; but, under Elizabeth and her two successors, more than one bearer of a famous name was brought near to ruin by the crowning catastrophe of a useful career.

So towering a superstructure required broad foundations. Too often they were lacking. The wealth of some of the nobility, and especially of the older families, was not infrequently more spectacular than substantial. It was locked up in frozen assets—immobilised in sumptuous appurtenances, at once splendid and unrealisable. More important, the whole structure and organisation of their estates was often of a kind, which, once a pillar of the social system, was now obsolescent. Side by side with more lucrative possessions, their properties included majestic, but unremunerative, franchises—hundreds, boroughs, fairs and markets; a multitude of knights' fees, all honour and no profit; free-holds created in an age when falling, not rising, prices had been the great landowners' problem, and fixed rents were an insurance; hundreds of prickly copyholds, whose occupants pocketed an unearned increment while the real income of their landlord fell. What was the use, a disconsolate peer expostulated with the Queen, of pretending to relieve his necessities by the gift of a manor whose tenants were protected by law against an increase in rents, and by custom against an increase in fines?[25] That cheerless condition was to be expected in properties which Elizabeth thought suitable for presents; but it was not, unfortunately, confined to them. The administrative machine which controlled a great estate had some of the vices of a miniature State department. It was cumbrous, conservative, difficult to divert from its traditional routine to new and speculative enterprises. The very magnitude and wide dispersion of the interests concerned—property of a dozen different kinds in a dozen different counties—made drastic reconstruction a formidable business, which it needed an exceptional personality to force through. It is not surprising that inherited opulence should sometimes have lacked the initiative to launch it.

Such difficulties confronted all conservative landowners, both peers and commoners, in proportion to the magnitude of their commitments and the rigidity of their incomes. The most that can be said is that the former usually carried more sail than the latter, and found it, when the wind changed, more difficult to tack. Mere majestic inertia, however, was an expensive luxury. As the tension tightened, something had to go. What went first was an aspect of life once of the first importance, but to which justice to-day is not easily done. The words "hospitality" or "house-keeping," its ordinary designation, were the description, not of a personal trait or a private habit, but of a semi-public institution, whose political dangers, once a menace to the State, were a thing of the past, but whose social significance had survived little abated. As the centre of a system of relations offering employment, succour, a humble, but recognised, niche to men helpless in isolation, the great household had performed somewhat the same rôle as was played, till yesterday, by the informal communism of the family system in China, and its break-up was attended by the same symptoms of disintegration as have followed in the Far East the shattering of ancient social *cadres* by western industrialism. The stream of lamentations voiced by popular opinion, conservative moralists, and the Government itself, all strike the same note. Their burden is that, as expenses are cut down, staffs reduced, and household economy put on a business footing, a cell of the social organism is ceasing to function. The plight of younger brothers, put off, like Orlando "with the stalling of an ox," or compelled—to the public advantage, but to their own exasperation—to take "to letters or to arms",[26] is a footnote to the same story; it is not a chance that attacks on primogeniture become more vocal at the moment when once prosperous families are feeling the pinch. The social dislocation, if exaggerated, was not a trifle; but the relief to the landowner was not proportionate to it. Since his real income, in default of other measures, continued to decline, it was, at best, only a respite.

The materials for generalisation have hardly yet been put together; but to say that many noble families—though not they alone—encountered, in the two generations before the Civil War, a financial crisis is probably not an over-statement. The fate of the conservative aristocrat was, in fact, an unhappy one. Reduced to living "like a rich beggar, in perpetual want,"[27] he sees his influence, popularity and property all melt together. Some, like Lord Howard of Effingham and the Earl of Sussex, part with their estates to their creditors, or sell outlying portions to save the remainder. Some resort to half-obsolete claims on their tenants, with which, as a Lancashire landlord remarked, the victims comply, "if not for love, then for fear";[28] claims resembling, in their pedantic and exasperating legality, those most criticised in the Crown, but which—so merciful is history to the victors—are commonly ignored in the case of private landowners. Some, like the Berkeleys, do both. The sixth earl,[29] for whom his admiring biographer—a lover of honorific titles—could find no more appropriate name than Lord Henry the Harmless, combined with the style and establishment of a medieval potentate the sporting tastes of a country gentleman; periodical plunges into the world of fashion in London; the maintenance of a *salon* as a concession to culture; and an heirloom in the shape of a lawsuit, which when he inherited it had already lasted a century, and which in 1609, four years before his death, he steered at last, with cries of self-congratulation, to a disastrous victory. While continuing to manage his Gloucestershire estates with a conservatism as agreeable to his tenants as it was fatal to himself, he sinks ever deeper into debt to tradesmen, to scriveners, to merchant-bankers; sells land outside the county to the value of £60,000; and ends his life in a maze of financial expedients, charged with a slightly exotic odour, as of the Seine rather than the Severn—collecting an aid from his freeholders to knight his eldest son, releasing his customary tenants from irksome obligations that had elsewhere long vanished, and raising a benevolence to pay for the ruinous results of his triumphs as a litigant. Other landowners again—Lord Compton, Lord Noel, Lord Willoughby, the Earl of Holderness—restore their fortunes by marrying City money.[30] Others, with a pull in the right quarter, plant themselves on the preposterous pension list of the Crown, angle—an odious business—for "concealed lands," or intrigue, with a kind of amateurish greed, for patents and monopolies.

Whether their embarrassments were increasing it is impossible to say; some debts, it is fair to remember, represented reproductive expenditure on development and improvements. But soundings, wherever taken, show much water in the hold. The correspondence of Burleigh,[31] in the last decade of Elizabeth, reads like the report of a receiver in bankruptcy to the nobility and gentry. A few years later, when, with the opening of the great boom which began in 1606, things should have been better, Cranfield, no financial leviathan, had a score of them in his books, while, to judge by stray references, Hicks the silk-man and banker—later Lord Campden—and Herriott, the goldsmith, may well have had more. Rubens, no stranger to the costly futilities of courts, still retained sufficient naïveté to lift his eyebrows at the orgy of extravagance and peculation—"business, public and private, sold cash down, over the counter"[32]—which distinguished that of James. Clarendon's[33] account of the notabilities of his day is a catalogue of splendid spendthrifts. When, in 1642, all went into the melting-pot, the debts owed to the City by Royalists alone were put, in a financial memorandum, at not less than £2,000,000.[34] Of the commercial magnates who, a few years later, scrambled for confiscated estates, not a few, as Dr. Chesney[35] has shown, were creditors entering on properties long mortgaged to them. It was discovered, not for the last time, that as a method of foreclosure war was cheaper than litigation.

III

For, if the new world had its victims, it had also its conquerors. That "the wanton bringing up and ignorance of the nobility force the prince to advance new men that can serve, which ... subvert the noble houses to have their rooms themselves,"[36] had been noted with uneasiness in the early years of Elizabeth, when suggestions were considered for redressing the balance. Half a century later, the consequences of the movement were visible to all, and there could be no question of reversing it. "The age was one," writes Miss Wake in her account of Northamptonshire under James, "which had recently seen the rise of the solid middle class of lesser landowning gentry on the ruins of the ancient aristocracy. The families were few which ... managed to survive the turbulent end of the middle ages. ... Many of the knights and squires belonged to families of local and extraneous origin who had made money early in the previous century by the law, trade, or sheep-farming."[37]

That picture is true of more counties than one. The conditions which depressed some incomes inflated others; and, while one group of landowners bumped heavily along the bottom, another, which was quicker to catch the tide when it turned, was floated to fortune. The process of readjustment was complex; but two broad movements can be observed, affecting respectively the technique of land-management and the ownership of landed property.

While the crisis of depreciation was not confined to one country, the English response to it had a character of its own. Partly for economic reasons, partly owing to the political and military conditions of a frontier region, parts of Eastern Europe had met the emergency by a servile reaction which gave villeinage a new life. In East Prussia, in particular, the great estate, half farm, half fortress, swollen by the holdings of evicted peasants, and worked by its owner with the aid of *corvées*, became the dominant institution, against which the reforming monarchy, when it took the matter up—not to mention its successors—would for long struggle in vain. France had felt the same tightening of the screw, but the French escape from the *impasse*—if it was an escape—took the opposite direction. Precluded by law from evicting the *censitaires*—the customary tenants—French landowners had been thrown back on the policy of a more remorseless exaction of customary dues, of which the last desperate gamble, when the clock had almost struck, was to be denounced under the name of the feudal reaction, but which in fact, other avenues being blocked, had gone on piecemeal for centuries. In England, as elsewhere, it was necessary for landlords, if ruin was to be averted, to play to the score; but the tune called by English conditions was neither the despotism of the *Junker* nor the half-abdication of the *Seigneur*. English agriculture had as its setting a commercial, increasingly individualistic society, in process of an industrialisation that was more than merely local. Landowners learned—when they did learn—from their environment, and cured their wounds with a hair of the dog that bit them. Fixed incomes falling, and profits rising, who could question that the way of salvation was to contract interests as a *rentier*, and expand them as an entrepreneur? The experts, at any rate, felt no doubts on the subject. Business is booming. They cry with one accord, "Go into business and prosper."

Business methods and modernisation, the fashionable specific, have different meanings in different ages. The stage at which matters stood under the early Stuarts was that, not of crops and rotations, but of marketing, management, tenures, the arrangement of holdings, and reclamation. If modern analogies are sought, they are to be found in the sphere, not of cultivation and breeding, but of rationalising the administration of estates and improving their lay-out. The problem was, in the first place, a financial one. Certain sources of income were drying up; a substitute must be found for them. Several lines of attack were possible, but the most characteristic were four. First, customary payments dwindling, the landlord could revise the terms on which his property was held, get rid of the unprofitable copyholders when lives ran out, buy out small freeholders, and throw the land so secured into larger farms to be let on lease. Rent at this period is an ambiguous category; but leasehold rents were certainly rising—on the view of Thorold Rogers[38] six-fold in half a century, on the estimate of a contemporary[39] five-fold in rather less, on the evidence of some estate documents about three to four-fold. Second, instead of, or in addition to, letting, he could expand his own business activities, run his home-farm, not to supply his household, but as a commercial concern, enlarge his demesnes, and enclose for the purpose of carrying more stock or increasing his output of grain. Third, if he had the means, he could invest capital in bringing new land into cultivation, clearing woodlands, breaking up waste, draining marshes. Finally, he could supplement his agricultural income by other types of enterprise, going into the timber trade, exploiting coal, iron and lead, speculating in urban ground-rents. Naturally, none of these departures was without abundant precedents. Naturally, again, the particular policy, or combination of policies, adopted depended both on local circumstances and on individual resources. But the tendency of all was the same. In each case, whatever the particular expedient used, the emphasis of the up-to-date landowner is increasingly thrown on the business side of land-management. He relies for his income on the rents or profits derived from it.

The situation confronting the landed classes in the half-century before the Civil War resembled in miniature that of 1850–70. Not only were prices rising, but, with the progress of internal unification, the development of specialised semi-industrial areas, and the growth of urban markets, demand was expanding. The advice to put estate management on a business footing was, in such circumstances, sound; but not everyone could take it, and not all who could would. Then, as now, rationalisation might look easy on paper, but was, in fact, no simple matter. Then, as now, therefore, what appeared at first sight a mere pedestrian improvement in methods of administration set in motion, as it developed, subtle social changes. It was to be expected that men with the resources and ambition to play the part of pioneers should gain at the expense of groups, whether below them or above, less qualified by means and traditions to adapt themselves to a new climate. The well-to-do yeoman, the *kulak* of the day, might maintain, or even improve, his position; but the extension of demesne farms, the upward movement of rents and fines, and encroachments on commons, combined in parts of the country to tilt the scales against the humbler peasants. To that chapter of the story, whose local diversities still remain to be worked out, but of which the outlines are known, must be added another, of which historians have said less, but by which contemporaries were impressed. There was a struggle for survival, not only between large landowners and small, but between different categories among the former.

It was primarily a struggle between economies of different types, which corresponded more closely with regional peculiarities than with social divisions. There are plenty of gentry who stagnate or go down hill. It would be easy to find noble landowners who move with the times, and make the most of their properties; the sheep-farming of Lord Spencer; the enclosures of Lords Brudenell, Huntingdon and Saye and Sele; the coal-mines of the Earl of Northumberland and the Earl of Wemyss; above all the grandiose reconstruction carried through by the Russells, are cases in point. The smaller the part, nevertheless, played by passive property, as compared with active enterprise, the larger the opportunities of rising; and the increased rewards

THE FEUDAL AND EARLY MODERN ECONOMY

to be reaped by the improving landlord favoured classes still ascending the ladder compared with those already at the summit. The charms of established wealth might be represented by an Earl of Newcastle, with a rent-roll of £22,000, or an Earl of Pembroke, with the ninety-three manors, four boroughs and estates scattered over ten counties from Middlesex to Yorkshire, which gave him, at his death in 1630, the reputation of one of the richest peers in England.[40] But, when experiment and innovation were the order of the day, the cards were in other hands. They were all on the side of the enterprising country gentleman.

Professor Kosminsky has described the owners of "small and medium-sized estates" in the thirteenth century as "all people less intimately involved in the economic system of feudalism, and early subject to capitalist transformation."[41] It is the representatives of much the same indeterminate middle class, with interests large enough to offer a secure base for manœuvre, but not so large as to be top-heavy, who, three centuries later, are quickest, when the wind shifts, to trim their sails. Such a man was not tempted by great possessions into the somnolence of the *rentier*; was less loaded than most noble landowners with heavy overhead charges in the shape of great establishments; did his work for himself, instead of relying on a cumbrous machine to do it for him; owned, in short, his property, instead of being owned by it. Usually, unless one of the minority of active administrators, he was freer from public duties in his county, and more immune to the blandishments of London. The problem confronting him, if he undertook reconstruction or development, was of manageable dimensions. It demanded practical experience of farming, common sense, attention to detail, not the rarer gifts of the business strategist.

Under the pressure of an environment in motion, several types emerge. Some strike no roots; others survive and become fixed. There is the gentleman farmer, leasing land, till he makes money, without owning it, and not infrequently—since the thing is his profession—running several farms at once. There is the man who works his land as a commercial undertaking—a John Toke in Kent, buying Welsh and Scottish runts to finish on Romney marsh for the London market; a Robert Loder in Berkshire, all piety and profits; a Sir Thoman Tresham in Northamptonshire, selling everything, from rabbits supplied on contract to a poulterer in Gracechurch Street, to wool to the value of £1,000 a year, whose dual rôle as a leader of the Catholic cause in England and the most hated encloser in his much disturbed county is a point on the side of those who dismiss as a mare's nest the alleged affinities of economic and religious radicalism; a Sir John Wynn in North Wales, cattle breeder, tribal chieftain, land-grabber, scholar, and prospector for minerals unknown to science, with the vanity of a savage and the credulity of his beloved alchemists, whose dealings with his tenants were too much for his own class, and cost him his seat on the Council of Wales. There are families like the Pelhams and Twysdens, living mainly on rents, but doing on the side a useful trade in grain, hops, wool and iron in local markets and in London.[42] Each type has its own idiosyncrasies, but none is in land for its health. All watch markets closely; buy and sell in bulk; compare the costs and yields of different crops; charge the rent, when custom allows, which a farm will stand; keep careful accounts. Mr. Fussell's[43] description of one of them—"before all things a business man"—is true of all.

It was agricultural capitalists of this type who were making the pace, and to whom the future belonged. Nor, if land supplied the base from which they started, were their interests confined to it. The lament that "it is impossible for the mere country gentleman ever to grow rich or raise his house, he must have some other profession,[44]" was uttered at a moment when pessimism was pardonable, and was too pessimistic. It is true, however, that many of the class, whether of necessity or by choice, were up to the eyes in other branches of business. Naturally, they turned first to the industries native to their own districts—iron in Sussex and the Forest of Dean; tin in Cornwall; lead in Derbyshire and North Wales; coal in Nottinghamshire, Durham and Northumberland; textiles in a dozen counties. But their business connections were not merely local. The habit of investment was spreading rapidly among the upper classes, and the starry host of notabilities, who lent lustre to the Virginia and East India Companies, contributed less to its development than did the web woven by the humbler ventures of hundreds of obscure squires. Some of them, too, held shares in those much advertised undertakings. More had relations in the City, and sent their sons into business. An increasing number—for the current did not run only one way—had been in business themselves.

"See," wrote Cobden to Bright, "how every successful trader buys an estate![45]" The remark might have been made with equal truth under James I. The movement from trade into land had long been an old story. Each successive generation made its bow to the proprieties by affecting surprise at it. It was not so long, indeed, since a statesman, alarmed at the crumbling of the social pyramid, had proposed to shore it up, by fixing a legal maximum to the real property which vulgar persons, like mere merchants, might buy.[46] Thirty years later that pose had worn thin. The Government of the first two Stuarts continued, on a more majestic scale, the Elizabethan policy of turning Crown estates into cash. So far from deprecating the acquisition of land by the business world, it threw land at its head. It was not surprising that a successful merchant, who had made his pile in trade, should prefer to the risks of commerce the decorous stability of what was regarded as a gilt-edged investment. By the middle years of James, if not, indeed, earlier, it is difficult to find a prominent London capitalist who is not also a substantial landowner; even such dubious cosmopolitans as Van Lore and Burlamachi, like Pallavicino before them, feel obliged to astonish the natives by setting up as country gentlemen. Fortunes made in law went the same way. Whether it is true or not, as was alleged, that leading barristers[47] were making, in the later years of Elizabeth, £20,000 to £30,000 a year, there was general agreement that their emoluments were not trifling. Their profession had taught them what, properly handled, land could be made to yield; naturally, they used their knowledge. Popham, who speculated heavily in Crown lands; Ellesmere, who left his son £12,000 a year; the odious, but indispensable, Coke, were all substantial landowners; the last, indeed, with his fifty odd manors, was well up in the first flight. In the twenties, the inroads of the London plutocracy on the home counties gave rise to complaints; and what was true of the neighbourhood of London was hardly less true of the environs of other growing cities, for example Bristol.[48] In such conditions, the social categories used to distinguish the landed and trading classes, which in France and Germany remained terms with a legal significance, lost in England any claim to precision which they may once have possessed. The landowner living on the profits and rents of commercial farming, and the merchant or banker who was also a landowner, represented, not two classes, but one. Patrician and *parvenu* both owed their ascent to causes of the same order. Judged by the source of their incomes, both were equally *bourgeois*.

IV

The advance of the classes representing a more business-like agriculture was accompanied by a second movement, which at once reflected its influence and consolidated its results. That movement was the heightened rapidity with which land was changing hands. The land-market deals in a form of capital, and, in many societies, the most important form. The article which it handles is not merely a commodity, but an instrument of social prestige and political power. It is most active, therefore, when a rise in incomes swells the surplus for investment, and when wealth, in addition to increasing, is passing into new hands. Commercial expansion, industrial progress, discovery and invention, but also financial recklessness, revolution and war, have all at different times set the wheel spinning with heightened speed. In the age of Elizabeth and her two successors, economic and political conditions combined to mobilise real property, while the hostility of the courts to entails gave both forces free play.[49] The former, apart from occasional severe depressions, acted continuously, and with increasing force, to augment the demand for it. The latter, by periodically bringing fresh blocks of land into the market, supplied recurrent opportunities for profitable speculation.

The economic causes which lent property wings need no lengthy explanation. By depreciating fixed incomes, and inflating profits, rising prices sapped the reluctance of conservative owners to sell, and heightened both the eagerness and the ability of the business classes, whether agriculturalists or merchants, to buy. The very customary arrangements—fixed freehold and copyhold rents, and, sometimes fixed fines—which, if maintained, threatened ruin, could be turned by a bold policy of innovation from a liability to an asset. Involving, as they did, the existence of a wide margin between the actual receipts from a property and its potential yield, they offered, like an old-fashioned company which has survived into a boom, a golden opportunity for a remunerative reconstruction. Given a knowledge of the ropes, manors could be refloated as easily as mills, with results as agreeable to those who got in on the ground floor, and equally unpleasant to everyone else. To the purchaser with the capital and capacity to undertake it, modernisation was as profitable as it was unpopular with his tenants. If himself a farmer, he sold his produce in a rising market. If he dealt in land as a speculation, he could count on reselling at a profit. If he bought to hold, he could feel a reasonable confidence that he would leave to his heirs an estate appreciating in value. In the event, many bought for a committee of enemies at Goldsmiths Hall. But none foresaw the war.

Our first formal accounts of the land-market seem to be subsequent to the Restoration.[50] The picture then drawn is of a stream of mortgages and sales in London, which, owing to its financial resources, had the bulk of the business, even from the remotest counties, in its hands. Before the end of the previous century, however, it had been realised that the increased volume of transactions raised some awkward problems. The later seventies and early eighties appear to have been a period of exceptional activity. There were compaints of malpractices, and legislation was passed to check them. An Act of 1585 voided fraudulent conveyances, imposed heavy penalties on the guilty parties, and required all mortgages to be entered with the clerks of recognizances, who were to keep a record, which intending purchasers could inspect on payment of a small fee.[51] The last provision appears to have remained a dead letter, but the issue raised did not die down. The unorganised condition of the market was thought to depress prices, and a patent was granted in 1611 for the establishment of a public office, which was to have as part of its business the provision of facilities for dealing in real property and the recording of transactions. Copyholds—it was an advantage to set against their inconveniences—were transferred publicly in the court of the manor, so that encumbrances on them could not be concealed. It was natural that it should be asked whether the purchaser of a freehold could not be given similar security. Registration of title, advocated and opposed on the same grounds as to-day, was being urged from the left by the forties, and found later a place in the abortive programmes of land reform prepared during the interregnum.[52]

Long before that date, a second unpleasant symptom of the increased scale of the business had attracted general comment. Lawyers were not beloved by laymen; "Peace and law," wrote an indignant country gentleman, who had seen much of the tribe, "hath beggared us all."[53] The portentous inflation of the legal profession—the figures of men called to the bar at Gray's

Inn and Lincoln's Inn rose[54] by almost two-thirds between 1591–1600 and 1631–40—was ascribed largely to the new opportunities open to the conveyancer. Nor, perhaps, is it without significance that it was in 1612, towards the end of the greatest orgy of speculation seen since the Reformation, that another body of practitioners which handled the same business, the growing trade of scriveners, applied for a charter of incorporation.[55] "Sell not thy land; ... rather feed on bread and water than be the confusion of thy house",[56] might be the motto of parents. Things were in the saddle and rode their sons. The earliest version of "clogs to clogs in three generations" was applied, not to Lancashire mills, but to Lancashire land.[57] The rapid absorption by absentee aliens of estates in Northamptonshire and Nottinghamshire was noted with disfavour under James I, and much the same statement as to properties in Berkshire was made half a century later by Fuller; while nearly two-thirds of the gentry owning land in Bedfordshire in 1620 were said to have sold it and left the county by 1668. The oft-quoted remark that half the properties in conservative Staffordshire had changed hands in sixty years does not, in the light of such evidence, appear too implausible.[58] The passing of familiar names, the break-up of patriarchal households, the unpleasantness of the *parvenus* who rose on their ruins, provided dramatists with materials for satire and moralists for sermons. If Sir Petronel Flash and Sir Giles Overreach were successful as parodies, it was that the nauseous reality was not too grossly caricatured.

Lamentations that the oaks are shedding their leaves are a piece of sentimental common form, too fashionable in all ages to throw much light on any one of them. Rising classes, like crowned heads, have always known how to grab and weep at once; nor, once in possession of the title-deeds, are they at a loss for a pedigree. In reality, the Bladesovers of England, repeatedly submerged beneath a flood of new wealth, have been refloated not less often, with undiminished buoyancy, as wealth has found a way to make novelty venerable. The statistical evidence of the dimensions of the movement has not yet been put together, nor is it often in the form most instructive to posterity. Contemporaries commonly thought in terms, not of acreage, but of manors; they spoke of a man owning manors, or selling them, much as to-day he might be said to hold, or to dispose of, large investments, in order to convey an impression, not to record precise facts. The category, needless to say, is a highly ambiguous one, embracing estates varying widely in magnitude, value and organisation. At best, it covers only one species of real property, and that not the most marketable. In the two generations before the Long Parliament such property seems, nevertheless, for what the fact is worth, to have changed hands with fair rapidity. Of 2,500 odd manors in seven counties, whose owners can be traced, just under one in three were sold once in the forty years between 1561 and 1600, and rather more than one in three between 1601 and 1640. In the case of the six hundred odd in

Hertfordshire and Surrey, which felt the wash of the London whirlpool, the figure in the second period was over 40 per cent.[59]

The only continuous register of sales of smaller parcels of land, which naturally came into the market more often, seems to be that supplied by the records of the Office of Alienations.[60] The land which it handled, being subject to awkward financial obligations to the Crown, was not attractive to purchasers. But the average sales per decade described a rising curve, in rough correspondence with the movement of foreign trade, which helped to determine the surplus available for investment. In the expansion of the 'seventies and early 'eighties the figure bounded up; declined with the slump which began on the eve of the Armada; rose again with the beginning of recovery at the turn of the century; reached the highest point yet attained in the boom of 1606-16; and fell sharply with the depression of the early 'twenties. It ended at a level which, from 1630 to 1639, stood well above twice that at which it had started. It is not, perhaps, an exaggeration to say that for two generations there was an intermittent real estate boom. Naturally land values bounded up. An observer who stated in the later years of Elizabeth that they had risen tenfold[61] within living memory over-stated his case; but there was general agreement that the rise had been impressive. Not much weight can be attached to the fact that under James I some Crown land was sold at the fantastic price of forty-five[62] years purchase, for such land—it was one of its attractions—was notoriously under-rented. Twenty-eight[63] years purchase, however, was quoted in the later 'twenties as the price at which some estates were then changing hands.

This mobilisation of property, the result of commercial expansion and inflation combined, was not peculiar to England. As Professor Bloch and M. Raveau have shown, a similar reshuffling of possessions was occurring at the same time in France.[64] But in England the results of an accelerated economic tempo were heightened by adventitious causes. The state threw its weight into the scales, and permanently depressed them. Intending to buttress its own foundations, it released currents which, in the end, carried them and it away.

Periodical redistributions of land by acts of public policy, to the gain or loss now of this class, now of that, are not the astonishing departure from pre-established harmonies which they appear to their victims. In one form or another, they are a recurrent feature of European history, whose repeated appearance lends colour to the view which sees in them, not an accident, but the prelude to a new era. The decorous story of England is no exception to that rule. In the century and a half between the Reformation and Restoration, such a redistribution took place on a scale not seen since the Conquest. There were two immense confiscations, the result of revolution and civil war, and a steady alienation, under financial duress, of estates formerly used to provide a revenue for public purposes.

The opening act of the drama is not here in place. But the story which had begun with the Dissolution had not ended with it. Like taxation, the fruits of confiscation do not always rest where they first light. It is an error to suppose that, when James skipped happily on to his throne of thorns, the results of that great transaction were already ancient history. Property producing a gross income equal to about half the then yield of the customs had been cut adrift from its moorings, and added to the acreage available for acquisition by influence or enterprise. When the first fever of speculation was over, it had continued to float from hand to hand in the ordinary way of business, coming at intervals to anchor only again to resume its exciting voyages. Nor had the Crown's interest in the matter ceased with the mere act of confiscation and the sales which followed it. For one thing, though it had disposed within a decade of the greater part of the spoils, those which it retained remained substantial. For another, part of the land with which it parted had not been sold outright, but had been leased for terms of years, and ultimately returned to it. In the third place, part of that which it sold came back to it later through escheats and confiscations. Two generations later, therefore, it still owned, as a result of the Dissolution, a great mass of property, which could be leased, mortgaged or sold, and which, when the Court of Augmentations was wound up in 1554, had continued to be administered by the Augmentations office of the Exchequer. A vast deal in Chantry lands brought temporary relief to the financial embarrassments of the early years of James. His son was disposing of monastic estates within a decade of the Long Parliament.

The continued redistribution of monastic property in the century following the Reformation was as momentous, therefore, as that which accompanied it. The transference to lay hands of part of the land owned by bishops and by deans and chapters—"their wings . . . well clipt of late by courtiers and noblemen, and some quite cut away"[65]—has been studied in detail only during the Interregnum, but the statements of contemporaries suggest that the scale on which it took place under Elizabeth was not inconsiderable. Nor was it only ecclesiastical property which came into the market in large blocks. Few rulers have acted more remorselessly than the early Tudors on the maxim that the foundations of political authority are economic. They had made the augmentation of the royal demesnes one of the key-stones of their policy.[66] They had enjoyed, as a consequence, not only a large revenue from land, but the extensive economic patronage which great estates conferred, and had been powerful as Kings partly because unrivalled as landowners. A shrewd foreigner remarked, as he watched in the next century the headlong plunge downhill of the Crown finances, that the Stuarts were on the way to be overshadowed in wealth by their subjects before they were overthrown by them.[67] There was some substance in the view, hinted more than once under James, that the New Monarchy was undermined by reversing for three generations the financial policy which had helped to establish it. Each of the three great crises of Elizabeth's reign carried its own block of Crown estates away; she sold in her forty-five years land to the value, in all, of some £817,000. Her two successors inherited the nemesis of living on capital, as well as of rising prices and of their own characters. They sold in thirty years nearly twice as much. In spite of half-hearted attempts to tie his hands, alienations of property under James reached about £775,000, and those of Charles I, in the first decade of his reign, over £650,000.[68] The estates remaining to the Crown, when the Long Parliament met, were still, of course, substantial; but how ruinously they had been dilapidated can be shown by a comparison. Between 1558 and 1635 Crown lands to the value of some £2,240,000 had been thrown on the market. When, in the crisis of the Civil War, the remains were swept together and put up to auction, the sum realised, it seems, was under £2,000,000.[69]

V

What, if any, were the social consequences of these portentous landslides? Did they, while changing, or reflecting a change in, the fortunes of individuals, leave unaltered the distribution of property between different groups? Or was the set of social forces such that some classes gained, while others lost? Is there truth in the suggestion of a later political theorist that "two parts in ten of all those vast estates" of the nobility, "by the luxury and folly of their owners, have . . . been purchased by the lesser gentry and commons," and that "the crown-lands, that is the public patrimony, are come to make up the interest of the commons"?[70]

As to the tendency of private transactions, little can at present be said. Some great estates can be seen disintegrating, and others being formed. A comparison of the distribution at different dates of certain categories of property reveals the results. But the threads in the intricate skein leading from the first stage to the last can rarely be unravelled.[71] The dealings in monastic and Crown lands left a trail which is easier to follow. Much is still obscure; but enough is known to suggest certain provisional conclusions.

The natural starting-point, in considering the former, is the classification of grantees made, some thirty years ago, by Dr. Savine.[72] His figures suggest that the lion's share of the spoils had passed, in the first instance, to two categories of persons. The first, the peers, received the largest individual grants; the second, the gentry and their connections, the largest aggregate share. What is known of the subsequent history of the land in question suggests that the second of these groups had the greater survival value. Properties dispersed, like the acquisitions of some noble grantees, over half-a-dozen different counties, were more readily sold than smaller and more compact estates, to which their owners were bound by strong local attachments. The squirearchy was less exposed to the vicissitudes which ruined some aristocratic families; while, keen farmers and business men as many of them were, they were in a better position to reap the fruits of commercial progress and improved methods of agriculture. Hence while, as a class, they had gained most by the Dissolution, they not only succeeded in retaining their acquisitions, but continued to add to them in the course of the next century.

"As the Gibeonites," wrote Fuller, "though by their mouldy bread and clouted shoes pretending to a long peregrination, were but of the vicinage; so most of those gentry [sc., in the later years of Henry VIII], notwithstanding their specious claims to antiquity, will be found to be . . . low enough in themselves, did they not stand on the vantage ground heightened on the rubbish of the ruins of monasteries."[73] The settlement of monastic estates into the hands of the most progressive element in rural society may be illustrated by the course of events in one small corner of the country. In Gloucestershire, Northamptonshire and Warwickshire about 317 manors, together with a mass of miscellaneous property —tithes, rectories and land in different places— appear to have changed hands at the Dissolution.[74] Of the manors, which are more easily traced than the smaller acquisitions, between 250 and 260 passed into the ownership of individuals, the remainder being obtained by bishops, deans and chapters, colleges and other corporations. The nobility had done fairly, though not immoderately, well; twenty-six[75] peers had acquired monastic property of some kind, and seventeen had secured just over forty manors. Crown officials, like Sadler and Kingston, the two largest grantees of Gloucestershire estates; big business, in the persons of Gresham, Sharington and Stump; and an ubiquitous group of professional speculators, had all got their share; while a number of smaller men picked up crumbs from the cake. The bulk of the property had gone, however, not to influential aliens, but to well-known local families. In Gloucestershire the beneficiaries had included Chamberlains, Poynzs, Thynnes, Throckmortons, Tracies, Dennises, Porters, Comptons and Botelers; in Northamptonshire Montagues, Knightleys, Kirkhams, Cecils and Fermors; in Warwickshire Knightleys, Aglionbys and Throckmortons. Precision is impossible; but it is probably not an exaggeration to say that from one-half to two-thirds of the property acquired by individuals had passed to men of this type and to humbler members of the same class. In so far as there had been competition between national notabilities and tenacious local interests, local interests had won.

Their victory became steadily more decisive in the course of the next century. Compared with the adventurers who dealt in properties that they had never seen, the local gentry were a settled population confronting mere marauders. As the revolution receded, and its first turmoil died down, their strategic advantage—the advantage of a settled base—asserted itself with ever-increasing force. Political convulsions shook down the estates of one group of absentees; financial embarrassments sapped the staying-power of another. As each over-rigged vessel went on the rocks, the patient watchers on the shore brought home fresh flotsam from the wreck. Long after the last monk had died, they were adding to their abbey lands, and, if not admitted on the ground floor, became shareholders at one remove. In Gloucestershire the estates of Cromwell, Northumberland and the Seymours drifted, some quickly, some gradually, into the hands of the Duttons, Winstons, Dorringtons and Chamberlains. The property of the Earl of Pembroke, who browsed juicier pastures elsewhere, passed, soon after its acquisition, to the Dennises and Comptons. The lands of Sir Thomas Gresham came by marriage to the Thynnes, and those of Lord Clinton and Sir Robert Tyrwitt to the Heydons; while, of the eight manors secured by Sir Anthony Kingston, more than half had passed by 1608 to other families, in particular the Baynhams and Sandys. Sir Ralph Sadler's descendants continued to be considerable landowners in the county; but the property acquired by him from the Abbey of Winchcombe, and four of the six manors taken from the college of Westbury-on-Trim, had left them by that date, some passing to the Actons and Bridges, others to less well-known families. In Northamptonshire, of the property acquired by peers at the Dissolution, some, by the beginning of the next century, had returned to the Crown; most of it had come to Kirkhams, Hattons, Spencers, Andrews, Stanhopes, Cradocks, Griffins and Ishams. In Warwickshire, the families who gained most by later re-shuffles were the Leighs, Dilkes, Throck-mortons and Spencers. The general result in these counties, in spite of the reputation of Northamptonshire as the Dukeries of the age, was that, of the forty odd manors which had gone to peers at the Reformation, those remaining to them two generations later numbered only six, while the remainder swelled the fortunes of rising middle-class families. Something between two-thirds and threequarters of the manors secured by private persons had gone originally to the squirearchy. By the early years of the next century, the proportion in their hands was over nine-tenths. Thus the ultimate consequences of the Dissolution, if similar in kind to its immediate effects, were different in degree. In this part of England, at any rate, it did not so much endow an existing nobility, as lay the foundations of a new nobility to arise in the next century.

"It is owing," writes Dr. Chambers in his study of Nottinghamshire, "to the elimination of these factors, the monasteries, the copyholders, the Crown, and the Church, as rivals to the gentry, that Thoroton is enabled to place them on the pedestal of unchallenged local supremacy."[76] The full effects of the dismemberment of Crown estates before the Civil War still remain to be worked out; but enough is known to suggest that it is not of one county alone that his statement is true. The individuals into whose hands the land in question passed fell, between 1600 and 1640, into three main categories. Part of it was acquired by the peasants on Crown estates; part, in the first instance, by syndicates of speculators, who bought land in large blocks, subdivided, and resold it; part by well-to-do landowners and business men. The Government's dealings with the first class in parts of Lancashire and

Yorkshire have been described by Dr. Tupling.[77] Their social effects were not without interest; but, as a solution of the financial problem, that method of disposing of Crown property was of worse than dubious value. It involved prolonged higgling with obstinate copyholders; years of surveying, hearings before commissions, and litigation; the extraction from thousands of petty transactions of sums which, in the end, were liable to be unimpressive. What the Government wanted was to get large tracts of land taken off its hands for prompt and substantial payments. If it was to secure that result, it must clearly look elsewhere than to the cautious avidity of impecunious peasants.

These reasons caused the best market for Crown property to be found, not among the smaller cultivators, but in the classes who could afford to deal on a large scale. Many well-to-do families had been interested in particular estates long before they came to be offered for sale. Among the lessees of Crown lands in the first decade of Elizabeth, appear, side by side with humble members of the Royal Household, distinguished civil servants and statesmen, like Smith and Cecil, judges and law officers of the Crown, and leading country gentlemen.[78] Down to, and after, the beginning of the century, much of the property in question was notoriously under-rented.[79] As a consequence, a would-be purchaser could offer a figure which appeared on paper impressive, but which in fact, especially if he bought to reconstruct, was money in his pocket. In such circumstances, it was natural that prosperous landowners, who already held Crown land on lease, should welcome the prospects of acquiring the freehold. The Irish war had brought one great opportunity. The accession of James was the occasion of a second. The great deals in Crown property were financed largely on credit;[80] one leading speculator professed to have raised £80,000 in the City, and to have burned his fingers. The boom in trade, which began with the peace of 1605, meant easy money. With a debt which by Michaelmas, 1606, was over £550,000, and showed signs of mounting, fresh spoils were in the offing. As usual, it was complained that Scots got more than their fair share; but there is no sign that the higher civilisation was backward in the scramble. "At court," wrote a future secretary of state, shocked—not for the last time—by the magnitude of the depredations, "every man findeth way for his own ends."[81] Coke was not alone in thinking that the thing threatened to become a ramp.

The dimensions of the business, and the anxiety of the Government to realise without delay, prompted the adoption of a technique which, if not new in principle, was now practised on a novel scale. The traditional expedient of sale through Special Commissions brought in, between 1603 and 1614, just over £180,000. What was done, in addition, was to use the financial machinery of the City. The procedure was somewhat analogous to the underwriting of a Government loan to-day by a group of issuing houses, except that what was involved was an actual transference of property. Instead of itself dealing with prospective purchasers, the Crown disposed of land wholesale to financial syndicates, who paid cash down, retained as much as they wanted for themselves, and peddled the remainder over a period of years. One group, for example, took over in 1605-6, and again in 1611, a mass of tithes, priory lands and chantry lands; a second just over 400 Crown mills, with the land attached to them; several others different blocks of property. The "contractors," as they were called, included, in addition to certain guinea-pigs in the shape of courtiers and officials, the leading business magnates of the day, such as Garway and Jones, two farmers of the Customs; Hicks, the silk merchant and banker; the masters and prominent members of certain city companies; and —the man who plunged most heavily, being engaged in seven separate deals to the value of £137,055— Arthur Ingram, the controller of the customs. The separate bargains made with these syndicates between 1605 and 1614 numbered seventeen, and the total sum thus obtained—apart from sales direct to individuals—amounted to just under half a million.[82]

The capitalists concerned bought primarily, of course, not to hold, but as a speculation, unloading partly on subsidiary rings of middlemen, whose names also are known, partly on the public, at the best price they could get. It was complained in the House in 1614 that they made 100 per cent., and skinned purchasers alive.[83] The procedure adopted masked the personalities of the ultimate beneficiaries; but, wherever the latter can be traced, while part of the land goes in small lots to obscure peasants or craftsmen in Devonshire, the Isle of Wight and elsewhere, the bulk of it is seen passing, as would be expected, to people of substance, such as leading lawyers, country gentlemen and business men.[84] The same tendency can be traced in greater detail in the transactions of the next reign. The most imposing deals were two. In the first place, a Commission[85] was set to work, which, between 1625 and 1634, disposed of property to the value of £247,597. In the second place, with a view to settling outstanding debts and to raising a further loan, the Crown transferred to the City Corporation land valued at £349,897.[86] The City marketed it gradually during the next twelve years, using the proceeds to pay the Crown's creditors.

The purchasers concerned in the first of these transactions numbered 218, and the value of the land which can be traced £234,437. The comment of a foreigner—that most of the property went to courtiers who had secured promises for it in advance—exaggerated the part played by influence, as distinct from money; but, in emphasising that the sales of Crown land under Charles, when the financial system of the monarchy was tottering to its fall, were, to an even greater extent than under his predecessors, a deal between the Crown, big business and the richer country gentry, he put his finger on a vital point. For obvious reasons of speed and economy, the policy of the Commission was to sell in large blocks. Lots of £1,000 and upwards, accounting for four-fifths of the land sold, went to less than one-third of the purchasers. The scale of the transactions naturally narrowed the market. Five merchants got one-tenth of the total; twenty-seven peers between one-quarter and one-third; a group of a hundred and thirty-three knights, esquires and gentlemen rather more than half. The second and larger deal, in which the City was the auctioneer, differed from the first only in the fact that the business world had a larger hand in it, and the nobility a smaller, the latter acquiring about one-tenth of the land and the former one-quarter. But the bulk of it went in the same direction as before. Among the three hundred and fifty odd purchasers the squirearchy and its dependants formed the largest group, and acquired well over half the total. It is not an exaggeration, in fact, to say that, apart from purchases effected through other channels, these two transactions alone had the effect that, in the course of something over fifteen years, several hundred families of country gentry added to their possessions land to the value of £350,000 to £400,000. Nor is that the whole story. Much of the property was sold as undeveloped land to men who, when the time came, would seize the chance to develop it. If an exasperated official, who put the difference in value between the two at twenty-fold,[87] over-stated his case, we know from other sources—for example, the margin between old rents and improved rents on private estates—that the difference sometimes ran into hundreds per cent. It was this margin—not merely the price at which Crown land was transferred, but the prospective increment of rack-rents, enclosure, exploitation of timber and minerals—which must be considered in estimating the gains accruing to its purchasers.

To complete the picture of property passing from the Crown to its wealthier subjects, it would be necessary, in the first place, to take account of further less obtrusive changes, which went on side by side with these grandiose deals. The process of piecemeal disintegration associated with the dubious business of "concealed lands," and with gifts and grants, such as the concessions of "drowned lands" to persons willing to reclaim them, still awaits its historian. Even the famous matter of the forests made little noise till near the end, when it made too much. The *de facto* transference of possessions involved in the absorption by neighbouring landowners of the last alone would seem not to have been a trifle. "The King loseth daily by intrusions and encroachments"; "wholly converted to the private benefits of the officers and private men"; "[private] claims do swallow up the whole forest, not allowing his Majesty the breadth of one foot"[88]—such lamentations, though uttered before the question entered politics, may sound like the voice of official pessimism; but the routine returns of encroachments contained in the records of some forest courts make them appear not unplausible. It would be necessary, in the second place, for the purpose of obtaining a comprehensive view, to compare the course of events in England with the history of those parts of the Continent where matters went a different way. Leaving these further questions, however, on one side, what significance, if any, it may be asked, is to be attached to the movement of which the dull transactions described above are specimens?

THE RISE OF THE GENTRY, 1558-1640

VI

Its financial consequences are obvious; they were those which led Hobbes to make his comment on the futility of attempting to support a State by endowing it with property subject to alienation.[89] The effect on the peasants of recurrent orgies of land speculation, if less conspicuous, is equally certain. In the third place, such figures as we possess suggest that the tendency of an active landmarket was, on the whole, to increase the number of mediumsized properties, while diminishing that of the largest.[90] Mr. Habakkuk has shown in a striking article[91] that "the general drift of property in the sixty years after 1690 was in favour of the large estate and the great lord," and has "explained the causes of that movement. During the preceding century and a half the current, as he points out, appears to have flowed in the opposite direction, with the result that, as the number of great properties was levelled down, and that of properties of moderate size levelled up, the upper ranges of English society came to resemble less a chain of high peaks than an undulating table-land. Is it too incautious, in the fourth place, to regard as one symptom of the change in the distribution of wealth the acquisition of new dignities by members of the class which gained most from it? Of 135 peers in the House of Lords in 1642, over half had obtained their titles since 1603. They included some lawyers and merchants, but the majority of them were well-to-do country gentlemen. The creation by the Stuarts of a *parvenu* nobility, like the sale of baronetcies to knights and esquires with an income from land of £1,000 a year, if politically a blunder, showed some insight into economic realities. It owed such fiscal utility as it possessed to the existence of a social situation which such expedients could exploit.

Nor, finally, were political attitudes unaffected by the same influences. With the growth of speculative dealings in land, the depreciation of the capital value of certain categories of real property by the antiquated form of land-taxation known as the feudal incidents became doubly intolerable. The more intimately an industry—agriculture or any other—depends on the market, the more closely is it affected by the policy of Governments, and the more determined do those engaged in it become to control policy. The fact that *entrepreneur* predominated over *rentier* interests in the House of Commons, was, therefore, a point of some importance. The revolt against the regulation by authority of the internal trade in agricultural produce, like the demand for the prohibition of Irish cattle imports and a stiffer tariff on grain, was natural when farming was so thoroughly commercialised that it could be said that the fall in wool prices alone in the depression of 1621 had reduced rents by over £800,000 a year. The freezing reception given by the Long Parliament to petitions from the peasants for the redress of agrarian grievances is hardly surprising, when it is remembered that one in every two of the members returned, up to the end of 1640, for the five Midland

Counties which were the disturbed area of the day, either themselves had been recently fined for depopulation or belonged to families which had been.[92] The economic reality behind the famous battle over the forests was the struggle between more extensive and more intensive methods of land utilisation, to which the increased profitableness of capitalist farming lent a new ferocity. Most of the attitudes and measures, in fact, which were to triumph at the Restoration can be seen taking shape between the death of Elizabeth and the opening of the Civil War.

To attempt an answer which went beyond these commonplaces would, perhaps, be rash. But it is not presumptuous to address the question to contemporaries; and some of them have left us in little doubt as to their opinion. Mr. Russell Smith,[93] in his interesting study of Harrington, has suggested that the thesis as to the political repercussion of changes in the distribution of landed property, which is the central doctrine of the *Oceana*, if partly inspired by a study of Roman history, derived its actuality from the English confiscations in Ireland under the Act of 1642 and the Diggers' movement in England. In reality, it was needless for Harrington to look so far afield as the first, or in spheres so humble as the second. In so far as he was in debt to previous writers, his master was Macchiavelli; but the process from which he generalised had been taking place beneath his eyes. His own relatives had been engaged in it.[94]

Had he shared the modern taste for figures, he would have found little difficulty in supporting his doctrine by some casual scraps of statistical evidence. He would have observed, for example, had he taken as a sample some 3,300 manors in ten counties, that out of 730 held by the Crown and the peerage in 1561, some 430 had left them (if new creations[95] are ignored) by 1640, while an additional 400 had been acquired by the gentry. He would have discovered that, as a consequence, the Crown, which in 1561 owned just one–tenth (9 per cent.) of the total, owned in 1640 one-fiftieth (2 per cent.); that the peers held one-eighth (12.6 per cent.) at the first date, and (ignoring new creations) one-sixteenth (6.7 per cent.) at the second; and that the share of the gentry had risen from two–thirds (67 per cent.), when the period began, to four-fifths (80 per cent.) at the end of it. His remarks on the social changes which caused the House of Commons "to raise that head which since hath been so high and formidable unto their princes that they have looked pale upon those assemblies," and his celebrated paradox, "Wherefore the dissolution of this Government caused the war, not the war the dissolution of this Government,"[96] were based on his argument as to the significance of a "balance" of property; and that argument took its point from his belief that in his own day the balance had been altered. To the sceptic who questioned its historical foundations, he would probably have replied—for he was an obstinate person—by inviting him either to submit rebutting evidence, or to agree that there was some *prima-facie* reason, at least, for supposing that, in the counties in question, the landed property of the Crown had diminished under Parthenia, Morpheus and his successor by three-quarters (76 per cent.), and that of the older nobility by approximately half (47.1 per cent.), while that of the gentry had increased by not much less than one-fifth (17.8 per cent.).[97]

In reality, however, as far as this side of his doctrines were concerned, there were few sceptics to challenge him. To regard Harrington as an isolated doctrinaire is an error. In spite of its thin dress of fancy, his work was not a Utopia, but partly a social history, partly a programme based upon it. Contemporaries who abhorred the second were not indisposed to agree with the first, for it accorded with their own experience. The political effect of the transference of property appeared as obvious to authors on the right, like Sir Edward Walker, whose book appeared three years before the *Oceana*, as to Ludlow, to that formidable blue-stocking, Mrs. Hutchinson, and to Neville, on the left.[98] If, in 1600, it could be said[99] that the richer gentry had the incomes of an Earl, and in 1628 that the House of Commons could buy the House of Lords three times over,[100] the argument advanced in some quarters in 1659 that, since the Peers, who once held two-thirds of the land, now held less than one-twelfth, the day for a House of Lords was passed, was not perhaps, surprising.[101] It overstated its case; but a case existed.

The next generation, while repudiating Harrington's conclusions, rarely disputed his premises. Dryden was not the only person to see political significance in the fact that

> The power for property allowed
> Is mischievously seated in the crowd.

Thorndike complained that "so great a part of the gentry as have shared with the Crown in the spoils of the monasteries think it in their interest to hold up that which ... would justify their title in point of conscience"; that the result had been "a sort of mongrel clergy of lecturers"; and that "it is visible that the late war hath had its rise here." Temple defended the plutocratic composition of his proposed new Council with the remark that "authority is observed much to follow land." Burnet wrote that the Crown had never recovered from the sales of land by James I, not merely for the reason of their effect on the revenue, but because they snapped the links which had kept the tenants of the Crown "in a dependence" upon it; Sidney that the nobility, having sacrificed "the command of men" to the appetite for money, retained "neither the interest nor the estates" necessary to political leadership, and that, as a consequence, "all things have been brought into the hands of the Crown and the commons," with "nothing left to cement them and to maintain their union"; an author—possibly Defoe—with the *nom-de-plume* of Richard Harley, that the "second and less observed cause" of the troubles of his youth was "the passage of land from its former possessors into the hands of a numerous gentry and commonalty"; Davenant that the case for a resumption, at any rate of recent grants, was overwhelming, though it would be prudent to try it, in the first place, in Ireland.[102]

The moral for Governments desirous of stability was drawn by a writer[103] who borrowed Burnet's name, and whose father—if the ordinary ascription is correct—had had much to say half a century before on the effects of the transference of land in his own county of Gloucestershire. He condemned the book of Harrington—"calculated wholly for the meridian of a Commonwealth"—but quoted its doctrines, and propounded a policy, which, but for his Republicanism, Harrington himself might have endorsed. The cause of all the trouble, he wrote, had been the reckless alienation of the estates of the Crown and nobility. Salvation was to be found by reversing the process. The Crown should by purchase gradually build up a new demesne, which should remain inalienable; and—"since a monarchy cannot subsist without a nobility"—should confine new peerages to persons with estates worth at least £6,000 a year and entailed on their heirs. Of these proposals, the first had long been impracticable, the second was superfluous.

Notes

1 The omission of some references, which should have been inserted, and the incompleteness of some others, require an apology. They are due to circumstances which, since the article was written, have made it difficult to consult some of the sources used.
2 Pierre Coste, *De l'éducation des enfants* (1695).
3 de Tocqueville, *L'ancien régime* (trans. by H. Reeves) pp. 15, 72, 77, 85; L. de Lavergne, *The Rural Economy of England, Scotland and Ireland* (trans. 1855), chaps. ix and x; H. Taine, *Notes sur l'Angleterre* (1872).
4 *Official Return of Members of the House of Commons* (1878).
5 The counties concerned are Herts, Beds, Bucks, Surrey, Hants, N. Riding of Yorks, Worcs, Glos, Warwick, Northants. The facts for the first seven in 1640 are taken from the lists of manors and their owners given in the V.C.H., and for the last three from Sir R. Atkyns, *The ancient and present state of Gloucestershire*; Dugdale, *Antiquities of Warwickshire*; J. Bridges, *History and Antiquities of Northamptonshire*. Those for 1874 are taken from John Bateman, *The Acreocracy of England, a list of all owners of three thousand acres and upwards . . . from the Modern Domesday Book*.
6 Sir W. Raleigh, *Concerning the Causes of the Magnificency and Opulency of Cities*.
7 Thomas Wilson, *The State of England Anno Dom. 1600* (ed. F. J. Fisher, Camden Miscell., vol. xvi, 1936), p. 23, put the number of gentlemen at "16,000 or thereabouts," plus some 500 knights. For the purposes of this article, no distinction is drawn between knights and gentry.
8 Samuel Butler, *Characters and Passages from Notebooks*, ed. A. R. Waller, and J. Earle, *Micro-Cosmographie* (1628). See G. Davies, *The Early Stuarts, 1603–1660*, pp. 264–272.
9 *The Examination and Confession of Captain Lilbourne* (B.M. E.130/33). I owe this reference to Miss P. Gregg.
10 See, for the tendency towards a "parity," Sir Edward Walker, *Historical Discourses upon Several Occasions* (1705), and, for the laxity of heralds, the same

writer's *Observations upon the Inconveniences that have attended the frequent Promotions to Titles of Honour and Dignity since King James came to the Crown of England* (1653).
11 *Hist. MSS. Com., MSS. of the Duke of Portland*, vol. ix, p. 5.
12 *De Republica Anglorun* (ed. L. Alston, 1906), pp. 39–40, "and, to be shorte, who can live idly and without manuall labour, and will bear the port, charge and countenance of a gentleman, he shall be ... taken for a gentleman."
13 Th. Wilson, *op. cit.*, pp. 23–4, gives £650–£1,000 a year as the income of a gentleman in London and the home counties, and £300–£400 as the figure for the remoter provinces. He describes knights as men of £1,000–£2,000 a year, but cites some with incomes of £5,000–£7,000.
14 E.g. H. Peacham, *The Complete Gentleman*, 1622; R. Braithwaite, *The English Gentleman*, 1633.
15 Thomas Wilson, *op. cit.*, pp. 18–24; Bacon, "Certain Observations upon a libel published this present year 1592," in *Works* (Bohn ed.) Vol. I p. 385; Dr. G. Goodman, *The Court of King James I*, ed. J. Brewer, Vol. I, pp. 311, 290–1, 322–3; Selden, *Table Talk*, under "Land" (see also under "Knight Service"); *Cal. S.P. Ven.*, *1603–7*, No. 729, 1617–19, No. 658, 1621–3, No. 603, 1629–32, No. 374; *Hist. MSS. Com., MSS. of the Earl of Cowper*, Vol. I, p. 129.
16 *The Works of Sir Walter Raleigh, Knt.*, ed. by Tho. Birch (1751), Vol. I, p. 9 (where the metaphor of a scales is used) and pp. 206–7.
17 Thomas Wilson, *op. cit.*, p. 18.
18 See the admirable article by Miss Helen M. Cam, "The Decline and Fall of English Feudalism," in *History*, vol. xxv, Dec. 1940, and *Trans. R.H.S.*, N.S., vol. xx, R. R. Reid, "The Rebellion in the North, 1569."
19 For the fall in the value of one item, profits of Courts, see *Cottoni Posthuma* (1651 ed.), p. 180, where it is stated that on Crown estates "the casual profits of courts never paid to the present officers their fees and expenses," and that in 44 Eliz. the costs of collection exceeded the receipts by £8,000. For a similar condition on a private property see *Bedford MSS.*, "Answere to my L. Treasurer's demands, and what may growe to the payment of my late lordes debts," 20 April, 1586, "the profyttes of Courtes will not be much moare than to answer the stuerdes and officers' fees, and in some places the same will not be discharged with their profyttes." I am indebted to Miss G. Scott Thomson for a transcript of this document.
20 M. Bloch, *Les Caractères Originaux de l'histoire rurale française*.
21 *Harl. Misc.*, vol. ii, pp. 515 *sq.*, "The Mirror of Worldly Fame," 1603, chap. iii.
22 Clarendon, *History of the Rebellion*, VI, 58.
23 Bacon, "Of the True Greatness of the Kingdom of Britain," in *Works* (Bohn ed.) I, p. 507.
24 L. Aikin, *Memoirs of Court of King James I*, p. 300.
25 *Bedford MSS.*, "Reasons to move her Mat[s] gracious consideration towards the Erle of Bedf.", February, 1579. I am indebted to Miss G. Scott Thomson for a transcript of this document.
26 Thomas Wilson, *op. cit.*, p. 24.
27 *Hist. MSS. Com., MSS. of Duke of Portland*, vol. ix p. 5.
28 *Chetham Misc.*, vol. iii, pp. 6–7, "Some Instructions given by William Booth to his stewards ..."
29 John Smyth, *Lives of the Berkeleys*, II, pp. 265–417, and Smyth Papers in the Gloucester Public Library.
30 Lord Compton married the daughter of Sir John Spencer, Lord Mayor in 1594, who died worth £300,000 (some said £800,000), Goodman, *op. cit.*, II, pp. 127–32;

Lord Noel a daughter of Sir Baptist Hicks, mercer, *Court and Times of Charles I*, vol. ii, p. 355; Lord Willoughby a daughter of Alderman Cockayne, "who brought him £10,000 in money . . . £1,000 a year pension out of the Exchequer, and a house very richly furnished," *ibid*, II, p. 220; the Earl of Holderness another daughter of Cockayne, with £10,000 as portion, *Cal. S.P.D. Jas. I, 1623–5*, CLXX, 54.

31 *See Hist. MSS. Com.*, *MSS. of the Marquis of Salisbury*, *passim*. Some references to the indebtedness of the nobility will be found in Thomas Wilson, *A Discourse Upon Usury*, Introduction, pp. 31–42.

32 Max Roose et Ch. Ruelens, *Correspondence de Rubens et Documents Epistolaires*, Vol. V, p. 116, ". . . molti altri, signori e ministri . . . sono sforzati a buscarsi la vita come possono, e per cio qui si vendono gli negoci publici e privati a dinari contanti."

33 e.g. *History of the Rebellion*, I, 131–6, 115–26, 131, 167, 170; III, 27, 93, 95, 283.

34 *S.P.D. Chas. I*, CCCCXCVII, No. 59, March, 1642–3.

35 H. E. Chesney, "The transference of lands in England, 1640–60," in *Trans. R.H.S.*, 4th ser., XV, pp. 181–210.

36 *Hist. MSS. Com.*, *MSS. of the Marquis of Salisbury*, Vol. I, pp. 162–5.

37 *The Montagu Musters Book, 1602–1623*, ed. by Joan Wake (Vol. VII of the Publications of the Northamptonshire Record Society), Introduction, pp. xiv–xv.

38 Th. Rogers, *A History of Agriculture and Prices*, V, p. 812.

39 *Harl. Misc.*, III, pp. 552 *sq.*, "The present state of England," by Walter Carey, 1627.

40 Marg. Duchess of Newcastle, *Life of the Duke of Newcastle* (Everyman ed.) pp. 98–100; *Abstract of Wilts Inquis. p/m.*, pp. 97–101; Clarendon, *History of the Rebellion*, I, 120–6.

41 E. A. Kosminsky, "Services and Money Rents in the Thirteenth Century," in *Econ. Hist. Rev.*, V, No. 2, April, 1935.

42 *The Account-book of a Kentish Estate, 1616–1704*, ed. by Eleanor C. Lodge (1927); *Robert Loder's Farm-Accounts*, ed. G. E. Fussell (Camden Society); Add. MSS., 39836, and *Hist. MSS. Com.*, *Report on MSS. in Various Collections*, Vol. III, 1904 (Tresham papers); Wynn Papers in Nat. Library of Wales, Aberystwyth, and published *Calendar of Wynn Papers*; Add. MSS., 33142 (agricultural accounts of the Pelhams) and 33154 (accounts relating to iron); Add. MSS., 34167–77 (Twysden papers).

43 *Robert Loder's Farm-Accounts*, Introduction.

44 *A Royalist's Note-book, the Commonplace Book of Sir John Oglander of Nunwell, 1622–52*, ed. Francis Bamford, p. 75.

45 Quoted by O. F. Christie, *The Transition to Democracy*, pp. 147–8.

46 *Hist. MSS. Com.*, *MSS. of the Marquis of Salisbury*, Vol. I, pp. 162–3, "Considerations delivered to the Parliament, 1559." See for earlier complaints King Edward VI's *Remains*, "Discourse Concerning the Reformation of many Abuses," and F. J. Fisher, "Commercial Trends and Policy in Sixteenth-Century England," in *Econ. Hist. Rev.*, Vol. X, No. 2, p. 110.

47 Thomas Wilson, *op. cit.*, p. 25.

48 *S.P.D., Jas. I*, XXII, No. 63, contains complaints of the purchase of Suffolk manors by Londoners. For Bristol see *S.P.D. Chas. I*, XXXV, No. 43, Sept. 8, 1626, and W. B. Willcox, *Gloucestershire 1590–1640*, p. 105.

49 The attitude of the Courts is well summarised in Mr. H. J. Habakkuk's article, "English Landownership 1680–1740," in *Econ. Hist. Rev.*, Vol. X, No. 1, Feb. 1940.

50 *Harl. Misc.*, VII, pp. 488–93, "Reasons and Proposals for a Registry ... of all Deeds and Incumbrances of Real Estate," etc., by Nicholas Philpott, 1671; *ibid*, pp. 493–501, "A Treatise concerning Registers ... of Estates, Bonds, Bills, etc., with Reasons against such Registers," by William Pierrepoint.
51 27 Eliz. Cap. IV. An earlier Act requiring the enrolment of sales of land had been passed in 1536. For an example of enrolments under it in one county, see Somerset Record Society, Vol. LI, "Somerset Enrolled Deeds," by Sophia W. B. Harbin.
52 *Harl. Misc.*, VI, p. 72, "A word for the Army and two words for the Kingdom," by Hugh Peters, 1647; *ibid.*, VII, pp. 25–35, "A Rod for the Lawyers," by William Cole, 1659.
53 *A Royalist's Note-Book*, etc., p. 14. An earlier complaint on the same subject is contained in Th. Wilson, *op. cit.*, pp. 24–5.
54 For Gray's Inn see Harl. MSS., 1912, no. 16, f. 207b, and for Lincoln's Inn *Records of Lincoln's Inn*, "The Black Books," Vol. II.
55 *Cal. S.P.D., Chas. I*, CXCIV, p. 87, June 20, 1631.
56 *A Royalist's Note-book*, p. 212.
57 *The Dr. Farmer Chetham MSS.* (Chetham Society, 1873) pp. 122–3.
58 *Hist. MSS. Com., MSS. of Duke of Buccleuch*, Vol. III, p. 182 (Northants); J. D. Chambers, *Nottinghamshire in the Eighteenth Century*, pp. 6–7; Thomas Fuller, *The History of the Worthies of England* (1840 ed.), Vol. I, p. 140; *Harl. Soc. Pub.*, Vol. XIX, 1884, pp. 206–8 (Beds); Sir Simon Degge in Erdswick's *Survey of Staffordshire*.
59 The counties concerned are Surrey, Herts, Beds, Bucks, Hants, Worcs and N. Riding of Yorks. The figures, which I owe to the kindness of Mr. F. J. Fisher, are taken from the lists of manors and their owners given in the V.C.H. They exclude transfers of leases, and transfers due to marriage, gift, inheritance, forfeiture, or other non-commercial transactions.
60 Excheq. Accounts, Alienations Office, *Entries of Licenses and Pardons for Alienations*.
61 Cotton MSS., Otho E X., no. 10, ff. 64–78 (*c.* 1590).
62 Lans. MSS., vol. 169, art. 51, f. 110, Contract made with Sir Baptist Hicks and others, Dec. 19,18 Jas. I, (by which land with an annual value of £1,000 was sold for £45,000).
63 *S.P.D. Chas. I*, CIX, 44, quoted by W. R. Scott, *English Joint Stock Companies*, I, p. 192. As Professor Scott points out, the price of land reflected not only the annual rent, but casualties, such as fines.
64 Marc Bloch, *op. cit.*, pp. 140–5; Paul Raveau, *L'Agriculture et les Classes Paysannes dans le Haut-Poitou au xvie siècle*, especially chap. II.
65 Thomas Wilson, *op. cit.*, pp. 22–3.
66 F. C. Dietz, *English Government Finance, 1485–1558*.
67 *Cal. S.P. Ven., 1603–7*, No. 709; 1617–19, No. 658; 1621–3, No. 603; 1629–32, No. 374.
68 For sales of Crown land under Elizabeth, see *S.P.D. Jas. I*, XLVII, Nos. 99, 100, 101, and S. J. Madge, *The Domesday of Crown Lands*, pp. 41–2; under James, Lans. MSS., Vol. 169, art. 51; under Charles I, Add. MSS. 18705, ff. 2–22, and *S.P.D. Chas. I*, CXXIV, 51; and under the two last, and 1649–56, Madge, *op. cit.*, pp. 47–64.
69 Madge, *op. cit.*, p. 256.
70 Henry Neville, *Plato Redivivus* (1763 ed.), p. 39.
71 One example may be given. John Smythe (*Lives of the Berkeleys*, Vol. II, pp. 356–61) gives particulars of property sold by Lord Henry Berkeley between

1561 and 1613 to the value of approximately £42,000. Sales of 25 manors and of the lease of one manor, realising £39,279 odd, were made to 13 persons (7 knights or baronets, 5 esquires and the trustees of a peer), the remainder, to the value of £2,789, going to 25 other persons of unspecified condition. Thus (i) 38 owners succeeded one; (ii) over nine-tenths of the property sold was acquired by purchasers relatively high in the social scale.

72 Dr. Savine's figures are printed in H. A. L. Fisher's *The Political History of England, 1485–1547*, App. ii, pp. 497–9.
73 Thomas Fuller, *op. cit.*, Vol. I, p. 60.
74 The following account of the fate of monastic property in three counties does not pretend to complete accuracy. It is based mainly on Sir Robert Atkyns, *The Ancient and Present State of Gloucestershire*, and *Men and Armour in Gloucestershire in 1608* (London, 1902, no editor stated), a list compiled by John Smythe from the Musters roll of 1608; J. Bridges, *History and Antiquities of Northamptonshire*; and Dugdale, *Antiquities of Warwickshire*.
75 i.e., eliminating duplication arising from the fact that several peers acquired monastic property in more than one of the three counties in question.
76 J. D. Chambers, *op. cit.*, p. 4.
77 G. H. Tupling, *The Economic History of Rossendale* (Chetham Society, N.S. Vol. 86, 1927).
78 The source of this statement is a list of lessees of Crown land 1–12 Eliz., contained (I think) in *S.P.D. Eliz.*, Vol. CLXVI, but the reference has been mislaid. The list includes among others, Sir William Cecil, Sir Thomas Smith, Anthony Brown (Justice of the Common Pleas), David Lewis (judge of the Court of Admiralty), Sir Francis Knollys, Sir Maurice Berkeley, Sir Henry Jernigan, Sir Walter Mildmay, Sir Gervase Clifton, Richard Hampden, etc.
79 Bacon, "Discourse in the Praise of his Sovereign" in *Works* (Bohn ed.) Vol. I, p. 371. For statistical evidence of under-renting, see S. J. Madge, *The Domesday of Crown Lands*, pp. 55–6.
80 This was so, e.g., in the case of Lionel Cranfield's speculation of 1609. His ledger shows that he and his partners borrowed £529 from Sir John Spencer, £427 from Lady Slanye, and £209 from Thomas Mun. I am indebted to Lord Sackville and Professor A. P. Newton for permission to examine the Cranfield papers.
81 *Hist. MSS. Com., MSS. of the Earl of Cowper*, Vol. I, p. 50.
82 A summary of these transactions, with the names of the principal contractors, is contained in Lans. MSS., Vol. 169, art. 51, f. 110. S.P.D. Jas. I, Vols. XL to LXXV, contain many references to the subject.
83 *C. J.* 1614, April 18, speech of Mr. Hoskyns.
84 I take these particulars from the Cranfield MSS. For the deal in which he was specially engaged see *S.P.D. Jas. I*, XLV, No. 159 (articles between the Commissioners for the sale and demise of Crown Lands and John Eldred and others, contractors for purchase of the same).
85 Add. MSS., 18795, ff. 2–22.
86 *Cal. S.P.D. Chas. I*, 1628–9, CXXIV, 51. The sale of land to the City was the result of a contract made in 1628 with Edw. Ditchfield and other trustees acting on behalf of the Corporation. Particulars as to the subsequent sale by the City of the properties concerned are contained in the Royal Contract Deeds in the Guildhall.
87 *Cal. S.P.D., Jas. I*, CXI, No. 80, Dec. 15, 1619. Sir T. Wilson to Master of Rolls. "The King was greatly deceived in the Chantry lands which he granted to discharge that debt, for he passed the lands with £5,000 or £6,000 a year at the

old rents, which are now worth 20 times as much.... The whole affair was a cozenage."
88 Cranfield MSS., 8236, 1622, Selwood forest; *ibid.* 8328, 1622, Crown forests in general, parts of Whittlewood, Barnwood and Sherwood being specially mentioned; S.P.D. Jas. I, LXXXIV, No. 46, Norden's Survey of Kingswood Forest.
89 *Leviathan*, chap. xxiv.
90 The following figures, which I owe to the kindness of Mr. F. J. Fisher, are based on the lists of manors and their owners contained in the V.C.H. They relate to manors whose ownership is known at all the four dates given below in the seven counties of Herts, Beds, Bucks, Surrey, Worcs, Hants and the North Riding of Yorks.

	1561	%	1601	%	1640	%	1680	%
Total	2547		2547		2547		2547	
Belonging to owners with 4 manors and under	1445	56.7	1457	57.2	1638	64.3	1684	66.1
Belonging to owners with 5 manors and under 10	490	19.2	544	21.3	488	19.1	556	21.8
Belonging to owners with 10 manors or more	612	24.0	546	21.4	421	16.5	347	13.6

91 H. J. Habakkuk, "English Landownership, 1680–1740," in *The Econ. Hist. Review*, Vol. X, No. 1, Feb., 1940, p. 2.
92 *Chanc. Petty Bag., Misc. Rolls*, No. 20, gives the names of persons fined for depopulation 1635–8. The five counties in question are Leicester, Northants, Notts, Hunts and Lincs, which accounted for 506 out of 589 individuals fined and for £39,208 out of £44,054 collected. The names of M.P.s are taken from the *Official Returns of Members of the House of Commons* (1878).
93 H. F. Russell Smith, *Harrington and his Oceana*, chap. III.
94 J. Wright, *History and Antiquities of Rutland* (1684), p. 135; E. J. Benger, *Memoirs of Elizabeth Stuart, Queen of Bohemia* (1825), pp. 68, 285; Grove, *Alienated Tithes*, under Leicestershire, parishes of Bitteswell, Laund, Loddington, Melbourne, and Owston; Add. MS. 18795, pp. 2–22, which shows Sir William Harrington and a partner buying Crown lands between Dec. 1626 and Feb. 1627.
95 Several of the families concerned had acquired peerages under James or Charles.
96 *Oceana*, ed. S. B. Liljegren, pp. 49–50.
97 The figures in this paragraph relate to the counties of Herts, Beds, Bucks, Surrey, Hants, Worcs, N. Riding of Yorks, Glos, Warwick, Northants. For those of the first seven counties I am indebted, as before, to Mr. F. J. Fisher.
98 Sir Edward Walker, *Observations upon the Inconveniences*, etc. (1653), especially his remarks on the effect of granting monastic lands to "mean families"; E. Ludlow, *Memoirs*, ed. C. H. Firth, Vol. II, p. 59; *Memoirs of the Life of Colonel Hutchinson* (Everyman ed.), pp. 59–60.
99 Thomas Wilson, *op. cit.*, p. 23.
100 *Court and Times of Charles I*, I, p. 331.
101 Burton's *Diary*, III, p. 408. See on the whole subject Firth, *The House of Lords during the Civil War*, pp. 21–32.
102 Dryden, *Absalom and Achitophel*, Pt. I, 777; H. Thorndike, *Theological Works*, V, pp. 440–2, 337–9, 371–3; Sir W. Temple, *Miscellaneous Writings*, Pt. III,

p. 16; Burnet, *History of his own Times* (1815 ed.), Vol. I, p. 12; Algernon Sidney, *Discourses Concerning Government* (1750 ed.), pp. 311–13; *Somers Tracts*, Vol. XIII, p. 679, Richard Harley, "Faults on both Sides"; C. Davenant, *A Discourse upon Grants and Resumptions.* See also P. Larkin, *Property in the Eighteenth Century* (1930) pp. 33–57.

103 *A Memorial Offered to Her Royal Highness the Princess Sophia* (*1815*). Foxcroft (*Life of Gilbert Burnet*, II, App. II, p. 556) ascribes the work to George Smythe of North Nibley.

34

MOHAMMED, CHARLEMAGNE AND RURIC

Sture Bolin

Source: *Scandinavian Economic History Review* 1, 1953: 5–39.

The association of Charlemagne with Mohammed is familiar to all students of the Middle Ages. It has arisen particularly in the various attempts which have been made from about 1920 to assess the significance of the political and cultural changes which took place in the early Middle Ages and are ascribed to, or at least associated with, Mohammed and Charlemagne, and to estimate the connexions between the events in the Arab and the Carolingian parts of the world. The two leading participants in the discussion are the Austrian Alfons Dopsch and the Belgian Henri Pirenne. Ruric, the Nordic viking chief in Russia, has, however, never been mentioned in the discussion.

There is no important difference between the interpretation of Dopsch and Pirenne of the transition from the ancient world to the Middle Ages. The collapse of the Roman Empire did not mean the end of an old world, nor did the Germanic migrations imply the birth of anything completely new. Neither the invasion of the Roman Empire by the Teutons, nor their assumption of political power led to any transformation of economic, social, political or cultural conditions. Changes had been continuously occurring in social, economic and intellectual life throughout the late Empire; these same processes continued during and after the barbarian invasions. Both Dopsch and Pirenne held that the similarities between the later Roman Empire and the Merovingian period were very significant while the differences were comparatively unimportant. Pirenne particularly stressed that the Mediterranean world remained a cultural and economic unit during the entire Merovingian period: the same religion and the same cultural influences still prevailed throughout; lively trading connexions were still maintained across the Mediterranean between western Europe and the many coastal towns of the Near East.

But although Dopsch and Pirenne are in agreement on all essentials concerning the Merovingian period, their opinions are in sharp contrast when they turn to the Carolingian period.

Dopsch maintains that social and economic life in the Carolingian period rested on the same foundations as Merovingian society. No gulf separated the two epochs; there were no essential differences in character between them. Dopsch resolutely rejects the view that during the Carolingian period agriculture attained a completely predominant position in western economy. It was not true that almost everywhere each separate farmstead primarily produced to supply its own needs; nor was the economic importance of the commercial and market towns reduced to a minimum. On the contrary, trade was not only active throughout the Carolingian period but was even on the increase.

On point after point, Pirenne maintained completely different opinions, exactly the opposite to those of Dopsch. The Merovingian age was a prolongation of the ancient world; the Carolingian period the true beginning of the Middle Ages. It was in Carolingian times that the transition occurred from the mercantile economy of the preceding epoch to the largely agrarian economy of the true mediaeval world. Internal trade declined within the Frankish empire and, except for a few isolated cases, the international exchange of goods ceased. The fundamental reason for this, says Pirenne, lay in the transformation which the map of Eurasia underwent in the seventh and eighth centuries. The Arab conquest of the eastern and southern coasts of the Mediterranean in the course of these centuries shattered the unity of the civilization that had existed until that time. Thereafter the Mediterranean no longer bound together the different parts of the same culture; instead it separated two alien and hostile civilizations, the Arab-Mohammedan world and the European-Christian world. There were very few connexions between these two spheres of culture. Peaceable trading ships no longer sailed the Mediterranean as before; the Sea was now dominated by the pirate fleets of the Arab Saracens. The Carolingians accepted the implications of the changed geopolitical structure of the world and moved the centre of their empire away from the Mediterranean coast to the region of the Rhine estuary. Charlemagne's palace at Aachen became a new political and cultural centre. The expansion of Charlemagne's empire was directed towards the east and the north; its economy was agricultural, its culture purely Germanic. The foundation of this new empire was, according to Pirenne, Charlemagne's most important contribution to world history. But the re-organization which he accomplished was made possible in the first place by the shattering of the Mediterranean world and thus indirectly by the developments which began with Mohammed. Pirenne epitomized his point of view in a striking paradox: without Mohammed, no Charlemagne.[1]

The writings of Dopsch and Pirenne provide a clear statement of the different interpretations of the Carolingian period and reveal the difficulties of the problem. Both writers are specialists in early mediaeval studies and they are the two leading authorities on the period. Nevertheless, their opinions on this fundamental question are as far apart as east and west.

That this can be so is due, of course, to the nature of the original sources on which mediaeval historians have to rely. For the early Middle Ages there is no documentary source material to make statistical comparisons possible. The widely scattered references in chronicles, legends, decrees and other sources, to trade, merchandise or economic conditions, can be used on either side of the argument. It can be shown for instance that papyrus ceased to be used in western Europe in the eighth century; on the one hand, this may be taken to indicate that the connexions with the Orient were much fewer; on the other hand, it can be held that this merely reflects changed governmental practices in the Frankish empire, since the conservative papal Chancery continued to use quantities of papyrus until the eleventh century. If one party quotes the many markets and fairs of the Carolingian period as evidence of a flourishing and growing trade, the other can interpret them as indicating that normal trade, conducted by a class of professional tradesmen, had declined. Circumstance after circumstance, source after source, may be interpreted in either of the two opposing ways.

There are two facts, however, in the mercantile history of the early Middle Ages which are so familiar and generally accepted that they need no further substantiation; they are so well known that it may seem banal to mention them. Firstly, whether or not trade ceased between western Europe and the Arab world during the Carolingian period, it is quite certain that, within the Caliphate, trade, industry and a town economy flourished as never before. Secondly, whether the internal trade of western Europe increased or decreased during this epoch, the ancient connexions between western Europe and the northern and Baltic countries became very much more important, especially in the first part of the Carolingian age.

If these two accepted facts are set in juxtaposition, however, the main problem again thrusts itself forward. One is led to ask whether the communications between the Frankish empire and the North became more lively in consequence of reduced communications between the West and the Orient, or whether the same factors were responsible for the prosperity of trade both in the Caliphate and around the North Sea.

Faced with this dilemma, we are obliged to look for some kind of original sources which permit comparisons to be made as directly as possible between different periods of time and different spheres of culture.

There is in this case only one type of study which can really provide the basis for direct comparisons between economic conditions at different ages and in different countries, namely numismatics. The history of coinage is abundantly rich in source material, – coins and coin hoards by the thousand. The coins run in unbroken series from the beginning of the period to the end of the Dark Ages; their date of minting can be ascertained to the year or at least within rather limited periods. They originate from every part of the civilized world of that time. It is always possible to determine the country in which they were minted, very often the exact place. If the basic problem which confronts us, of discovering the main commercial developments during the Carolingian period, can be solved at all, then it is through a study of the coins which have been discovered.

Coin hoards play an important part in discussions on commercial relationships in early times. Discoveries of Roman and Byzantine coins in Germanic territories and in India from the first six centuries A. D., of Arab and western coins in northern and eastern Europe from the period 800–1100, of Bohemian coins in Russia from the last centuries of the Middle Ages, of Portuguese and Dutch coins in India from more recent times, all bear witness to the changing pattern of international trading connexions. It may therefore appear that an examination of the hoards of coins from Carolingian times will show fairly directly how close the connexions were between the Frankish and Arab worlds and whether trade within the Frankish empire increased or declined. It could be assumed that, if connexions between East and West were close, many Arab coins would have been discovered in western Europe or many western coins inside the Caliphate. The absence of such discoveries might indicate that there were no close connexions between the two spheres of culture. In the same way, by studying the composition of the coin hoards found in western Europe and the radius of circulation of the coins, it would seem possible to determine the main lines of the development of internal trade; if the radius of circulation tends to become smaller and smaller, – that is to say, if the hoards in course of time tend to be dominated by coins minted in towns near to the place of discovery while coins from distant places become rare, – it might be taken as a sign of reduced trade; if the opposite is shown to be the case, – that the treasures contain greater numbers of coins from distant mint-cities, – it might be assumed that trade had expanded.

No information is available from this era concerning discoveries of western European coins in the East, but there is some evidence regarding discoveries of Arab coins in the West. These are not, however, so frequent that they can be considered to prove that close connexions existed between the two cultures. On the contrary, they are so few that, if we were compelled to draw a conclusion only from this evidence, we would have to infer that trans-Mediterranean intercourse had practically ceased.[2]

An inspection of the radius of circulation of the coins from the Frankish treasures reveals that this radius was wide during Merovingian times: the hoards from this period consist of coins originating from the most distant parts of the Frankish kingdom. The same applies to the hoards from the reigns of Charlemagne and Louis the Pious. But in the later Carolingian treasures, from about the middle of the ninth century onwards, the coins often have a limited radius of circulation: in some cases all the coins discovered in one place originate from a single mint not far away. Certainly, the main trend is a contraction of the area of circulation, and this might be taken as a sign of diminished trade; there have been pronouncements to that effect from students of the age.[3]

This would, however, be an over-simplified reading of the coin hoards. The two facts that Arab coins in western Europe are so few and that the coins of the later Carolingian hoards show a contracted radius of circulation cannot in themselves give much information about the state of trade. These phenomena must first be regarded in the light of the prevailing currency arrangements.

Certain fundamental currency principles were applied from the outset in the Carolingian kingdom. They persisted into the High Middle Ages and are called the principles of feudal coinage. One was that precious metal was worth more when minted than unminted. Another, – and this has greater relevance to our present study, – was to the effect that any type of coins was valid only within a limited area and that, within the area, only one type of coin could be used. Thus, within the Frankish empire, currency was limited by national boundaries as early as Merovingian times and by the beginning of the Carolingian period. The limitation was rigid: for the purposes of internal trade only the national coinage might be used and the area of validity of the coins thereafter became still more restricted. From the middle of the ninth century, coins only had territorial validity. This implied that, from the beginning of the Carolingian period, no foreign coins at all could be used within the boundaries of the Frankish empire; all foreign coins had to be reminted as Frankish coins, – that is they were melted down and the metal was used to make Frankish deniers. As, then, coins came to have this merely territorial validity, the deniers from one area of circulation in the Empire had to be melted and reminted in exactly the same way whenever they crossed a territorial frontier. These principles were strictly observed, as may be seen from various hoards discovered near the Loire. During the later part of the ninth century the southern boundary of one area of circulation ran just south of the river, the area reaching to the north as far as the Channel. Some hoards of this period have been found near the Loire, both south and north of the river. These hoards contain coins from all parts of northern France but none at all from the southern currency areas which were outside the boundaries of the territory, although geographically much nearer to the places where the hoards were buried.[4]

It is thus obvious that, no matter how close the trade connexions may have been between the Caliphate and western Europe, they could not have left behind any more than the slightest trace in the evidence found in the coin discoveries. Furthermore, it is obvious that the limitation of the area of validity of the coins must result in a contraction of their radius of circulation. We may thus conclude that the coin hoards from western

Europe can be of no direct assistance in helping to unravel the complex problems in dispute.

It will, therefore, be necessary to examine and compare the Frankish and the Arab coins themselves.

Our starting point is with the metal of the coins. At the height of the Merovingian period, gold was practically the only metal used for coinage in the Frankish empire, just as everywhere else around the Mediterranean. Towards the end of the Merovingian period, silver began to be used in France but it was not until about 700 that silver coins began to be of importance. From the middle of the eighth century, silver was almost the only metal used in minting.[5]

What was the state of affairs in the East? In those parts of the Caliphate which had been part af the Byzantine empire, only gold coins were minted in the earliest Arab times, whereas silver was and remained the coinage metal of the eastern parts which had been Persian. As early as the seventh century, however, silver coins were also to be found in the former Byzantine territories and towards 700 a fully bimetallic currency of silver and gold was in use. From 725 and for a long time thereafter, silver was the predominant coinage metal in the western parts of the Caliphate, the exclusive metal in Spain and the principal metal in Africa (i. e. Algeria with Tunis). Silver coins were minted extensively in the last-named territory in the latter part of the eight century.[6]

These facts indicate that, by and large, silver began to be an important coinage metal at roughly the same time both in the Frankish empire and in the Caliphate; likewise it became the dominant coinage metal almost simultaneously in both territories.

We may proceed from here to examine the type of coins. It is generally known that the Arab silver dirhem provided the model for the Carolingian silver denier. Merovingian coins usually bore a degenerate form of a bust of the emperor, – a legacy from Roman times; this type of engraving became rare early in the Carolingian period and was replaced by an inscription in large lettering, arranged in rows. From that time on, coins with lettering only were in circulation both in the Caliphate and in the Frankish empire; in the former they were the only coins, in the latter incomparably the most common. Exactly the same tendency is to be found in the silver coinage of the Byzantine empire from the mid-eighth century onwards. A well-known extreme example of early Arab influence on western European coinage is an Anglo-Saxon gold coin from the time of King Offa inscribed with an Arabic religious text. Another example is less extreme and has been little noticed, but is very significant: when the Carolingian coins began to be minted in the reign of Pepin the Short, the Latin letters used in the inscription were designed in such a way as to reveal clear Cufic characteristics.[7] These coins show a strong and fundamental Arabic influence on western culture.

Can the inscriptions themselves tell us anything? The currency of the Caliphate was reformed in 696 by 'Abd-al-Malik. The coins took on the Cufic characteristics and were inscribed with religious texts, features which became permanent. Arab coins proclaimed: "There is no God but God, the only God, and Mohammed is His Prophet." The emperor Justinian II was the contemporary of 'Abd-al-Malik in Constantinople. He abandoned the type of coin which had prevailed until that time (a gold coin bearing the inscription "Victoria Augusti" on the reverse) and introduced a new type of coin which, after the final victory of the iconodules, became the chief Byzantine coin: it bears a head of Christ, surrounded by the inscription, "Jesus Christus rex regnantium". The Cufic coins carried the Caliph's title, "The servant of God"; Justinian II called himself on his new coins "Servus Christi". Thus, after the Mediterranean world had been divided into two cultures, even coins were used to propagate the respective religions; they took part in the fight waged with both pen and sword between the creeds. About a hundred years later the Frankish denier began to take part in the controversy; a new inscription suddenly appeared on coins which are attributed to Charlemagne and became usual on coins of the time of Louis the Pious. It read simply "Christiana religio". It is self-evident that this struggle of the coins reflects the schism, but it also shows, not isolation, but points of contact between the cultural spheres in which the coins originated.[8]

A further circumstance is worth mentioning in this connexion. It was the custom in the Carolingian empire for coins to bear the name of their place of origin, whether city, castle or province, after the Merovingian pattern. This also applies to the coinage of the Caliphate which followed the Sassanian pattern.[9] Around 800, however, a new development occurred in the Caliphate. A coin from the year 796 bears the inscription "Ma'âdin al-Shâsh"; another from 799 reads "Ma'âdin Bajanis"; another from 810, "Ma'âdin". These inscriptions mean "the Shâsh mine", "the Bajanis mine" and "the mine". Similar inscriptions are to be found on Carolingian coins. "Metallum", "Metall(um) German-(icum)", "Ex met(allo) nov(o)", i. e. "the mine", "the German mine" and "from the new mine". The earliest of these coins has been dated between 794 and 800. This means that, in addition to the earlier inscriptions which still remained, a new form of inscription appeared on coins both in the Frankish empire and on the most easterly border of the Caliphate, the region around Tâshkand, separated in time by only a few years at the most.[10]

Thus we can observe on different points and in different respects important and even intimate similarities between Frankish and Arab coins. They have still further points in common and these make it possible for us to see more clearly the nature of the general development.

In the course of time, a given type of coin usually decreases in value; its face value corresponds to a smaller and smaller amount of precious metal.

But this was far from true of the Frankish silver denier in the early Middle Ages. The Merovingian denier had an average weight of 1.13 grammes. The weight of the denier increased as early as the first Carolingian reign, that of Pepin the Short; a number of coins preserved from that time have an average weight of 1.25 grammes. By the beginning of the reign of Charlemagne, the denier had probably become somewhat heavier still; coins preserved from the later part of his reign have an average weight of 1.59 grammes. The coins of Louis the Pious averaged 1.67 grammes and this weight was maintained throughout the ninth century. The denier of Charles the Bald had an average weight of 1.62 grammes; Odo's, of 1.60 grammes. From about 900 the process began to be reversed. The coins of Charles the Simple and of his successors had an average weight of only 1.31 grammes.[11] (The fluctuations in the weight of the Frankish denier are shown in the graph on page 16).

If we turn to the Arab coins, we find in one respect a similar trend. The weight of the silver coins also increased in the Caliphate during the eighth and ninth centuries. In the early part of the eighth century the dirhem had an average weight of 2.78 grammes; towards the end of the century it was 2.83 grammes, during the early ninth century 2.87 grammes and during the later ninth century 2.96 grammes. The first of these increases in weight can be fixed closely in date; it took place at the transition from the Umayyad to the Abbasid period, that is, at precisely the same time that the first increase in weight of the Frankish denier occurred, in the reign of Pepin the Short.[12]

Arab coinage, unlike the Carolingian, was a bimetallic system. Coins were minted in the Caliphate both in gold and silver. Changes took place in both types of coin but the gold coins decreased in weight while the silver dirhems increased. In addition, the relation between the gold and silver coins changed; at different times there were different numbers of dirhems to the dinar. These facts complicate the question and make it impossible to reach historically valid conclusions simply by a direct comparison of the two series of weights of Frankish and Arab silver coins. But it gives us another possible line of approach: by comparing the weight of Arab gold and silver coins in conjunction with documentary references in Arab sources to the relation between the dinar and the dirhem, we can trace the fluctuations in the relative values between gold and silver within the Caliphate.

A considerable amount of relevant information is available about the relation between the dinar and the dirhem. It is stated in several places that, at the time of Mohammed and of the Caliph 'Omar, – i. e. during the first part of the seventh century, – the dinar was worth 10 or 12 dirhems. The dinar was then the Byzantine solidus, the dirhem the Persian drachma. These quoted rates of exchange between the two coins correspond approximately to ratios of 9:1 and 11:1 between the value of gold and silver. In a summary of a revenue account at the time of the Caliphate of Hârûn-ar-Rashîd

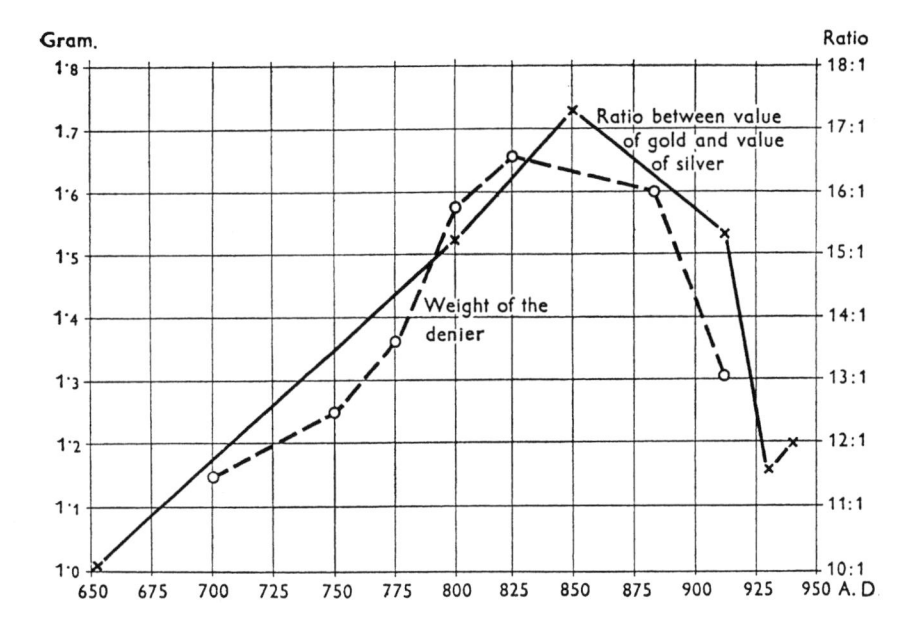

(786–809) quoted by a tenth century historian, the dinar is reckoned as 22 dirhems; this ratio is obviously appropriate in these accounts and thus may be dated around 800; the corresponding gold-silver ratio is 15.2:1. In Yâkût's Geographical Dictionary, compiled during the thirteenth century, but largely describing far older conditions, it is expressively stated that under the Caliph Mutawakkil (847–861), the dinar was equivalent to 25 dirhems; the corresponding gold-silver ratio was 17.33:1. There are several statements from the tenth century about the relative values of the dinar and the dirhem which show that the ratio changed greatly from one time to another and between place and place, particularly in the later part of the century; this was obviously connected with the fact that the weight and fineness of the coins varied considerably among the small principalities into which the Caliphate was rapidly being sub-divided. Nevertheless, some statements relating to the first part of the tenth century should be noted. A budget from the Caliphate of Muktadir (907–932) counts 20 dirhems to the dinar, giving a relative value of 15.43:1 between gold and silver. The geographer Kudâmah, writing soon after 928, passed a number of comments on the caliph's revenues during the first part of the ninth century, using an exchange rate of 15 dirhems to 1 dinar for that period, implying a relative value of 11.57:1 between the precious metals. Both the values mentioned here, – 15 and 20 dirhems to the dinar, – are also found among the many local variants of the exchange ratio in the tenth century. A final point to mention is a reform of 941 referred to in many places, which fixed the relation at 13 dirhems to the dinar, meaning that gold was valued about 12 times more highly than silver.[13]

The fluctuations in the relative values of gold and silver to which these comments bear witness, are shown in the graph on the opposite page. The graph indicates that up to the middle of the ninth century the value of silver declined in terms of gold but thereafter increased. To maintain the position of silver coins in a bimetallic currency while the value of silver was falling could be accomplished in three ways: by decreasing the weight of gold coins; by increasing the weight of silver coins; or by changing the relation between the two coins, counting more silver coins to one gold coin. As we have already seen, all three methods were used in the Caliphate.[14]

But if the situation is quite different, – if it is a question of maintaining the position and purchasing power of silver coins in a monometallic currency where they are the only coins in existence, – only one expedient is available: to increase the weight of the silver coins. Conversely, if silver increased in value, it was necessary to reduce the weight of the silver coins. This is precisely what happened in the Frankish kingdom. Until the middle of the ninth century, while silver was losing its value in the Caliphate, the weight of the Frankish denier increased. From the middle of the ninth century onwards, when the value of silver in relation to gold was increasing, the weight of the Frankish denier fell back again. The graph shows how closely the weight of the Frankish denier adapted itself to the gold-silver ratio in the Caliphate. In other words, through changes in its weight, the Frankish denier corresponded constantly to one and the same amount of gold.

Can these fluctuations, – especially the fall in the value of silver before the middle of the ninth century, – be traced in any different way in other original sources? Attention may be drawn, perhaps, to one Persian source which, although difficult to interpret, seems to indicate a decline in the price of silver from an index of 100 in 793 to an index of 85 in 835.[15]

Certain events in the Frankish empire are more revealing. A capitulary issued in 864 contains the only known instance from the early Middle Ages of a maximum price being fixed for gold. The fixed maximum price, – 12 pounds of deniers to one pound of gold, – unfortunately cannot be compared with the Arab exchange rate between the precious metals, among other reasons because the capitulary referred to unminted gold; in accordance with prevailing currency principles, minted metal was considerably more valuable than unminted.[16] The very fact that it was considered necessary to fix a maximum price bears itself eloquent witness to the rising price of gold. It was exactly at this time that gold reached the highest value in relation to silver known to us in the monetary system of the Caliphate.

There are three particularly interesting Frankish capitularies from the period around 800. Two of them (issued in 794 and 806) contained provisions for fixing maximum prices for grain of different kinds; the third (805), for certain clothing and furs. Thus, within fifteen years of the introduction of the new and heavier silver coins, maximum prices had been fixed both for necessities and for luxuries. The significance of this is quite clear. It is to be remembered that law-making in the Middle Ages was always realistic and closely concerned with specific cases; one may therefore justifiably conclude that the provisions of these capitularies are definite evidence that prices in the Frankish empire were increasing, in other words, that the value of silver was declining, thus confirming the clear evidence of the increased weight of coins.[17]

The next problem must be to attempt to account for these fluctuations in the values of the precious metals which were common to both the Caliphate and western Europe, namely, first the fall and then the increase in the relative value of silver. The obvious question to investigate first is the possibility that changes had taken place in the production of precious metals.

Very little attention has so far been paid to an examination of the world's supply of silver in the period before the opening of the Saxon mines in the tenth century.

The Frankish inscriptions mentioned earlier, Metallum, Metallum Germanicum and Ex metallo novo, show that silver was mined to some extent in the Frankish empire. But it could not be supposed by anyone that this mining was sufficient to bring about a world-wide decline in the price of silver on the scale that we have now established.

The corresponding types of coin in the Arab world have also been considered earlier. There are, in addition, many references in Arabic literature and in other written sources to silver mines and silver production. From these sources we know of silver mines in Spain, Africa, Armenia and, – in quite considerable numbers, – in Persia. But the references are often obscure, short, vague and uninformative; sometimes they indicate that the mines were not very productive and that they had quickly been abandoned.

The information which is available about the silver mines in the most easterly parts of the Caliphate, Khurâsân and Transoxania, however, tells quite a different story.

In the Hindu Kush range in modern Afghanistan was the mine of Banjahîr, described as the largest and most productive in the world. Thus one reads in Yâkût's Geographical Dictionary: "The people of Banjahîr are a mixed race; passion and wickedness prevail in the territory; murder is common. Their dirhems are large and plentiful; it is impossible to buy anything, even a bunch of vegetables, for less than one dirhem. The silver is found at the top of the mountain which, as a result of the many pits which have been dug, looks like a sieve. It can happen that one single man who mines silver has a yield of 300,000 dirhems (a sum corresponding to about a ton of silver). He often makes enough to keep himself and his descendants prosperous. He often retrieves at least his outlay but he often is left destitute also, for instance if water or other adverse circumstances gain the upper hand. It can happen that the man who is rich in the morning is poor in the evening and that the man who is poor in the morning is rich in the evening."

Yâkût's description can, without any exaggeration, be said to refer to a mediaeval Klondyke. There is little difference between the silver town of that era and the gold-diggers' camp at a much later date. Fortunes were made and lost just as easily in both; the inhabitants were collected together indiscriminately from many different quarters; in both they were prone to violence. A consequence of the super-abundance of silver was that the purchasing power of silver, and of the dirhem, was small.

As we noted earlier, Yâkût wrote in the thirteenth century although his description of conditions in Banjahîr refer to a much earlier period. The different facts which he states are to be found in tenth century sources, with but occasional variations. As is so often the case, Yâkût is clearly repeating the story of a much earlier writer.

The oldest certain trace of this mine is a coin of the year 911 with the inscription "Ma'âdin Banjahîr", "the mine of Banjahîr". Nevertheless, coins were minted regularly in the town of Banjahîr from the middle of the ninth century. There is no reason to doubt that the extraction of silver dated back at least to the same time.

Another mining district of great importance lay in Transoxania, especially in the neighbourhood of Shâsh, i. e. Tâshkand. There are no such lively accounts of mining there comparable with Yâkût's description of Banjahîr, but the mines can be traced further back in time: several coins with the inscription Ma'âdin al Shâsh are known from as early as the closing decades of the eighth century, when, after a long interruption, regular minting was restarted in the eastern provinces of the Caliphate. The Transoxanian mines were, according to Arab geographers, the richest silver mines in the whole of the Mohammedan world, with the exception of Banjahîr. Dirhems were minted in large quantities in Shâsh; coins originating from that town are so numerous that one is almost tempted to doubt the truth of the statement by the geographers that the Shâsh mine was less rich than that at Banjahîr. There can be no question about the very great importance of the Shâsh mine. The extent of the mining may be estimated in the following calculations, though they may be considered beyond the bounds of historical criticism and based on material which is far too insubstantial. In a list of the items of the caliph's income from his eastern provinces in the early part of the ninth century, one entry is of 607,100 dirhems from Shâsh and its mines. Certain items of information given by the geographer Mukaddasî also correspond with the items of the tax-roll, with one significant exception. The exception concerns Shâsh, to which Mukaddasî attributes an income of only 180,000 dirhems, without making any mention of the mine. The most satisfactory explanation of the discrepancy is that Mukaddasî did not include in the caliph's income anything from the silver mine at Shâsh; his income from the mine would in that case have amounted to about 400,000 dirhems, or 1.2 tons of silver.

If the contribution which the caliph received from the mine was paid in accordance with Mohammedan law, it should have been 1/25 of the total production; in that case the mine at Shâsh must have produced about 30 tons of silver annually, a quantity equal to about two thirds of the total world production of silver around 1500 when the output of the Saxon and Bohemian mines was at its greatest. These estimates contain such grave uncertainties that the finding is of no scientific value, – but it is not unreasonable.

However this may be, it is quite certain that unexampled quantities of silver were found in the Caliphate. A viceroy might be fined as much as 2,700,000 dirhems, or about 8 tons of silver, – a sum which is approximately the same as the amount for which Sweden redeemed Scania in the fourteenth century and which Denmark paid in ransom for King Valdemar Sejr, – sums which ruined the two countries. In the ninth century the Viceroy of Khurâsân levied between 40 and 50 million dirhems annually, – between 120 and 150 tons of silver, a quantity twice or three times more than the estimated world production in 1500. On the basis of official documents it has been calculated that the Caliph's total income in silver around 800 was some 400 million dirhems, or 25 times the world production in 1500. There can thus be no doubt that the silver resources of the Caliphate reached fantastic proportions at this time; or that the production of silver from several mines, principally in the eastern parts of the Caliphate, was quite extraordinary. The fall in the price of silver which, it is established, occurred between the seventh century and the middle of the ninth century can now be explained in all respects. At the beginning of the eighth century the Arabs finally joined together in a single political, cultural and economic unit, the rich silver-producing region of Transoxania and the eastern parts of the Mediterranean; during this period the Arabs began to produce silver from the two mines at Shâsh and Banjahîr, described as the largest in the Caliphate. Production on such a scale, creating such a superabundance of silver, must have led to a fall in its price and it is known that this took place in the currency of the Caliphate, of the Frankish empire, and elsewhere. It also provided a natural background for the considerable increase which took place in the use of silver as a minting metal, alike in the East and in the West.

What then lies behind the increase in the price of silver in relation to gold during the period from the middle of the ninth century to the beginning of the tenth? The circumstances connected with this trend can only be dealt with here in brief. One possible reason is that the silver-producing East went its own way from the late ninth century onwards after the foundation of the Samanid dynasty, virtually independent of the caliphs; the ties between Transoxania and Baghdad were severed. But there was certainly another factor which affected the relative values of gold and silver. From information found in a work written around 1400 by the learned historian al-Makrîzî which he derived from writings by the tenth century historian 'Abd

Allah ibn Ahmad, we know that, shortly after the middle of the ninth century, Nubia, a gold-producing region since ancient times, was finally conquered by the Arabs and that shortly afterwards new and rich gold discoveries were made. The same author, – and also the geographer Ya'kûbî writing around 900, – gives us vivid descriptions of life in this mining area. Wâdî-al-Allaki, situated in the district, was like a vast town, swarming with people, in which Arabs and non-Arabs alike tried their fortune; fairs were held, business was transacted. After the Arab conquest, the country flourished so greatly that as many as 60,000 camels were needed to carry its provisions from Assuan, even though other supplies arrived by sea. These accounts are the counterparts of the story of Banjahîr. It is natural that the increase in the production of gold which occurred after 850 brought precisely the same consequences as the earlier increase in silver production had done: gold sank in value and the relative value of silver increased again.[18]

The increased production of silver within the Caliphate in the period before 850, the increased production of gold in the subsequent period both left their marks not only on the coinage of the Caliphate but also on that of the Frankish empire. Under these circumstances it becomes impossible to agree with Pirenne's view that western Europe and the East were isolated from one another in the Carolingian period.

In fact, a re-examination of the European source material was undertaken by Pirenne's pupil, E. Sabbe, and in one vital respect led to a similar conclusion. Sabbe found that passages mentioning the use of silk, purple and brocade are far more numerous in the ninth and tenth centuries than earlier. He does not, however, take a standpoint in direct opposition to Pirenne; the fact may simply be due, he says, to the deficiency of the records from Merovingian times. He formulates his final conclusion in this way: trade in oriental cloths continued in western Europe in the ninth and tenth centuries despite the difficulties caused by the Arab conquests and Saracen piracy, and remained a regular feature of life in Carolingian times.[19]

If we leave the European sources and turn to the Arab, we find numerous pieces of evidence of trade and shipping activity on the Mediterranean. The best known and the most descriptive account is that of world trade in the ninth century given by the geographer Ibn Khurdâdbih. "The Jewish Radanites speak Arabic, Persian, Roman, Frankish, Spanish and Slavonic. They travel from east to west and from west to east. They board ships in Frankish territory and proceed to Faramâ. There they load their wares on camels and travel by land to Kulzum; from there they cross the eastern seas to the seaports for Medina and Mecca, to Sind, Hind and China. On the return some of them make for Constantinople to sell their goods to the Romans; others go to the place of abode of the Frankish king to dispose of them there. Sometimes the Jewish merchants sail from Frankish lands across the western sea to Antioch and go from there by Baghdad to Oman, Sind,

Hind and China. These journeys can also be made by land. The merchants coming from Spain go to Morocco, thence to Africa and so across Egypt and by Damascus to Fâris, Kirmân, Sind, Hind and China. Sometimes they make their way round the back of Rome and travel through the lands of the Slavs to the capital of the Khazars and also across the Caspian Sea to Balkh and from there by land across Transoxania to China."[20]

We are here shown a picture of an active and widely ramified international trade in which the Mediterranean certainly does not play an unimportant part. It is very much a world-wide trade; one's thoughts are transported to the epoch 700 years later when America was newly discovered and a great flood of silver poured into the old world whose inhabitants went out on ever more frequent and further distant journeys in search of trade.

Let us return at this point to Pirenne's epigram on Mohammed and Charlemagne. The facts we have just described certainly speak for the existence of a bond uniting the two, but not in the sense intended by Pirenne. His view was that the Arab conquests led to a break-up of the world culture as it was known until then and to an end of trade across the Mediterranean.

Instead we may summarize the position as follows: through the wars of conquest begun by Mohammed the unity of world culture was shattered and civilization was divided into separate spheres; but it was also enlarged, for, far to the east, new countries, the lands of Khurâsân and Transoxania, both rich in silver, were brought into the Mohammedan orbit. Silver production increased to very large proportions. So began a new era, the age of oriental silver. From this newly-won territory there issued a mighty flood of silver over the whole world fructifying trade and economic life, – just as 700 years later a similar flood issued from other recently discovered lands. The flood did not stop at the boundaries of the Caliphate but penetrated into western Europe, where also it led to changes in economic life: we observe that maximum prices had to be fixed and the currency system modified. Commercial life flourished within the Frankish empire as well as internationally.

In other words, the Carolingian renaissance had not merely its intellectual but also its material pre-requisites in the Caliphate. In this sense one may reiterate Pirenne's paradox, without Mohammed, no Charlemagne, but in disagreement, not in accord, with his views.

In order to assess completely the connexions between the Frankish empire and the Caliphate we must establish what goods were the basis of trade between the two territories.

An Arab source which has little reliability as evidence says that silver was imported by the Franks from the Mohammedan world; for the rest, historical writings contain no more than occasional surmises.[21] The foregoing exposition should establish beyond any doubt that silver was exported from the Mohammedan world to western Europe. Moreover, spices and oriental luxury goods of various kinds were imported into western Europe just as during an earlier period.[22]

The question therefore arises of what the Franks gave in exchange. It has not been possible for writers who have relied solely on western sources of information to supply a complete answer. The Monk of St. Gall relates that Charlemagne sent to Hârûn-ar-Rashîd red fabrics which were very highly valued in the Arab world. This has been quoted as proof that textiles were exported from western Europe to the Orient. It is clear from western European sources that France and Italy exported slaves to the Caliphate; this fact has already been stressed by scholars whose conclusions derive from those sources: slaves certainly were an item of import into the eastern countries as early as Merovingian times.[23]

Far more detailed information about the imports of the Caliphate from western Europe is to be found in Arab writings. The ninth century geographer Ibn Khurdâdbih states that the Franks exported to the Mohammedans eunuchs, male and female slaves, brocade, beaver-skins, marten-skins, other furs, swords, the perfume of the styrax and the mastic drug. Other statements, from tenth century writers, are worth noting. Istakhrî writes that from Maghrib came white eunuchs, brought thither from Spain, and valuable girls. Ibn Hawkal, whose work is closely allied to that of Istakhrî but contains more detailed and more useful information, relates that beaver-furs were brought to Spain from the Slav territories; among the articles of trade which came from Spain to Maghrib and Egypt were male and female slaves of Frankish and Galician nationality and Slav eunuchs. Mukaddasî was aware of the export from Spain of Slav eunuchs. An eleventh century geographer describes how the Franks took Slav prisoners of war and had them castrated by Jews living within the country or in neighbouring Mohammedan lands after which they were sold to Spain. The Italian writer Liutprand confirms this in the tenth century: according to him, merchants from Verdun made incalculable profits out of making men into eunuchs and then selling them to Spain.[24]

These Arab sources show that the Frankish exports were, except for occasional examples of less important goods, weapons, brocade, (the account of the Monk of St. Gall does not seem to have been entirely invented out of thin air), furs and slaves. There can be no doubt that, of these, the last two were the most important.

But, as far as is known, furs were never produced in the Frankish empire on any significant scale; on the other hand many sources indicate that northern Europe and the territory inhabited by the Slavs were the principal fur-producing regions. Nor did the slaves, the other leading article of export from the Frankish empire to the Caliphate, originate in the empire. We have seen already from the passages quoted from Arab writings, that the slaves sold by the Franks to the Caliphate were Slav. A decision of the Council of

Meaux in 845 is of interest in this connexion: Jewish and other merchants travelled with heathen slaves across Christian lands and sold them to infidels; this practice should be prohibited in the future. It is true that cases are known of Christian slaves also being sold to Spain, – the anti-Semitic letter-writer Agobard lays the blame for this upon the Jewish merchants. But as a general rule Christian slaves were not sold to infidels. Thus, after the conversion of the Saxons to Christianity, the slaves sold to the Caliphate from the Frankish empire must have come largely from the same regions as the furs, the Slavic territory east of the Elbe, or northern Europe.[25]

Once the fact is established that the chief articles of export of the Franks to the Caliphate were furs and heathen slaves, the part played by the Frankish empire in the international trade of the time is set clearly into perspective. The main Frankish exports were primarily not its own products. Instead, the Frankish empire was a country of transit between the fur- and slave-producing territory in northern, central and eastern Europe and the Mohammedan world. This conclusion may be somewhat startling but it is incontestable. Indeed, it supplies us with the key to an understanding of many problems relating to the development of and changes in world trade during the early Middle Ages.

It now becomes possible to understand why there were such active connexions in the early Carolingian period between the Frankish empire and the North. Ancient trading routes linked the East with the Frankish empire as well as the Frankish empire with the North and the Baltic lands. When the supply of silver greatly increased in the Caliphate, slaves and furs were imported in increasing quantities. Naturally, the routes used for this trade were the old lines of communication between the Orient and western Europe. But the increased export of slaves and furs from the Frankish empire most certainly had its counterpart in the increased import of these two commodities into the Frankish empire from their countries of production. Consequently, trade increased and commerce became livelier along the old route between western Europe and the northern and Baltic lands at precisely the same time.

We have here an answer to the problem which confronted us at the beginning of this enquiry. The livelier trade on the North Sea and the commercial prosperity of the Mohammedan world were not isolated phenomena. They were intimately connected and were both symptomatic of the worldwide economic boom during the age of oriental silver.

There is indeed a great deal of evidence of the active connexion between northern and western Europe in early Carolingian times. It was in the 790's that Nordic Vikings set out on their first raid on the west, when they went to England. The earliest Nordic coins minted at home follow the pattern of Frankish coins of precisely this epoch, the later part of the eighth century. The first treasures buried in Scandinavia and the immediately surrounding territory during the time of the Viking conquests consist exclusively of

Frankish coins of the reigns of Charlemagne and Louis the Pious. Coins from western Europe are found to some extent up to the middle of the ninth century in graves and in other scattered places in the North. The ancient towns known to have been in existence around 800, – Reric, Slesvig-Hedeby, Ribe and Birka, – are unmistakable evidence of the importance of trade in the Baltic region. Visits to these towns by Frisian merchants, as well as journeys by Northmen to Duurstede, the trade metropolis of Frisia, are described in written documents. Archaeologists and philologists alike stress the importance of these links between the North and Frisia in their respective studies. Both the political intercourse between Franks and Danes in the first three decades of the ninth century and the attempt which started about this time to convert the Nordic peoples to Christianity show plainly how Frankish interests tried to assert themselves in the North.[26]

Of course, the links between northern and western Europe were never broken, but hardly any western European coins are to be found in any Nordic discoveries from a very long period after 850. References in western European writings to conditions in the North become rare after 830. The Frankish intervention in the Danish wars of succession ceased; by the middle of the ninth century the Frankish missionary activity had ended. But after 830 the Viking excursions to the West increased in strength and number.

Thus, a change seems to have occurred in the relations between the North and western Europe and this change should be regarded against the background of developments in international trade.

It was natural, indeed essential, that when the age of oriental silver began, the trade in furs and slaves should follow the old paths which for centuries had linked the Orient with western Europe and western Europe with the North and the Baltic lands. But it was by no means essential, hardly even natural, for such a roundabout commerce to persist.

The Frankish empire was the entrepot but the market was the Caliphate. In 750 the centre of the Caliphate moved from Syria to Iraq. Economic life flourished in Persia in the Abbasid period; the silver was won still further to the east; there was a considerable development of industry.

The territory which offered the best opportunities for procuring slaves was the Slavic lands which at this time extended in the east as far as the Upper Volga. Furs were to be obtained in the North and the Baltic regions and in the countries to the east. The great eastern European rivers provided excellent means of transport. In other words, circumstances were more favourable for a more direct connexion between producers and consumers than was provided by the circuitous method of using the old traditional routes by way of Frankish territory.

The Nordic expansion eastwards and the creation of "the great Svitjod", the area of Swedish dominance in eastern Europe, must be seen against this background. Later sources attribute the foundation of the Russian state to the Viking chieftain Ruric of the people of Rus and date it at 862. Ruric may be only a legendary figure but his name may remain as a symbol of a historical reality. The year 862, which was once regarded as a corner-stone in the chronology of the history of eastern Europe, is certainly the product of a late and hypothetical reconstruction of events on the basis of known sources; modern research attaches no value at all to it.[27]

The Nordic expansion towards the east across the territory of the eastern Slavs had begun earlier. Swedish influence was strongly felt in the Baltic coastal areas before 800, although not further inland. But Swedish archaeological evidence from the early part of the ninth century bears witness to long-range connexions between the North and the territory north of the Caspian Sea; it shows that the eastward expansion had progressed very far. From the same period there are questionable archæological traces of Nordic settlement south of Lake Ladoga. It is certain that in 839 Swedes advanced along some of the rivers of eastern Europe as far as Constantinople; they pretended to be emissaries from the Khan of the Rus. In 860 the first Viking expedition took place in the direction of Constantinople. Perhaps as early as about 846, certainly before the end of the century, Ibn Khurdâdbih says that merchants of the Rus visited Constantinople and Baghdad. Modern historians have every reason to put the date of the Nordic penetration of East Slavia in the early part of the ninth century.[28]

The nature of the Nordic expansion is fairly well known. The Norsemen in the east were typical equivalents of the Spanish conquistadors of the sixteenth century. They were conquerors in foreign lands, callously exploiting a subdued people.

They acted like marauding pirates, – less, however, in the east than in the west: only two assaults on Constantinople and three or four on the Caliphate are definitely established as historic facts.[29]

The Norsemen came as mercenary soldiers. The Varangian Guards of the Byzantine emperors in Constantinople are well known. The Arab author Mas'ûdî gives us to understand that men of the Rus, – and Slavs, – found employment as soldiers and servants to the Jewish khan of the Khazars in his realm north of the Caspian Sea.

The Norsemen settled inside the east Slavic territory and forced their subjects to support them and furnish them with commercial merchandise. The Arab Ibn Rustah relates that the Rus owned no arable land but lived on what they took from the Slavs; they forced them to surrender goods of all kinds. Constantin Porphyrogennetos describes how the Rus passed the winter living among the conquered Slavs and then spent the spring and summer in Kiev and on trading journeys.[31]

They came to look for slaves. Ibn Rustah and Gardîzî say that the Rus made war on the Slavs, carried them off as slaves and sold them. In these comments describing conditions at the beginning of the tenth century, there are accounts of actual slave-hunts made by the Norsemen in the eastern parts.[32]

The Norsemen were not only dealers in slaves; they appeared, in the east more than in the west, as merchants in general. It has truly been said that the ruler of Kiev himself was a great merchant who traded in the goods he received in taxes from his subjects.[33]

There are many references in Byzantine and Arab literature to the activities of the Norsemen as merchants in eastern Europe. One of their trading routes ended at Constantinople where, according to an Arab source, they sold furs and swords. A fact of a greater interest in this investigation is that the trading journeys of the Norsemen regularly took them to the capital city of the Khazars on the Lower Volga as well as to the town of Bulgar situated in the lands of the Volga Bulgars near the junction of the River Kama with the Volga. Mohammedan influence was strong in both these places; it is true that in the Khazar empire the khan and the nobility had been won over to the Jewish faith but there were also many Mohammedans in the country; the Emir of the Volga-Bulgars went over to Islam before 922. Both places were termini of Arab routes, one of which came from the north of Persia across the Caspian Sea to Khazaria, the other from Transoxania across Khwarizm to Bulgar. The tenth century writer Mas'ûdî describes the ceaseless passage of caravans along this latter route; they were provided with military escort as a protection against the nomadic tribes wandering on the Steppes.[34]

It is easy to ascertain what the Arabs bought in Khazaria and Bulgar. Mukaddasî baldly enumerates all the merchandise which came from Bulgar by Khwarizm: sable, miniver, ermine, marten, fox, beaver, the many-coloured hare, goatskin, wax, arrows, birch-bark, caps, fish-glue, fish-teeth, castor, ambre, granular leather, honey, hazelnuts, hawks (falcons?), swords, armour, maple, Slavic slaves, sheep, goats, pigs and cattle. Several of these items were produced by the Volga-Bulgars themselves. This was certainly true of birch-bark, caps, maple, nuts, sheep, etc., goatskin and fish-glue, and probably of wax and honey. On the other hand, the other items which were not produced locally, were more important. They were principally of three types: furs, slaves and weapons. According to several authorities, including Ibn Rustah and Ibn Hawkal, the Rus in Khazaria and Bulgar supplied the first two of these articles. Ibn Fadlân who personally met merchants of the Rus on the Volga in 922, describes how, on arrival in a market town, they used to invoke the assistance of their God: "I have brought with me so-and-so many sableskins and so-and-so many bondwomen. Give me a buyer, rich in dinars and dirhems." His comment that the Russians carried Frankish swords should not pass unnoticed.[35]

The principal exports from the Rus to the Mohammedan countries were obviously slaves and furs. As we have already seen, these had been imported into the Caliphate by way of the Frankish empire.

The evidence about the Frankish transit trade is, however, commonest and most important in the early Carolingian period. The Arab influence on the

Frankish coinage made itself felt particularly strongly around the middle of the eighth century. The most reliable evidence of the transport of slaves across the Frankish empire is from the years before 850; after 900 no export of slaves to the Caliphate is spoken of, other than of eunuchs. These were luxury slaves from which Frankish merchants, as we are told, certainly made great fortunes, but they obviously could not have had the same importance in world trade as the virile slaves and bondwomen.

The situation concerning the sources for the direct Nordic-Arab trade is entirely different. Not until after 800 can the connexions along the eastern route be traced in literary and archæological sources but they appear with increasing frequency as the century progresses.

In the tenth century the Arab geographer Ibn Hawkal compares the importance of the two routes in the fur- and slave-trades. He says that the beaverhides which were brought to Spain from the rivers of Slavia were only a very small proportion of the total quantity produced. The majority of beaver-hides, – almost all, – came direct from the territory of the Rus, from Yâjûj and Mâjûj, and were sold from there to Bulgar, Khwarizm and Khazaria. Ibn Hawkal further states that the Slavic slaves which were taken via Spain were usually eunuchs, while those taken by the eastern route were not so; the majority of Slavic and Khazar slaves came by way of Khwarizm.[36]

The sources make it clear, therefore, that in due time the Frankish transit trade between the fur- and slave-producing regions in northern and eastern Europe was outflanked by a direct Nordic-Arab trade along easterly routes.

As lords of the great Svitjod, the Norsemen controlled a region with a very great productive potential. It produced slaves and furs in greater quantities than any other European country. Slaves provided labour force; furs were the only raw materials of clothing which the Mohammedan world could not itself produce in any appreciable measure. These two commodities were imported in mass into the Caliphate. In addition the Norsemen controlled the best routes to the Orient, to the economic and cultural centre of the age; and the Norsemen were the nearest European neighbours to the country from which sprang the source of oriental silver.

It is fairly clear that under these circumstances the stream of silver was bound to spread all over eastern and northern Europe. It was a stream of no small dimensions. Ibn Rustah and Gardîzî state that the Norsemen refused to accept payment for their goods in anything but silver coins. Ibn Fadlân gives us another description of the situation: when a Rus merchant had made a profit of 10,000 dirhems, he usually gave his wife a necklace and there were many Rus ladies who owned several. The numismatic material bears out the truth of this and other information in Arab literature. The discoveries of Cufic coins show that the stream of silver had already penetrated into eastern Europe in 825 and that not long afterwards, certainly before the middle of the ninth century, it was pouring into the northern countries. An examination of the composition of the coin hoards establishes beyond doubt that silver was entering eastern Europe across the Caspian Sea and by the caravan route across Khwarizm as early as the beginning of the ninth century. The point which is of greatest interest to us is that the coin hoards from northern and eastern Europe reveal the intensity of the flow of silver. Their geographic distribution extends from Norway and northern Sweden in the north as far as Silesia and the Ukraine in the south, from Schleswig-Holstein and Mecklenburg in the west to the Urals in the east. The hoards of Arab coins here can be counted in hundreds; they often contain very large numbers of coins. There are reports of treasure troves as rich as Aladdin's cave. The largest find known with certainty is imposing enough: it consisted of more than 11,000 dirhems, in addition to an indeterminate number of fragments, and weighed more than 65 lbs. Hoards containing many hundreds or a few thousands of dirhems are common.[37]

The great reorientation of international trade meant that the North became its centre. It is significant that Ibn Khurdâdbih mentions the Rus of the North along with the Radanite Jews as the leading carriers of international trade; after the description we quoted earlier of the journeys of the Jews on and around the Mediterranean, he continues: "the Rus come from the most distant parts of the Slav lands, cross the Roman Sea to Constantinople where they sell their wares, furs of beaver and black fox as well as swords. Or, they sail up the Don (?), the river of the Slavs, and make for the capital of the Khazars. There they embark in boats and cross the Jurjân Sea to various points on its coastline. Sometimes they carry their merchandise on camels from Jurjân to Baghdad where Slavic eunuchs act as interpreters for them."[38]

The politico-commercial position in which the Norsemen found themselves is without parallel in their history. Conditions at this time were the direct opposite of normal conditions at all other times. At other times the Baltic region has always imported precious metals from the west and exported to the west the lion's share of their own produce. But during the age of oriental silver its most important products went east and the flow of silver came from the east.

It now remains to investigate the nature of the trade connexions between northern and western Europe during this period.

The archæological evidence from Sweden shows that several commodities such as swords, glass and ceramics were imported from the Frankish empire. Discoveries in eastern Europe show that Frankish swords even went so far. The references in Arab literature to Rus exports of swords to Byzantium and of Arab imports of swords from Bulgar should establish beyond doubt that the Norsemen in eastern Europe carried on not only an important trade in slaves and furs but also a transit trade in Frankish swords.[39]

It is more difficult to discover what the Norsemen gave the west in exchange. Probably it was still furs, but hardly on the same scale as in early Carolingian times. The main question now becomes whether the flow of silver from the east stopped at the western boundaries of northern and central Europe or whether it crossed these boundaries, with the result that silver became part of the exports from the North to western Europe.

It was remarked earlier that, in consequence of the currency principles which prevailed, the coin hoards found in western countries cannot reflect the importation of foreign coins, no matter how large, to any appreciable extent. The same holds good. The western European hoards from the time after about 850 to the beginning of the tenth century are not particularly plentiful but there are undoubtedly some which include dirhems which have come by way of the northern countries. There are not many of these coins, but certainly many times more than the number of western deniers in the abundant treasures from the same period found in the North.[40]

It is not to be expected that evidence could be found in literary sources either for or against the existence of a heavy drain of dirhems into western Europe across its eastern border. It would indeed be remarkable if documentary evidence relevant to this investigation could be found. Nevertheless, this is the case: towards the end of the reign of Otto I, a Jew from Spain was staying at Mainz and he was shown some dirhems which he recognized. They were exactly of the type and from exactly the same period as those which are the most common in Scandinavian coin hoards. There can be no doubt that they came to Mainz by way of eastern Europe, perhaps also via the North.[41]

A final answer to the question whether the flow of silver from northern and central Europe went further west can only be found from a thorough comparison of the eastern and the western European coin hoards. Such an examination shows the following. Throughout the ninth century the composition of the eastern and northern treasures was the same at all points of time. It can be seen in the discoveries from this century that coins which were predominant in the earlier treasures have completely disappeared in the later. This position changed in the course of the tenth century and two essentially different types of hoard are found, one in the North, the other in eastern Europe. Northern treasures are now characterized by the dominance of older coins, – a Nordic hoard, for instance, from the 950's consists mostly of dirhems from the first two decades of the tenth century. But the hoards from the same time in eastern Europe contain considerably fewer coins from earlier times but many from the decades immediately preceding the year, when the latest coins in the hoards were minted. Shortly after the middle of the tenth century, a further differentiation took place within the eastern European region. The treasures found in Volga-Bulgaria with the last coins from the period after 970 are still consisting to a large extent of dirhems from the most recent decades. The treasures in the eastern Slav territory now take on a different structure: the dirhems from the period immediately preceding the minting year of the last coin are here no longer the commonest; coins of the 950's and 960's predominate. As the hoards from northern Europe still are dominated by coins from the beginning of the century, we thus have from this time onwards three types of treasures: the northern type, characterized by the predominance of dirhems from the beginning of the 900's, the eastern Slav type in which the dirhems are mostly from the middle of the century, and the Volga-Bulgarian type characterized by the predominance of dirhems from the decades immediately preceding the minting year of the last coin of the collection.

It is not difficult to explain the differentiation between the east Slav and the Volga-Bulgarian treasures. It occurred just at the time when, according to the evidence from Northern coin hoards, the import into the North of dirhems from eastern Slav territory ceased.[42] Formerly, the coins had passed beyond the latter territory further towards the north-west and, as long as this was the case, the number of older coins in eastern Slavia declined in relation to the coins newly arrived from the east, from Volga-Bulgaria. After the export of coins from eastern Slavia to the North had come to an end, the older coins, the dirhems of the 950's and 960's, remained in East Slavia; the movement of dirhems from Volga-Bulgaria largely brought with it newly minted dirhems but also, – although to a steadily decreasing extent, – older dirhems from the middle of the tenth century, but this flow was neither strong enough nor of sufficiently long duration to counterbalance the excess of the older coins. In that way there arose about that time an important difference between the East Slavic and the Volga-Bulgarian treasures.

It now also becomes easy to find an explanation for the difference between the treasures of eastern and northern Europe which arose in the first part of the tenth century. As long as the dirhems were exported from eastern Europe to the North, the older coins became increasingly rare in the former territory compared with the new dirhems arriving from the east. On the other hand, from the beginning of the tenth century, the coins were not re-exported from the North and so the old coins accumulated there. The flow of coins from the East continued to bring dirhems to the North, mostly including recent coins, but with older coins as well. The flow was not strong enough nor lasting enough, however, to deprive the coins minted at the beginning of the century of their preponderance among the coins in the treasures. On the basis of material which is certainly imperfect, and assuming undiminished imports from the east and the complete cessation of exports from the north, it can be calculated that the dirhems from the first two decades of the tenth century should account for 86 per cent of the coins in the treasures of the 930's and 56 per cent of those of the 960's. In the extensive discoveries of coins in Gotland it is found that in fact the proportions were 84 per cent during the 930's and 54 per cent towards the 960's.[43]

It would, therefore, seem that the continued recurrence in the hoards of the older coins, taken in conjunction with the appearance of other coins, is a phenomenon of very great significance; the territories where the older coins accumulated, – the North up to the 970's and East Slavia thereafter, – formed the territorial limits to the flow of oriental silver.

But why, in the ninth century, are no such differences to be found between the variously located treasures as they are in the tenth? Why, in the ninth century, is there no visible boundary line to the flow of oriental silver, marked by the accumulation of older coins? The simplest explanation must be that there was no such boundary line in the ninth century, but that the dirhems moved uninterruptedly across the whole territory of the discoveries, without running up against an impassable barrier anywhere, – not even on the western frontier. Thus the flow of silver during the ninth and early tenth centuries must have, in fact, moved into western Europe.

Of course, no decisive proof of this can be presented, but there are strong arguments that, in the period immediately after the Nordic expansion across eastern Europe, Scandinavia held in yet another respect a position in relation to western Europe which was unique in its history: precious metals were apparently flowing across its territory from the East towards the West.

Whether the North exported silver to western Europe or not, the changed relationship between these two regions in the ninth century should certainly not be regarded in isolation from the new world situation.

After 830 and particularly after 850, western Europe became less influential in the North: the missions were withdrawn, the flow of coins from the west ended, the Frankish kings ceased to intervene in Danish domestic struggles. All this was natural if we remember how greatly conditions were changed by the growth of the direct Nordic-Arab trade in comparison with the situation at the time when slaves and furs from the Baltic region were transported to the Caliphate by way of the Frankish empire.

But, in reverse, Nordic incursions to the west became much more common and much more vigorous. At the same time as the Saracens were masters of the Mediterranean after the 830's, the Nordic Viking expeditions developed into great waves of conquest, reaching a climax after 850. The great Viking fleets captured London and beleaguered Paris. Kings and emperors made considerable cessions of territory to the Vikings and paid them tribute. The Norsemen founded kingdoms and principalities in Germany, France, England, Scotland and Ireland. They peopled large regions in those parts and colonized the expanses of Iceland and, later, Greenland.

Enterprises on such a scale have set out from the North at no other time before or since. To this period in the history of the North, there is neither economic nor political parallel. And these two aspects cannot be isolated. The two are closely inter-connected: the Vikings who terrorized the Western world came from a country where oriental silver was common.

This then is the background of the Viking expeditions to the west which culminated in large-scale enterprises and conquests. The background is not at all that of an impoverished northern land extended to bursting point by over-population, but rather of the region further east which, according to the legend, had been conquered by Ruric and his men. The conquistadors of the North exploited the Slavic population tyrannously and ruthlessly and conducted a large trade with the principal centres of civilization in the commodities they thus acquired. The Nordic vessels brought up towards the Baltic and the North by the rivers of eastern Europe from Khazar and Bulgar precious metal from as far away as the most important silver producing regions of Central Asia. They formed, – if this article may be concluded with yet another comparison between Viking times and the next great period of great discoveries, increased silver supply and expanding trade, – a miniature of the treasure fleets of the Spaniards bringing silver from the New World in the sixteenth and seventeenth centuries.

Notes

This study is based upon, and in part reproduces unchanged, the manuscript of a lecture which I delivered when I took up a chair of history at Lund University in February, 1939. I expanded the manuscript by adding some discussion of sources and a few foot notes and published it in Swedish in the '*Scandia. Tidskrift för historisk forskning*' 1939. It was, of course, by no means my intention to put forward a scientifically documented presentation of my views, but only to give a summary of certain parts of two books, that had been, provisionally but with full documentation, completed in 1935–38. For their final presentation several complementary investigations in continental museums and libraries were necessary. The Second World War and my post-war duties made it impossible for me to continue the work and bring it to a conclusion. Now I have again taken up the subject and I hope before long to begin publishing the results at greater length. But as this will presumably take a considerable time I have thought it opportune to give an account of some of my results in the Scandinavian Economic History Review.

Editor's note. At a meeting of Scandinavian historians in Gothenburg in 1951, Professor Bolin read a paper on the nature and origin of the feudal currency system, *Denarius tributarius* and *denarius aratralis*. A summary of this paper, has been published (see footnote 4 below) and is now being translated. It will be published in this journal in the near future.

1 On the above, see principally A. Dopsch: Wirtschaftliche und soziale Grundlagen der europäischen Kulturentwicklung aus der Zeit von Caesar bis auf Karl den Grossen 1–2, 1920–23, Die Wirtschaftsentwicklung der Karolingerzeit 1–2, 1912–13, Naturalwirtschaft und Geld-wirtschaft in der Weltgeschichte, 1930; H. Pirenne: Mahomet et Charlemagne, Revue belge de philologie et d'histoire 1, 1922, Un contraste économique: Mérovingiens et Carolingiens, Revue belge de philologie et d'histoire 2, 1923, Le commerce du papyrus dans la Gaule mérovingienne, Comptes rendus des séances de l'Académie des inscriptions et belles-lettres 1928, Histoire de l'Europe des invasions au XVI:e siècle, 1936, Economic and social history of medieval Europe, 1936, Mahomet et Charlemagne, 1937. Cf. E. Patzelt: Die fränkische Kultur und der Islam, Veröffentlichungen des Seminars

für Wirschafts- und Kulturgeschichte an der Universität Wien, 4, 1932. A detailed bibliography is given by A. Riising: The fate of Henri Pirenne's theses on the consequences of the Islamic expansion, Classica et Mediaevalia 13, 1952.

2 Discoveries of Cufic coins in western Europe are listed or referred to in A. Markov: Topografiia kladovvostochnykh monet, 1910; P. C. J. A. Boeles: Les trouvailles de monnaies carolingiennes dans les Pays-Bas, 1915; Bulletin des Musées royaux des arts décoratifs et industriels à Bruxelles 10, 1911; A. E. Cahn: Versteigerungs-Katalog no. 49, Sammlung eines rheinischen Gelehrten, 1922; C. M. Fraehn: Erklärung der im J. 1830 bei Steckborn im Thurgau ausgegrabenen Münzen, Bülletin scientifique, publié par l'académie impériale des sciences de Saint-Petersbourg 2, 1837; F. Jecklin: Der langobardisch-karolingische Münzfund bei Ilanz, Mitteilungen der bayerischen numismatischen Gesellschaft 25, 1906–07; H. Christmas: Discovery of Anglo-Saxon coins at White Horse, near Croydon, Numismatic Chronicle N. S. 2, 1862; J. Kenyon: Discovery of ancient coins and other treasure near Preston, Numismatic Chronicle 3, 1840; E. Hawkins: An account of coins and treasure found in Cuerdale, Numismatic Chronicle 5, 1842; W. S. W. Vaux: An account of a find of coins in the parish of Goldborough, Numismatic Chronicle N. S. 1, 1861; A. Smith: On Anglo-Saxon coins found in Ireland, Numismatic Chronicle N. S. 3, 1863; J. Evans: A new Saxon mint, Weardbyrig, Numismatic Chronicle 3 S. 13, 1893; S. Grieg: Vikingatidens skattefund, Universitetets old-saksamlings skrifter, 2, 1929.

3 Regarding coins and coinhoards of the Merovingian and Carolingian periods see particularly A. Luschin von Ebengreuth: Der Denar der Lex Salica, Sitzungsberichte der philosophisch-historischen Klasse der Kaiserlichen Akademie der Wissenschaften, 163, 1909; M. Prou: Les monnaies mérovingiennes, Catalogue des monnaies françaises de la Bibliothèque Nationale, 1892; M. Prou: Les monnaies carolingiennes, Catalogue des monnaies françaises de la Bibliothèque Nationale, 1896; E. Gariel: Les monnaies royales de France sous la race carolingienne, 1885. Cf. F. Vercautern: L'interprétation économique d'une trouvaille de monnaies carolingiennes faite près d'Amiens, Revue belge de philologie et d'histoire 13, 1934.

4 No exhaustive study exists on the nature and origin of the feudal currency system. I have published a short summary concerning this subject (S. Bolin: Skattpenning och plogpenning. Nordiska historikermötet i Göteborg 1951, Berättelse utg. av mötets arbetsutskott 1952). On the feudal currency system see A. Soetbeer: Beiträge zur Geschichte des Geld- und Münzwesens in Deutschland, Forschungen zur deutschen Geschichte 1, 2, 4, 6, 1862–66; K. T. Eheberg: Ueber das ältere deutsche Münzwesen und die Hausgenossenschaften, Staats-und socialwissenschaftliche Forschungen 2: 5, 1879; É. Bridrey: La théorie de la monnaie au XIV:e siècle, Nicole Oresme, 1906; E. Babelon: La théorie féodale de la monnaie, Mémoires de l'institut national de France 38: 1, 1909; A. Dieudonné: La théorie de la monnaie à l'époque féodale et royale d'après deux livres noveaux, Revue numismatique 1909; E. Born: Das Zeitalter des Denars, Wirtschafts- und Verwaltungsstudien mit besonderer Berücksichtigung Bayerns 63, 1924; W. Taeuber: Geld und Kredit im Mittelalter, 1933.

5 Concerning the part played by silver in the currency history of the Frankish kingdom see, in addition to the works enumerated in footnote 3 above, a number of studies by B. Hilliger in Historische Vierteljahrschrift from 1903 onwards.

6 There is no full account of the history of the Arab currency system or of Arab numismatics. The Arab coinage of Spain has been treated by G. C. Miles: The coinage of the Umaayyads of Spain, Hispanic Numismatic Series 1: 1–2, 1950. Most of the facts in the present article on Arab coins, types of coins, metals used

for coins, mints, and weights of coins are derived from a study of the material and the notes contained in printed catalogues of the great European collections of Muhammedan coins and in description of discoveries. The most important catalogues are H. Lavoix: Catalogue des monnaies musulmanes de la Bibliothèque Nationale 1–3, 1887–96; H. Nützel: Königliche Museen zu Berlin, Katalog der orientalischen Münzen 1–2, 1898–1902; R. S. Poole: Catalogue of Oriental coins in the British Museum 1–10, 1875–90; C. J. Tornberg: Numi cufici regii numophylacii Holmiensis, 1848.

7 See especially the reproduction in Gariel, *op. cit.*, pl. III, Nos. 49, 51–54, 65, 66.
8 Little attention has been paid by numismatic research to these coins, and their importance and the meaning of their propaganda have been overlooked. Isolated observations have been made by J. v. Karabacek: Zur orientalischen Altertumskunde 2, Sitzungsberichte der philosophisch-historischen Klasse der kaiserlichen Akademie der Wissenschaften, 161, 1909, p. 33 f.; Lavoix, *op. cit.* p. XXX; A. Suhle: Christiana religio, Wörterbuch der Münzkunde, edited by F. v. Schrötter, 1930. – Regarding Byzantine coins, on which no comprehensive study is available, see W. Wroth: Catalogue of the imperial Byzantine coins in the British Museum 1–2, 1908.
9 Sassanid coins are dealt with in F. Paruck, Sāsānian coins, 1924.
10 On the Arab coins referred to see the literature given in footnote 6 above; the Frankish coins and their dating are treated in Soetbeer, *op.cit.*, p. 346 ff., who alone interprets the inscriptions in a natural and satisfactory way. Cf. A. Richard: Observations sur les mines d'argent et l'atelier monétaire de Melle sous les Carolingiens, Revue numismatique 1893; A. Engel-R. Serrure: Traité de numismatique du moyen âge 1, 1891 p. 220; Prou *op. cit.* p. LXXVIII *et passim;* Gariel, *op. cit.* p. 124 f.
11 The data on weights have been taken from, or calculated on the basis of, information contained in the works listed in footnote 6 above.
12 These average weights are calculated on the basis of weight data given in the catalogues by Lane-Poole, Nützel and Lavoix of coins in the British Museum, the Kaiser Friedrich Museum, Berlin, and the Bibliothèque Nationale (cited in footnote 6 above).
13 The relative value of the dinar and the dirhem and to some extent that of gold and silver are discussed by E. von Bergmann: Die Nominale der Münzreform des Chalifen Abdulmelik, Sitzungsberichte der philosophisch-historischen Classe der kaiserlichen Akademie der Wissenschaften 65, 1870; A. von Kremer: Ueber das Einnahmebudget des Abbasiden-Reiches vom Jahre 306 H (918–919), Denkschriften der kaiserlichen Akademie der Wissenschaften, Philosophisch-historische Classe, 36, 1888; A. von Kremer: Culturgeschichte des Orients 1, 1875; A. von Kremer: Ueber das Budget der Einnahmen unter der Regierung des Hârûn alras'îd, Verhandlungen des VII. internationalen Orientalisten-Congresses 1888, Sem. Sect. The information contained in the text will be found in these works and in: Jacut: Geographisches Wörterbuch, ed. F. Wåstenfeld, 2, 1867 p. 86; Kodâma ibn Dja'far: Kitâb al-Kharâdj, Bibliotheca geographorum arabicorum 6, edited and translated by M. J. de Goeje, 1889, p. 180, 190; H. Sauvaire: Matériaux pour servir à l'histoire de la numismatique et de la métrologie musulmanes, Journal asiatique 7 sér. 14, 1879, 19, 1882; C. Defrémery: Mémoire sur les émirs al-Oméra, Mémoires présentés par divers savants à l'académie des inscriptions et belles-lettres 2, 1852.
14 During the period after the middle of the ninth century when the value of silver rose in relation to that of gold, the dirhem became not lighter but heavier, but gold coins became steadily lighter. At this time, therefore, it was exclusively through

changes in the dinar-dirhem relation that adjustment to the altered price-relationship of the precious metals took place.

15 Mohammed Nerchakhy: Description topographique et historique de Boukhara, Publications de l'école des langues orientales vivantes, edited by C. Schefer, 1892 p. 34 ff. Cf. V. Veselovskii in Zhurnal ministerstva narodnago prosveschcheniie, Dec. 1897.
16 On the monetary system at this period see the works cited in footnote 4 above.
17 See on these capitularia Soetbeer, *op.cit.*, 6 p. 73 ff.; K. T. von Inama-Sternegg: Deutsche Wirtschaftsgeschichte bis zum Schluss der Karolingerperiode 1, 1909 p. 660 ff.; Th. Sommerlad: Die wirtschaftliche Tätigkeit der Kirche in Deutschland 2, 1905 p. 116 ff.; A. Dopsch: Wirtschaftsentwicklung der Karolingerzeit 2 p. 264 ff.
18 The principal source for the silver mine at Banjahîr is Yâkût, *op. cit.*, p. 743 (cf. N. Tiesenhausen: Uber drei in Russland gemachte kufische Münzfunde, Numismatische Zeitschrift 3, 1871). This mine, like other mines in the eastern provinces of the Caliphate, is mentioned in various places by the geographers Ibn Hawkal, Istakhrî, Mukaddasî, Ibn Fakîh, Ibn Rustah, Ibn Khurdâdbih etc. The main sources regarding the extraction of gold in Nubia are al-Jakûbî: Kitâb al-Boldân, Bibliotheca geographorum arabicorum 7, 1892, edited by M. J. de Goeje p. 334 f.; al-Maqrizi: Description topographique et historique de l'Égypte, translated by U. Bouriant 1, 1895 p. 561 ff., Mémoires publiés par les membres de la mission archéologique française du Caire, 17. Cf. E. Quatremère: Mémoires géographiques et historiques sur l'Égypte 2, 1811, p. 2 ff. 81 ff. The best treatment of Arab gold and silver production is to be found in A. Mez: Die Renaissance des Islams, 1922. Notes on mining, without any important comments, are contained in G. Le Strange: The lands of the eastern Çaliphate, 1930; P. Schwarz: Iran im Mittelalter nach den arabischen Geographen 2–7, Quellen und Forschungen zur Erd- und Kulturkunde 3, 6, 9, 1910–21, Quellen und Forschungen zur Kultur- und Religionsgeschichte 1–3, 1924–29. On the resources of silver in the Caliphate see the works by von Kremer cited above in footnote 13, and on the production of precious metals *circa* 1500 A Soetbeer: Edelmetall-Produktion und Wertverhältniss zwischen Gold und Silber seit der Entdeckung Amerika's bis zur Gegenwart, Dr. A. Petermanns Mitteilungen zur Justus Perthes' geographischer Anstalt, Ergänzungsband 13: 57, 1879.
19 E. Sabbe: L'importation des tissus orientaux en Europe occidentale au Haut Moyen Age (IXe et Xe siècles), Revue belge de philologie et d'histoire 14, 1935.
20 Ibn Khordâdbeh: Kitâb al-masâlik wa'l-mamâlik, Bibliotheca geographorum arabicorum 6, 1889, edited and translated by M. J. de Goeje p. 114 ff.
21 Maçoudi: Les prairies d'or, edited and translated by C. Barbier de Meynard-P. de Corteille, 1, 1861, p. 367. Cf. Born *op. cit.* p. 40 ff.
22 On this see *i. a.* W. Heyd: Geschichte des Levantehandels im Mittelalter 1, 1879 p. 104 ff.; A. Schaube: Handelsgeschichte der romanischen Völker des Mittelmeergebiets bis zum Ende der Kreuzzüge 1, 1906 p. 3 ff.; A. Schulte: Geschichte des mittelalterlichen Handels und Verkehrs zwischen Westdeutschland und Italien mit Ausschluss von Venedig 1, 1900, p. 71 ff.; J. W. Thompson: The commerce of France in the ninth century, Journal of political economy 23, 1915; H. Pirenne: Mahomet et Charlemagne p. 62 ff.
23 See the works mentioned in footnote 22.
24 These sources, together with others, are given in translated extracts in G. Jacob: Welche Handelsartikel bezogen die Araber des Mittelalters aus den nordisch-baltischen Ländern?, 2. Aufl., 1891.

25 On the above cf. G. Caro: Sozial- und Wirtschaftsgeschichte der Juden im Mittelalter und der Neuzeit, 1908, p. 137 ff.; B. Hahn: Die wirtschaftliche Tätigkeit der Juden im fränkischen und deutschen Reich bis zum 2. Kreuzzug, 1911 p. 28 ff.
26 Cf. on the above E. Nöbbe: Der karolingische Münzschatz vom Krinkberg, Festschrift zur Hundertjahrfeier des Museums vorgeschichtlicher Altertümer in Kiel 1936; O. Rydbeck: Ett silverfynd från vikingatiden, Fornvännen 1906; N. L. Rasmusson: Nordens tidigaste import av engelska mynt, Fornvännen 1934; N. L. Rasmusson: Kring de västerländska mynten i Birka, Från stenålder till rokoko, Studier tillägnade Otto Rydbeck 1937; E. Wadstein: Norden och Västeuropa i gammal tid, 1925; H. Arbman: Schweden und das karolingische Reich, 1937.
27 The problem of the Nestor chronicle and the date 862 are dealt with in A. A. Shakhmatov: Khronologiia drevneishikh russkikh letopisnykh svodov, Zhurnal ministerstva narodnago prosveshcheniia 1897; A. A. Shakhmatov: Razyskaniia o drevneishikh russkikh letopisnykh svodakh, 1908; V. M. Istrin: Zamechaniia o nachale russkago letopisaniia, Izvestiia otdeleniia russkago iazyka i slovesnosti rossiiskoi akademii nauk 26, 1921; W. Kliutschewskij: Geschichte Russlands 1, 1925, p. 71 ff.
28 B. Nerman: Svenskarna i ostbaltiska länder och i Ryssland, Nordisk kultur 1, 1937; T. J. Arne: La Suède et l'Orient, 1914; V. Thomsen: Ryska rikets grundläggning, 1882; N. Brian-Chaninov: Les origines de la Russie historique, Revue des questions historiques 102, 1925; G. Laehr: Die Anfänge des Russischen Reichs, Historische Studien 189, 1930; K. Stählin: Geschichte Russlands von den Anfängen bis zur Gegenwart 1, 1923, p. 32 ff. On the time of Ibn Khurdâdbih's work see M. de Goeje in Ibn Khurdâdbih *op. cit.* p. XVIII ff. and J. Marquart: Osteuropäische und ostasiatische Streifzüge, 1903, p. 18 f., 390.
29 On the Viking raid on Constantinople see G. Laehr, *op. cit.*, and on the expeditions against the Caliphate see especially B. Dorn: Caspia, Mémoires de l'académie impériale des sciences de St. Pétersbourg 7. sér. 23, 1877.
30 Mas'ûdî *op. cit.* 2 p. 11 f.
31 Ibn Rostah: Kitâb al-a'lâk an-nafîsa, Bibliotheca geographorum arabicorum 7, 1892, edited by M. J. de Goeje p. 145 ff.; Constantinus Porphyrogenitus: De administrando imperii 9, edited by I. Becher p. 74 ff., Corpus scriptorum historiæ byzantinæ, 1840.
32 Ibn Rustah *op. cit.*,; Gardîzî is cited by V. Bartold: Otchet o poezdke v sredniuin Aziiu, Mémoires de l'académie impériale des sciences de St. Pétersbourg 8. sér. 1: 4, 1897, p. 124.
33 J. Kulischer: Russische Wirtschaftgeschichte 1, 1925, p. 28 ff.; Laehr *op. cit. passim;* M. Pokrowski: Geschichte Russlands, 1929, p. 21 ff.
34 Arabic sources on Khazaria and its inhabitants are assembled in B. Dorn: Beiträge zur Geschichte der kaukasischen Länder und Völker aus morgenländischen Quellen 4, Mémoires de l'académie impériale des sciences de St. Pétersbourg 6. sér. 6, 1844; C. M. Fraehn: Veteres memoriae chasarorum ex Ibn-Foszlano, Ibn-Haukale et Schems-ed dino Damasceno, Mémoires de l'académie impériale des sciences de St. Pétersbourg 8, 1822. The most important notes on the Bulgars are to be found in M. Fraehn: Die ältesten arabischen Nachrichten über die Wolga-Bulgaren aus Foszlan's Reiseberichten, Mémoires de l'académie impériale des sciences de St. Pétersbourg 6. sér. 1, 1832.
35 Most of the Arabic sources dealing with the commodities entering into the trade between Russia and Arabia have been collected and translated by G. Jacob, *op. cit.* Of the Arabic sources in which Slavs and Rus are mentioned, most are

to be found translated into Russian in A. Kharkavi: Skazaniia musulmanskikh pisatelei o slavianach i russkikh, 1870. C. M. Fraehn: Ibn-Fozlan's und anderer Araber Berichte über die Russen älterer Zeit, 1823; Bartold: *op. cit.* J. Markwart: Ein arabischer Bericht über die arktischen (uralischen) Länder aus dem 10. Jahrhundert, Ungarische Jahrbücher, 4, 1924. The best text of Ibn Fadlân's relation is to be found in A. Z. V. Togan: Ibn Falân's Reisebericht, Abhandlungen für die Kunde des Morgenlandes 24: 3, 1939.

36 Cf. P. 25–27 above. See also the works cited in footnotes 34–35 above.
37 European discoveries of Cufic coins to 1900 are listed in Markov, *op. cit.* This is of particular value as far as eastern Europe is concerned. It is supplemented by a number of excellent surveys and descriptions by R. Vasmer: Spisok monetnykh nakhodok, zaregistrovannykh sektsiei numismatiki i gliptiki akademii istorii materialnoi kultury v 1920–1925 gg., Soobshcheniia, Gossudarstvennaia akademiia istorii materialnoi kultury, 1, 1926; Spisok monetnykh nakhodok, Soobshcheniia, Gossudarstvennaia akademiia istorii materialnoi kultury, 2, 1929; Ob izdanii novoi topografii nakhodok kuficheskikh monet v vostochnoi Evrope, Izvestiia akademii nauk SSSR, 1933; Klad kuficheskikh monet, naidennyi v Novgorode v 1920 g.; Izvestiia rossiiskoi akademii istorii materialnoi kultury 4, 1925; Der kufische Münzfund von Friedrichshof in Estland, Sitzungsberichte der gelehrten estnischen Gesellschaft 1925; Ein im Dorfe Staryi Dedin in Weissrusslad gemachter Fund kufischer Münzen, Kungl. Vitterhets historie och antikvitets akademiens handlingar 40: 2, 1929; Zavalishinskii klad kuficheskikh monet VIII–IX v., Izvestiia gossudarstvennoi akademii istorii materialnoi kultury 7: 2, 1920; Dva klada kuficheskikh monet, Trudy numismaticheskoi komissii 6, 1927; Die kufischen Münzen des Fundes von Luurila, Kirchspiel Hattula, Finska fornminnesföreningens tidskrift 36, 1927. Descriptions of a number of Swedish hoards are contained in two notebooks by C. J. Tornberg preserved in Lund University Library. Notes from other countries are to be found mostly in articles in historical and numismatic journals.
38 Ibn Khurdâdbih *ed. cit.* p. 115 f.
39 On the above see especially Arbman, *op. cit.*
40 See above p. 8–12, especially the literature cited in footnote 2 and 4.
41 G. Jacob: Arabische Berichte von Gesandten an germanische Fürstenhöfe aus dem 9. und 10. Jahrhundert, Quellen zur deutschen Volkskunde 1, 1927, p. 31.
42 Also after the middle of the tenth century Arab coins were brought to Scandinavia. These late Arab coins, however, cannot have been brought there from eastern Europe, as they were minted further to the west than contemporary Arab coins found in eastern Europe.
43 In several of the works cited in footnote 37 above Vasmer has noted some of the characteristics of the material referred to here. Owing mainly to unsatisfactory statistical treatment of the material he has, however, been unable to elucidate the significance of the features in question. His attempt to interpret them must be regarded as quite unsuccessful.

35

THE COMMON FIELDS[1]

Joan Thirsk

Source: *Past and Present* 29, 1964: 3–25.

It is now nearly fifty years since H. L. Gray published his detailed study of *English Field Systems*, and nearly twenty-five years since the first appearance of *The Open Fields* by C. S. and C. S. Orwin.[2] Both books made an attempt to explain the origin of the common-field system, Gray regarding it as a ready-made scheme of cultivation imported by the Anglo-Saxons from the Continent, the Orwins considering it as a common-sense method of farming in pioneer conditions when cooperation was the best insurance against hunger and famine. Both theories still command a certain measure of support for the simple reason that no alternatives have yet been offered in their place. But in the last two decades and more, a number of studies on agrarian subjects have contained evidence that does not fit comfortably in the old framework, and a fresh appraisal of the subject is overdue. Moreover, since all countries in western Europe have the same problem to solve — they have all had experience of common-field systems existing side by side with enclosed farms — it behoves us to take account of the large amount of foreign literature that has accumulated in recent years, since it may not be irrelevant to the English situation.

But first a definition of the common-field system is necessary. It is composed of four essential elements. First, the arable and meadow is divided into strips among the cultivators, each of whom may occupy a number of strips scattered about the fields. Secondly, both arable and meadow are thrown open for common pasturing by the stock of all the commoners after harvest and in fallow seasons. In the arable fields, this means necessarily that some rules about cropping are observed so that spring and winter-sown crops may be grown in separate fields or furlongs. Thirdly, there is common pasturage and waste, where the cultivators of strips enjoy the right to graze stock and gather timber, peat, and other commodities, when available, such as stone and coal. Fourthly, the ordering of these activities is regulated by an assembly of cultivators — the manorial court, in most places in the Middle

Ages, or, when more than one manor was present in a township, a village meeting.

Since all four elements — strips, common rights over the arable and meadow, common rights over the pasture and waste, and disciplinary assemblies — are necessary to make a fully-fledged common-field system, it is unthinkingly assumed that they have always existed together. This, however, is almost certainly not the case. The oldest element in the system is in all probability the right of common grazing over pasture and waste. It is the residue of more extensive rights which were enjoyed from time immemorial, which the Anglo-Saxon and later Norman kings and manorial lords curtailed, but could not altogether deny. By the sixteenth century we are familiar with commons that were enjoyed by one township alone. But even at this date there are examples of commons which were still enjoyed by two or three townships, such as Henfield common, grazed by the commoners of Clayton-le-Moors, Altham, and Accrington, Lancashire. Earlier still we have examples of commons that were used by the townships of a whole Hundred, such as the common called Kentis Moor in Kentisbeare, which belonged to the Hundred of Hayridge, Devon, in the early fourteenth century, and the common of the Hundred of Colneis, Suffolk, so described in 1086. A century earlier than this we hear of commons which were reserved to the inhabitants of a whole county: thus, the men of Kent had common rights over Andredsweald, and the men of Devon over Dartmoor. There is some reason to think, then, that common rights over pasture and waste were ancient, were once extensive, but underwent a process of steady erosion, which even in the sixteenth century was not everywhere complete.[3]

The existence of strips in the arable fields and meadows is first attested in one of the laws of King Ine of Wessex, issued between A.D. 688 and 694. Since the interpretation of the passage is of some importance, it must be quoted in full:

> If ceorls have a common meadow or other shareland to enclose, and some have enclosed their share while others have not, and cattle eat their common crops or grass, let those to whom the gap is due go to the others who have enclosed their share and make amends to them.

The meaning of the passage is not crystal clear, and with our knowledge of later common-field systems in mind, it is, of course, tempting to assume that one such is depicted here. In fact, there is nothing in this law to prove the existence of a mature common-field system. It states explicitly that peasants could have shares in arable and meadow, bearing "common crops or grass", but it does not say that all the fields of the community were organized together for the purposes of cropping and of grazing when the land lay fallow. It is perfectly possible that one set of parceners or neighbours shared one field, while another group shared another field. Indeed, this is the meaning taken for granted by Vinogradoff, who described the law as one imposing on parceners the duty of maintaining the hedges of a meadow. If this interpretation is correct, then such arrangements as parceners may or may not have made about cultivating and grazing their land in common were likely to be their own private concern.[4]

There is nothing in Ine's law, then, to support the idea that in the late seventh century common grazing after harvest was practised in common fields or meadows on a village basis. And where no evidence exists, there is no place for assumptions. There are examples from the later Middle Ages onwards, in the fens of south Lincolnshire and in Kent, of strip fields in which there were no common rights of pasture and none were felt to be necessary. If and when cultivators grazed their arable, they tethered their beasts on their own parcels. In another county, where common rights over the arable were customary in the later Middle Ages, there are hints that they had been established only recently. It is the opinion of Dr. Cunliffe Shaw that when, in the period 1250–1320, manorial lords began to make grants of common rights over ploughland in the Royal Forest of Lancaster, such rights were an innovation. Before this, common grazing had been confined to the *Moors* — the relatively small pastures attached to every Lancashire vill. In short, there is a case for thinking that in the earliest strip fields cultivators may not have enjoyed common rights over all the arable fields of the township. If so, an essential ingredient of the mature common-field system was missing.[5]

Early evidence of communally-agreed crop rotations is also elusive. The authors of some detailed studies of medieval estates as late as the fourteenth and fifteenth centuries have confessed themselves completely unable to disentangle any system of cropping, despite the presence of fields divided into strips. In some cases, it is clear that the lands of the demesne were subject to a rotation while tenants' lands lack any signs of having been similarly organized. In other cases, even the demesne lands seem to have been cropped hazardly. Miss Levett's study of the manors of St. Albans Abbey, for example, showed that in 1332 the demesne fields were divided into three main groups (*prima, secunda, et tertia seisona*), presumably for the purpose of a three-course rotation, but there was no indication that the tenants' lands were similarly grouped. She concluded her study of all the manors of St. Albans with the judgement that the three-field system was imperfectly developed or else decaying. Professor Hilton, writing of the distribution of demesne arable on the manor of Kirby Bellars, Leicestershire, and observing the variety of crops, both spring and winter sown, which were grown in the same field, was driven to conclude that "the lord of the manor had a flexible agricultural system within the framework of the supposedly rigid three-field system." On the estates of Stoneleigh abbey at Stoneleigh, Warwickshire, he concluded that there was no regular division of the common fields into two, three, or four large fields, that widely separated furlongs were cropped together, and that tenants' holdings were unevenly distributed throughout the fields. Miss Davenport in her study of Forncett manor, Norfolk, thought that "probably Forncett was a three-course manor", but at the same time admitted that there were no clear indications of three great fields, cultivated in rotation. On the contrary, there were abundant references to fields which were numerous and small. A more recent study of the fields of Church Bickenhill, Warwickshire, has shown "not the classic arrangement of two or three large open fields; instead ... we are confronted by a bewildering complexity of many small open fields or furlongs ... there is no way of discovering whether the six or seven apparently independent open fields were separate cropping units in the fourteenth century, and if so how they were related to each other." Moreover, in all but one of the few deeds in which the holdings of tenants were specified in detail, there was no equality in the acreage which each tenant held in each field. From all these examples, then, we have to conclude that another ingredient of the common-field system — regulated crop rotations — was missing from at least some villages in the later Middle Ages.[6]

The account of Church Bickenhill carries us a stage further, however, because its authors pursue the problem beyond 1500, and demonstrate how the field pattern was later immensely simplified. A deed of 1612 and a survey of 1677 show that Church Bickenhill's ploughland then consisted of three common arable fields, whose many furlong names had been discarded. In short, a simplification of field lay-out and/or nomenclature had occurred somewhere between the fourteenth and seventeenth centuries.[7]

Our knowledge of the origins of the common-field system is woefully incomplete, but what there is does not support the view that the four elements composing the system were present in all villages from the very beginning of settlement. In many places, some of the essential elements seem still to be missing in the later Middle Ages. Yet from the sixteenth century onwards manorial documents contain more and more explicit rules and regulations about the workings of the system until in the seventeenth and eighteenth centuries they are at their most emphatic and lucid. On the eve of Parliamentary enclosure some maps of common-field villages present a more orderly pattern of strips, furlongs, and fields than anything available earlier. Here then are grounds for the hypothesis that the system evolved slowly. Common rights of pasture on the waste were ancient; arable fields seem to have been divided into strips before any village agreements were reached to regulate rotations and graze the stubble and fallow in common. The careful supervision exercised by manorial officers over all aspects of common-field farming is not everywhere apparent in early manorial documents, and in some manors not until the sixteenth century: court roll material survives from the thirteenth century onwards, and although there is much evidence of penalties imposed on those who damaged the property of others, particularly at harvest time, there are few hints of crop rotation or common pasture rights. Since this view of the common-field system as a gradual development is already the considered opinion of German scholars, has won the assent of Scandinavian and Yugoslavian colleagues, and is now being more seriously considered by the French, it is worth paying some attention to their argument and the evidence for it. While some of the steps in the argument have to rest upon the balance of probability, most lie upon a sound foundation of archaeological and documentary evidence.[8]

In Germany the first farms for which there is archaeological proof from the later Iron Age were farms in severalty. Some were isolated, some were grouped in hamlets. By the sixth century of our era German settlements were still small, consisting not of twenty or thirty households, as Meitzen once supposed, but of two or three families with perhaps twenty inhabitants all told. As population increased, new households were at first accommodated in the old settlements. It was this increase which led to the emergence of nucleated villages. Other changes accompanied the growth of population. Farms were split up to provide for children, and fields were divided again and again. Ancient field names, such as *Spalten*, meaning *slits*, point to this development, while later documents and plans amply prove it. A multitude of German examples can be cited of townships consisting at one stage of large, undivided, rectangular fields, which became subdivided into hundreds of strips in two centuries or less. There are Yugoslavian examples, authenticated by detailed maps, which show this transformation taking place in the nineteenth and twentieth centuries in an even shorter period.[9]

If it be asked why the division of holdings resulted in the creation of long strips rather than small rectangular fields, then the answer of German scholars is that the strip was a more convenient shape for cultivation by the plough. It did not, as English historians have sometimes argued, influence the lay-out of fields at the time of colonization, but it did influence the method of partitioning holdings at a later date.[10]

As farms were divided into smaller units and population rose, the production of food had to be increased. The arable land was enlarged by assarts and the fields became more numerous. The waste diminished, and the arable had to be worked more intensively. The former field-grass economy, under which land had been used alternately for arable crops and then left for years under grass, gave way gradually to a more intensive rotation of arable crops and fewer years of grass until finally a two- and later a three-course rotation, allowing only one year of fallow, was arrived at. It is unlikely, however, that in the first instance this system of cropping was communally organized. More probably it was adopted by individuals or by parceners cooperating for mutual convenience in one field.[11]

Eventually, as fields multiplied whenever new land was taken into cultivation from the waste, and as the parcels of each cultivator became more and more scattered, regulations had to be introduced to ensure that all had access to their own land and to water, and that meadows and ploughland were protected from damage by stock. The community was drawn together by sheer necessity to cooperate in the control of farming practices. All the fields were brought together into two or three large units. A regular crop rotation was agreed by all and it became possible to organize more efficiently the grazing of stubble and aftermath. Thereafter, the scattering of strips, which had at one time been a handicap, became a highly desirable arrangement, since it gave each individual a proportion of land under each crop in the rotation. Some exchanges of land took place to promote this scattering. The partition of holdings was in future contrived to preserve the same effect. And when new land was colonized in the Middle Ages by the inhabitants of old-established settlements, it was not uncommon for this too to be divided into strips. Indeed, such was the force of example that the inhabitants of some East German villages, colonized for the first time in the high Middle Ages under lordly direction, allotted their arable from the start in intermingled strips.[12]

German scholars also recognize the possibility that, when cropping regulations were introduced and peasants did not have adequate representation in all the fields, a complete re-allotment of strips may have taken place, and a new pattern of occupation introduced to replace the old. One case of re-allotment occurred in unusual circumstances in 1247 when the abbot of the monastery owning the village of Isarhofen ordered a fresh apportionment of holdings on the grounds that war and the desertion of farms had caused such confusion that no one knew the boundaries of his land. Similar re-arrangements in more peaceful circumstances may perhaps be inferred from fourteenth-century documents showing tenants' holdings that were more or less equally distributed throughout the fields.[13]

The evolution of common fields in Germany was a long-drawn-out process. Many came into existence gradually after sites, deserted in the Middle Ages, had been re-occupied. It is possible to observe the gradual parcelling of rectangular fields into strips as late as the seventeenth and even the eighteenth centuries. But for our purpose, of comparing German with English experience, it is more important to be able to date the earliest examples of a complete common-field system. Unfortunately, the German evidence is, if anything, more scanty than the English in the Middle Ages. There is enough to suggest the existence of fields, divided into strips, in the high Middle Ages. Examples of crop rotations are found on monastic demesne as early as the eighth century and may be assumed to have spread to tenants' holdings by 1300 when rising population compelled people to use their land with the utmost economy. A rotation on tenants' lands may be inferred from documents from the Wetterau *circa* 1300 showing tenants' holdings that were divided more or less equally between three fields. Finally, since the multiplication of strips seems to be associated in Germany with periods of increasing population, in the sixteenth, and again in the eighteenth and nineteenth centuries, it is argued by Dr. Annaliese Krenzlin that the first complete common-field systems probably developed in the previous period of rising population, somewhere between the tenth and thirteenth centuries. It will be noticed that, in answering this final and most important question of all, the documents fail and German scholars are driven to an assessment of probability.[14]

With the steps of this argument in mind, it is now time to review the English evidence, looking for clues to the gradual evolution of the common-field system. The task is difficult because so many of the earliest references impart only scraps of ambiguous information, and it is tempting when the presence of one element of the common-field system is proved, to take the others for granted. This temptation must be resisted.

Nucleated villages and common fields are generally believed to have been an innovation of the Anglo-Saxons, who introduced to England a system of farming with which they were already familiar in their homeland. This theory could only prevail so long as German scholars adhered to the argument, put forward in its clearest form by August Meitzen in 1895 in *Siedelung und Agrarwesen der Westgermanen und Ostgermanen, der Kelten, Römer, Finnen, und Slawen*, that the field systems portrayed in German maps of the eighteenth and nineteenth centuries, so strongly reminiscent of English common-field villages of the same period, were a more or less faithful representation of the lay-out of fields from the time of original settlement. Modern German scholars who have consulted earlier maps and plans than those available to Meitzen, however, no longer hold this view. As we have seen, they now regard the common-field system as the outcome of a long and slow process of development. In these circumstances, it is no longer possible for English scholars to argue that the Anglo-Saxons brought from Germany in the sixth century a fully-fledged common-field system.

Anglo-Saxon laws refer to parceners, to "common meadow", and "shareland", the charters to land lying "acre under acre", to land lying in "common fields", "in common land", in "two fields of shareland", to headlands and gores. The significance behind these terms and phrases is uncertain, but it is just as legitimate to interpret them as a description of lands in which parceners were associated as to conclude that a mature common-field system embracing the whole village was in existence. With even more reason, this interpretation can be put upon the chapter in the "Venedotian" lawbooks, which has frequently been used to illustrate the cooperative method of farming from which emerged the common-field system in Wales. This chapter on co-tillage (*cyfar*) describes how land, when ploughed with a team assembled by a group of cultivators, was then divided between them, one strip being allotted to the ploughman, one to the irons, one to the exterior sod ox, one to the exterior sward ox, and one to the driver. Since we are also told about "whoever shall engage in co-tillage with another", and about "tillage between two co-tillers", it is reasonable to assume that these laws refer to partnerships between a few cultivators, such as parceners, and not to a system of cultivation involving the whole township. But in any case, these Welsh regulations can no longer be safely used as evidence for tenth-century conditions, since most if not all of them are of much later date.[15]

If laws and charters fail to establish the existence of a mature common-field system, they nevertheless give ample evidence of the division of land into strips. Was this due to division of land at death, or, as Continental scholars assume, to the effects of partible inheritance? Almost nothing is known from any period as yet about the customs of the English peasantry when devising land by will. But there were few manors in the Middle Ages, whatever the official manorial custom of inheritance, which did not allow customary tenants to create trusts on their death beds and so dispose of their land in any way they pleased, and at all times freeholders were entitled to dispose of their land freely. Primogeniture was never popular with the peasantry: it was the subject of adverse comment by pamphleteers during the Interregnum, when it was called "the most unreasonable descent." Even in the nineteenth century, a writer on primogeniture in England was constrained to remark that "primogeniture is not rooted in popular sentiment or in the sentiment of any large class except the landed aristocracy and those struggling to enter their ranks". We are left with a shrewd suspicion that the English peasant preferred, if he could, to provide for more than one of his children.[16]

As for the influence of partible inheritance, this is a subject almost totally neglected by English historians, who have been too readily persuaded of the supremacy of primogeniture by the lawyers and by medieval evidence from the later twelfth century onwards from a few highly manorialized and carefully administered ecclesiastical estates where partible inheritance did not find favour with the landlord. It is generally thought that partible inheritance was once the dominant custom in England. Domesday Book shows that it was still a common custom among members of the upper classes in the eleventh century. It is usual to argue that the custom began to be displaced after the Conquest when land held by knight service was made subject to the rule of primogeniture. By the end of the thirteenth century lawyers applied the rule of primogeniture to all free land unless special proof was given of a custom of partibility. Primogeniture thus became the law of England in cases of intestacy. So far the argument is unexceptionable. But it would be a mistake to pay too much attention to the lawyers' assertions concerning the subsequent supremacy of primogeniture, particularly among the peasantry. Partible inheritance was still the custom of the manor in the sixteenth century in many of the less densely-settled pastoral areas of the north — Furness, Rossendale, highland Northumberland and the West and North Yorkshire dales — as well as in parts of Kent and the East Anglian fenland. Indeed, I have argued elsewhere that it was liable to persist in all weakly-manorialized areas where the lord's authority was frail, and land was plentiful — usually only pastoral regions by the Tudor period.[17]

But even if we concede only a small place in our calculations for the effects of inheritance in partitioning land, we have to be prepared for large consequences. H. L. Gray has demonstrated its effects in a township of 205 acres in Donegal, Ireland, which was at one time divided between only two farms. In 1845, after two generations of partitioning, these two farms had dissolved into twenty-nine holdings consisting of 422 separate parcels. The plan of the township without accompanying explanation would suggest a common-field township on the way to being enclosed. In fact, it was an enclosed township on the way to becoming a common-field one. Similar effects were described by the inhabitants of the Welsh lordship of Elvell, Radnorshire, before the statute of 27 Hen. VIII put an end, in law if not in practice, to the custom of gavelkind in Wales. It was not unusual, declared the natives, for a small tenement to be divided into thirty, forty, and sometimes more parcels in three or four generations. They had seen the lordship, numbering 120 messuages, increase to 400.[18]

If the partition of inherited land could have the effect of dividing fields into a multitude of strips, what evidence is there to show that it had this effect in England? There are some illustrations to show single fields which became subdivided into strips: an example, cited by Professor Hilton, concerns Swannington, Leicestershire, where an assart, *Godebertes Ryding*, held in severalty by Roger Godeberd in the thirteenth century, was found later subdivided among several tenants and incorporated in the common fields. In this case the reason for the partition is unknown. More conclusive is the example of a number of villages in the East Riding of Yorkshire in which the creation of strips led on to the emergence of a complete common-field system. These villages lay in a district that was devastated in 1069 and lay waste for almost a century. When the land underwent reclamation in the mid-twelfth century, charters show that the tenants occupied farms in severalty. They provided for their sons by dividing their lands and, when necessary, reclaiming more. Their assarts bore the names of those who first cleared the land, and by the end of the thirteenth century they too were divided among several occupiers, all heirs of the original tenant. Indeed, the townships were full of selions and bovates. And although this is not adequate evidence by itself of a fully-fledged common-field system, it was well established by the sixteenth century. Here then is convincing proof that when farms in severalty are divided among heirs, fields of arable strips can emerge in a comparatively short time out of farms in severalty, and eventually become absorbed into a full common-field system.[19]

These examples from the East Riding carry us silently over several vital stages in the evolution of the common-field system. They explain the appearance of intermingled arable strips, but they do not tell us how and when the cultivators resolved upon rationalizing this complex arrangement by adopting a common crop rotation and agreeing to share common rights after harvest throughout the village fields. To illuminate this phase of development we have to examine evidence from other places and periods.

When once the number of tenants and the number of arable fields in a village increased substantially, the problem of ensuring access to land and water and of preventing encroachments must have become acute. Our knowledge of assarting which took place in the thirteenth century tells us much if we have imagination enough, for many assarts were divided into strips at the outset, others in the course of several generations. But we can also illustrate the problem more exactly. Professor Finberg has drawn attention to an unusual charter, probably belonging to the early eleventh century, which describes the boundaries of an estate at Hawling, Gloucestershire. It defines the area of *feld*, or pasture, in the south of the parish, and the area of woodland in the north. These boundaries exclude a piece of land in the centre occupied by the village and its arable. Thus, we are able to compare the arable land of Hawling in the early eleventh century with the lay-out of the parish some seven hundred years later, when in 1748 a new plan of the common fields of Hawling was drawn. There were then three arable fields. The original nucleus of arable was now Middle Field, the smallest of the three; the West Field was part of the former *feld*, and stretched to the parish boundary; the East Field was also an assart from the *feld* in the south-east of the parish. The arable was some five or six times its size in the eleventh century, and we may guess that the parcels or strips of individual tenants were perhaps ten or even twenty times as numerous.[20]

Ine's law hints at cooperation between parceners or neighbours who possessed strips in the same fields. And it may be that (as the later Welsh evidence suggests), such cooperation extended to choice of the crops to be grown in a particular field and assistance in cultivation. If men cooperated to this extent, did they also pasture their fields in common after harvest, and if so, how? We cannot attempt to answer these questions until we have considered whether the stubble was grazed at all. It afforded useful feed for animals but was not indispensable if pasture and waste were plentiful. The fields needed the manure to keep them in good heart and it was obviously more convenient to graze stock on the fields than to cart the manure from elsewhere. But the need for manure might not be urgent until the fields were fairly intensively cropped. Under a rotation of crops and long years of grass, men could have managed without. Thus, until population grew and land had to be used economically, we can envisage the possibility that the stubble in the arable fields was not grazed. But by the thirteenth century, certainly, and how much earlier we do not know, the value of dung was fully recognized and received due attention in Walter of Henley's treatise on husbandry.[21]

We must now consider the second question: when and how was the stubble grazed? When once parceners and neighbours cooperated in cultivating their fields, *and* also recognized the need to graze the stubble, we may assume that in some places, at least, common grazing would suggest itself naturally. It may not always have happened this way: the example of Kentish fields, in which stubble was always grazed in severalty, springs to mind. But grazing in common was obviously convenient, for it eliminated the tedious and always unsatisfactory business of hurdling strips to contain the sheep and of tethering great cattle.

We are still dependent on Ine's law (apart from the dubious later Welsh evidence) for our assumption that cultivation of the arable and the grazing of the fields in common concerned only parceners and neighbours who were sharing fields, and did not necessarily involve the whole community of tenants. This belief is strengthened by Bracton's treatise on the *Laws and Customs of England*, written in the mid-thirteenth century, which also discusses rights of common pasture on the same basis, that is, as a grant of a right from one person to another or between members of a small group who are parceners or neighbours. Indeed, his examples make it abundantly clear that the word *common* had a more restricted meaning than that which historians normally accord it.[22] Medieval charters and court rolls lend further support to this view by yielding examples of such agreements between neighbours possessing intermingled or adjoining land. The charters of Missenden Abbey, Buckinghamshire, record a grant of land in Missenden in 1161 from Turstin Mantel. With it Mantel granted rights of common over all his own land, presumably because it lay intermingled with, or adjoining, that newly granted to the abbey. In 1284 each side agreed to forgo rights over the other's arable, and the monks received permission to build a dyke and hedge to divide their land from Mantel's. In another charter from the same cartulary, dated 1170–79, Alexander de Hampden confirmed a grant to the monks of Missenden Abbey of a virgate of land in Honor, minus four acres which Alexander kept for himself. He substituted in their place four acres from his demesne elsewhere. He allowed the monks to pasture a certain number of animals on his land "in wood and field (*in bosco et plano*)", and in return Alexander received rights of common over the third field of the abbey grange, which lay next to Alexander's land, when it was not in crop. Another agreement (1240–68) recorded in the same cartulary was between Thomas Mantel and Robert Byl. Thomas held land within the bounds of Robert Byl's estate and agreed to enclose his portion with a ditch and not to claim rights of pasture beyond it. Here, then, are three agreements, each of which refer to the grant of rights of common over arable between two parties. Bearing in mind the possibility that such agreements between neighbours might continue in some places long after they had given way in others to a common-field system on a village basis, we may treat as equally relevant other examples from later periods.[23]

In the Wakefield manor court rolls of 1297 a dispute between Matthew de Bosco and Thomas de Coppeley concerning grazing rights in open time (i.e. after harvest) was settled by an agreement that in open time "they ought to intercommon". Another quarrel at Alverthorpe in the same manor in December 1307 concerning common rights in a certain *cultura* of the arable fields was set down in the court rolls not as a quarrel between the complainant, Quenylda de Alverthorpe, and the whole township but between her and four other named persons. In 1299 in the manor court of Hales, Worcestershire, Richard de Rugaker made amends to Geoffrey Osborn because he drove off Geoffrey's animals from a field which was common between themselves *and others* (not, it should be noted, between them and the whole township). Similarly, when German Philcock of Stanley, in Wakefield manor, was accused in November 1306 of making a fosse in the fields of Stanley, he said it was not to the injury of *his neighbours*, because it was always open in open time. Yet again, Prior Walter and the canons of Selborne Priory, Hampshire, granted in 1326 to Henry Wyard and his wife Alice common pasture for all their beasts except pigs and goats in the field (described in detail) belonging to the Prior, in exchange for a release from Henry and Alice of all their right in sixteen acres of land in Theddene and in the common pasture above *La Bideldone*. Finally, another citation from a later period, from the court orders of Lowick, Furness, in 1650, wherein it was laid down that Christopher Harries, Bryan Christopherson, and James Penny "shall stint their after grass when their corn is gotten equally according to their share".[24]

Alongside the early grants of common pasture rights between individuals and small groups, we must set examples of grants of wider scope, some embracing all tenants, though not, so far as our evidence extends, embracing all fields, others proving conclusively that all tenants commoned all fields. In a grant dated between 1235 and 1264 Roger de Quincy forbade his tenants in Shepshed to pasture their animals on the fields of the monks of Garendon "except in the open season when neighbours common with neighbours". This saving clause — "set in seysona quando campi aperti sunt et vicini cum vicinis communicare debent" — stresses once again the rights of neighbours to common with one another. Nevertheless, it is significant that the right of common pasture mentioned here is a grant to *all* tenants to pasture the fields of the monks. A custumal of the late thirteenth century (temp. Edward I) tells us that tenants of land in Crowmarsh, Oxfordshire, had common of pasture on the stubble of the lord's land as soon as the grain had been gathered. A custumal of Laughton, Sussex, dated 1272, declared that rights of common pasture over the demesne were the privilege of the free tenants in return for services to the lord. Finally two convincing examples of tenants' common rights over all fields. According to the customs of Stanbridge and Tilsworth, Bedfordshire, in 1240 "when a field of Tilsworth lies out of tillage and to fallow, then likewise a field of Stanbridge ought to lie out of tillage and fallow, so that they ought to common horn under horn"; the court roll of Broughton, Huntingdonshire in 1290 lists the names "of those who sowed in the fallow where the freemen and bondmen ought to have their common pasture". If we assimilate these examples into one generalization, we may say that rights of grazing over arable land were still being shared by neighbours in the twelfth century, but before the middle of the thirteenth century there were villages in which all tenants shared common rights in all fields. Further search, of course, may well produce evidence of the latter in the twelfth century. Alternatively, we may reach the same goal by approaching the problem from another direction.[25]

The grazing of all the fields of a village in common could not take place until they were all incorporated into a scheme of cropping which ensured that all the strips in one sector lay fallow at the same time, that all the strips in another were sown in autumn, or in spring, and that the fields were harvested and cleared at the same time. Thus, in places where common rights over the arable were still a matter of agreement between neighbours, we should not expect to find crop rotations organized on a village basis. We need not be surprised, then, that many villages in the Middle Ages appear to have contained numerous fields, not apparently arranged in any orderly groups, and that no distinction was preserved between furlongs and fields. In such cases, it is likely that the distinction was of no practical significance.

Not all manors, however, exhibit the same puzzling appearance of disordered cultivation even in the thirteenth century. Some early references to cropping imply that an intensive rotation of one or two crops and a fallow was observed on ecclesiastical demesne in the twelfth century. A lease of Navestock manor, Essex, in 1152, for example, mentions winter and spring corn and a season of fallow. An extent of 1265–6 shows that some lands of the monastery of St. Peter at Gloucester, situated in Littleton and Linkenholt, Hampshire, were cropped for two years out of three. In 1299 a two-course rotation, including one year of fallow, prevailed on various Worcester episcopal estates. And, indeed, since three thirteenth-century treatises of husbandry imply that a regular two or three-course rotation was an essential of good farming, we may guess that it was fairly commonplace practice among responsible farmers by that time.[26]

None of these examples, however, can be taken as proof that tenants' lands were subject to the same rotation, or, indeed, any rotation. But on Lincolnshire manors in the twelfth and thirteenth centuries we find clues to the division of all the village land into two halves for cropping purposes, and here we are on firmer ground: tenants' lands must have been drawn into the same field courses as that of their lords. Sir Frank Stenton assures us that the practice of dividing the land of the village into two halves was not unusual in Lincolnshire: it was common in every part of Lindsey, and less frequently found in Kesteven; it has not been found in Holland, but we should not expect this, for there is no evidence of a common-field system ever having developed in the fens. To illustrate this arrangement, two of Sir Frank Stenton's earliest examples must suffice. Early in Henry II's reign (between 1154 and 1170) Thorald, son of Warin, gave to the nuns of Bullington in East Barkwith "15 acres of arable land on the one side of the village and as much on the other side and half the meadow which belongs to all my land of the same village, and pasture for a hundred sheep with all things pertaining to the same land". In 1156–7 Peter Cotes granted to Catley priory 20 acres of land on one side of the village of Cotes and 20 acres on the other. The purpose of equally dividing the land between two halves of the village is made clear in at least two leases which said that the land was to be cropped in alternate years.[27]

If we now discount the possibility that these holdings had been equally divided between the two halves of the village from the time of original settlement, we have to explain how this equal division had been brought about. German scholars, as we have mentioned already, envisage the possibility that at some stage in the evolution of a common-field system a radical redistribution of land was necessary in order to facilitate the introduction of new common-field regulations on a village basis. Such a re-organization is not inconceivable in English villages; it would not have been repugnant to tenants. We are already familiar with the annual re-apportionment of meadow by lots, which was customary in many English villages. The re-allotment of arable land was a common, though not, of course, annual, practice in Northumberland — a normal common-field county — in the sixteenth century and later: in a number of villages the fields were divided into two halves and the strips re-allocated in order to give tenants land in one half or the other and reduce the distances they had to walk to their parcels. It was also customary in parts of the northern counties, possessing an infertile soil, to change the arable fields at intervals by putting the old ploughland back to common pasture and taking in a new field from the common. It is clear that people did not always cling tenaciously to their own plots of land.[28]

Clues to the re-allotment of land in the Middle Ages are not explicit, but indirect. They are of two kinds. Some documents show holdings comprising strips that lay in a regular order between the strips of other tenants. Professor Homans has cited several examples from the thirteenth and fourteenth centuries. Seebohm drew attention to an outstanding example from Winslow, Buckinghamshire, where in 1361 John Moldeson held seventy-two half-acre strips, of which sixty-six had on one side the strips of John Watekyns, while on the other side forty-three lay next to the strips of Henry Warde and twenty-three next to those of John Mayn. However, knowing as we do from the experience of German, Welsh, and Irish villages that, in a matter of two generations, a pattern of land occupation could be changed out of recognition through conveyances of pieces and the division of fields among parceners, we cannot believe that this orderliness dates from the time of original settlement. Indeed, we could say with some confidence that the allotment of land, depicted in a document in 1361, had taken place not more than one hundred years before. Do these examples, then, denote deliberate re-allotments of village land in the not very distant past for the sake of facilitating common-field regulations? It is possible. But there are equally plausible, alternative explanations. They may be the result of a redistribution of land following the Black Death, for many new tenancies had to be created after this calamity. Alternatively they may represent isolated examples in their villages of the partition among heirs of one holding comprising scattered fields. Such an effect can be demonstrated from English documents occasionally, from German records frequently. In short, none of these cases is any use for clinching an argument.[29]

Other clues to the re-distribution of village land lie in the evidence of holdings that were equally divided between two or more sectors of the village lands. But when we look for such examples, they turn out to be far from numerous. The vast majority of tenants' holdings did not consist of strips evenly divided between two or more cropping units. The distribution was more often highly irregular, and this fact has been a constant source of bewilderment to historians. Even the examples from Lincolnshire of estates comprising equal amounts of land in two halves of the village prove to be less tidy than we imagined. Peter Cotes's grant of land in Cotes, already quoted, consisted of forty acres divided into two equal halves. But the details of the parcels composing it are as follows: $13^{1}/_{2}$ acres lay on the north side of the village upon Lechebek, 3 acres less one rood upon Northills; on the south side 9 acres lay upon Lekbek, 8 acres upon Rodewale, 3 acres next Gilbert's court, and a further selion on the other side of the trench opposite the toft. Far from indicating an orderly allocation of tenants' lands throughout the village, the composition of this estate strongly suggests a collection of pieces, deliberately selected at this date or earlier to make an estate that conformed to some prior division of all the village lands. It prompts the suggestion that the division of village fields into halves, and later into thirds or quarters was intended to facilitate cultivation and grazing, but was implemented without much regard to the distribution of individual tenants' strips. After all, it would not have been difficult, within a generation, for the individual to rectify any irksome unbalance of crops by buying, leasing, or exchanging land. Moreover, additional land was being assarted at the same time: some of it was held in severalty; some of it was assarted by cooperative effort and immediately divided into strips and added to the existing field courses. There were plenty of occasions for re-shaping a lopsided holding, even though many peasants did not apparently deem it necessary to do so. If this is a reasonable hypothesis, it removes some of the problems of explaining how field courses could be re-organized from time to time without any elaborate preliminaries or consequences. When we encounter a decision in the court roll of the manor of Crowle, Isle of Axholme, in 1381 to divide the fields into four parts in order to fallow a quarter each year, and when the villagers of Marton, north Yorkshire, in the fourteenth century appointed men "to do and ordain as best they can to cast the field into three parts so that one part every year be fallow", we do not have to look for a wholesale re-allocation of tenants' land.[30]

This survey of some of the early evidence of common-field practices does not allow us to say with any certainty when the first village took a decision to organize the cultivation *and* grazing of its arable fields on a village basis. A much more thorough examination of all the evidence will be necessary before this stage is reached. All we have been able to do so far is to recognize in documents of the twelfth and thirteenth centuries some of the steps in the development of a common-field system. The earliest case cited here of regulated cropping by the whole village is dated 1156–7. It may have involved common grazing as well, but we cannot be certain. The first unmistakable statement about commoning by a whole village dates from 1240. With some assurance, then, we can point to the twelfth and first half of the thirteenth centuries as possibly the crucial ones in the development of the first common-field systems.

To reach this stage of our argument, we have been obliged to use scraps of information from many different manors and villages, and it may not have escaped the notice of the observant reader that some of the illustrations used here are drawn from districts of England in which the final system did not usually contain two or three arable fields on the classic model, but one or many fields. Some explanation is called for. The distinction between the two- and three-field system, on the one hand, and systems with other numbers of fields on the other, is not, I submit, a fundamental one that indicates a different origin, as H. L. Gray maintained. The two systems coincide with, and arise out of, the distinction between arable and pasture farming types. The two- and three-field system characterized arable, that is mixed farming districts. Villages with more or fewer common fields were mainly pasture-farming communities. I have argued elsewhere that the principal difference between the communal farming practices of the forest and pastoral areas, on the one hand, and the arable areas on the other was that in the latter the common-field system reached a more mature stage of development. In the pastoral areas, common arable fields were not unknown, but they were small in comparison with the acreage of pastures. Grassland was the mainstay of the economy and arable crops were grown for subsistence only. Hence the arable fields did not have to be cropped with the utmost economy; their small area lessened the problems of ensuring access to all tenants' parcels; and the stubble did not have to be economically grazed owing to the abundance of other pasture. For these reasons, there was no urgent necessity to control rigorously the cultivation of the ploughland. In the pastoral villages of the Lincolnshire fenland, for example, no attempt was ever made to order the strip fields on a village basis.[31]

If pastoral areas were slow to regulate their ploughland as a village concern, we begin to understand why enclosure was for them a painless and peaceful process. For agreements between two persons or a small group to extinguish common rights over the arable were far more easily reached, as the charters of Missenden abbey readily demonstrate, than agreements between all the inhabitants of the village. Far-reaching conclusions follow from this argument if it is pursued to its logical end. The areas of England which we are accustomed to label as "early enclosed" — central Suffolk, most of Essex, Hertfordshire, parts of Shropshire, Herefordshire, Somerset, Devon, and Cornwall — were pastoral districts in the sixteenth century, and were "early enclosed" only because they had never known a fully developed common-field system.

Finally, it is necessary to revert again to the unanswered question, posed in this paper, namely the date of the earliest complete common-field system to be found in England. It is clear that the mature system was liable to come into operation at different times in different parts of the kingdom. Professor Hilton's introduction to the Stoneleigh Leger Book shows that common fields in this forest area were in process of creation in the period 1250–1350. Mr. Elliott's study of Cumberland common fields hints at an even later process of evolution, as well as supplying some excellent examples of one phase in gestation when closes were shared between several tenants. Mr. Glanville Jones has recently argued that Welsh bond hamlets with their open field share-lands are well documented in the Middle Ages and go back to the Early Iron Age; if the argument presented here is at all acceptable, then we may recognize in this case too the first signs of a field pattern that might evolve later into a common-field system. For there is no reason to regard Wales, or England, for that matter, as a special case. One point is established beyond reasonable doubt by the comparisons drawn here between English and Continental experience, namely, that in those West and East European countries in which field systems have been analysed with some care, the evolution of the common fields appears to have followed much the same course. In all cases the presence of a sufficiently large and growing population, compelled to cultivate its land more intensively, was a pre-condition of growth: this condition seems to have been first fulfilled in the twelfth and thirteenth centuries. It should also be said that there is no reason to think that the social framework in which common-field systems emerged necessarily influenced their form. They could evolve in a thoroughly authoritarian society, in which the lord allotted land to his men — there are German examples to show this occurring in a pioneering community under the close surveillance of the lord. They could just as well take shape in a society of free colonists, such as that depicted in the East Riding of Yorkshire in the twelfth and thirteenth centuries.[32]

Notes

1 For many helpful comments and criticisms I wish to thank Mr. Trevor Aston, Dr. A. R. H. Baker, Mr. T. M. Charles-Edwards, Dr. Cunliffe Shaw, Professor Rodney Hilton, Dr.W. G. Hoskins, and Professor M. M. Postan, and most of all Professor H. P. R. Finberg, who has read every one of the innumerable drafts of this paper.
2 H. L. Gray, *English Field Systems* (Cambridge, Mass., 1915); C. S. and C. S. Orwin, *The Open Fields* (Oxford, 1938).
3 L. Dudley Stamp and W. G. Hoskins, *The Common Lands of England and Wales* (London, 1963), pp. 5–13; *Trans. Devon Assoc.*, xxxii (1900), p. 546. I wish to thank Prof. H. P. R. Finberg for this reference.
4 Ine's laws, c. 42 (ed. Liebermann, i, pp. 106–9). This law is translated and discussed in F. M. Stenton, *Anglo-Saxon England*, 2nd edn. (Oxford, 1947), p. 277; P. Vinogradoff, *The Growth of the Manor* (London, 1905), p. 174. See also H. R. Loyn, *Anglo-Saxon England and the Norman Conquest* (London, 1962), pp. 156–7.
5 Joan Thirsk, *English Peasant Farming*, p. 14; A. R. H. Baker, "The Field Systems of Kent" (London Ph.D. thesis, 1963), pp. 23–6. See also A. R. H. Baker, "The Field System of an East Kent Parish (Deal)", *Archaeologia Cantiana*, lxxviii (1963), pp. 96–117; "Open Fields and Partible Inheritance on a Kent Manor", *Econ. Hist. Rev.*, 2nd ser., xvii (1964), pp. 1–23; "Field Systems in the Vale of Holmesdale", forthcoming article in the *Agric. Hist. Rev.;* Dr. Cunliffe Shaw in correspondence with the author.
6 A. E. Levett, *Studies in Manorial History* (Oxford, 1938), pp. 338–9, 184; R. H. Hilton, *The Economic Development of some Leicestershire Estates* (Oxford, 1947), p. 152; R. H. Hilton, *The Stoneleigh Leger Book* (Dugdale Soc. Publications, xxiv, 1960), p. lv; F. G. Davenport, *The Economic Development of a Norfolk Manor, 1086–1565* (Cambridge, 1906), p. 27; V. H. T. Skipp and R. P. Hastings, *Discovering Bickenhill* (Dept. of Extra-Mural Studies, Birmingham Univ., 1963), pp. 15–18.
7 Skipp and Hastings, *op. cit.*, pp. 20, 22.
8 I wish to thank Professor W. O. Ault for allowing me to see his manuscript, shortly to be published, on early village by-laws. It is mainly on his very full collection that the above remarks about court rolls are based. For Continental literature on common-field systems, see Gunner Bodvall, "Periodic Settlement, Land-Clearing, and Cultivation with Special Reference to the Boothlands of North Hälsingland", *Geografiska Annaler*, xxxix (1957), pp. 232, 235; Svetozar Ilešič, *Die Flurformen Sloweniens im Lichte der Europäishen Forschung* (Münchner Geogr. Hefte, xvi, 1959), *passim;* E. Juillard, A. Meynier and others, *Structures Agraires et Paysages Ruraux* (Annales de l'Est, Mémoire xvii, 1957), p. 54.
9 W. Abel, *Geschichte der deutschen Landwirtschaft* (Stuttgart, 1962), pp. 15–16, 27, 70–74; Annaliese Krenzlin, *Die Entstehung der Gewannflur nach Untersuchungen im nördlichen Unterfranken* (Frankfurter Geogr. Hefte, xxxv, 1961), part 1, p. 110; A. Krenzlin, "Zur Genese der Gewannflur in Deutschland", *Geogr. Annaler*, xliii (1961), pp. 193–4; S. Ilešič, "Die jüggreen Gewannfluren in Nordwestjugoslavien", *ibid.*, pp. 130–7.
10 Krenzlin, *Die Entstehung der Gewannflur*, p. 96; Abel, *op. cit.*, p. 72.
11 Krenzlin, *op. cit.*, pp. 104–7, 111–7.
12 Abel, *op. cit.*, p. 75; F. Steinbach, "Gewanndorf und Einzelhof", *Historische Aufsätze Aloys Schulte zum 70 Geburtstag gewidmet* (Duëseldorf, 1927), p. 54;

Krenzlin, *op. cit.*, p. 114; *Kolloquium über Fragen der Flurgenese am 24–6 Oktober, 1961, in Göttingen*, ed. H. Mortensen and H. Jäger (*Berichte zur deutschen Landeskunde*, xxix, 1962), p. 313. I wish to thank Dr. Karl Sinnhuber for drawing my attention to this report of the latest German conference on the origin of common fields.
13 Abel, *op. cit.*, p. 75. It has been suggested that the Swedish re-organization of strips, known as *solskifte*, was also associated with the introduction of a communal crop rotation: Staffan Helmfrid, *Östergotland "Västanstång, Geogr. Annaler*, live (1962), p. 260.
14 Abel, *op. cit.*, p. 75; Krenzlin, *op. cit.*, pp. 102–7, 111; *Kolloquium, op. cit.*, pp. 232, 246. Controversy still rages among German scholars, but the main differences of opinion concern explanations for the different shapes of common fields, a subject which is almost totally ignored by English scholars. One exception, however, is *Valley on the March* (London, 1958) by Lord Rennell of Rodd, chapter iv. See also Harald Uhlig, "Langstreifenfluren in Nordengland, Wales, und Schottland", *Tagungsbericht und Wissenschaftliche Abhandlungen, Deutscher Geographentag, Würzburg, 29 Juli bis 5 August 1957*, pp. 399–410.
15 Vinogradoff, *op. cit.*, p. 262, note 29; H. P. R. Finberg, *Gloucestershire* (London, 1955), pp. 39–40; F. Seebohm, *The English Village Community* (Cambridge, 1926 edn.), pp. 118–21; *The Welsh History Review*, 1963, "The Welsh Laws", *passim, esp.* p. 55; J. G. Edwards, "The Historical Study of the Welsh Lawbooks", *Trans. Roy. Hist. Soc.*, 5th ser., xii (1962).
16 Margaret James, *Social Problems and Policy during the Puritan Revolution, 1640–60* (London, 1930), pp. 26, 98, 310 (I wish to thank Mr. Christopher Hill for drawing my attention to these references); J. W. Probyn, ed., *Systems of Land Tenure in Various Countries* (London, 1876), p. 375.
17 Professor G. C. Homans and Dr. H. E. Hallam are honourable exceptions to this generalization at the beginning of this paragraph; T. H. Aston, "The Origins of the Manor in England", *Trans. Roy. Hist. Soc.*, 5th Ser., viii (1958), pp. 78–9; W. Holdsworth, *History of English Law*, iii (London, 1903), p. 173; Joan Thirsk, "The Farming Regions of England", in the forthcoming *Agrarian History of England and Wales*, vol. iv, *1500–1640*.
18 H. L. Gray, *op. cit.*, pp. 190–1; E. G. Jones, *Exchequer Proceedings (Equity) concerning Wales, Henry VIII-Elizabeth* (Univ. of Wales, History and Law Series, iv, 1939), p. 313; I owe this reference to the kindness of Mr. Glanville Jones. For a discussion showing that this custom of inheritance had exactly the same effect upon land in China, see Hsiao-Tung Fei, *Peasant Life in China* (London, 1943), pp. 194–5.
19 *Vict. County Hist. of Leicester*, vol. ii, p. 158; T. A. M. Bishop, "Assarting and the Growth of the Open Fields", *Econ. Hist. Rev.*, vi (1935–6), pp. 13 ff. For the effects of partible inheritance on Kentish fields, see articles by A. R. H. Baker cited in note 5.
20 H. P. R. Finberg, *The Early Charters of the West Midlands* (Leicester, 1961), pp. 188–96.
21 *Walter of Henley's Husbandry* . . . , ed. E. Lamond (London, 1890), pp. 18–23.
22 Henry de Bracton, *De Legibus et Consuetudinibus Angliae*, ed. G. C. Woodbine (New Haven, 1915–22), vol. iii, pp. 129–30, 166–70, 182, 184. The Welsh evidence seems to come from rather the same period (above, n. 15).
23 E. C. Vollans, "The Evolution of Farm Lands in the Central Chilterns in the Twelfth and Thirteenth Centuries", *Trans. Institute of British Geographers*, xxvi (1959), pp. 204–5, 208, 222, citing charters from *The Cartulary of Missenden Abbey*, part i, ed. J. G. Jenkins (Bucks. Arch. Soc., Records Branch, ii, 1938), pp. 66–8, 184–5, 128.

24 *Court Rolls of the Manor of Wakefield*, vol. ii, *1297–1309* (Yorks. Arch. Soc. Rec. Ser., xxxvi, 1906), pp. 20, 131, 58; *Court Roll of the Manor of Hales, 1270–1307*, part ii (Worcs. Hist. Soc., 1912), p. 391; *Calendar of Charters and Documents relating to the Possessions of Selborne and its Priory* (Hants. Rec. Soc., 1894), p. 41 — see also p. 38, and Hants. Rec. Soc., 1894, pp. 38–9, 49, 64; G. Youd, "The Common Fields of Lancashire", *Trans. Hist. Soc. Lancs. and Cheshire*, cxiii (1962), p. 10.

25 L. C. Lloyd and D. M. Stenton, *Sir Christopher Hatton's Book of Seals* (Northants. Rec. Soc., xv, 1950), p. 14; *Custumals of Battle Abbey in the Reign of Edward I and Edward II*, ed. S. R. Scargill-Bird (Camden Ser., N.S., xli, 1887), pp. 89, xxxv; *Custumals of the Manors of Laughton . . .*, ed. A. E. Wilson (Sussex Rec. Soc., lx, 1961), pp. 3–4; G. C. Homans, *English Villagers of the Thirteenth Century* (Cambridge, Mass., 1942), pp. 422, 57–8.

26 *The Domesday of St. Paul's . . .*, ed. W. H. Hale (Camden Ser., 1858), p. 133; *Historia et Cartularium Monasterii Sancti Petri Gloucestriae*, ed. W. H. Hart (Rolls Series, 1863–7), vol. iii, pp. 35–6, 41; *The Red Book of Worcester*, ed. Marjory Hollings (Worcs. Hist. Soc., lxxii, lxxiv, 1934), pp. 125, 126, 151; *Walter of Henley's Husbandry*, pp. 6–9, 66–7, 84–5.

27 *Transcripts of Charters relating to the Gilbertine Houses . . .*, ed. F. M. Stenton (Lincs. Rec. Soc., xviii, 1920), pp. 94, 83; *Registrum Antiquissimum . . . of Lincoln*, vol. iv, ed. C. W. Foster (Lincs. Rec. Soc., xxxii, 1937), pp. 69–70, 233. Other possible twelfth-century examples are listed in H. L. Gray, *op. cit.*, pp. 450–509, but the evidence given there is not sufficient to prove anything either way.

28 M. W. Beresford, "Lot Acres", *Econ. Hist. Rev.*, xiii (1943), pp. 74–9; Lord Ernle, *English Farming Past and Present* (London, 1961 edn.), pp. 26, 230; R. A. Butlin, "Northumberland Field Systems", *Agric. Hist. Rev.* xii (1964), pp. 99–120; H. L. Gray, *op. cit.*, pp. 208–9.

29 G. C. Homans, "Terroirs ordonnés et Champs orientés: une Hypothèse sur le Village anglais", *Annales d'histoire économique et sociale*, viii (1936), pp. 438–9; Seebohm, *op. cit.*, p. 27, P. F. Brandon, "Arable Farming in a Sussex Scarp-foot Parish during the late Middle Ages", *Sussex Arch. Coll.*, c (1962), p. 62.

30 Lincs. Archives Office, Crowle manor 1, 34; Homans, *English Villagers*, p. 56.

31 Thirsk, "The Farming Regions of England," cited in note 17. The importance of arable husbandry in forcing the growth of the common-field system is also stressed in Ilešič, *op. cit.* (cited in note 8 above), pp. 73, 75, 114.

32 Hilton, *The Stoneleigh Leger Book*, p. liv; G. Elliott, "The System of Cultivation and Evidence of Enclosure in the Cumberland Open Fields in the Sixteenth Century", *Trans. Cumb. and Westm. Antiq. and Arch. Soc.*, N.S., lix (1959), pp. 85, 87, 95, 99; Glanville Jones, "Early Territorial Organization in England and Wales", *Geogr. Annaler*, xliii (1961), pp. 175–6.

36
THE EFFICIENCY AND DISTRIBUTIONAL CONSEQUENCES OF EIGHTEENTH CENTURY ENCLOSURES*

Robert C. Allen

Source: *Economic Journal* 92, 1982: 937–53.

Between the fifteenth century and the nineteenth century the open fields of England were enclosed. Although the consequences of enclosures have been the subject of controversy since the process began, the proximate cause of enclosure has always been clear. Enclosures were invariably initiated by landowners because they expected their tenant farmers would pay higher rents after the parish was enclosed (Chambers and Mingay (1966, p. 8) and Tate (1967, p. 154)). The landowners' expectations seem generally to have been fulfilled. The great mystery is why rents rose. There are two possibilities: first, enclosed farming was more efficient than open field farming, so enclosed farms could afford to pay a higher rent. In that case the rise in rent indicates the rise in efficiency upon enclosing. Second, enclosures might have redistributed income from farmers to landowners. When land was enclosed, the existing leases were replaced by newly negotiated ones. If open field farms had been let at rents less than the value of the marginal product of land, then the rise in rents might simply indicate a redistribution of income (Yelling, 1977, pp. 209–13).

Eminent historians have championed both possibilities;[1] however, the evidence which they have brought to bear on this issue has not been sufficient to distinguish between these alternatives. In this paper the impact of enclosure will be assessed on the basis of statistical returns for 231 farms collected by Arthur Young in his tours of England in the late 1760's. The results would have surprised Young, who was an influential proponent of the view that enclosure increased efficiency, for they show that in the late eighteenth century, the enclosure of open field arable did not have that effect. Instead, enclosure caused a massive redistribution of income from farmers to landowners.

Arthur Young was secretary of the Board of Agriculture, editor of the *Annals of Agriculture*, and author of numerous books and pamphlets. He was one of the most prominent 'agricultural improvers' of the late eighteenth century. In 1768–70, early in his career, he travelled throughout England. His observations of farming practice and rural economy were embodied in nine volumes totalling 4,500 pages (Young, 1769, 1771, 1967). In these books Young presented detailed and uniform descriptions of agricultural practices in the villages he travelled through. In many cases he reported the 'particulars of representative farms'. The particulars included the actual rent the farmer was paying as well as enough information to estimate the prices or opportunity costs, and quantities of all of the inputs (including those supplied by the farmer such as farm family labour), and products of the farms. Young appears to have been careful and thoughtful in collecting his data. When judgement was required he proceeded in ways in which a modern economist would approve. For instance, wage rates frequently included payments in kind. Young valued these payments at local retail prices and added them to the money payment to obtain the wage (Young (1769), p. 320; (1771), vol. IV, pp. 311–2; and (1967), vol. 11, pp. 292, 297). Thoroughness of this sort commends the data Young collected as the basis for a serious study of enclosure.

Nonetheless the data are not without their difficulties. Some difficulties are a result of incompleteness on Young's part. He did not, unfortunately, detail the quantity of every input and output used on every farm. It was necessary to impute values of some variables (like crop yields) reported for a village to all of the farms in the village. Young failed to report the quantities of some inputs (e.g. implements) so their quantities were estimated on the basis of various farm accounts. These estimation procedures are described in the Appendix.

A second sort of difficulty is a consequence of the organisation of eighteenth century farms. The common was an important component of the land input on many farms, especially open field farms. Since commons were used jointly by several farms, it is impossible to reduce their size to an acreage that can be added to the other land of the farm. Later in the paper, indices of the characteristics of land are used to incorporate commons into a measure of the land input.

In interpreting the results, the geographical distribution of the farms must be kept clearly in mind. From one point of view, the location of the farms is desirable. There were many in East Anglia, reputedly the most efficient region. Most of the farms were situated in the Midlands or in the northern counties of Yorkshire, Durham, and Northumberland. With the exception of the latter county, this was the classic region of open field farming (Gray, 1915) and includes the districts where parliamentary enclosure was most intense. On the other hand, the variation among the farms in soil and environmental characteristics is not as great as the geographical spread might suggest. The farms were mixed farms; the sample lacks farms in permanent pasture districts.[2] Moreover, while some farms were located on heavier soils than others, none of the farms were situated on the really heavy boulder clays where the cultivation of turnips was impractical. Consequently, Young's data do not illuminate the efficiency gains (if any) of enclosure where the result was the conversion of land to permanent pasture or the installation of better drainage systems (Vancouver, 1794, 1795). What we do observe is the effect of enclosure in areas where farming remained heavily arable and where the introduction of turnips and clover into farm management was the basis of advance. Since the history of the agricultural revolution has often been told in terms of the diffusion of these crops, the results are still of considerable interest.

In assessing the results, one ought also to consider the representativeness of the data. The farms do not constitute a random sample; however, randomness is not necessary for this study since its aim is not to estimate unconditional population parameters like the average yield of wheat in England. Instead, the object of the study is to estimate parameters like farm efficiency *conditional on a farm's being open or enclosed*. Thus it is immaterial, for instance, if Young visited a disproportionate number of enclosed villages as long as he did not systematically search out enclosed villages more efficient than the average enclosed village or open field villages less efficient than average. Given Young's belief that enclosure raised efficiency, such a sampling strategy is the most likely way he might have been non-random. The results reported in this study hardly support that possibility. One remark in the preface to the *Northern Tour* does suggest that many of the farms were included because they shared one characteristic in common. Young reports that he arranged much of that tour when he met landlords at the annual horse races in York (Young, 1967, vol. 1, pp. v–vi). It is difficult to see how that selection criterion might have biased the conditional distributions studied here.

The 231 farms that comprise the data used in this study are treated as one cross section. Of the farms 159 are classed as enclosed, 27 as open, and 45 as partially open. Enclosed farms are ones in which all the arable was enclosed. Open farms are ones in which the arable was predominantly open. Farms classed as partially open contain appreciable quantities of both sorts of land. This latter class was created in recognition of the fact that by the late eighteenth century piecemeal enclosure had made appreciable inroads into the fields of many villages. The distinction between enclosed farms, on the one hand, and open or partially open farms on the other, is sharp. In contrast, the distinction between open and partially open is fuzzy. Even the most pristine open village contained some enclosed land, and many villages classed as partially open were subsequently enclosed by Parliamentary Act. In this study, a conservative course has been followed, and farms were classified as open only if they appeared quite undisturbed by piecemeal enclosures. It should be noted that the empirical results presented subsequently usually show open and partially open farms to be similar to each other and decisively different from enclosed farms.

I. The scope for redistribution

Rents rose when villages were enclosed either because the efficiency of agriculture increased and hence the value of the land rose or because open field rents were less than the value of the land and rents were raised at enclosure to eliminate the disequilibrium. The crucial first step in distinguishing between these hypotheses is to compare the rents paid with the value of the land. This comparison can be made using the data Arthur Young collected since for each farm it is possible to compute the Ricardian surplus, i.e. revenues minus the opportunity cost of all non-land inputs, and compare it to the rent actually paid. When making this comparison, it is also necessary to include tithes and rates, the principal taxes. Their burden was light and, in this study, is presumed to have fallen entirely on land. Under this assumption, the test for competitive equilibrium in the land rental market is that rents were bid up to the level such that surplus minus rent minus taxes, which I shall call farmer's surplus, equalled zero. If this condition is satisfied for both open and enclosed farms then it is likely that enclosure raised rents by raising efficiency. On the other hand, if farmer's surplus equalled zero for enclosed farms but was positive for open farms, then the rise in rents that accompanied enclosure probably indicates a redistribution of income.

Table 1 shows the frequency distribution of farmer's surplus per acre for enclosed, open, and partially open farms. The distribution for enclosed farms is centred near zero with a mean of £0.2351 per acre. In contrast, farmer's surplus is positive for almost every open or partially open farm and the means of those distributions are £1.2233 and £0.8847 per acre respectively. In all cases (even enclosed farms) the null hypothesis that the means of the populations equal zero can be rejected. However, the magnitude of the divergence from equilibrium is very small in the case of enclosed farms. Indeed, since in these calculations the farmer's time was valued only at an agricultural worker's wage, the computed farmer's surplus per acre of £0.2351 in enclosed farms may indicate a return to the farmer's entrepreneurship. The hypothesis that the mean farmer's profit per acre is equal for the three kinds of farms can easily be rejected given the test statistic $F(2, 228) = 14.947$.

Table 2 shows the mean surplus per acre, rent per acre, and taxes per acre for the three kinds of farms and puts the degree of disequilibrium into perspective. In open and partially open farms, rents absorbed about one

Table 1 Farmer's Surplus per Acre.

Farmer's surplus per acre £	Number of farms		
	Enclosed	Open	Partially open
Less than −1.5	4	—	—
−1.0 to −1.5	4	—	—
−0.5 to −1	13	1	3
0 to −0.5	46	2	6
0.5 to 0	38	3	11
1.0 to 0.5	31	5	6
1.5 to 1.0	8	7	7
2.0 to 1.5	5	5	6
2.5 to 2.0	5	1	1
3.0 to 2.5	4	1	3
3.0+	1	2	2
Number	159	27	45
Mean farmer's surplus per acre	0.2351	1.2233	0.8847

Farmer's surplus equals a farm's surplus minus taxes and tithes paid minus the rent actually paid.

Table 2 Surplus, Efficiency, and Prices.

	Surplus per acre (£)	Rent per acre (£)	Tithes and taxes per acre (£)	Farmer's surplus per acre (£)
Open	2.16	0.73	0.21	1.22
Partially open	1.62	0.57	0.17	0.88
Enclosed	1.00	0.65	0.12	0.24

Notes: Surplus per acre equals the farm's revenues per acre minus the opportunity cost of all non-land inputs per acre. Rent per acre equals the rent actually paid. Farmer's surplus per acre equals surplus per acre minus rent per acre minus tithes and taxes per acre.

third of the surplus. If rents in these farms were increased to absorb all the surplus, they would rise by a factor of 2½. This result is consistent with the conventional wisdom of the eighteenth century that enclosure doubled or trebled rents.

The numbers in Table 2 are also consistent with conclusions drawn in the Board of Agriculture's *General Report on Enclosures* (Young, 1808). In discussing the impact of enclosure on farmers, the *Report* notes:

> If profit be measured by a percentage on the capital employed, the old system [open field arable] might, at the old rents, exceed the profits of the new [enclosed]; and this is certainly the farmer's view of the comparison.[3]

If one imputed the farmer's surplus shown in Tables 1 and 2 to the capital invested by farmers, the implied rates of return would be in accord with this observation.

II. Prices and efficiency comparisons

These results indicate that enclosure offered considerable scope for the redistribution of agricultural income. The results do not preclude the possibility that enclosure also raised farm efficiency, a possibility now to be explored. This inquiry is made urgent by other aspects of Table 2. The table shows that, strangely, rents per acre were similar in open and enclosed farms:[4] the reason rents could be increased when farms were enclosed was not that open field rents were low but rather that the surplus per acre of open field farms exceeded the surplus of enclosed farms. If surpluses measure efficiency, then the implication of Table 2 is that enclosure lowered farm efficiency. This implication is not only inconsistent with everything that is known about eighteenth century farming, but it is also inconsistent with the movement of rents since it suggests that the disequilibrium in the open field rental market would be eliminated by surpluses falling rather than by rents rising.

A major reason for the curious pattern in Table 2 is the treatment of common rights. They have thus far been ignored. The divisor in the calculations is a farm's acreage of arable and grass. Since common rights were particularly extensive for open and (to a lesser degree) partially open farms, surplus per acre for these farms is artificially raised relative to enclosed farms.[5] In addition, there are two factors other than the quality of the farming that might account for the lower surplus per acre of enclosed farms. Either the enclosed farms were less favourably located so that on average they faced lower output and higher input prices (the von Thünen effect), or they were located on poorer land than the open field farms (the Ricardo effect). Either effect would cause open field farms to generate higher surpluses per acre even if the two farming systems were intrinsically of the same efficiency. This section is concerned with assessing the importance of the von Thünen effect by examining how efficiency differences can be inferred from surplus differences in the face of varying input and output prices. In this section the assumptions that land was homogeneous and that common rights did not vary across farms are maintained. These assumptions are relaxed in the next section.

To develop a procedure for decomposing surplus per acre variations into price and efficiency variations, it is necessary to develop an economic model of a farm. Imagine the farm to possess a particular acreage of land, L, and to face exogenous product prices $P = (P_1, \ldots, P_m)$ and variable input prices $W = (W_1, \ldots, W_n)$ for all inputs besides land. These inputs are regarded as variable. Suppose the farm has a neoclassical technology and the farmer chooses to produce those outputs $Q = (Q_1, \ldots, Q_m)$ and to utilise variable inputs $X = (X_1, \ldots, X_n)$ that maximise Ricardian surplus, $S = \sum_{i=1}^{m} P_i Q_i - \sum_{i=1}^{n} W_i X_i$. In that case, maximised Ricardian surplus is a function[6] of P, W, and L: $S = S^*(P, W, L)$. Suppose further that the technology set exhibits constant returns to scale and that the level of efficiency can be represented by a multipliatively separable parameter, A. Then the function $S^*(\cdot)$ has the form:

$$S = AS(P, W)L. \tag{1}$$

Empirical implementation of equation (1) requires the assumption of a particular form for $S(\cdot)$. I will assume it is a weighted geometric average of the input and output prices:

$$S(P, W) = \prod_{i=1}^{m} P_i^{\alpha_i} \bigg/ \prod_{i=1}^{n} W_i^{\beta_i}. \tag{2}$$

$S(\cdot)$ is linearly homogeneous which implies the restriction $\Sigma \alpha_i - \Sigma \beta_i = 1$. $\alpha_i = P_i Q_i / S$ and $\beta_i = W_i X_i / S$ are shares in surplus. Define Ricardian surplus per acre as $r = S/L$. Product and input shares in revenue and total cost can then be defined as $v_i = P_i Q_i / R$ and $u_i = W_i X_i / R$ and $u_L = S/R$ where u_L is land's share. Here $R = \Sigma P_i Q_i = \Sigma w_{iXi} + vL$ is farm revenue or total cost. Consequently, $v_i = u_L \alpha_i$ and $u_i = u_L \beta_i$.

Suppose one observes the Ricardian surplus per acre of two farms, r_1 and r_2, whose technologies and behaviour satisfy the assumptions made here. By combining equations (1) and (2) and the definitions of the shares, one can infer relative efficient (A_2/A_1) by deflating r_2/r_1 by a geometric index of output and variable input prices:

$$\frac{r_2}{r_1} \frac{\prod_{i=1}^{n} \left(\frac{W_{2i}}{W_{1i}}\right)^{u_i/uL}}{\prod_{i=1}^{m} \left(\frac{P_{2i}}{P_{1i}}\right)^{v_i/uL}} = \frac{A_2}{A_1}. \tag{3}$$

In this paper, the efficiency, E, of the farm in case 2 will be defined to be a function of A_2/A_1:

$$E = \left(\frac{A_2}{A_1}\right)^{uL}. \tag{4}$$

This definition is made since E equals a conventional index of real output divided by real input, as minor manipulation of equations (3) and (4) shows:

$$\frac{\dfrac{R_2}{R_1} \Big/ \prod_{i=1}^{m}\left(\dfrac{P_{2i}}{P_{1i}}\right)^{v_i}}{\dfrac{R_2}{R_1} \Big/ \left(\dfrac{r_2}{r_1}\right)^{uL}\left[\prod_{i=1}^{n}\left(\dfrac{W_{2i}}{W_{1i}}\right)^{u_i}\right]} = E. \tag{5}$$

The left-hand side of equation (5) is an implicit index of real output divided by an implicit index of real input.

Equations (3) and (4) provide a basis for decomposing relative surplus per acre into relative efficiency and relative output-input price variations. For convenience, define the relative excess of output and input prices in case 2 to the base case 1 to be:

$$D = \frac{\prod_{i=1}^{m}\left(\dfrac{P_{2i}}{P_{1i}}\right)^{v_i}}{\prod_{i=1}^{n}\left(\dfrac{W_{2i}}{W_{1i}}\right)^{u_i}}. \tag{6}$$

Substituting equations (4) and (6) into equation (3) yields:

$$\frac{r_2}{r_1} = D^{(1/uL)} E^{(1/uL)}. \tag{7}$$

Equation (7) indicates how relative surplus per acre can be decomposed into price and efficiency effects.

The only limitation to the analysis developed thus far is that E can be computed only if $r_2/r_1 > 0$. Eighteen farms in the sample earned negative surpluses. Rather than discard them another efficiency index is defined.

$$E^* = \frac{\dfrac{R_2}{R_1} \Big/ \prod_{i=1}^{m}\left(\dfrac{P_{2i}}{P_{1i}}\right)^{v_i}}{\left(\dfrac{L_2}{L_1}\right)^{uL} \prod_{i=1}^{n}\left(\dfrac{X_{2i}}{X_{1i}}\right)^{u_i}}. \tag{8}$$

In this index the implicit index of inputs in the denominator of equation (5) is replaced with a direct index of inputs. A corresponding index of relative output to input prices can be defined as:

$$D^* = \frac{(r_2/r_1)^{uL}}{E^*}. \tag{9}$$

157

Table 3 Efficiency and Price Indices.

	Efficiency I	Price I	Efficiency II	Price II
Open	1.12	1.11	1.22	1.05
Partially open	1.05	1.07	1.05	1.06
Enclosed	0.95	1.03	0.94	1.04

Notes: Efficiency I is E as computed by equations (3) and (4); Price I is D as computed by equation (6); Efficiency II is E^* as computed by equation (8); Price II is D^* as computed by equation (9).

To decompose surplus per acre variations into price and efficiency components, price and efficiency indices were computed for every farm. The shares in revenue of all the inputs and outputs were computed for every farm and then averaged across all farms.[7] These average shares were used in all computations. For each farm, efficiency and price indices were computed according to equations (5), (6), (8) and (9). The base values (i.e. P_{1i}, W_{1i}, r_1, L_1, X_{1i}), in all of these calculations were the overall average prices, surplus per acre, and quantities of inputs.[8] Therefore, as the computed E, E^*, D, and D^* for a farm exceed or fall short of one, so its efficiency or the relative prices it faced exceed or fall short of this overall average.

Table 3 shows the mean values of E and D (labelled efficiency and price indices I) and E^* and D^* (labelled indices II) for the open, enclosed, and partially open farms. The variation of the average price indices is small compared to the variation in efficiency. This result is especially strong in the case of E^* and D^* but is also apparent in the case of E and D. When analogous comparisons are made among the farms in each of the three groups, the same pattern is observed; namely, that the variations in surplus per acre are associated with variations in E and E^* but not with D and D^*. It appears, therefore, that the von Thünen effect does not account for the variation in surplus per acre. When land is treated as a homogeneous input, the high surplus per acre of open field farms implies they were much more efficient than enclosed farms.

III. Land characteristics, commons and efficiency comparisons

That greater measured efficiency, however, might simply have been caused by the open field farms' having been situated on more fertile land. In this section that possibility is explored. This inquiry is much more difficult than the inquiry of the last section since it is not possible to measure all of the characteristics that influence the capacity of land to generate surplus. The empirical work is restricted to exploring only some of the major determinants of land quality. Nevertheless, the results are reasonably strong: Depending on how one chooses to interpret them, anywhere from half to all of the differences in efficiency between open and enclosed farms is explained by variations in the quality of the land, as measured here.

Three characteristics of land are analysed: predominant soil type (sand, loam, clay or moor), average rainfall, and degree-days of heat. In addition common rights can be incorporated into the model systematically by treating them as a characteristic of the arable and grass of the farm. Common rights are difficult to measure. A farmer acquired such rights by occupying land in the fields of a village possessing a common. In some villages there was no limitation on the number of animals a farmer could pasture on the common, but in most villages the common was stinted, and a farmer's stint, i.e. the number and type of animals he could pasture on the common depended on the acreage he held in the fields. The appropriate measure of a farm's common rights would be its stint, which might be infinite. The stint rights of the farms in this data set are not known. A variety of proxies for their rights were explored but only one gave plausible results in the statistical estimations. That measure of stint rights took on a value of zero if a farm was located in a village without a common but equalled the number of sheep the farm possessed if the farm was located in a village with a common. Since the farms located near very large areas of common waste (like the Yorkshire wolds or the Wiltshire downs) used the commons for grazing sheep and kept large flocks, it is not surprising that this proxy for stint rights works well.

As a first experiment to see whether land characteristics influence efficiency, the equations shown in Table 4 were estimated. In regressions 1–3, E^* was the dependent variable and the sample consisted of all 231 farms. In equation (1) E^* is regressed on a constant and dummy variables for enclosed and partially open farms. (The corresponding dummy variable for open farms is excluded.) The coefficient of the dummy variable for enclosed farms is negative and strongly significant. In equation (3) variables representing the land characteristics are also included in the regression. Adding these variables substantially reduces the absolute magnitude of the coefficient of the dummy for enclosed farms and makes it insignificantly different from zero. The coefficient of the partially open farm dummy also becomes inconsequentially different from zero. Taking account of land characteristics, therefore, eliminates the differences in efficiency among open, enclosed and partially open farms.[9]

Similar but more modest results are shown in equations (4–6). In those equations the dependent variable is E and the sample consists of the 213 farms with positive surpluses. Equation (5) shows that the mean value for E is significantly less for enclosed farms than for open farms. In equation (6), when the variables representing land characteristics are added, the coefficient of the enclosed dummy is closer to zero than it was in equation (4) but is still significantly different from zero.

The regressions on Table 4 particularly those involving E^*, lend support to the view that it is the superior quality of their land and their extensive

Table 4 Efficiency on Characteristics (*t* ratios in parentheses).

Regression...	1	2	3
Dependent variable...	E*	E*	E*
Constant	1.217	0.326	0.434
	(17.692)	(1.429)	(1.707)
DE	−0.278	—	−0.114
	(−3.735)		(−1.362)
DP	−0.163	—	−0.018
	(−1.878)		(−0.197)
DL	—	−0.033	−0.033
		(−0.604)	(−0.593)
DC	—	0.050	0.026
		(0.682)	(0.324)
DM	—	0.037	−0.006
		(0.370)	(−0.057)
R	—	0.006	0.007
		(1.472)	(1.893)
H	—	0.019	0.016
		(2.701)	(2.226)
T	—	0.176	0.157
		(6.790)	(5.655)
R^2	0.064	0.240	0.252
N	231	231	231

Regression...	4	5	6
Dependent variable...	E	E	E
Constant	1.123	0.319	0.431
	(25.502)	(2.043)	(2.499)
DE	−0.175	—	−0.112
	(−3.651)		(−2.008)
DP	−0.073	—	−0.017
	(−1.290)		(−0.289)
DL	—	−0.045	−0.044
		(−1.191)	(−1.170)
DC	—	−0.010	−0.035
		(−0.203)	(−0.664)
DM	—	0.866	0.043
		(1.301)	(0.642)
R	—	0.006	0.008
		(2.465)	(3.076)
H	—	0.021	0.018
		(4.390)	(3.676)
T	—	0.069	0.051
		(3.891)	(2.698)
R^2	0.075	0.174	0.204
N	213	213	213

Variables
E* efficiency index II in Table 3 and defined by equation (8).
E efficiency index I in Table 3 and defined by equations (3) and (4).
DE dummy variable with a value of one for enclosed farms.
DP dummy variable with a value of one for partially open farms.
DL dummy variable with a value of one for loam soil.
DC dummy variable with a value of one for clay soil.
DM dummy variable with a value of one for moor soil.
R inches per year of rain.
H hundreds of degree days of heat per year.
T common rights.
See the Appendix for the sources and detailed definitions of variables.

common rights which account for the high surplus per acre generated by open field farms. A sounder test, however, can be developed by incorporating the characteristics of land into the model of the farm developed in the last section. Rather than assume that the land input of a farm can be measured by the sum of its arable and grass, it ought to be measured as a linearly homogeneous aggregate of the characteristics of the land, including the appurtenant common rights. Equation (1), the function describing the farm's behaviour, is then modified by replacing L with the aggregate $L = F(\mathbf{C})$, where $\mathbf{C}$ is the vector of land characteristics:

$$S = AS(P, W)F(\mathbf{C}). \tag{10}$$

In the empirical work, the characteristics of land are taken to be RL, the volume of rain falling on the farm in inch-acres, HL, the useful heat the farm receives in hundreds of degree-days, T, the common right, and L, the area of the farm. $F(\mathbf{C})$ was taken to be linear in these variables.

$$F(\mathbf{C}) = B_1 RL + B_2 HL + B_3 T + B_4 L \tag{11}$$

subject to the restriction $\sum_{i=1}^{4} B_i = 1$ which imposes linear homogeneity. The coefficients B_i are the marginal valuations of the characteristics. Analogously with equation (3) and (4), the relative efficiency of two farms can be measured as:

$$\left[\frac{S_2/S_1}{F(\mathbf{C}_2)/F(\mathbf{C}_1)}\right]^{uL} \frac{\prod \left(\frac{W_{2i}}{W_{1i}}\right)^{u_i}}{\prod \left(\frac{P_{2i}}{P_{1i}}\right)^{v_i}} = \left(\frac{A_2}{A_1}\right)^{uL} = E_c. \tag{12}$$

Equation (12) suggests an obvious test of the hypothesis that it is the superior quality of the land upon which open field farms were situated and their more extensive common rights which was responsible for their higher measured efficiency. If E_c is computed for every farm, its average value for open, enclosed, and partially open farms should be equal if the hypothesis is correct.

In order to carry out the test, it is necessary to estimate the coefficients of equation (11) so that E_c can be computed. The coefficients were obtained by estimating the following equation, which was suggested by equations (10) and (11):

$$\frac{S/L}{D^{1/uL}} = B_1 R + B_2 H + B_3(T/L) + B_4. \tag{13}$$

The restriction $\sum_{i=1}^{4} B_i = 1$ was imposed to guarantee linear homogeneity in the characteristics. The result was:

$$\frac{S/L}{D^{1/uL}} = 0.00384\, R + 0.0201\, H + 0.319\, (T/L) + 0.657. \qquad (14)$$
$$\phantom{\frac{S/L}{D^{1/uL}} =\ } (0.644) \quad\ \ (2.337) \quad\ \ (4.475) \qquad (8.949)$$
$$R^2 = 0.1187 \quad t \text{ ratios in parentheses.}$$

There is little basis for forming alternative estimates of the shadow prices of the environmental variables in equation (14). One can, however, construct alternative estimates of the value of T/L (common rights per acre of land in the fields) and compare those alternative estimates with the coefficient of T/L. The coefficient of T/L in equation (14) indicates that a farmer facing average input and output prices (so $D = 1$), would be willing to pay about 6 shillings (£0.3188) more in rent for an acre of land if it carried with it the right to pasture one sheep (the measure in which common rights have been measured) on a common. An alternative estimate of the value of a common right to a farmer would be the value of the products of a sheep minus the non-land costs incurred in obtaining those products. Most farmers sold their flocks after a year and bought new sheep to replace them. Young frequently reports the 'profit' of sheep, i.e. the value of a sheep's products less its purchase price. For sheep kept on commons, the average 'profit' was 5–8 shillings per sheep. From this, one ought also to subtract the shepherd's wage per sheep, but that was a very small number[10] that can be safely ignored. Hence, this alternative estimate of the shadow price of commons, 5–8 shillings per sheep, is strikingly consistent with the shadow price implied by equation (14). This consistency is important confirmation of the equation.

The positive and significant shadow price of common rights conveys another important lesson about eighteenth century agriculture. It is often loosely argued that commons were common property resources and overgrazed to the extent that all rent was dissipated. If that argument were true, no farmer would be willing to pay a higher rent for arable simply by virtue of any common rights appurtenant to it. Since farmers were willing to pay higher rents for such land, the value of their commons had not been dissipated.

The coefficients in equation (14) were used to compute E_c defined by equation (12). Table 5 shows the results obtained when E, E^*, and E_c were regressed on a constant and dummy variables identifying enclosed and partially open farms. In all three regressions, the sample consisted of the 213 farms showing positive surpluses, and, to facilitate comparison, E^* and E_c were normalised, so that their mean values for open field farms equalled the mean value of E. The regressions involving E and E^* both show enclosed farms significantly less 'efficient' than open field farms. However, in the regression of E_c as the dependent variable, the coefficient of the enclosure dummy is much closer to zero and is no longer significantly different from it. Thus,

Table 5 Efficiency Index Incorporating Characteristics.

Regression... Dependent variable...	1 E	2 E*	3 E_c
Constant	1.123	1.123	1.123
		(18.469)	(13.502)
DE	−0.175	−0.233	−0.093
	(−3.65)	(−3.525)	(−1.135)
DP	−0.076	−0.112	0.135
	(−0.59)	(−1.446)	(1.267)
R^2	0.075	0.066	0.047
N	213	213	213

Variables: E_c defined by equation (12). All other variables defined in Table 4.

when land is correctly measured, i.e. as an economically well defined index of its characteristics rather than simply by its spatial dimensions, the systematic difference in efficiency between open and enclosed farms disappears. The result is a consequence of the fact that open field farms were located on drier but warmer land than enclosed farms. The most prominent cause of the greater 'efficiency' of open field farms, however, was their more extensive common rights.

The finding of no difference in efficiency among the three classes of farms gains plausibility when one examines the details of farm management. Table 6 presents average values for some important characteristics of the farms. In all cases the average sizes were well above minimum efficient size. The average size of open and enclosed farms were quite similar (247 and 274 acres, respectively) while partially open farms were considerably larger (566 acres). These sizes, in fact, under-represent the quantities of land utilised by the farms, for common rights are not included. All classes of farms had a high proportion of their land under grass. The proportion is smallest in the case of open field farms, but this disproportion is at least partly due to the omission of common pasture.

Arable husbandry was similar on the three sorts of farms. The enclosed farms had gone a bit further in eliminating fallows and introducing clover and turnips than had the open farms, but the open farms were certainly not static. Their rotations were far from the early modern practice of a year of wheat or barley followed by a year of peas or beans, and then a year fallow. The partially open farms, likewise, had modernised to a considerable degree. Moreover, there was little difference in the crop yields among the three types of farms. Mean yields on the open farms, in fact, were slightly higher than on the enclosed farms. However, it was only in the cases of barley and oats that the differences were statistically significant. Overall, the differences in arable husbandry were not dramatic.

Table 6 Land Use Patterns and Crop Yields.

	Open	Enclosed	Partially open
	Major division (acres)		
Grass	70.148	143.201	275.556
Arable	177.148	130.956	290.111
	Distribution of the arable (%)		
Wheat	22.768	18.788	22.061
Barley	17.144	16.997	20.950
Oats	9.471	16.593	9.873
Peas	10.976	5.754	8.633
Beans	5.917	2.699	7.032
Turnips	8.488	11.964	11.214
Clover	4.286	11.507	6.281
Fallow	20.950	15.698	13.956
	Crop yields (bushels per acre)		
Wheat	24.519	22.470	25.756
Barley	36.185	30.723*	33.511
Oats	40.667	36.371*	47.489
Peas	20.815	21.440	20.800
Beans	30.467	27.947	27.107

* The difference between this mean and the corresponding open field mean is statistically significant at the 5% level.

IV. Conclusion

The data collected by Arthur Young in his tours of England support two conclusions. First, only half of the surplus generated by open field farms accrued to the landlord as rent and to the church and state as tithes and rates. Hence, introducing free competition into the farm lease market would approximately double rents and substantially lower farmer's incomes. Second, enclosure did not raise efficiency. Indeed, the first comparisons undertaken showed enclosed farms to be less efficient than open field farms. However, when differences in the characteristics of the land (treating common rights as one of those characteristics) were incorporated into the comparison it was possible to accept the statistical hypothesis that open and enclosed farms were equally efficient. The data on crop yields and land use patterns buttress this result. The overall conclusion to which these findings point is that the major economic consequence of the enclosure of open field arable in the eighteenth century was to redistribute the existing agricultural income, not to create additional income by increasing efficiency. The major limitation to this conclusion is that the data pertain to farms located in places where the optimal land use strategy involved a heavy commitment to arable farming and where the soil was light enough to permit the cultivation of turnips. In other environments, open field farming may not have been as successful *vis-à-vis* enclosed farming.

The finding that enclosure did not raise efficiency contradicts the influential work of early twentieth century historians like Ernle (1961) who contended that enclosure was a prerequisite to the adoption of advanced methods. Although that view became the conventional wisdom, it has been seriously undermined by recent agricultural historians who have shown that open field farmers did indeed adopt modern practices (Havinden, 1961; Kerridge, 1969; Yelling 1977). The conclusions of this study extend those findings and, in turn, are made more plausible by them.

The finding that open and enclosed farms were equally efficient is interesting in the light of much recent work on the efficiency of agriculture in developing countries. At one time, it was widely believed that small scale peasant farming was inefficient. Much recent research, however, has shown that those farmers are indeed as efficient as large capitalist farmers (e.g. Yotopoulos and Nugent (1976, pp. 87–106)). While the parallels with eighteenth century England are loose, an analogous rehabilitation of the once maligned open field farmer is underway. To carry the parallel further, the enclosure movement itself might be regarded as the first state sponsored land reform. Like so many since, it was justified with efficiency arguments while its main effect (according to the data analysed here) was to redistribute income to already rich landowners.

The most difficult finding of this paper to account for is the renting of open field land at less than its value. Such a pattern would be inconsistent with a competitive market for tenancies in which rents were frequently renegotiated. The institutions of the open fields, however, seem to have departed from these arrangements in two ways. First, some land may have been let for long terms at low customary rents. It was indeed the case that virtually every enclosure act contained a clause cancelling existing leases and thus allowing renegotiation at competitive rents. Second, bilateral bargaining between the farmers as a group and the landlords may have been important in setting open field rents. Such bargaining would emerge when the adoption of new cropping patterns was discussed. In the late eighteenth century, it was the tenant farmers (not the landowners) who chose the cropping pattern (Yelling, 1977, p. 147). The farmers would have had no incentive to modernise unless they received some of the benefits. Since enclosure, which broke village control over cropping, was costly, the landlords would find it advantageous to concede some benefit to the farmers in the form of low rents. Unfortunately, Young was silent on the tenancy arrangements of the villages he visited so these conjectures cannot be explored with his data.

Appendix

The purpose of this Appendix is to describe the main principles and procedures used in putting together the data set. Allen (1979) is a more complete explanation and is available on request.

In compiling the data, it was necessary to determine the price and quantity of every input and output for every farm. Farm revenues consisted of the sales of arable crops and livestock products. Farm costs consisted of the cost of seed, livestock, labour, and implements. With some minor exceptions discussed in Allen (1979), these magnitudes were estimated as follows:

(1) Crops and seed

Young indicated the acreage of each farm devoted to wheat, barley, oats, peas, beans, clover, turnips, and fallow. Following Marshall (1796, vol. II, p. 140) and subject to some internal checks, it was presumed that all farms were self sufficient in forage so crop revenues equalled the sale of wheat, barley, oats, peas, and beans. Production and seed requirements of these crops were estimated by multiplying the farm acreage by the average yields and sowing rates for the crops in the village where the farm was located. The prices of the crops were taken to be the average 1771 London *Gazette* prices in the principal market towns of the county in which the farm was located. Peas and beans were presumed to sell at the same price. The prices of seed were taken to be the same as the corresponding crop prices except that the seed prices were increased by 5% to include the foregone interest on the investment in seed.

(2) Livestock

For each farm Young recorded the number of dairy cows, sheep, 'fatting beasts', young cows, and draught animals. The first four kinds generated revenue. Dairy revenue was computed as the number of cows multiplied by the 'average value of the products of a cow' for the village where the farm was located. Dairy cows were capital goods and were assumed to be worth £5. Annual rental prices were computed on the basis of a 5 % interest rate and a 15 % depreciation rate.

Sheep, fatting beasts, and young cows were treated as though they were bought at the beginning of a year and sold (along with wool and lambs in the case of sheep) at the end of the year. They were presumed to cost 12 shillings, £5, and £3 respectively. In the case of sheep, revenues were taken to be 12 shillings plus the 'profit of a sheep' which Young reported for each village; fatting beast revenue equalled £5 plus the analogous profit figure (again reported for the village); young cows were presumed to sell for £5.

The prices of the various sorts of livestock products were taken to be the prices ruling in the village where the farm was located for cheese (for dairy products), mutton (for sheep products), and beef (for fatting beast and young cow products).

Draught animals were assumed to be worth £10 and interest and depreciation on them was computed at 5 and 15%, respectively. For horses, the cost of oats and shoeing was computed by subtracting the summer joist (assumed to be accounted for elsewhere) from the annual cost of keeping a horse. These values were reported at the village level and imputed to all the farms in the village.

(3) Implements

Implements were treated as capital goods. Since Young rarely recorded details of their quantities, the numerous farm descriptions in Young (1770) were used to estimate for each farm the number of wagons, broad-wheeled wagons, carts, three-wheel carts, harrows, rollers, and sacks as well as the value of dairy furniture, harness, and miscellaneous equipment.

Fortunately Young recorded for each village the purchase prices of these implements. Interest and depreciation were figured at 20%.

(4) Labour

Young recorded the number of servants, dairy maids, boys, and labourers employed. The first three kinds of labour were hired on annual contract and provided with room and board in addition to a money payment. Young records the money payment for each village. Room and board was taken to be £9 per year for servants, £6. 10s. for boys, and £5 for maids, following Young (1967), vol. IV, p. 356. The wage rate for labourers was taken as fifty-two multiplied by the average weekly wage reported for each village by Young.

It was necessary to estimate the quantity and opportunity cost of family labour. Farms run by gentlemen were presumed to use no family labour (Young 1770, vol. 1, pp. 246-80). Other farm families were presumed to supply one first class servant, one maid, and one boy. This labour was valued at the local money wage plus the cost of room and board.

It was also necessary to estimate harvest labour. Following Young (1771, vol. IV, p. 460), the quantity of this labour was estimated at 25 % of the number of labourers employed. This labour was valued at the same wage rate as the labourers.

(5) Tithes and rates

Local rates were estimated by multiplying each farm's rent (which Young reported) by the village rate. Where tithes were compounded, the composition of the village was used to compute the tithe liability. Average compositions for each county were worked out and used to estimate tithe liabilities for farms where tithes were collected in kind.

(6) Environmental variables

Rainfall was taken to be average annual rainfall in inches for the years 1916-50 as plotted on Ordnance Survey (1967). Soil type was determined from Bickmore and Shaw (1963, p. 40). Degree-days (in hundreds of degrees Fahrenheit) were obtained from Gregory (1954, p. 65).

A further line of research pertaining to the data must be noted. Young did not always indicate whether a village was open or enclosed. It was consequently necessary to examine printed and archival sources in order to classify the farms. Large scale eighteenth century county maps, many of which were drafted around 1770, were the most helpful printed sources, for they usually indicated, by varying the symbol identifying a road, whether it was passing through open or enclosed fields. In addition, archival material was examined for villages in which most of the farms were located. Twenty-seven county record offices or comparable archives were visited. The principal object was to examine manuscript maps, made about 1770, to ascertain the predominant field patterns. The property descriptions in glebe terriers, estate surveys, mortgages, deeds, conveyances, and leases were occasionally also useful.

Notes

* This research was supported by grants from the Canada Council and the British Columbia Ministry of Labour Youth Employment Program. I am indebted to Nancy South and Don Andrews for outstanding research assistance. I am also grateful to G. C. Archibald, R. Barichello, C. Blackorby, P. Chinloy, E.J. T. Collins, J. G. Cragg, W. E. Diewert, S. Engerman, S. Fenoltea, E. Hoffman, E. L. Jones, D. Landes, F. Lewis, P. Lindert, D. McCloskey, D. G. Paterson, M. B. Percy, M. Turner, J. Vanous, G. Wright, J. Yelling and a referee of this JOURNAL for helpful discussions and advice. I also thank the participants at the 1979 Cliometrics Conference and the U.B.C. Department of Agricultural Economics Workshop for their spirited remarks.

1 Ernle (1961) vigorously supports the view that enclosure raised efficiency; Hammond and Hammond (1924) that enclosure redistributed income.
2 Young did report on a few purely grassland farms but they were too few to support the sort of analysis reported here and so have not been included in the sample. Also farms located in Cumberland, Westmoreland, Lancashire, and Cheshire have not been included since their natural environments were so different from the rest of the country.
3 Young (1808, pp. 31–2). It should also be noted that, in contradiction to this conclusion, the *Report* (*ibid.*, pp. 37–8) also argues that the rise in rent indicates a rise in efficiency. Recently McCloskey (1972, 1975) has elaborated the argument that the rent rise indicates a rise in efficiency.
4 Yelling (1977, p. 210) notes the same phenomenon in comparing rents in 'Common-field' parishes and 'enclosed "arable" ' parishes in Rutland.
5 This characteristic of Table 2 does not impair the finding of Table 1; namely, that rents in open field farms were about half of surplus, while rents in enclosed farms were close to surpluses.
6 The requisite regularity assumptions and the resulting properties of the variable profit function are presented in Diewert (1974, pp. 133–7).
7 These computations were made before the exclusions mentioned in the footnote 1 on p. 938.
8 To use these values as base values, one must assume that the average t and X_i are optimal values given the average P_i, W_i, and L.
9 It will be noted that the R^2 values for these regressions and the others reported in this paper are not notably high. Two factors (other than the specifications) might amount for this. First, there is some error in the measurement of the variables. Second, not all relevant variables are included as independent variables. In particular, there are no variables that capture the farmer's competence. Farmers must

have varied enormously in this regard, and that variation must have accounted for much of the variation in farm efficiency.

10 For instance, the calculation of Young (1771, vol. III, p. 330) indicate that the shepherd's wage cost per sheep was 0.2 shillings.

References

Allen, R. C. (1979). 'The efficiency and distributional consequences of eighteenth century enclosures.' Department of Economics, University of British Columbia, Discussion Paper no. 79–18 (April).

Bickmore, D. P. and Shaw, M. A. (1963). *The Atlas of Britain and Northern Ireland.* Oxford: Clarendon Press.

Chambers, J. D. and Mingay, G. E. (1966). *The Agricultural Revolution, 1750–1880.* New York: Schoken Books.

Diewert, W. E. (1974). 'Applications of duality theory.' In *Frontiers of Quantitative Economics*, vol. 11 (ed. M. D. Intriligator and D. A. Kendrick). Amsterdam: North-Holland Publishing Company.

Ernle, Lord (1961). *English Farming Past and Present.* London: Heinemann Educational Books and Frank Cass.

Gray, H. L. (1915). *English Field Systems.* Cambridge: Harvard University Press.

Gregory, S. (1964). 'Accumulated temperature maps of the British isles.' *Transitions of the Institute of British Geographers*, vol. 20, pp. 59–73.

Hammond, J. L. and Hammond, B. (1924). *The Village Labourer, 1760–1832.* London: Longmans, Green.

Havinden, M. A. (1961). 'Agricultural progress in open field Oxfordshire.' *Agricultural History Review*, vol. 9.

Kerridge, E. (1969). *Agrarian Problems in the Sixteenth Century and After.* London: George Allen and Unwin.

McCloskey, D. (1972). 'The enclosure of open fields: preface to a study of its impact on the efficiency of English agriculture in the eighteenth century.' *Journal of Economic History*, vol. 32, no. 1, pp. 15–35 (March).

—— (1975). 'The economics of enclosure: a market analysis.' In *European Peasants and their Markets* (ed. W. N. Parker and E. L. Jones), pp. 123–60. Princeton: Princeton University Press.

Marshall, W. (1796). *The Rural Economy of the Midland Counties*, 2nd ed. London: G. Nicol.

Ordnance Survey (1967). *Rainfall: Annual Average, 1916–1950.* Chessington, Surrey: Ordnance Survey.

Tate, W. E. (1967). *The English Village Community and the Enclosure Movement.* London: Victor Gollancz.

Vancouver, C. (1794). *A General View of the Agriculture of the County of Cambridge.* London.

—— (1795). *A General View of the Agriculture of the County of Essex.* London.

Yelling, J. A. (1977). *Common Field and Enclosure in England, 1450–1850.* Hamden, Connecticut: Archon Books.

Yotopoulos, P. A. and Nugent, J. B. (1976). *Economics of Development: Empirical Investigations.* New York: Harper and Row.

Young, A. (1769). *A Six Weeks Tour Through the Southern Counties of England and Wales*, 2nd ed. London: W. Strahan and W. Nicoll.

—— (1770). *The Farmer's Guide in Hiring and Stocking of Farms*. London: W. Strahan and W. Nicoll.

—— (1771). *The Farmer's Tour through the East of England*. London: W. Strahan and W. Nicoll.

—— (1808). *General Report on Enclosures*. London: Board of Agriculture.

—— (1967). *A Six Month's Tour through the North of England*. New York: Augustus M. Kelley.

37

THE CAUSES OF SLAVERY OR SERFDOM

A hypothesis

Evsey D. Domar

Source: *Journal of Economic History* 30(1), 1970: 18–32.

I

The purpose of this paper is to present, or more correctly, to revive, a hypothesis regarding the causes of agricultural serfdom or slavery (used here interchangeably). The hypothesis was suggested by Kliuchevsky's description of the Russian experience in the sixteenth and seventeenth centuries, but it aims at a wider applicability.[1]

According to Kliuchevsky, from about the second half of the fifteenth century Russia was engaged in long hard wars against her western and southern neighbors. The wars required large forces that the state found impossible to support from tax revenue alone. Hence the government began to assign lands (*pomest'ia*) to the servitors, who were expected to use peasant labor (directly and/or via payments in kind and/or money) for their maintenance and weapons. In exchange, the servitor gave the peasants a loan and permitted them, free men as yet, to work all or part of his land on their own. The system worked rather badly, however, because of shortage of labor. Severe competition among landowners developed, the servitors being bested by lay and clerical magnates. Things became particularly difficult for the servitors after the middle of the sixteenth century when the central areas of the state became depopulated because of peasant migration into the newly conquered areas in the east and southeast. Under the pressure of the serving class and for certain other reasons, the government gradually restricted the freedom of peasants, already hopelessly in debt to their landlords, to move. They became enserfed by the middle of the seventeenth century, though the process itself continued for many decades to come.

This is a very rough summary of Kliuchevsky's story which hardly does him justice but which will serve my purposes until Part II. Like many a historian, he assembled and described the relevant facts (and in beautiful Russian at that) and stopped just short of an analytical explanation.

The economist would recast Kliuchevsky's account as follows: The servitors tried to live off rents (in one form or another) to be collected from their estates. But the estates could not yield a significant amount of rent for the simple reason that land in Russia was not sufficiently scarce relative to labor, and ironically, was made even less scarce by Russian conquests. The scarce factor of production was not land but labor. Hence it was the ownership of peasants and not of land that could yield an income to the servitors or to any non-working landowning class.

A simple economic model may sharpen the argument (if any sharpening is needed) and help to develop it further. Assume that labor and land are the only factors of production (no capital or management), and that land of uniform quality and location is ubiquitous. No diminishing returns in the application of labor to land appear; both the average and the marginal productivities of labor are constant and equal, and if competition among employers raises wages to that level (as would be expected), no rent from land can arise, as Ricardo demonstrated some time past. In the absence of specific governmental action to the contrary (see below), the country will consist of family-size farms because hired labor, in any form, will be either unavailable or unprofitable: the wage of a hired man or the income of a tenant will have to be at least equal to what he can make on his own farm; if he receives that much, no surplus (rent) will be left for his employer. A non-working class of servitors or others could be supported by the government out of taxes levied (directly or indirectly) on the peasants, but it could not support itself from land rents.

As a step toward reality, let us relax the assumption of the ubiquity of uniform land, and let capital (clearing costs, food, seeds, livestock, structures and implements) and management be included among the factors of production. Owners of capital, of superior skill and of better-than-average land will now be able to pay a hired man his due (or to use a tenant) and still obtain a surplus. But so long as agricultural skills can be easily acquired, the amount of capital for starting a farm is small, and the per capita income is relatively high (because of the ample supply of land), a good worker should be able to save or borrow and start on his own in time. Most of the farms will still be more or less family-size, with an estate using hired labor (or tenants) here and there in areas of unusually good (in fertility and/or in location) land, or specializing in activities requiring higher-than-average capital intensity, or skillful management. But until land becomes rather scarce, and/or the amount of capital required to start a farm relatively large, it is unlikely that a large class of landowners, such as required by the Muscovite government, could be supported by economic forces alone. The American

North in the Colonial period and in the nineteenth century would be a good example of an agricultural structure of this type.

So far the institutional structure has been shaped by economic forces alone without direct interference by the government.[2] Suppose now that the government decides to create, or at least to facilitate the creation of, a non-working class of agricultural owners. As a first step, it gives the members of this class the sole right of ownership of land. The peasants will now have to work for the landowners, but so long as the workers are free to move, competition among the employers will drive the wage up to the value of the marginal product of labor, and since the latter is still fairly close to the value of the average product (because of the abundance of land) little surplus will remain. The Russian situation prior to the peasants' enserfment corresponds to this case.

The next and final step to be taken by the government still pursuing its objective is the abolition of the peasants' right to move. With labor tied to land or to the owner, competition among employers ceases. Now the employer can derive a rent, not from his land, but from his peasants by appropriating all or most of their income above some subsistence level.[3] That Russian serfs could stay alive, and even to multiply, while working for themselves half-time and less suggests that the productivity of their labor (with poor technique, little capital, but abundant land) must have been quite high.

To recapitulate, the strong version of this hypothesis (without capital, management, etc.) asserts that of the three elements of an agricultural structure relevant here—free land, free peasants, and non-working landowners—any two elements but *never all three can exist simultaneously*. The combination to be found in reality will depend on the behavior of political factors—governmental measures—treated here as an exogenous variable.

The presence of this exogenous political variable seriously weakens the effectiveness of my model: it makes the presence of free land by itself neither a necessary nor a sufficient condition for the existence of serfdom. It is not a necessary condition because so long as marginal productivity of labor is high, serfdom may continue to exist even if free land is no longer present; it may even be imposed at this stage, as it was in the Russian Ukraine in the eighteenth century. Free land is not a sufficient condition because, as I stated above, without proper governmental action free land will give rise to free farmers rather than to serfs.

For the same reasons the model cannot predict the net effect of a change in the land/labor ratio on the position of the peasants. Suppose that with constant land, technology, and per capita stock of capital, population increases. The economic position of the peasants will worsen (even serfs can be exploited more), but the landowners will be less inclined to interfere with the peasants' freedom. Let population decline instead. The peasants will be better off provided they do not become less free. Thus a change in the land/labor ratio can set in motion economic and political forces acting in opposite directions.

The strength and usefulness of the model could be increased by making the political variable endogenous. But this I cannot do without help from historians and political scientists.

These difficulties notwithstanding, I would still expect to find a positive statistical correlation between free land and serfdom (or slavery). Such a correlation was indeed found by H. J. Nieboer of whom you'll hear more in Part III.

What about the end of serfdom (or slavery)? Traditionally it was assumed that it would or did disappear because of the inherent superiority of free labor. This superiority, arising from the higher motivation of the free man, was supposed to increase with greater use of capital and with technological progress. Let us disregard the possibly greater reliability of the slave and the longer hours he may be forced to work (particularly in traditional societies where leisure is highly valued), and let us assume that the economy has reached the position where the net average productivity of the free worker (P_f) is considerably larger than that of a slave (P_s). The abolition of slavery is clearly in the national interest (unless the immediate military considerations, such as of the Muscovite government, overwhelm the economic ones), but not necessarily in the interest of an individual slave owner motivated by his profit and not by patriotic sentiment. He will calculate the difference between the wage of a free worker (W_f) and the cost of subsistence of a slave (W_s) and will refuse to free his slaves unless $P_f - P_s > W_f - W_s$, all this on the assumption that either kind of labor can be used in a given field.[4]

As the economy continues to develop, the difference $P_f - P_s$ can be expected to widen. Unfortunately, the same forces—technological progress and capital accumulation—responsible for this effect are apt to increase W_f as well, while W_s need not change. We cannot tell on a priori grounds whether $P_f - P_s$ will increase more or less than $W_f - W_s$. Therefore we cannot be sure that technological progress and greater use of capital *necessarily* reduce the profitability of slave as compared with free labor. Much will depend on the nature of technological progress. Thus Eli Whitney's gin greatly increased the profitability of slavery, while a transition from raising crops to breeding sheep in medieval England might have acted in the opposite direction by creating a surplus of workers. (See Part II.) American planters must have used better agricultural techniques and more capital than their Latin-American and particularly Russian colleagues, but the Americans defended slavery with much greater zeal.

In a traditional society without technological progress and capital accumulation, the end of slavery is, paradoxically, more certain. As population continues to increase and the society eventually becomes Malthusian, the marginal product of labor descends to the subsistence level. Now the free man costs little more to employ than the slave, while, hopefully, being less bothersome and more productive. The ownership of human beings becomes pointless because of the great multiplication of slaves, and they become free provided they stay poor.[5] It is land that becomes valuable, and rents collected from estates worked by free laborers or tenants without any non-economic compulsion are sufficient to support an army of servitors or idlers. If the Muscovite government could have only waited a few hundred years!

II

Where I come from, an economic model without empirical testing is equated with a detective story without an end. My attempts to test the present model, however, merely taught me that the job is not for the amateur. I shall report to you the results of my skin deep investigation in the hope that my mistakes will stimulate the specialists. I concentrate on the Russian case, with short excursions into the histories of Poland-Lithuania, Western Europe and the United States.

1. Russia

The phenomenon to be explained here is not only the development of serfdom but its particular timing: before 1550 Russian peasants were free men; a hundred years later they were serfs. The relevant variables are:

(1) the number of servitors required by the military needs of the Moscow state, and (2) the population density.

According to Kliuchevsky, prior to the middle of the fifteenth century, Moscow, still a Tatar vassal surrounded by other Russian lands, fought very few foreign wars; its population became dense because Moscow was the safest spot in the area with few outlets for emigration.[6] We may conclude that there was no need as yet for a large class of servitors, and that the landowners could derive rents from their estates (patrimonies, to be exact) without enserfing the peasants. It is true that Russia, from the Kievan times onward, always had a substantial number of slaves. At the time, these were mostly household servants and retainers rather than peasants.[7]

From the middle of the fifteenth century the situation changes drastically. Having become independent from the Tatars (officially in 1480, actually earlier), and having gathered a number of Russian lands, Moscow was confronted with powerful enemies: with Poland-Lithuania and Sweden in the west and northwest, and with the Crimean Tatars in the south. The struggle with the latter went on continuously, while 50 out of the 103 years from 1492 to 1595 were spent in wars against Poland-Lithuania and Sweden, as were the following 30 out of 70 years from 1613 to 1682, not to mention the Time of Troubles, 1598–1613, filled with both civil and foreign wars.[8]

The military proficiency of the Muscovite armies being poor, refuge was sought in large numbers. More than 300,000 men were reported to have been under arms during Ivan the Terrible's Livonian War. There must have been a great increase in the number of servitors. With trade and industry making no significant progress, the government had to assign land to them. This process began on a large scale in the second half of the fifteenth century and was accelerated throughout the sixteenth century.[9]

In the meantime, the central areas of the country became depopulated. The conquest of the whole expanse of the Volga river (begun in 1552) opened up large areas of better soil and attracted large masses of peasants fleeing from high taxes, Ivan the Terrible's oppression (the famous oprichnina) and Crimean invasions. And then came the Time of Troubles which devastated the country once more. Already in the sixteenth century there was fierce competition for peasant hands among the landowners. It must have intensified after 1613.[10]

Thus both ingredients for the development of serfdom—a high land/labor ratio and the government's determination to create a large class of servitors— were present. In addition, there were several other forces working in the same direction. The first was the decline in the power of the great magnates, both at the hands of Ivan the Terrible and during the Time of Troubles. By offering the peasants privileges and protection, these magnates had been quite successful in bidding the peasants away from the servitors; for this reason the magnates favored the free movement of peasants, while the servitors, quite naturally, opposed it. Now the peasants lost the support of their "friends."[11] The second reason lay in the fiscal interest of the state: peasant migrations, particularly from the center to the periphery of the state, disorganized tax collections.[12] And finally, the peasant communities objected to the emigration of their members because the community carried a collective responsibility for the tax liabilities of its members (until in later years this responsibility was taken over by the masters); the departure of several members would leave the rest overburdened until the next census.[13]

Space does not allow me to give additional details of the process which gradually enserfed the peasants, or to discuss the disagreement between Kliuchevsky, who emphasized the hopeless indebtedness of the peasants to their landlords as the main obstacle to their movement, and Grekov and Blum who put greater stress on legislative enactments (particularly on the so-called "Forbidden Years," *zapovednye gody*).[14] Let me mention instead two further reflections of the scarcity of labor in Russia: the first manifested itself in the replacement of the basic land tax by a household tax in the seventeenth century, and by a poll tax under Peter the Great.[15] The second is an interesting cultural trait which remained long after its cause had probably disappeared: as late as in the first half of the nineteenth century, the social position of a Russian landowner, as described in contemporary literature, depended less on the size of his land holdings (which are seldom mentioned) than on the number of souls (registered male peasants) that he owned.[16]

2. Poland-Lithuania

On the theory that the length of a report should be proportional to the intensity of research done, this section will be very short. The relevant facts are as follows:

(1) In the fourteenth century vast open and very sparsely populated territories in the Ukraine were conquered by the Lithuanians.[17]
(2) In the fifteenth and sixteenth centuries, Ukraine was repopulated by immigrants from the more central areas of the state. The migration depopulated the central areas to such an extent as to constitute, according to Grekov, a threat to the Polish state.[18]
(3) By the end of the sixteenth century, the peasants were enserfed.[19]

What is not clear to me is the time sequence of events (2) and (3). In Vol. III (p. 110), Kliuchevsky dates the repopulation of the Ukraine in the sixteenth century; in Vol. I (p. 293), in the fifteenth century. But in both places he attributes the migration of peasants to the intensification of serfdom in Poland-Lithuania. Polish serfdom, according to him, had been established already in the fourteenth century, and Lithuanian, in the fifteenth century.[20] On the other hand, Grekov asserts that according to the Polish constitution of 1493, each peasant could still leave the land, having settled accounts with his landlord. But he also reports that in 1444 the Galician gentry demanded that the government prevent other landlords from interfering with the peasant movements.[21] Evidently, such interference was taking place even then.

In Poland-Lithuania great gaps between legal enactments and the actual state of affairs were quite possible. There were probably considerable regional variations, both in law and in practice as well. I would be happier if it could be established that migration to the Ukraine preceded the development of serfdom, but I am certainly not in a position to settle the matter. It is quite possible that migration and serfdom were reinforcing each other.

Since I have not studied the development of serfdom in other East European countries, I can make only two brief comments on Blum's well-known and very interesting article on "The Rise of Serfdom in Eastern Europe." His stress on the increasing power of the nobility and on the general depopulation of the area "from the Elbe all the way across to the Volga . . ." is heartily welcome.[22] But his use of alternating periods of prosperity and depression as important causes of the rise and decline of serfdom cannot be evaluated until he presents an analytical explanation of the causation involved.

THE FEUDAL AND EARLY MODERN ECONOMY

3. Western Europe

We shall deal here very briefly with four events:

(1) The emergence of serfdom in the late Roman Empire
(2) The decline of serfdom by 1300
(3) Its non-recurrence after the Black Death
(4) The relationship between sheep breeding and serfdom.

The depopulation of the late Roman Empire is, of course, well known. Referring to Byzantium, Georg Ostrogorsky states: "And so ever-increasing masses of the rural population were tied to the soil. This is a particular instance of the widespread compulsory fastening of the population to their occupation which scarcity of labour forced the later Roman Empire to pursue systematically."[23]

This is the clearest statement on the relation between scarcity of labor and the development of serfdom that I have come across in my reading of European economic history.

Similarly, the great increase in population in Western Europe by the end of the thirteenth century when serfdom was declining is also well known. Thus Ganshof and Verhulst talk about ". . . a considerable and growing reserve of surplus labor . . ." in France, and Postan discusses signs of overpopulation in England: a growing number of wholly landless men, sub-holdings of many tenants, shortage of pasture, etc.[24] The same information for Western Europe in general is supplied by Smith, who adds that: "The problem therefore for western landowners, at any rate before the demographic collapse of the mid-fourteenth century, was not to keep tenants, but how to get the most out of them.[25] Since these facts fit my hypothesis so nicely, let me stop here while I am still winning.

But when we come to the depopulation caused by the Black Death after 1348 (though, according to Postan, English population stopped growing even earlier),[26] my hypothesis is of little value in explaining the subsequent course of events. (See Part I.) Why did serfdom fail to come back after such a sharp increase in the land/labor ratio?

I address myself only to England. Except for one rather queer economic explanation to be discussed presently, I have none to offer and have to fall back on political factors. Serfdom could not be restored unless the landowners were reasonably united in their pressure on the government, and unless the latter was willing and able to do their bidding. But it is most unlikely that every estate lost the same fraction of its peasants. Hence, those landowners who had suffered most would welcome the freedom of peasant movement, at least for a while, while those who had suffered least would oppose it. If so, the landowners could not be united. Postan also suggests the probability that the main pressure behind Richard II's legislation came not from feudal landowners, but from smaller men;[27] English magnates, like their Russian colleagues (see above), could evidently take care of their own interests. Though I cannot judge the "spirit" of medieval legislation, it seems to me that the measures undertaken by Richard's government were somewhat halfhearted.[28] In any case, they were ineffective. So economic forces could reassert themselves and help the peasants.

The queer economic explanation which I have just mentioned would delight an economist if only it squared with facts. It is the expansion of sheep breeding, an activity which is land-using and labor saving.[29] Unfortunately such data as I could find do not support the contention that there was an expansion of sheep breeding in the hundred years following the Black Death. The legal exports of English wool, in raw and in cloth, fell from 12 million pounds in 1350 to 8.7 million in 1400—a drop of 27 percent. Another fall of 12 percent (of the 8.7 million) took place by 1450.[30] My authorities do not state the proportions of wool consumed at home and smuggled out of the country.[31] Perhaps these were affected by the Hundred Years' War. But as things stand, I certainly cannot claim that an expansion of English sheep breeding took place after 1350 and that it helped to save the peasants from the return of serfdom.[32]

Judging by Thomas More's famous passage about sheep devouring men, by Bishop Latimer's "Sermon of the Plough" (1549), and by other more direct evidence, there must have been considerable expansion of sheep breeding at the expense of crops and of people in the sixteenth century.[33] By that time, however, English peasants hardly needed the help from the sheep in staying free.

But is it possible that the early expansion of sheep breeding which must have taken place sometime prior to 1350 *had* helped the English serfs to gain their original freedom after all?

4. The United States

The American South fits my hypothesis with such embarrassing simplicity as to question the need for it. The presence of vast expanses of empty fertile land in a warm climate, land capable of producing valuable products if only labor could be found seems to me quite sufficient to explain the importation of slaves. What is not clear to me is the failure of the North to use them in large numbers. Besides social and political objections, there must have been economic reasons why Negro slaves had a comparative advantage in the South as contrasted with the North. Perhaps it had something to do with the superior adaptability of the Negro to a hot climate, and/or with his usefulness in the South almost throughout the year rather than for the few months in the North.[34] I have a hard time believing that slaves could not be used in the mixed farming of the North; much food was produced on southern farms as well, most of the slave owners had very few slaves, and many slaves were skilled in crafts.[35] A study of the possible profitability of slavery in the North, along Conrad and Meyer's lines, which could show whether the North could have afforded paying the market price for slaves, would be most welcome.

I have not come across any good evidence that slavery was dying out in the United States on the eve of the Civil War, and I side here with Conrad and Meyer, though, in truth, I am not sure that such a thorough investigation was required to prove the profitability of slavery in the South.[36]

III

In conclusion, let me say a few words about the origin of my hypothesis and about its place in economic history. Although I had discussed it in my classes for a good dozen years, I did not write it up until 1966 because I had been told on good authority that the idea was old and well known. My source was indeed correct because a brief search in the library revealed quite a few predecessors. The most important of them was the Dutch scholar Herman J. Nieboer whose magnum opus of 465 pages under the title of *Slavery as an Industrial System: Ethnological Researches* was published in 1900.[37] The hypothesis which I have immodestly called "mine" was stated by him time and again, and tested against a mass of anthropological and historical data. As you might expect, he was satisfied with his results.

But the hypothesis was not really original with Nieboer. He in turn referred to A. Loria's *Les Bases Economiques de la Constitution Sociale* of 1893, and to E. G. Wakefield's *A View of the Art of Colonization* published in 1834. Some glimpses can be found even in Adam Smith's *The Wealth of Nations*.[38]

I have two disagreements with Nieboer. First, his definition of free land has too much legal and not enough economic content to my taste, though he seems to have been unclear rather than wrong. Second, he exaggerated the importance of the hypothesis by claiming, though not in so many words, that free land or other free resources are both necessary and sufficient for the existence of slavery or serfdom: ". . . Only among people with open resources can slavery and serfdom exist, whereas free labourers dependent on wages are only found among people with close resources."[39] He protected himself with a note on the same page by excluding simple societies of hunters, fishers, and hunting agriculturists, hardly a fit company for the farmers of the American North. He disregarded the possibility that serfdom, once established, could exist for a long time after its initial cause—free land— had disappeared, or that serfdom may be even introduced in the absence of free land. He ignored the role of government. These, however, are minor defects in an important major contribution.

On the other hand, my source may have been a bit wrong. If historians have always known about the relation between the land/labor ratio and serfdom (or slavery), they must have tried hard not to scatter too many good, clear statements in places where I could find them, though the students of the American South have been much kinder to me than others.[40] Nieboer could also lodge some complaints. His name can be found neither in the bibliography nor in the index of the 1966 edition of the first volume of *The Cambridge Economic History of Europe*. And it is absent from Blum's classic study of Russian serfdom. I did find Nieboer's name in Genovese's *The Political Economy of Slavery* in connection with some insignificant point, but with a further notation that "Phillips read and referred to this book." Phillips had read it, and confirmed that "hired labor was not to be had so long as land was free."[41]

Perhaps in history this hypothesis occupies a place similar to that enjoyed by economic growth in economic theory not long ago. That place was once described as "always seen around but seldom invited in." If so, why not invite it? After all, the land/labor ratio is readily quantifiable.

Notes

For many helpful comments on an earlier draft, I am grateful to the following persons: Abraham Becker, Oleg Hoeffding, Clayton La Force, Edward Mitchell, William Parker, George Rosen, Matthew Edel, Peter Temin, Helen Turin and Charles Wolf, Jr. Alexander Gerschenkron's earlier suggestions were also very helpful. Thanks are also due Ann Peet for her excellent research assistance.

I am also grateful to the RAND Corporation for its support of an earlier version of this study (20 October 1966), and to the National Science Foundation for its assistance (Grant No. NSF-GS-2627) in revising and extending the first draft. Neither these two organizations, nor the persons listed above, are responsible for the views expressed here.

1 V. Kliuchevsky, *Kurs russkoĭ istorii* (Moscow: Gosudarstvennoe sotsial'no-ekonomicheskoe izdatel'stvo, 1937). The original work was published in 1906. All my references apply to the 1937 edition. An English translation by C. J. Hogarth, *A History of Russia*, was published in New York by Russell and Russell in 1960. For specific references, see Part II.

2 I mean by the "government" any organization capable of maintaining some measure of law and order and particularly of using non-economic compulsion. It can be a king, an assembly of landowners, a magnate, etc.

3 He may be restrained by custom and by the fear that his serfs can run away— a common occurence in Russia.

4 Actually, it is not easy to compare the relative profitability of free and slave labor. Since the free worker is paid more or less concurrently with his work, while a slave must be either reared or purchased, and may have children, etc., the streams of receipts and expenditures from the two kinds of labor must be properly discounted. It is assumed in the text that all indirect costs of using slaves, such as medical expense, extra supervision, etc., are included in W_8.

In a well-organized slave market, the price of a slave will approximate the present value of his discounted net lifetime marginal product. A buyer who pays this price will discover that he will earn not much more than the going rate of interest; he will complain about the high cost of slaves and express doubt regarding the profitability of slavery in general, because at the margin he will be fairly indifferent between employing free or slave labor. But so long as the supply of food and of similar items for the maintenance of slaves is elastic (which it is likely to be), the slave-breeder should do very well. He benefits from the chronic perpetual disequilibrium in the slave market created by the abundance of land and by the limited human capacity to procreate (assuming no importation of slaves). But if the slave-breeder computes his rate of return on the current value of his slaves and land, he may not record much more than the market rate of interest either. In other words, the market mechanism transforms the profit from slaves into capital gains.

On this see Lewis Cecil Gray, *History of Agriculture in the Southern United States to 1860*, published in 1933 and reproduced in part in Harold D. Woodman, *Slavery and the Southern Economy: Sources and Readings* (New York: Harcourt, Brace & World, Inc., 1966), pp. 106–09, and Alfred H. Conrad and John R. Meyer, *The Economics of Slavery and Other Studies in Econometric History* (Chicago: Aldine Publishing Company, 1964), pp. 43–92.

5 It is possible that even in a Malthusian society slavery (or serfdom) may linger on. Slaves may be kept for reasons of social prestige (a relic from the times when slavery was profitable), or simply because a slave is more reliable than a hired man. On the other hand, the use of a tenant (with a limited lease) or of a hired man allows the landowner to choose the best among several applicants with much greater ease than among slaves or serfs protected by custom.

6 Kliuchevsky, Vol. I, p. 379; Vol. III, pp. 9–10, 121. Blum, however, talks about depopulation already in the fourteenth and fifteenth centuries. See Jerome Blum, *Lord and Peasant in Russia from the Ninth to the Nineteenth Century* (Princeton: Princeton University Press, 1961), pp. 60–61. It is possible that Kliuchevsky describes the relative position of Moscow among other Russian lands, while Blum refers to the whole country.

7 Kliuchevsky, Vol. I, pp. 282–83; Vol. II, pp. 182–83.

8 *Ibid.*, Vol. II, pp. 121, 125, 221–22; Vol. III, p. 135.

9 *Ibid.*, Vol. II, pp. 221, 229–42, 248; Vol. III, pp. 63–64, 230–31, 257, 283. Blum, pp. 93, 157.

10 Kliuchevsky, Vol. II, pp. 254–57, 339–44; Vol. III, pp. 182, 244. Blum, pp. 147, 152–54, 157, 160, 252. B. D. Grekov, *Krest'iane na Rusi s drevneĭsheikh vremin do XVII veka* (Moscow-Leningrad: Izdatel'stvo Akademii Nauk SSSR, 1946), pp. 794–96, 849.

11 Kliuchevsky, Vol. II, pp. 259, 307. Blum, pp. 253–54. Grekov, pp. 870–71, 903, 909. Grekov, *Glavneĭshie etapy v istorii krepostnogo prava v Rossii* (Moscow-Leningrad: Gosudarstvennoe sotsial'no-ekonomicheskoe izdatel'stvo, 1940), p. 46.

It is interesting to note that when the leaders of the gentry militia were negotiating a treaty with the Polish king Sigismund regarding the accession of his son to the Moscow throne in 1610 and in 1611, they demanded the inclusion of a provision forbidding the movement of peasants. Kliuchevsky, Vol. II, p. 349.

12 Kliuchevsky, Vol. III, p. 188.

13 *Ibid.*, Vol. II, pp. 317–18, 336–37, 340. Blum, pp. 96, 234.

14 Kliuchevsky, Vol. II, pp. 321–23, 331–50; Vol. III, pp. 181–88. Blum, pp. 254–55. Grekov, *Krest'iane*, pp. 826, 850. Grekov, *Glavneĭshie*, pp. 64–65.

If the peasants' debts tied them to their lords as strongly and as hopelessly as Kliuchevsky asserts, it is puzzling that the government had first to limit and then to forbid their movement by law.

15 Kliuchevsky, Vol. III, pp. 243–46; Vol. IV, pp. 142–48. Grekov, *Glavneĭshie*, pp. 71–72.

16 Here are a few examples: In Pushkin's *Dubrovsky*, the old Dubrovsky is identified as the owner of seventy souls, and Prince Vereisky, of three thousand; in *The Captain's Daughter*, the commandant's wife is impressed by Grinev's father's ownership of three hundred souls; in Gogol's *The Dead Souls*, Pliushkin owns more than a thousand souls; in Goncharov's *Oblomov*, the principal hero owns three hundred and fifty; in his *A Common Story*, a certain Anton Ivanich has twelve, mortgaged over and over again....

17 Kliuchevsky, Vol. I, p. 293.

18 *Ibid.*, Vol. I, pp. 293–94. Grekov, *Krest'iane*, p. 387.

19 Jerome Blum, "The Rise of Serfdom in Eastern Europe," *American Historical Review*, LXII (1957), pp. 807–36. See particularly pp. 821–22.

20 Kliuchevsky, Vol. III, pp. 101–02.

21 Grekov, *Krest'iane*, pp. 381–83. There seems to be considerable disagreement among the authorities he cites. He mentions a number of legislative enactments passed at the end of the fifteenth century and in 1510, 1519, 1520, 1532 limiting the freedom of peasants to move (p. 387).

22 Blum, "The Rise of Serfdom," p. 819.

23 Georg Ostrogorsky, "Agrarian Conditions in the Byzantine Empire in the Middle Ages," *The Cambridge Economic History of Europe*, Second Edition (Cambridge: Cambridge University Press, 1966), I, 206. See also pages 11, 27–28, 33, 66 and 257 of the same volume. Also, W. R. Brownlow, *Lectures on Slavery and Serfdom in Europe* (London and New York: Burns and Oates, Ltd., 1892), pp. 49–50.

24 François Louis Ganshof and Adriaan Verhulst, "Medieval Agrarian Society in its Prime: France, The Low Countries, and Western Germany," *Cambridge Economic History*, I, 294; M. M. Postan in his essay on "England," same volume, pp. 552–56, 563–64, 624; Blum, "The Rise of Serfdom," pp. 810–11.

25 R. E. F. Smith, *The Enserfment of the Russian Peasantry* (Cambridge: Cambridge University Press, 1968), p. 4.

26 Postan, essay on "England," *Cambridge Economic History*, I, 566–70.

27 *Ibid.*, p. 609.

28 Brownlow, *Lectures on Slavery*, pp. 157–83. Smith, *Enserfment*, pp. 4–5.

29 The idea that sheep-breeding may have had something to do with serfdom was suggested by Nieboer in his book (pp. 371–75) discussed in Part III.

30 K. G. Ponting, *The Wool Trade Past and Present* (Manchester and London: Columbine Press, 1961), p. 30. The figures are based on a chart facing p. xviii of *Medieval Merchant Ventures* by E. Carus Wilson.

31 According to Postan, p. 568, domestic consumption of cloth is not known. Peter J. Bowden arbitrarily assumed it to be 50 percent. See his *The Wool Trade in Tudor and Stuart England* (London: Macmillan & Co., Ltd., 1962), p. 37.

32 Data on the size of the sheep population, or more correctly on increments in it, would not be sufficient for our problem. We would have to know how many crop-raising peasants were replaced, say, by 1,000 extra sheep.

33 See E. Lipson, *The History of the Woollen and Worsted Industries* (London?: Frank Cass & Co., Ltd., 1965), p. 19; E. Nasse, *On the Agricultural Community of the Middle Ages, and Inclosures of the Sixteenth Century in England* (London: Macmillan & Co., 1871), pp. 77–78; Brownlow, *Lectures on Slavery*, p. 184; Bowden, *Wool Trade*, p. xvi.

34 Woodman, *Slavery and the Southern Economy*, p. 7.

35 Conrad and Meyer, *Economics of Slavery*, p. 80; James Benson Sellers, *Slavery in Alabama* (University, Alabama: University of Alabama Press, 1950), pp. 71, 120, 162–63; Rosser Howard Taylor, *Slaveholding in North Carolina: An Economic*

View (Chapel Hill: University of North Carolina Press, 1926), p. 72; Harrison Anthony Trexler, *Slavery in Missouri* (Baltimore: The Johns Hopkins Press, 1914), pp. 13, 19; Woodman, *Slavery and the Southern Economy*, pp. 14–15.

36 As the authors practically admit on p. 78. On the profitability debate see Stanley L. Engerman, "The Effects of Slavery Upon the Southern Economy: A Review of the Recent Debate," *Explorations in Entrepreneurial History*, Second Series, IV (1967), pp. 71–97.

37 It was published in The Hague by Martinus Nijhoff. A republication is scheduled in 1970 by Burt Franklin, Publisher, New York.

38 Adam Smith, *The Wealth of Nations* (London: Cannan's edition, 1922), II, 66–68. There is another book by Wakefield on the same subject: *England and America: A Comparison of the Social and Political State of Both Nations* (London: Richard Bentley, 1833), Vol. II. Other sources: J. E. Cairnes, *The Slave Power* (London: Parker, Son, and Bourn, 1862); J. S. Mill, *Principles of Political Economy*, 1848 (New York: D. Appleton and Co., 1920), I, 316.

39 Nieboer, *Slavery as an Industrial System*, pp. 312, 389.

40 A clear statement by Ostrogorsky was quoted in Part II. For the American views, see Woodman's collection.

41 Eugene D. Genovese, *The Political Economy of Slavery* (New York: Vintage Books, 1967), p. 84. Ulrich B. Phillips, "The Economic Cost of Slaveholding in the Cotton Belt," *Pol. Sci. Q.*, XX (June 1905), partially reproduced in Woodman, *Slavery and the Southern Economy*, p. 36.

38

THE RISE AND FALL OF A THEORETICAL MODEL

The manorial system

Stefano Fenoaltea

Source: *Journal of Economic History* 35(2), 1975: 386–409.

I

Douglass North and Robert Thomas recently proposed a model of the rise and fall of the manorial system.[1] There is much to be admired in this work, which explores an unusually broad historical vision with great analytical acumen; but my purpose here is to examine some of its less compelling features. In section II, I consider the nature of feudalism, and develop empirical arguments against the wholly voluntaristic and non-exploitative interpretation proposed by North and Thomas. Section III examines their analysis of the "classic" manor, which I believe errs both in limiting the feasible contracts to forms of direct barter and in attributing the lowest transaction costs to labor dues even within that restricted set. Section IV reviews the proposed explanation of the later evolution of the manorial system, disputing both the continued use of the transaction costs model and the extensions of it that consider custom as an institutional barrier to efficiency, and population growth and inflation as the exogenous motors of change. Section V provides a brief concluding summary and evaluation.

II

North and Thomas tell us that "serfdom in Western Europe was essentially a contractual arrangement where labor services were exchanged for the public good of protection and justice" (p. 778). Given "the absence of an effective central political authority," and "the constant threat of piracy and brigandage," the professional military man was "welcomed by peasants unskilled in warfare and therefore otherwise helpless" (p. 788).[2] His authority was willingly accepted as the only way to deal with "the classic case of a public good, since protection of one peasant family involved protection of his neighbors as well. Each peasant therefore would have been inclined to let his neighbor pay the costs; in such a case, some form of coercion was required to raise the resources necessary for defense" (*ibid.*). In any event, no central coercive authority inhibited escape from the manor (pp. 779, 782) and "land of arable quality was freely abundant" (p. 782); if the peasants remained serfs, it had to be because feudalism—the lord's "protection and justice"—made them better off than free peasants. Serfdom cannot therefore be considered "a form of involuntary servitude" (p. 778); feudalism was not "an exploitative arrangement" (p. 778)[3] but "a fiscal system" (p. 781 n)—a solution, and indeed "an efficient solution" (p. 802), to the problem of obtaining the public goods desired by the peasants in the troubled world of the early Middle Ages.

This ingenious interpretation seems empirically unacceptable: the a priori argument from the peasants' demand for public goods is contradicted by a variety of facts, from the pattern of manorial organization to the technology of medieval warfare; and the revealed preference argument misconstrues the alternatives to serfdom in a largely anarchic environment. Let us consider these in order.

From a theoretical standpoint, the most obvious difficulty with the notion that the manor provided the public goods desired by the village stems from the ample non-coincidence of manors and vills. "One manor, one vill" may have been the rule; but in a large minority of cases things were not so neat. Manors could be dispersed, vills fragmented. How did that detached portion of a manor share in the (local) public goods provided elsewhere? And why should the cost of "protection and justice" have been lightest in villages where these public goods were provided not by one *dominus* but by half a dozen?[4] These problems—problems for the proposed interpretation, not for the traditional view of a manor as a unit of authority and exploitation—are symptomatic; upon closer examination, indeed, the "public goods" model appears to collapse altogether.

Consider the military protection provided by the lord. Technology favored static defense, and military power was embodied in fortifications; but the village was outside, not inside, the walls. The fortified manor house did not protect the peasants[5] against the sudden, unannounced violence that is presumably the hallmark of piracy and brigandage, though it did protect the lord (against all who were outside, his own peasants not necessarily excluded); it did not discourage raids, though it did discourage the raiders' metamorphosis from transient spoliators into resident exploiters. The suggestion that the lord protected his role in the village more than the village itself is only too clear.

The villeins could of course take shelter behind the lord's walls—if time allowed, and if the lord admitted them. But admission can be selective: any villager who was not under the lord's protection could be refused entrance. Unlike the mutual deterrence of modern states, or the peripheral fortification of the medieval commune, the lord's fortified buildings did not automatically and inevitably protect every member of the community. The lord's military protection was not a public good at all: no coercive fiscal system was required to impose the cost on those who reaped the benefit, and the *authority* of the lord cannot be legitimated by the nature of the service he provided.

The protection of the laws—"justice"—admits of largely parallel arguments. Justice is not a public good either, as any individual can be outlawed, that is, deprived of legal protection. Until the great simplifications operated by the capitalist revolutions, indeed, legal recognition of privilege and inequality was the rule rather than the exception. Neither is it clear that the lord provided a service for the benefit of the village: the English sources, at least, are replete with evidence of villages themselves administering justice the profits from which accrued to the lord.[6] Once again, then, the lord's authority appears rooted in threats rather than in blandishments.

The notion that feudalism was exploitative would of course have to be abandoned, whatever the evidence in its favor, if—as North and Thomas claim—the peasants' choices revealed that their servitude was in fact voluntary. This does not however appear to be the case, as migration was not by any means a costless path to freedom.

Top-quality arable land may have been available at constant cost, but surely not at *zero* cost, as the land had to be prepared—cleared, drained, whatever—before being put under the plow. Travel would also be costly, particularly since the migrants had to transport *in natura* the capital that would sustain them until their first harvest, and in the prevailing anarchy travelers had no protection beyond that which they could provide themselves. And what prospects did even successful migrants face? A small group would pay for its freedom with a permanently lower standard of living, as it lost those benefits (whether economies of production or pleasures of social intercourse) that justified nucleated settlement in the first place. A large enough group (if one can be imagined actually getting organized before the lord discovered the conspiracy and put an exemplary end to it) would avoid this particular cost; but by the same token it would be large enough to attract an armed parasite, and central authority did not restrain such self-appointed "protectors."

The serfs' options were thus to bear serfdom where they were, or to bear significant moving and setting-up costs for either isolation (with its attendant costs) or probable serfdom elsewhere. The lord could therefore reduce his peasants' welfare below what it would be if the village were free and still retain their services; one cannot argue from revealed preference that the lord's "protection and justice" were true goods, *freely* and willingly acquired, rather than vehicles for extortion. Indeed, peasant attempts at liberation by force of arms (in the face of their highly probable outcome) and their willingness to pay for their freedom (later, when a higher authority could make the bargain stick) suggest a revealed-preference argument diametrically opposed to that advanced by North and Thomas.

An effective territorial authority may be essential to outright slavery, but it is hard to believe that in its absence the world will know only voluntary, non-coercive "contractual arrangements." When the state is too weak (or unwilling) to protect the peasants against the magnates, and military technology is such that a peasant force is markedly inferior to a professional one, exploitation of the peasantry by the military class may be inevitable[7]; and if a peasant then does well to commend himself to a protector, he does so in strict analogy to the contemporary merchant who does well to buy the "protection" that extralegal authority may offer him.[8] Logic, the documents, and the very stones argue for the traditional view and against the proposed alternative.

III

Whether the feudal "contract" was mutually beneficial or exploitative, the nature of the serfs' "payment" to the lord needs to be explained. Consider first the "classic" manorial arrangement: why did the serfs "pay" the lords (so largely) in labor? The answer, North and Thomas tell us, is that such an arrangement minimized transaction costs. "The high risk incurred when transporting goods between manors," even as the "similar resource endowments between neighboring manors limited the potential gains from trade," "militated against any organized market economy: the exchanges that did take place were ... individual face to face bargains [requiring] "haggling," ... the expenditure of much time and effort. Thus the possibilities for exchange were severely limited" (pp. 787–788). In turn, "the general absence of a market requires that ... the consumption bundle must also be negotiated in any fixed rent, fixed wage, or crop sharing contract—an expensive procedure" since "the substantial natural variation in the size of output [requires] some agreement as to acceptable substitutions for the specified goods" and "the major difficulty is to agree on the rate at which other goods might be substituted.... The sharing of inputs, however, avoided this cost [of negotiation] by allowing each participant to grow the product-mix he preferred without the agreement of the other party" (pp. 784–785; see also pp. 789–790). To be sure, "the enforcement costs for sharing inputs ... are probably the highest of any of the contractual forms": since the laborer "had a considerable incentive to shirk [the] lord was ... forced to devote resources to supervision, and labor gangs came into being" (p. 790). Given that these high enforcement costs were outweighed by the attendant saving in negotiation costs, however, "the contractual arrangements of the classic manor can be seen as fully rational.... The general absence of any market for goods ... justified the sharing of inputs as the contractual arrangement having the lowest transaction costs" (p. 790).

In attributing the manorial system of labor dues to the absence of trade and the lack of markets, North and Thomas may recall the traditional explanation of the history books; but in comparing labor dues to the possible alternative arrangements they come to grips with a fundamental problem which the traditional histories do not even perceive. The key insight here is the recognition of the relatively high enforcement costs associated with labor dues. In particular contrast to a rental arrangement, in which production is wholly self-policing[9] because the worker always reaps the full benefit of his diligence and bears the full burden of his sloth, labor sharing reduces the available effective labor: if the lord's share of labor is unsupervised, it will be ineffective; if it is supervised, the effectiveness of direct labor is conserved only at the cost of diverting some labor to supervision. The threat of punishment for inadequate work, coupled perhaps to the definition of "a specified amount of achievement for a day's obligations" (North and Thomas, p. 790), might provide some escape from this dilemma[10]; but supervision remains necessary to establish *individual* responsibility within the group performing a task, and the *quality* of achievement, as opposed to its mere "amount," is notoriously difficult to control.[11] From the perspective of enforcement costs alone, then, labor dues appear inferior at least to rents,[12] and therefore wasteful; if their existence is to be explained, a suitable countervailing advantage must be found.

The solution North and Thomas propose seems, however, less compelling than their statement of the problem. Even among systems of direct barter, with payments in kind, labor dues do not appear to minimize transaction costs; and the exclusion of indirect barter, with payments in money and market exchange, seems both analytically and empirically unwarranted. Labor-sharing may have been cheaper to negotiate than rents in kind, but the latter were cheaper to enforce; and for a number of reasons the relative costs of enforcement appear altogether more significant than those of negotiation.

In the first place, agricultural output depends not just on the total labor input, but also, and crucially, on the *distribution* of that input over the year: the marginal product of a given flow of labor services varies from season to season and even from day to day, as the crop and weather cycle limits the time available for certain essential operations. In a relatively undeveloped economy, moreover, the nonagricultural sectors are too small to permit the temporary reallocation of labor to agriculture on a scale large enough to eliminate the periodic peaks in its marginal product; the variations in the flow of agricultural labor thus correspond to "slack" and "busy" periods in the economy as a whole, and "national income" is essentially constrained by the availability of effective labor at the busiest times of the agricultural production cycle.[13] Now the costs of negotiation may be incurred in the slack season, when time is cheap; the costs of supervision are instead necessarily incurred in rough proportion to the work being performed, that is, mostly when time is dear. A man-day spent haggling in the dead of winter thus had a far lower opportunity cost than a man-day spent supervising workers-with-a-tendency-to-shirk in those busy periods when time lost was output lost: hour for hour, negotiation costs would appear closer to negligible than equivalent to supervision costs.[14]

Neither would the negotiation necessary for a rental agreement have been the extremely time-consuming affair North and Thomas suggest, since the variability of output did *not* necessitate agreement as to acceptable substitutes for the stipulated consumption bundle at all. Even in the absence of any carryover from year to year, the periodicity of production guaranteed that current consumption would draw largely on accumulated stocks rather than current flows: once the harvest was in, a year's rent could be negotiated on the basis of a payments-fund that was known with virtual certainty.[15] In fact, average inventories appear to have been well above such inevitable minima, and credit was commonplace[16]; a rent could thus be fixed for years to come, to be paid largely out of future production, without for all that requiring the specification ex ante of acceptable substitutes in case the stipulated payment in kind could not be made out of the current harvest.

This recalls the further fact that negotiation costs are largely capital costs; and it is precisely because of this that on the appropriate per-period basis the time spent negotiating appears very slight indeed. Once a contract has been negotiated, any renegotiation need deal only with marginal changes to the current agreement; in a largely static system, the need even for marginal changes in the rental contract would be relatively infrequent, and normal renewal could be essentially automatic and virtually costless. Supervision costs, in contrast, are strictly current costs, that need to be incurred over and over again, year in and year out; the appropriate comparison is thus not directly between the negotiation costs of a rental contract and the supervision costs of a labor-sharing contract, but rather between the whole of the latter and the mere interest and amortization, as it were, on the former.

This capital-cost aspect of negotiation costs is in fact mentioned by North and Thomas, albeit only in a footnote explaining how the serfs' obligation "to provide certain minor amounts of goods in kind, firewood being an example"—the apparent exception, as it were, to the rule—also involved "the lowest transaction costs." The reason given is that "in the case of firewood, the consumption by the lord varied little from year to year. It was cheaper to negotiate once for a fixed amount and then to check the amount on delivery, than to fix a certain number of hours in a day for gathering firewood and then having to supervise each hour of labor" (p. 790 n). But doesn't this argument prove too much? If the lord's consumption of firewood varied little from year to year, his consumption of grain presumably varied even less: the former surely varied with the severity of the winter, the latter did not (or surely not as much). If wood is easy to check on delivery, grain is even easier: wood must be checked for quality as well as quantity (as fallen wood is easier to collect but harder to burn than dry standing deadwood); grain is much more nearly homogeneous. If an hour spent supervising the collection of wood is expensive, an hour spent supervising field-work is even more so: wood-gathering can take place when the opportunity cost of labor is relatively low; field-work, for the reasons noted, cannot. If the transaction cost of labor dues exceeded that of a rental contract in the case of firewood, then, it did so a fortiori in the case of the staple foodstuffs grown on the arable.

There is thus every reason to believe that labor dues did not minimize transaction costs even among forms of direct barter, and on both logical and empirical grounds it is difficult to accept the notion that these were in fact the only available arrangements in "the general absence of a market."

Granting for the sake of argument that markets and market-using arrangements were absent in fact, they would still appear to have been *possible:* for all its familiar, Pirennian flavor, the argument to the contrary advanced by North and Thomas is finally beside the point. In the prevailing anarchy, the high cost of travel and transportation may have interfered with exchanges *between* manors (or, better, villages or clusters of villages), but the issue here is that of the possibility of such exchange *within* these islands of order. North and Thomas make no attempt to explain why *external* trade should be considered necessary for *internal* trade, and the traditional argument of the history books—that with the decline of (interlocal) commerce cash became too scarce to support a full-fledged market ("money") economy—hardly remedies the omission. To an economist's mind institutions are the determinants, rather than the result, of the physical nature, quantity, and circulation of money, and on our usual definition of money as "the most saleable commodity" the notion that money disappeared from Western Europe is all but absurd. Even if "the" precious metals became too scarce to serve as money (perhaps by becoming so valuable that the typical transaction would involve an inconveniently small mass of metal), other commodities were there to take their place: less precious metals, ornaments, trinkets of magical or religious value, the staples of food or drink or widespread vices—all *can* serve, and indeed *have* served, as money.[17] Whether external commerce existed or not, then, *within* the village community a system of indirect barter—exchanging goods through a commodity that is in general, by definition, "money"—was as thoroughly feasible as direct barter, with payment "in kind."

Clearly, then, the "absence" of a market cannot be considered a given which determines the relative cost of various forms of economic coordination and exchange: it is rather the choice among the various possible forms of organization which determines whether or not particular markets exist.

Labor dues thus clearly reduce the need to exchange goods[18]; rents paying the lord something other than his preferred consumption bundle would by the same token "create the market," increasing goods-exchange and lowering its cost. In a proper analytical perspective, then, the transaction costs associated with "money" rents must be calculated on the basis of the inexpensive market exchange that would have obtained with such a system; and on that basis, North and Thomas agree, rents would in fact prove cheaper than labor dues. Since the historical cost of exchanging goods is thus only an upper bound to the relevant (counterfactual) magnitude, labor dues cannot be said to have minimized transaction costs whether markets actually "existed" or not.[19]

As an empirical matter, furthermore, money and markets do not appear to have been "absent" at all: in the *Capitulare de Villis*, for instance, exchange in foodstuffs markets appears to have been a routine event, in part from a preference for purchased seed.[20] Indeed, it now seems accepted that "demesne farming and independent cultivation with money rents exist side by side from Carolingian times on; rented land was already more extensive than demesne land in the Carolingian period . . . ."[21] If this utter revision of once prevalent views is in fact sound, the premise on which North and Thomas base their explanation of the "classic" manor is empirically untenable as well as analytically inappropriate.

In sum, it does not seem possible to justify labor dues as the contractual arrangement having the lowest transaction costs. The market for goods does not appear to have been as thin, or exchange as costly, as North and Thomas postulate; and in any case the feasibility of a system of indirect barter, with active exchange, cannot be ruled out a priori. Labor-sharing appears costlier even than rents in kind: the negotiation of the lord's "consumption bundle" could be relatively simple, avoiding contingent clauses; unlike the enforcement of the labor-dues contract, moreover, it did not have to be repeated in toto every year, and it could take place during the dead season, when workers had "free" time.

From the perspective of transaction costs, then, the superiority of rents over labor dues is clear, whether the lord was to be paid in goods or in money. The alleged superiority of rents in money over rents in kind is less certain: if the lord were to spend his money to purchase goods and services from his very tenants, and those purchases were forseeable even in detail, a single contract "in kind" could easily be preferred to a double contract in money.[22] Depending on the extent to which the underlying real exchange (or transfer, as argued in section II above) was bilateral rather than multilateral, and stable rather than unstable, a system which minimized transaction costs might thus utilize rents in kind rather than rents in money; but labor dues on the arable would not be part of such a system. In the early Middle Ages, as noted, rents in money or in goods were in fact so common that transaction costs may be taken to account for much, and perhaps most, of the prevailing manorial structure[23]; but the widespread preference for labor dues is to be explained, if it can be at all, in terms of some other impetus.[24]

IV

North and Thomas (pp. 791–799) also seek to explain the evolution of manorial agriculture according to the (English) chronology established by M. M. Postan.[25] Their attention is mostly devoted to the twelfth-century transition from labor dues to rents and to the thirteenth-century restoration of labor dues; the fourteenth-century return to rents, and even more the final disappearance of the manorial system, are altogether more briefly elucidated. These developments are claimed to have somehow minimized transaction costs, and are attributed to the action or interaction of population growth, inflation, and custom; from century to century, however, the details of the proposed explanations are quite different. I will consider each of these explanations in succession, with an eye, once again, to those features I find least plausible.

North and Thomas attributed the "classic" manorial system of labor dues to the absence of a goods market; the proposed explanation of the twelfth-century shift from labor dues to rents utilizes exactly the same transaction-costs model. In their words, "The development ... of a market for goods ... eventually eliminated the need to specify the consumption bundle if a contract were based on a fixed wage, a fixed rent, or a sharing of the output.... When this point was reached, the traditional labor-sharing arrangement no longer enjoyed a relative advantage in terms of transaction costs" (p. 793). The substance of this argument has already been examined, and I shall not review it here. Consider, rather, the variety of arrangements from place to place. With one exception, these differences are dismissed as unsystematic: "Precisely how the contractual form would change" in response to the growth of the market, we are told, "depended, among other things, upon current local customs. This accounts in part for the diversity of arrangements between manors found by historians" (p. 794). If diversity is explained by differences in custom rather than by differences in the local environment, the departures from the (efficient) norm are considered irrational, and custom is treated as an institutional obstacle to efficiency; in the strict language of economics or econometrics, this empirical variety is not "explained" at all.[26] The exception deals with the expansion of settlement: "The market for commodities was obviously more efficient in densely settled areas than on the frontier. Thus, it is not surprising to observe labor dues being implemented in newly-settled areas poorly serviced by the market, even while they were being modified or dying out in older settled areas. Within the context of our explanation, there is more reason to expect diversity than uniformity of economic organizations in the feudal world" (pp. 795-796). In fact, however, the frontier appears to have been *ab initio* a land of "freedom," of rents rather than labor dues;[27] and as Postan himself pointed out,[28] labor dues survived longest in the areas closest to the great markets of the age.

The more interesting novelty, at this juncture, is rather the rest of the proposed model, according to which the rise of a market economy was due to population growth (p. 794). As North and Thomas explain it, "these influences which . . . were radically to alter the manorial economy can be traced directly to changes in the level of the population of medieval Europe. From the tenth century onward . . . a growing population took up more land. . . . As migrants settled in geographic areas where different climate and resources were encountered, conditions were created that raised the gains from specialization and trade. . . . A powerful incentive in the form of increased gains was thus created to break down the previously iron barriers to trade. . . . The nobility were thus encouraged to found . . . market places and to join voluntarily with other lords to police these and surrounding areas. However, the protection of entire trade routes [was] beyond the realm of the local manor or a coalition of neighboring manors. [Thus] it now became essential to create or to strengthen larger political units. These regional or national states eventually came to hold jurisdiction over extensive areas. . . . Stemming initially from population growth and the resulting frontier movement, the increased potential for trade created the conditions for the establishment of local, then regional, and ultimately interregional markets for produced goods" (pp. 791-792). One might of course express dissatisfaction with the assumption that population growth was wholly exogenous, but even as far as it goes, the relation linking the rise of the market to population growth appears invalid.

In the first place, Europe's climate and resources vary more or less systematically right across the continent. The notion that opportunities for exchange were created by migration would thus be tenable only if people had spread out over Europe from a single relatively compact "older settled area." This is not implausible, of course—the shmoos spread out of Dogpatch in precisely this fashion—but if it ever happened this way in Europe it was not "from the tenth century onward" but millennia before then. Medieval trade did not follow hard upon the creation of comparative advantages: from the shores of the Channel to those of the Mediterranean the greatest of the medieval European trade routes linked areas of ancient and unbroken settlement.[29] Even apart from this, it is difficult to accept the notion that trade developed over progressively greater distances as the holders of political power recognized the opportunity for it and voluntarily coalesced into progressively larger political units to permit it. Long-distance trade in wool, wine, spices, metals, and salt, predicated precisely on major differences in climate or resource endowment, appears to have preceded rather than followed local trade between neighboring agricultural units. With the short-lived exception of the wine trade from Aquitaine to Britain, every major trade route crossed major political boundaries—and the *furiosa insania* of the Rhine trade[30] shows how difficult it was for neighboring lords to coalesce to reap the benefits of trade even where the benefits of coalescing were uniquely apparent and the boundaries to the coalition uniquely well-defined. Apart from the occasional marriage between a man and a woman who *both* ruled in their own right, the larger political units were in any case the product not of voluntary coalition but of conflict and dynastic accident—conquest, the gradual creation of the Crown's prerogatives, or the assimilation of a great fief[31]; and the example of France, first of the large Continental states yet not economically unified until the Revolution swept all before it, tells us how little the regional or national states were the creatures (or creators) of medieval trade.[32]

In interpreting the twelfth century, North and Thomas suggested that custom may have explained irrational deviations from the contractual norm; in interpreting the thirteenth, they would have custom explain the irrationality of the norm itself. The initially prevailing system of cash rents was optimal (at least, they aver, in the presence of a goods market), yet rents were abandoned in favor of labor dues. The reason, they tell us, is that "the thirteenth century witnessed a striking inflation; the price level in England ... tripled early in the century and ... climbed consistently thereafter.... Although ... a fixed crop rent ... would have dealt adequately with the problem of inflation, it would not only have proved costly or impossible to adopt within the traditional environment but would also have required costly periodic renegotiations to adapt to the changing land-labor ratio" as population continued to grow on the now scarce land. "Goaded by inflation, the lords increasingly chose to ... reclaim their leased demesne lands as they became available and to refuse to commute the labor dues needed to work them.... Since both actions were clearly within the lord's prerogatives, they did not run afoul of the customs of the manor and could be instituted with relatively low transaction costs.... The thirteenth-century adjustment of contractual arrangements between lord and tenant was, therefore, an efficient adaptation to the new economic situation subject to the constraints of the existing customs or institutional arrangements" (pp. 796–797). Efficiency subject to an institutional constraint is precisely what we call inefficiency *tout court;* according to the proposed interpretation, then, the (unlucky?) thirteenth was the first and only century, of those considered, to have embraced an irrational system on a large scale.[33]

Once again, however, the historical analysis scarcely seems acceptable. Custom, no doubt, served as "the fundamental institutional arrangement" of the time, but it did not limit choices to traditional rents or labor dues, and the record is replete with examples of alternative adaptations to rapidly changing circumstances, including specifically the periodic renegotiation of "precarious" rents.[34] At best, rather, custom guaranteed established rights,[35] without in any way proscribing mutually profitable contractual innovations. The lord might thus have had the option to be paid in money or in labor, and come to prefer the latter as inflation reduced the real value of the former; but if transaction costs had been the dominant consideration labor *services* (payments) would not have reappeared with labor *dues* (obligations), as both lord and peasant would have gained by a suitable contractual substitution.[36] This mutually beneficial exchange could take a variety of forms: the peasant might compensate the lord with an ad hoc payment added to the existing structure of financial obligations, much the way entry fines had been added in the preceding century[37]; or the rent might be renegotiated and fixed, whether in money or goods, at a suitably higher level.[38] Both parties would have gained by such a change, precisely as they did when labor dues were first commuted for cash[39]; and precisely because both gained, there was no need to invoke precedent to make the change legitimate and consonant with local custom.

The argument that labor services were preferable to rents because rents "would have required costly periodic renegotiations" to adapt to changing circumstances is equally difficult to accept. In the first place, changes in relative prices as in the price level do not by themselves create either the opportunity or the need for renegotiation: if the rent contract were agreed to once and forever, in perpetuity, relevant changes in circumstances would do no more than alter the distribution of real income in favor of one of the parties. The parties might of course *prefer* to agree to a short-term contract, to be renegotiated when it expires. They would do so if their expectations as to future developments differed appropriately in direction (so as to preclude agreement to a long-term contract) and sufficiently in magnitude (so as to warrant accepting the prospect of renegotiation). In the second place, periodic renegotiation would be justified in and by the very same circumstances whether the prospective payment were in output (crop rent) or input (labor dues): "the changing land-labor ratio" would have "required... renegotiations" in both cases, and this "requirement" is clearly not the deficiency of rents *as opposed to labor dues* that North and Thomas suggest it is. In point of fact, they tell us (p. 797), labor dues *were* renegotiated, and "in the process the extent of these burdens was generally increased to correspond to the reduced value of labor"[40]; but this tantamount concedes that labor dues were not inferior to rents, and that customary payments could be renegotiated.

North and Thomas also extend their analysis of the interaction of custom, inflation, and demographic change to explain the fourteenth-century return to rents and the eventual disappearance of the manorial system. "Early in the fourteenth century," we are told (pp. 798–799), "the ultimate consequences of centuries of population growth caught up with Western Europe.... The combined result of famine and pestilence was to drastically reduce the population, thus raising the land-labor ratio.... The lords initially attempted to force their surviving tenants to take up vacancies on the old customary terms ... [but] the competition between lords anxious to attract tenants ... defeated these attempts [and] led to the innovation of lengthy leases, ... under which labor obligations were combined with customary rents in one fixed rent contract. Inflations of the previous centuries had reduced substantially the real value of the nominal customary fixed rents, so they provided a close approximation to the current real value of rents and made mutual agreement easy. A life lease ... was the price lords were now willing to pay to obtain tenants.... But since recurrent plague did not allow the population to expand for several generations, these agreements themselves took on the force of custom and eventually the tenants obtained by customary practice the right of inheritance.... A secularly rising price level during the sixteenth century reduced this [rent] to a purely nominal payment by the year 1600. The manorial economy thus met its death ... ; land was now tilled by free tenants and/or by workers ... free to seek their best employment." Perhaps because they were intended as no more than a brief coda to the preceding elaboration, these arguments are not developed in detail, but they raise a number of fundamental questions, which deserve to be noted even at the risk of misinterpreting their thrust.

The fourteenth-century return to rents is once again ascribed to demographic developments, but these are no longer considered exogenous. The attribution of the fourteenth-century contraction to the preceding centuries' growth, however, is difficult to accept: North and Thomas make no attempt to justify it, and the traditional explanation by the exhaustion of the (marginal) soil[41] hardly accounts for large-scale decline. An agricultural economy, after all, lives not by drawing down a limited stock of previously accumulated resources, but by transforming an inexhaustible flow of new ones. No doubt, virgin land is supernormally fertile, and the frontier does benefit from an unrepeated decumulation of a finite resource, but the special fertility of the frontier is lost in a few years, and Europe's population had been growing—and the frontier moving—for centuries past, so that only a minuscule share of the population could have been subsisting on the frontier and off its non-recurring yield. Even if fourteenth-century Europe had run out of land, then, the resulting population decline would have been infinitesimal; if one can envision limits to growth set by land and technology, it is in terms of a stationary state that is approached through a broadly monotonic increase in population, and not through massive overshoot and collapse. Given the economy of the age, the logic of the resource-constraint model evokes Malthus and Ricardo, not the Club of Rome. It may explain the apparent leveling off of population in the late thirteenth century, perhaps even the incidence of famine in the early fourteenth—but it will not explain the tremendous mortality of the bubonic plague.[42] Indeed, the ensuing improvement in average living standards to apparently unprecedented levels, and the very scale on which land was abandoned, are compelling evidence that pestilence drove population far below what the land would otherwise have supported[43]; and pandemic plague can hardly be tied to the preceding population growth.[44]

North and Thomas appeal to "the competition between lords anxious to attract tenants" as the mechanism which raised the equilibrium real wage as population declined.[45] "Only an effective central coercive authority," they claim (p. 798), "could have prevented competition for the now very scarce labor"; in fact, if the great mortality of the fourteenth century redounded to the benefit of the poor,[46] it was no doubt thanks rather to the growing strength of a sovereign state jealous of its power than to its enduring weakness. The state admittedly, and without success, lent its influence to the status quo and tried by legislative fiat to keep wages from rising; but at the same time, by protecting the weak from private violence, it obliged the lords to recruit a labor force with positive inducements in lieu of the threats and coercion they could and did resort to a few centuries earlier. In the wake of the Conquest, the Crown may have returned runaway serfs, and helped the lords control the newly subjected population[47]; but later the Crown seems to have protected the runaway rather than the lord, allowing the latter only four days to repossess his serf without going through the courts which "were not very eager to further his interests and the perpetuation of villeinage."[48] In view of such evidence, then, even the failure of the state to control wages in the landowners' interests cannot strictly be considered evidence of administrative weakness rather than ill will.

In the wake of the rise in the equilibrium wage-rent ratio, North and Thomas claim, agreement to a rent was particularly easy since the centuries-old, depreciated "nominal customary fixed rents" were again close to equilibrium prices. Here too, then, they choose to focus on the transaction costs of altering the contractual arrangement in the presence of customary constraints.[49] But the change in the land-labor ratio was not quite a one-shot, overnight affairs; adaptation to *gradual* change would no doubt have been more easily achieved simply by adjusting the burden of labor dues, following the more recent precedent, than by altering the very form of the contractual arrangement. In fact, of course, the contractual alteration was not at all constrained by established precedent[50]: so little was it a revival of the customary tenure *ad censum* that the latter also, like the contracts *ad opera*, was displaced on a large scale by the new *arentata*.[51] What is less clear is that these contracts introduced "the innovation of lengthy leases," particularly as "the price lords were now willing to pay." Neither lessor nor lessee has, as such, a vested interest in either short or long agreements; on the argument sketched above, rather, the term of the contract depends in the first instance on the structure of expectations. There is thus reason to believe that leases were shortened, not lengthened, in the wake of the plague, as the situation it created was not expected to last, and a term contract was the simplest way to adapt to a complex pattern of expectations; and the evidence appears to support this interpretation. Postan, for instance, contrasts the new term leases to the earlier perpetual tenures, emphasizing "their short span—as a rule one life only"[52]; and the Ramsey records indicate that long leases were used only "sparingly" right after the Black Death, but "more frequently and universally" two decades later, when the new situation had presumably been recognized as stable.[53]

The proposed explanation of later developments is also perplexing. The major difficulties are empirical[54]: it is hard to accept the notion that after the Black Death rents remained constant to the point of becoming customary and inalterable. Most observers, rather, refer to a progressive decline in rents right through the fifteenth century.[55] Again, heritability in England appears to have waned just when North and Thomas would have it wax: "In the fourteenth and fifteenth centuries they [the English manorial judges] became more and more reluctant to recognize the heritability of villein tenure. ... There was one brief period, towards the end of the fifteenth century, when the king's judges at last ... started to intervene in manorial affairs. ... In most cases [however] the change to non-permanent tenures was already complete, and where this was so the judges had to admit it as accepted custom."[56] Finally, and perhaps principally, the transition to a world of *free* tenants and wage-workers involves changes in status as well as, or rather than, the changes in agricultural organization with which North and Thomas are here exclusively concerned. The issue is not (just) the repurchase of labor dues, but the purchase of freedom itself, and the liberation of the peasant from what they call "the public goods" of lordly protection and manorial justice. It is, if one will, the transformation of "feudalism" rather than of "manorialism" as such—and the merging of these two concepts[57] is here critically misleading. For all these reasons, then, the epilog to the proposed explanation of the manorial system is as little satisfying as that explanation itself.

V

The theoretical model proposed by North and Thomas is thus open to criticism on a number of points. Their view of feudalism as a strictly voluntaristic system whereby the peasants obtained public goods seems empirically untenable, given the nature of the services actually provided by the lord, and the narrowness of the alternatives among which the peasants could choose. The argument that the "classic" manorial arrangement of labor services minimized transaction costs also seems erroneous, since North and Thomas appear to misspecify the feasible alternatives (which in fact included indirect barter and market exchange) and misrank the alternatives they consider (as even rents in kind appear superior to labor dues). Their account of later developments is equally unsatisfactory, since it draws on a dubious interpretation of demographic and political history, and appeals to institutional constraints to an extent that is both empirically unjustified and analytically alarming.

But one must also recall their ambitious attempt to encompass centuries of change in a unified explanation, the pioneering application of transaction-cost analysis to economic history, and the proper formulation of the problem of efficiency with respect to labor obligations. All these remain, and will continue to claim both our gratitude and our admiration.

Notes

For their helpful criticism of a long earlier paper from which this one is drawn, I wish to thank my students, the Columbia University Seminar in Economic History, and the University of Chicago Economic History Workshop, Hugh Aitken, Howell Chickering, Jonathan Hughes, Arcadius Kahan, Charles Kindleberger, John Lambelet, Donald McCloskey, Walter Nicholson, John Pettengill, Nathan Rosenberg, Sylvia Thrupp, Frank Westhoff, and, very particularly, Frederic Cheyette, on whose expertise I have repeatedly drawn. Errors, of course, are mine alone.

1. Douglass North and Robert Thomas, "The Rise and Fall of the Manorial System: A Theoretical Model," JOURNAL OF ECONOMIC HISTORY, XXXI (December 1971), 777–803.
2. The nature of feudalism is discussed on pp. 778–783, but the a priori argument appears most explicitly somewhat later, at the point of transition to the transaction-cost argument for labor dues. The argument that "the lord was necessary to the peasant"—as protector ("against raiders, or against thieves") of the growing crops—may also be found in John R. Hicks, *A Theory of Economic History* (London: Oxford University Press, 1969), p. 102.
3. Note that the criterion of "exploitation" is here the difference between the actual welfare of the serfs and their hypothetical welfare as free peasants (on *all* the land of the village, demesne included). I shall also use the term in this sense, which is closer to common usage than the less interesting neoclassical definition (to which North and Thomas occasionally revert, e.g., p. 788 n).
4. See most recently M. M. Postan, *The Medieval Economy and Society* (London: Weidenfeld and Nicolson, 1972), p. 111 ff. None of this is new, of course: see for instance F. W. Maitland, *Domesday Book and Beyond* (Cambridge: Cambridge University Preses, 1897), pp. 114, 129 ff.; also R. H. Hilton, *A Medieval Society* (London: Weidenfeld and Nicolson, 1966), p. 143.
5. Nor, a fortiori, the growing crops; see note 2 above.
6. Postan, *Medieval Economy*, p. 111 ff.; Maitland, *Domesday Book*, pp. 80 ff., 258 ff., and esp. pp. 101–102.
7. Unless the peasants are protected by their very poverty: the freedom of mountain peasants may thus be as readily explained by the lack of expropriable surplus as by the inaccessibility of their crops. Contrast Hicks, *Theory*, pp. 102–103.
8. Thus Alexander Gerschenkron in "Mercator Gloriosus," a review of Hicks, in *Economic History Review*, XXIV (1971), 655. See also for instance M. Bloch, *Feudal Society* (Chicago: University of Chicago Press, 1961), esp. ch. XVIII. Documented cases of seigneurial gangsterism as late as the early fourteenth century are reported by Hilton in *A Medieval Society*, pp. 42, 223.
9. I am ignoring here the need for supervision to ensure that the owner's capital is adequately maintained; this enforcement cost is common to all contracts, and is in fact minimal in very long-term rental arrangements. Note that the present

issue of rents *versus* labor dues concerns the organization of labor and production within the manor: whether production should be carried out exclusively in petty tenancies, or in demesne farms as well; whether the surplus should be appropriated in goods or in labor; whether labor should be "independent" or "dependent." It must not be confused with the quite separate issue of rents ("farms") *versus* direct exploitation of entire manors, which does not concern workers' incentives at all.

10 Both of these devices illustrate the partial substitutability of negotiation and enforcement costs. The detailed specification of the worker's obligations makes enforcement easier, as their effective content is no longer disputable; but it does so at the cost of added negotiation costs due to the greatly increased complexity of the share contract. The threat of punishment operated in the opposite direction: rather than dismissing the lazy worker, and then renegotiating his payment (perhaps increasing the extent of his labor obligations to reflect his lower productivity), it was simpler to retain the contract and adjust (judicially) ex post.

11 The root problem is thus that of internalizing, for the individual worker, penalties and rewards that would otherwise be largely external. Even collective responsibility, though it might allow a somewhat greater scope for peer pressure and "moral incentives," in the main simply transfers (without eliminating, and perhaps without "shifting") the burden of enforcement. The experience of contemporary Socialist systems provides a rich body of evidence on the stubbornness of these problems.

12 The statement that labor dues are the contractual form with the *highest* enforcement costs (North and Thomas, p. 790) does not appear warranted, however, as in a wage system the production of *all* income is heir to the internalization problems labor-sharing encounters in the production of the surplus alone. (The term of the contract is not at issue, as all contractual forms admit of short and long terms, dismissal for cause, etc.)

13 See W. Kula, *Théorie économique du système féodal* (Paris: Mouton, 1970), p. 53. Data on the temporal distribution of work in a system of traditional (two-or three-course, naked fallow) agriculture may be found in A. V. Chayanov, *The Theory of Peasant Economy* (Homewood: Irwin, 1966), esp. pp. 74 ff., 107 ff.

14 The argument is not that leisure has a lower marginal utility than labor; it is, rather, that while these two marginal utilities are indeed equalized at any point in time (excluding "corner solutions"), they need not be constant *over* time, since we cannot transfer days from one season to another.

15 The financial year of manorial accounts and agreements thus began at Michaelmas, close after the harvest; see for instance J. Z. Titow, *English Rural Society, 1200–1350* (London: George Allen and Nnwin, 1969), p. 27 ff.

16 See my "Risk, Transaction Costs, and the Organization of Medieval Agriculture" (forthcoming).

17 In point of fact, standard coins are a comparative novelty, and it takes no little expertise to measure the metal content of a coin whose weight and fineness are uncertain. In the agricultural society of early medieval Europe such perfectly familiar, widely used, relatively homogeneous, and readily divisible commodities as grain or salt might well have been more saleable than gold or silver (even though the latter would of course have remained better stores of value, particularly with burial as the common form of safe-keeping). One thus finds in R. A. L. Smith, *Canterbury Cathedral Priory* (Cambridge: Cambridge University Press, 1943), p. 143, a tantalizing reference to a "very ancient wheat market": but to what extent was wheat at first the commodity rather than the means of exchange? Much more

indirect barter may thus have taken place than has been recognized by modern observers in whose experience money is only paper or metal, and households acquire (other) goods only to consume them themselves; see however that traced by Eli F. Heckscher, *An Economic History of Sweden* (Cambridge: Harvard University Press, 1963), p. 33 ff.

18 To the extent that expectations are not realized, *all* contractual arrangements, labor dues included, could witness the opportunity for mutually beneficial exchange after the harvest had been brought in; but this is here of secondary importance.

19 The position of the lord—party to every labor-sharing or rental contract, and empowered not only to create markets but to compel their use—suggests that the manor would not be locked into systems in kind even if markets were "absent" and a quantum change was necessary to reach the superior solution represented by (widespread) indirect barter.

20 See G. Duby, *Rural Economy and Country Life in the Medieval West* (Columbia: University of South Carolina Press, 1968), pp. 25–27, 44–46, 361 ff.; note that seed may have represented over half of total output. Even if markets were thin, moreover, moral incentives could substitute for market opportunities as a means of reducing "haggling" and transaction costs, as the imperative of custom facilitated agreement at the customary, "just" price. This argument applies to contingent contracts as well: one wonders, in fact, whether relative "just" prices corresponded to *expected* marginal rates of transformation.

21 Thus E. R. Wolf on A. Dopsch, in "The Inheritance of Land among Bavarian and Tyrolese Peasants," *Anthropologica* (1970), 106.

22 Rents in kind were thus widespread throughout the Middle Ages; not surprisingly, they appear to have been most durable where life was most carefully ordered —on the monastic estates. See Duby, *Rural Economy*, pp. 178 ff., 376 ff.; P. Vinogradoff, *English Society in the Eleventh Century* (Oxford: Clarendon Press, 1908), pp. 327 ff., 384 ff.; J. A. Raftis, *The Estates of Ramsey Abbey* (Toronto: Pontifical Institute of Medieval Studies, Studies and Texts, 3, 1957), pp. 10 ff., 61 ff.; P. D. A. Harvey, *A Medieval Oxfordshire Village: Cuxham, 1240 to 1400* (Oxford: Oxford University Press, 1965), p. 119. Nowadays also universities, for instance, do not pay their faculty entirely in money, and then sell them library privileges and office space; part of the faculty's services are bartered directly, "in kind," for an assortment of perks. Some of these (e.g., access to athletic facilities) are of course so obtained as a means of reducing income tax payments, but payments for office space, library privileges, and the like would represent tax-deductible expenses.

23 Transaction costs also appear to account for the scattering of peasants' plots; see my "Risk, Transaction Costs."

24 North and Thomas themselves suggest a possible candidate, as they claim for labor-sharing "the possible advantage of spreading the risk between parties according to their relative shares" (p. 789, and see p. 784); the validity of this argument is examined in my "Risk, Transaction Costs." I find it more plausible to argue that labor dues were valued as a means of exercising authority over the labor force for the sake of implementing a superior technique, or of reinforcing social roles. See my "Authority, Efficiency, and Agricultural Organization in Medieval England and Beyond: A Hypothesis" (forthcoming).

25 M. M. Postan, "The Chronology of Labour Services," *Transactions of the Royal Historical Society*, XX (1937), 169–193; see North and Thomas, p. 782 n.

26 In fact, it is difficult to believe that the interaction of lord and peasant did not eliminate inefficiency, and thus that local variations were in fact random; see my "Authority, Efficiency."

27 Thus for instance Duby, *Rural Economy*, pp. 113–114; the freedom of the frontier is there taken to explain the decline of labor dues in the older settled areas as well.
28 Postan, "Chronology," p. 171; see also pp. 192–193.
29 The Eastern half of the Hanseatic trade route might be considered an exception; but even the German migration to the East appears to have done little more than displace an alternative ethnic group—and what difference would it have made if the Baltic trade had been rather less intra-German and more international than it actually was? As North and Thomas suggested earlier (p. 782), of course, the relative lack of trade appears best attributed not to a lack of possible gains from it (assuming free transport) but to the high cost of transporting goods in the troubled anarchy most of Europe had lapsed into.
30 See for instance, Eli F. Heckscher, *Mercantilism*, 2d ed. (New York: Macmillan, 1955), I, p. 56. In the absence of a coalition, of course, such behavior may have been perfectly rational from the perspective of the individuals concerned. A Cournot solution in which each takes the tolls set by the others as given, for instance, is analogous to the usual oligopoly case, but with the axes reversed—i.e., assuming a linear "demand" (surplus) curve, and taking n as the number of "firms" (lords levying a toll), the *volume* of trade will tend to $1/(n + 1)$ of the volume unrestricted by tolls, and the total toll to $n/(n + 1)$ of the toll that would just eliminate trade; with "free entry," trade would virtually disappear as n grew.
31 See for instance, Bloch, *Feudal Society*, p. 422 ff. The term "accident" is used advisedly: at the level of the sovereign state, only small numbers of individuals are involved, and the corresponding analysis cannot draw on the statistical predictability of mass behavior.
32 See for instance Heckscher, *Mercantilism*, I, p. 78 ff.
33 "When the fundamental institutional arrangements are not those of private property rights, the possible new contractual responses to changing parameters may not be 'ideal': that is, a more efficient contractual arrangement could be envisioned by an economist, given the existence of private property. The response of the manorial economy to the inflation of the thirteenth century is an example" (North and Thomas, p. 799).
34 Thus, by mid-century, some of Ely's villein land was "held 'de anno in annum ad voluntatem domini' for money rents": see E. Miller, *The Abbey and Bishopric of Ely* (Cambridge: Cambridge University Press, 1951), pp. 109–110, also pp. 107–108, 136.
35 And often it did not even do that: see for instance M. Bloch, *French Rural History* (Berkeley: University of California Press, 1966), p. 70. As to the thirteenth century in particular, Postan, "Chronology," p. 192, roundly contradicts the claim (North and Thomas, p. 797) that the lord could not violate existing agreements.
36 In abstract terms, the lord had his choice of two endowment points in money-labor space, one point defining a bundle (mostly) of labor and the other a bundle (mostly) of money. The prevailing wage (explicit, or implicit in marginal productivity and goods prices) would expand each point into a line of a given slope; normally, one endowment point would wholly dominate the other, the money-basket being preferable at low money wages, the labor-basket at high ones. Inflation could thus redefine the obligations (the endowment) the lord chose to claim; but what needs to be explained is the shift in the composition not of the endowment point but of the preferred "consumption" basket, i.e. of the observed equilibrium. Of the commutability of those labor services for (increased) rents there can be no doubt: see Miller, *Ely*, p. 102; also Postan in the *Cambridge Economic History of Europe*, vol. I, 2d ed. (Cambridge: Cambridge University Press, 1966), pp. 606–607.

37 North and Thomas, p. 795; also Postan, *Cambridge Economic History*, p. 611.
38 See for instance Miller, *Ely*, p. 110.
39 The obvious difficulty with the proposed interpretation is of course that the very institutional conditions which supposedly explained the return to labor dues would never have allowed their abandonment in the first place. North and Thomas appear to finesse this problem by changing perspective in mid-argument: the successive systems *before* the thirteenth century had been analyzed with an eye to the transaction costs associated with the system itself, in a static context, rather than with the introduction of a new system as circumstances changed over time. While the latter approach is in some sense more sophisticated, it is not superior if the objective is to explain not short-run disequilibria but the system's long-term evolution.
40 This involved "reimposing, in specified detail, the labor obligations which formerly were unspecified." The impact of such specification on the structure of transaction costs has been discussed above; see also North and Thomas, p. 790.
41 See for instance Postan, *Cambridge Economic History*, pp. 556–559, and B. H. Slicher van Bath, *The Agrarian History of Western Europe A.D. 500–1850* (London: Arnold, 1963), p. 89.
42 This is not to deny that pestilence thrived in famine's wake; see for instance Slicher van Bath, ibid., p. 89, and E. Le Roy Ladurie, *Les paysans de Languedoc* (Paris: S.E.V.P.E.N., 1966), pp. 141, 325, and 423–424. The point to note, however, is the much higher mortality for *given* levels of population and malnutrition from the mid-fourteenth century.
43 See for instance Postan's analysis of "The Fifteenth Century," *Economic History Review*, IX (1939), 160–167; Le Roy Ladurie, *Les paysans*, p. 179 ff.; Slicher van Bath, *Agrarian History*, p. 163 ff.; and L. Génicot in the *Cambridge Economic History of Europe*, vol. I, 2d ed. (1966), pp. 661–664.
44 See John Saltmarsh, "Plague and Economic Decline in England in the Later Middle Ages," *Cambridge Historical Journal*, VII (1941), 23–41. J. F. D. Shrewsbury has recently argued that diseases *other* than bubonic plague were responsible for most of the epidemics of the later Middle Ages; see *A History of Bubonic Plague in the British Isles* (Cambridge: Cambridge University Press, 1970), esp. ch. 5. What matters here, however, is not the exact identity of the illnesses but their unusual virulence at that time.
45 This fact is further evidence against the proposed model of political innovation. Trade arose, we were told, when the lords coalesced in response to the opportunity to enrich themselves by doing so; but they failed to coalesce as buyers of labor even though the *damnum emergens* as they bid wages up was surely far easier to perceive than the *lucrum cessans* from not allowing trade to begin at all. In point of fact, as noted above, the modern Western state was not the product of a coalition at all, let alone a coalition of the aristocracy.
46 Assuming, of course, that the rise in real wages was not more than offset by the increased uncertainty that one would live to enjoy it . . .
47 See for instance Bloch, *Feudal Society*, p. 271; contrast North and Thomas, e.g., p. 779.
48 H. Nabholz in the *Cambridge Economic History of Europe*, vol. I (Cambridge: Cambridge University Press, 1941), p. 511.
49 See above, n. 39.
50 North and Thomas concede as much, again undermining their own argument, with the statement that the customary rents were combined with labor obligations in one (new, surely) fixed rent contract, which moreover introduced lengthy leases (about which more forthwith).

51 Raftis, *Ramsey Abbey*, p. 251.
52 Postan, *Cambridge Economic History*, p. 616.
53 Raftis, *Ramsey Abbey*, pp. 259–260.
54 There is also a problem of internal consistency: why should the inflation of the sixteenth century have spelled the death of the manorial economy, if that of the thirteenth century had instead revived it in its "classic" form?
55 See for instance Nabholz, *Cambridge Economic History*, p. 519; Postan, *Cambridge Economic History*, p. 596; Raftis, *Ramsey Abbey*, p. 288. Where the rents *did* remain constant over the fifteenth century and became "customary," moreover, they were increased (through the medium of entry fines) early in the sixteenth century; see A. J. Pollard, "Estate Management in the Later Middle Ages: The Talbots and Whitchurch, 1383–1525," *Economic History Review*, XXV (1972), 558.
56 Bloch, *French Rural History*, pp. 127–128. On heritability as the norm in earlier centuries, see Titow, *English Rural Society*, p. 18 n.
57 See North and Thomas, p. 781 n. Bloch, for instance, argues instead that "the manor in itself has no claim to a place among the institutions which we call feudal" (*Feudal Society*, p. 279), and treats the decline of "manorialism" and of "feudalism" as quite separate in time as well as in identity (*French Rural History*, pp. 77 ff., 102 ff.). See also Pollard, "Estate Management," 558–559. On a broader scale, it is of course the changing relation between the lords and the increasingly powerful state (rather than that between the lords and the peasants) which is crucial to the change in the "fundamental institutional arrangement" and "the rise of the Western World."

Part 6

FREE TRADE, MERCANTILISM, AND IMPERIALISM

39

MANPOWER AND THE FALL OF ROME

M. I. Finley

Source: M. I. Finley, *Aspects of Antiquity*, Penguin, 1960, pp. 153–61.

The second half of the fourth century was not one of the more creative periods in western history, at least not outside the Church. One would be hard put to think of a dozen names which merit our attention, and the man who interests me here has no name known to us at all. He addressed a pamphlet to an emperor, probably Valentinian I, in which he put forward proposals for army reform and a number of ingenious, though perhaps not very practical, military inventions. In explaining his motives, which he did at some length and with much carefully self-protective language, he delivered a detailed and slashing attack on the costs of the almost perpetual warfare of his time, on the oppressive taxation and the corrupt and extortionate provincial administration of the empire.

One did not lightly criticize in that way in the fourth century; no wonder our man remained anonymous. There is no way of knowing whether the emperor ever received the document, but we need have no hesitation in asserting that the pamphlet, which was probably written shortly before the shameful disaster at Adrianople at the hands of the Goths in 378, had not the slightest effect on imperial behaviour or thinking.

Yet the pamphlet survived somehow in manuscript, under the title of *De rebus bellicis* ('On Military Affairs'). It was first printed in a book, with illustrations of the inventions, in Basle in 1552 and it was reprinted at least five times in the next two hundred years.* It was read by humanists and others, who were fascinated by the machines, and by occasional writers on military history. It could have been read by Gibbon, who is known to have possessed two copies and who went through masses of rare and abstruse Latin and Greek texts in preparation for writing his *Decline and Fall of the Roman Empire*. But Gibbon did not read it so far as I can tell, and that is a fact of some significance. To be sure, by Gibbon's time interest in Anonymous's inventions had disappeared and there were better and fuller sources of information about imperial corruption and extortion. However, Anonymous also threw out strong hints about one factor which has impressed some modern students, and that is what we should call manpower shortage. The saving of manpower was one of his strong and explicit arguments in favour of his schemes, and this aspect of the later Roman Empire needs to be looked at with some care.

At its greatest extent, at the accession of Hadrian in 117, the territory of the Roman Empire embraced something like 2,000,000 square miles. If we deduct some very temporary acquisitions we get a more meaningful total of about 1,600,000 square miles. Such a figure may no longer leave us gasping by comparison, say, with the United States or the Soviet Union, but it was still impressive enough. The empire extended from the Euphrates river in Iraq all the way to the Atlantic, the whole of North Africa, Europe below the Rhine-Danube line (and a bit above), and most of Britain along the way. When the empire was functioning properly, furthermore, it was a unified state in fact and not just in name (unlike the Holy Roman Empire of mediaeval and early modern times). It included a large enough number of people, too, but there the figure bears no modern comparison. Actually we do not know the number, nor did any contemporary, not even the emperor himself or his bureau heads. That need not cause any surprise. Modern habits of counting and recording everybody and everything had not yet become sufficiently widespread or necessary (though they were not unknown). A fair guess would be that at its maximum, in the first two centuries of our era, the total population was something like 60,000,000, and that meant everybody—men, women and children, free men and slaves.

The precise numbers do not matter so much when they reach that level. What matters are trends and distribution. How was the population moving in the course of the history of the empire: up or down, or not at all? And how was the population distributed among the social classes and the necessary (or unnecessary) employments? In particular, what proportion was in the army, which was now a wholly professional body, and was that enough?

In the heyday of the empire, say from Augustus to Marcus Aurelius, the army was a fairly modest one of about 300,000 men. Gibbon noticed that this figure was equalled by Louis XIV, "whose kingdom", as he said, "was confined within a single province of the Roman Empire". But the army was sufficient for its purposes; it kept the peace within the empire; it could cope with rebellions, such as the Jewish revolt of 66–70, though that might require time; it protected the frontiers; it was even able to make a few further conquests, including Britain. Then one day it became inadequate, too small in number and sometimes unreliable in performance. The turning point was the reign of Marcus Aurelius (who died in the year 180). The Germanic tribes in central Europe, which had been fitfully troublesome for several centuries, now began a new and much heavier pressure on the frontiers which never stopped until the western empire finally came to an end as a political organism.

We must be careful here not to make too much use of our hindsight. Yet surely there were few Roman leaders, whether emperors or senators or field commanders, so stupid that they did not realize the enormity of Rome's difficulties and the need for effort on a greater scale than had been required before. They did make efforts, and they failed. It is astonishing that they did not fail earlier. In the third century the armies were busier with civil war and politics than with the frontier menace, as they had been once before after the assassination of Nero. For fifty years emperors and claimants to the throne came and went in an endless succession. Then Diocletian restored order, reorganized the administration and the defences, and doubled the army strength, at least on paper. And still the Germans came and the losing struggle against them went on, while civil wars and general disorganization kept recurring.

There was the open symptom of the coming fall of Rome. And this is how Gibbon saw it:

> The timid and luxurious inhabitants of a declining empire must be allured into the service by the hopes of profit, or compelled by the dread of punishment.... Such was the horror for the profession of a soldier, which had affected the minds of the degenerate Romans, that many of the youth ... chose to cut off the fingers of their right hand to escape from being pressed into service.

Note the language carefully: "timid and luxurious", "declining empire", "degenerate Romans". Even if one were to accept the characterization—and I am not concerned to argue that now—it does not explain. One would still have to give reasons why the Romans had become "timid" and "degenerate", if that is what they now were. Professor A. H. M. Jones does not use language of that kind in his great three-volume work on the later Roman Emperor. That is not simply because he has a different set of values from Gibbon's, but because historians now put different questions to the past, and therefore come out with a different picture. Jones's *Later Roman Empire* covers the same ground as the first half of Gibbon's *Decline and Fall*. The chief actors are the same; so are the dates and the battles and the defeats. But the history somehow is not the same in the end; the focus has been changed, as is clear on this question of manpower.

The paper strength of the army after Diocletian was about 600,000, a very small figure by contrast with the armies which a modern state with the same total population can muster in wartime. Why, then, were Diocletian and his successors unable to put even their full paper strength into the field against the barbarians, let alone increase the levies? Certainly the stakes were high, the emergency critical. Patriotism in the Roman Empire may have been lukewarm at best: the ordinary man, regardless of class, felt no personal obligation to fight to defend it. That is true, but it is equally true that they wanted even less to have the empire ripped apart by invading Germans. The Roman Empire, despite all its troubles, its burdensome taxation and terrible poverty, its bitter conflicts between Christians and pagans and then among the orthodox Christians and the heretics, was nevertheless an integral part of the order of things, central and eternal. When a Visigothic army led by its king Alaric captured the city of Rome in the summer of 410, St Jerome, then living in Bethlehem, added these words to the preface of the *Commentaries on Ezekiel* he was writing: "... the brightest light of the whole world was extinguished ... the Roman Empire was deprived of its head ..., to speak more correctly, the whole world perished in one city ...."

One reason for the astonishment was that Roman armies still fought well most of the time. In any straight fight they could, and they usually did, defeat superior numbers of Germans, because they were better trained, better equipped, better led. What they could not do was cope indefinitely with this kind of enemy. They were not warring with a neighbouring state like themselves, but with migratory tribes who wanted to loot or to settle in the richer world of the empire. As early as the reign of Marcus Aurelius groups of Germans were allowed to settle on the land and to join the Roman army themselves. That did not work either, though the attempt was repeated many times, partly because they would not be Romanized but chiefly because it simply encouraged more Germans on the outside to demand the same. It was physically impossible for 600,000 men to protect a frontier that ran from the mouth of the Rhine to the Black Sea and then on to the borders of the Persian kingdom in the east.

More men seemed the obvious answer—or a technological revolution, and that raises the critical point. It was in a sense misleading when I noted that we throw a far greater proportion of our manpower into battle in an emergency. When we do that, our whole civilian life is at once readjusted, not merely by austerity programmes and general belt-tightening, but also by increasing the *per capita* production of those (including women) who remain on the farms and in the factories. And that no ancient people could do because their technology was too primitive, resting almost entirely on the muscles of men and beasts; and because most of the population, the free as well as the half-free *coloni* and the slaves, had nothing to sacrifice to an austerity programme to begin with. Furthermore, the modern comparison fails for still another reason. Contemporary states have been able to make these extraordinary efforts for a limited time, on the assumption that the war will end soon enough. But this was not the Roman problem. They were not engaged in a war in that sense but were undergoing a persistent hammering, and it is pointless to talk about tightening the belt and working overtime seven days a week for a period of 200 years.

The Roman position can be presented in a simple model. With the stabilization of the empire and the establishment of the *pax Romana* under Augustus, a sort of social equilibrium was created. Most of the population, free or unfree, produced just enough for themselves to exist on, at a minimum standard of living, and enough to maintain a very rich and high-living aristocracy and urban upper class, the court with its palace and administrative staffs, and the modest army of some 300,000. Any change in any of the elements making up the equilibrium—for example, an increase in the army or other non-producing sectors of the population, or an increase in the bite taken out of the producers through increased rents and taxes—had to be balanced elsewhere if the equilibrium were to be maintained. Otherwise something was bound to break. Stated the other way round, if the boundaries of the Roman Empire had been at the ends of the earth, so that there were no frontiers to defend, and if the court and the aristocracy had been content to keep its numbers and its level of consumption unchanged, then there was no obvious reason why the Roman Empire should not have gone on indefinitely.

But of course none of the 'ifs' happened. The parasitic classes (and I use the word in its strictly economic sense with no moral judgments implied) kept growing larger, with the triumph of Christianity an important contributing factor after Constantine. So did the pressures on the frontier. A larger military establishment and more frequent battles in turn meant greater demands on the peasantry who made up the bulk of the population in this fundamentally agrarian world. With their primitive technology, there came a time when they could no longer respond, whatever their will may have been in the matter.

As the final insult in this tale of frustration, the population was apparently not even able to reproduce itself any longer. This is a difficult subject because we lack figures. Yet there are signs of some decline in the total population, at least from the time of Marcus Aurelius, the reign we keep returning to as the pivot. The surest sign is the increasing frequency of abandoned farmland, in Italy, North Africa, and elsewhere. In an age without technological advances, occupation of the soil is a gauge of the movement of population. When the population is going up, marginal lands have to be brought into cultivation, and then they are abandoned when the curve goes down. The documents of the period make it clear that manpower shortage was a problem, and a recognized problem, particularly in agriculture. The efforts of landed magnates to keep their peasants out of the army played a greater part in the military manpower difficulties than the occasional young man who chopped off his fingers. And the peasants, in their turn, showed a tendency to flee from the land into the cities or to become outlaws.

Decline in the birth-rate is a mysterious business. I know no satisfactory explanation for it in the Roman Empire. Some historians have tried to blame it on the low life-expectancy of the time, but an equally low life-expectancy was the rule everywhere until the nineteenth century, and still is in large parts of Asia, and we all know about the explosions in their population. I find the same difficulty with Professor Jones's suggestion that the peasantry had become too poor and too starved to rear children. I doubt if they were hungrier than the peasants of modern India or Egypt; and the upper classes, who ate far too much for their own good, did not seem to be breeding at a satisfactory rate either.

Whatever the explanation, the word 'depopulation' is too strong. It overstates the situation. Manpower shortage is a relative term. All resources —and manpower is another resource—are, or are not, sufficient not by some absolute measuring-stick but according to the demands made on them and the conditions of their employment. In the later Roman Empire manpower was part of an interrelated complex of social conditions, which, together with the barbarian invasions, brought an end to the empire in the west. The army could not be enlarged because the land could not stand further depletion of manpower; the situation on the land had deteriorated because taxes were too high; taxes were too high because the military demands were increasing; and for that the German pressures were mainly responsible. A vicious circle of evils was in full swing. Break into it at any point: the final answer will be the same provided one keeps all the factors in sight all the time.

I concede that this is neither a dramatic nor a romantic way to look at one of the great cataclysms of history. One could not make a film out of it. But it provides the necessary underpinning for the military and constitutional history and the magnificent moralizing of Gibbon. The Roman Empire was people and institutions, not just emperors, degenerate or otherwise. And it was the inflexible institutional underpinning, in the end, which failed: it could not support the perpetual strains of an empire of such magnitude within a hostile world.

Note

* Most recently by E. A. Thompson in *A Roman Reformer and Inventor* (1952).

40

ELI HECKSCHER AND THE IDEA OF MERCANTILISM

D. C. Coleman

Source: *Scandinavian Economic History Review* 5(1), 1957: 3–25.

It is more than a quarter of a century since the late Professor Eli Heckscher's *Mercantilism* first appeared, in Swedish (1931), and nearly as long since it became available in German (1932) and in English (1935). The recent publication of a revised English edition[1] offers an opportunity for a reappraisal both of the work and of the concept with which it is concerned. The latter has loomed large in the writing of economic history and in the study of economic thought. What is its value? What did it become in Heckscher's hands?

I

Adam Smith saw political economy as having two distinct objects: to provide revenue or subsistence for the people or to enable them to provide these for themselves; and to supply the state with revenue for the public services. There were two different systems by which these ends were achieved: the commercial or mercantile system and the system of agriculture. The former was 'the modern system'.[2] He spent the whole of Book IV of the *Wealth of Nations* constructing it, examining it and denouncing it. In reality, the 'system' was the reverse of systematic: a jumble of devices, assembled over the course of a century or more to meet the demands of state finance, sectional interests and power politics. But there was enough theoretical similarity in its constituent parts for Smith, superb systematizer that he was, to be able to present it as a systematic absurdity.

But Smith's presentation of the mercantile system was limited in scope. It assumed, he said, that wealth consisted in gold and silver; and that, for a country not possessing gold and silver mines, the favourable balance of trade was the only way of securing this wealth. Therefore, it became the object of political economy to discourage imports and encourage exports. And this was done by the following means: two sorts of restraints upon imports—high duties and prohibitions; and four sorts of encouragement for exports—bounties, drawbacks, treaties and colonies.[3] Smith saw the system thus defined as prevailing from the end of the seventeenth century, presumably supposing that economic life was previously unencumbered by it, for he admitted that he thought it improbable that 'freedom of trade should ever be entirely *restored* in Great Britain' (my italics).[4] Though exempting from his condemnation the Navigation Act of Charles II, on the grounds of political expediency,[5] he damned this apparatus of government action comprehensively and vigorously. He damned it in order to construct, on the wreckage of its absurdities, his own theoretical structure of economic *laissez-faire*. Though he wrote the following words in particular relation to English colonial rule, they summarise adequately his particular blend of economic and moral fervour:

> To prohibit a great people ... from making all that they can of every part of their own produce or from employing their stock and industry in the way that they judge most advantageous to themselves is a manifest violation of the most sacred rights of mankind.[6]

The Wealth of Nations preached doctrines allegedly of universal validity and in practice peculiarly apt for the expanding, industrializing Britain of the time. It became the Bible of a new politico-economic era. For nearly a century after its publication little was heard in Britain of the out-dated 'mercantile system', save for occasional shouts by some of the popularisers of classical economics, deriding the evident fatuity of its supposed principles. In the later decades of the nineteenth century, however, it re-appeared on the stage, refurbished by the opponents of *laissez-faire*, and inflated by them into a gigantic theoretical balloon. Its re-appearance was a reflection of the changing economic relationships of the time; the rising power and wealth of Germany was being developed with substantial government protection; and the challenge to British economic supremacy, both from Europe and from across the Atlantic, brought a challenge to the creed of *laissez faire*—a notion taken over from a Frenchman, developed by a Scotsman and put into practice by the English.

Although there were writers outside the German historical school who had earlier questioned the classical economists' denigration of the economics of an earlier era, Gustav Schmoller in Germany and William Cunningham in England may be taken as the outstanding actors in the revival of the idea of 'the mercantile system'.

Archdeacon Cunningham's *Growth of English Industry and Commerce* was first published in 1882. Cunningham had studied in Germany and, like certain other English historians and economists of the time, had come under the influence of German thought which had remained unenthusiastic about the merits of Smithianism. To the volume of his work which covered the period from the sixteenth to the eighteenth centuries, in the 1892 edition, Cunningham gave the title, 'The Mercantile System'. This he came to describe, in the 1903 edition, as 'a national system of economic policy'.[7] The pursuit of power was his *Leitmotiv;* and the apparatus of government economic action developed from Tudor to Hanoverian England was the way in which power was secured. 'The *rationale* of the whole', he wrote, 'was the deliberate pursuit of national power; the means of attaining this end had been made the object of repeated experiment and now they were organised by statute.'[8] He saw the flexibility of the Statute of Artificers as serving to maintain it as an effective system of 'industrial regulation' until the advent of machine production made it inapplicable. And the shifting, sectional conflicts of eighteenth-century English economic politics were dressed up as 'Parliamentary Colbertism'.[9]

Schmoller, concerned with the history of Brandenburg from the fifteenth to the seventeenth centuries, came to believe that 'the creation of the German territorial state was not merely a political but also an economic necessity'.[10] And in this process of state-making, the mercantile system—now blown up into *Merkantilismus*—had a vital part to play. Indeed, mercantilism *was* state-making, shaped in the conflict between the growing state policy and that of the town, the district or the various estates. It was the making of 'real political economies as unified organisms' which was at stake. And those who won were the governments which succeeded in putting political power at the service of the economic interests of the nation and state.[11] Accordingly, as he wrote in 1884:

> in its innermost kernel [mercantilism] is nothing but state-making.
> . . .
>
> The essence of the system lies not in some doctrine of money, or of the balance of trade; not in tariff barriers, protective duties, or navigation laws; but in something far greater:—namely in the total transformation of society and its organisation, as well as of the state and its institutions, in the replacing of a local and territorial economic policy by that of the national state.[12]

Thus to Smith's relatively limited concept of commercial policy were added the new ingredients of national power and state-building. The notion of mercantilism was being expanded. With the growing vigour of national rivalries in the twentieth century and the abandonment, largely under economic and social pressures, of *laissez-faire* policies, it was not long before a mirror was held up to the past and the increasingly important part played by governments in economic and social matters labelled as 'neo-mercantilistic'. Sundry books and learned articles examined and developed the ideas and policies of the 'mercantilists'.[13] As a text-book lable for three centuries of European, or at least of English, history, 'the age of Mercantilism' proved tenacious: thus did E. Lipson label the second and third volumes of his *Economic History of England* when they were published in 1931, treating mercantilism here as 'the pursuit of economic power in the sense of economic self-sufficiency'.[14] The broad synthesis of the whole notion was evidently due and it came in the form of Heckscher's great work.

Heckscher treated mercantilism under five main heads: as a system of unification (covering attempts to unify tolls, weights and measures and the like; various other elements in the transference of municipal to national policies; industrial regulation; the establishment of national trading companies and other business organisations); as a system of power; as a system of protection; as a monetary system; and as a conception of society. The approach was at once sceptical and humane. Mercantilism's continuity with medieval ideas was stressed; its alleged achievements analysed and found wanting; its theoretical content compared unfavourably with *laissez-faire;* and its moral attitude towards humanity castigated. In this process, the notion became still bigger. This was the apogee of the idea of mercantilism.

II

The building-up of the notion of mercantilism had not proceeded without attack. Cunningham's approach was tartly condemned by W. A. S. Hewins in 1892 in a review of the new edition of Cunningham's book in that year.[15]

Later George Unwin poured much cold water on the belief in the efficacy of policy to do what it was said to do. Unwin's attitude here may be summed up by his views on 'a tendency which is as misleading as it is all but universal—the tendency to overestimate the active part which wise forethought and the deliberate pursuit of clear ideas has played in the economic history of nations'.[16] This was in 1913, though the remarks did not appear in print until 1927. Sir John Clapham played down the notion of mercantilism and his text-book on English economic history before 1750 will have little to do with it.[17] But it was with the varied reception accorded to Heckscher's work, and especially to the English edition, that there began to show a real reaction against the tyranny of a long word, as well as a questioning of Heckscher's particular approach.

The questioning came predominantly from the historians rather than from the economists. The theorists or those whose interest lay in the history of economic thought beamed upon this superbly systematic presentation of the idea of mercantilism. Professor A. Montgomery noted that Heckscher had raised 'some very pertinent objections against any tendency to overstress the reaction of economic conditions on the growth of economic thought'.[18] Professors Jacob Viner and B. F. Haley also picked upon this point as an especially commendable attribute of the work. Heckscher had succeeded in 'making mercantilism intelligible';[19] and 'by avoiding the simple explanation of economic policy in terms of the economic conditions which called forth that policy, Heckscher has successfully avoided the error of attempting to justify the policy on the basis that it was the product of economic conditions'.[20] Though Viner raised an important objection to Heckscher's treatment of mercantilism as a system of power, for the most part criticism from economists was confined to comments on certain limitations in the scope of the book, and these were overshadowed by the very justifiable praise for the scholarship, erudition and skill of the work.

But if the idea of mercantilism thus remained intact for the economists, it was given a nasty jolt by the historians, though they, too, expressed admiration for the obvious qualities of Heckscher's work. Marc Bloch cast a doubtful eye upon Heckscher's indiscriminate use alike of economic tracts and of legislative enactments; and on more than one count reproached him for failing to pay adequate heed to historical context, or to 'les grands phénomènes de masse de l'économie et l'influence exercée par les intérêts et les passions des groupes humains'.[21] Professor T. H. Marshall wrote of Heckscher's inability to 'establish a complete synthesis between the three elements, the situation, the ideas and the action, and demonstrate in this synthesis the presence of the unique character which he claims for his subject'. Did mercantilism have historical significance? 'In spite... of his enormously illuminating analysis, Professor Heckscher has not established beyond dispute the validity and utility of the term which is the title of his work.'[22] By his very expansion of the notion of mercantilism Heckscher was thus helping to create doubt as to its very existence.

Probably the most penetrating criticism was that which came from Professor Heaton in 1937.[23] Like other critics, he noted the attitude to sources, too readily drawn upon to support Heckscher's general argument, without reference to the context from which they were drawn; he took this further and emphasised the need to examine the effect, on policy and ideas, of short-term fluctuations in economic activity. He drew attention, as had Marc Bloch, to Heckscher's failure to take cognizance of particular groups or classes in society; and he further elaborated upon the absence from the work of discussion of particular governmental problems, as they affected public finance, policies of provision or protection, or the export of bullion. But he reserved his most devastating onslaught for the onus which Heckscher put upon the transition from a natural economy to a money economy and for the unreality of his elaborately theoretical treatment of the desire for precious metals. Heckscher dates his 'policy of provision' from the twelfth century to the mid-fourteenth century, and sees the 'policy of protection' as beginning in the early thirteenth century in Northern Italy, spreading to the Low Countries in the fourteenth and to England in the fifteenth. So, as Heaton pointed out, there was generally only 100 years between the two policies.

Was the crucial change in that hundred years the emergence of a money economy? Was twelfth century Italy or thirteenth century Flanders in the grip of natural economy? Did the economies of these two countries change so markedly in such a short space of time that a fundamental change in attitude towards commodities was inevitable? Was the policy of provision as portrayed in the tenth century *Book of the Prefect* of Constantinople due to the fact that the metropolis of the Eastern Empire was operating on a natural economy? Was fourteenth century England, which supplies Heckscher with his statistics of export control, on a natural economy?[24]

And so, of course, to the recurrent questions: What was mercantilism? Was there ever such a thing? The growth and implications of the idea were discussed at some length by Professor A. V. Judges in a paper published in 1939.[25] He examined it by reference to two main criteria: that a system must be capable of systematic demonstration; and that an '-ism' must 'offer a coherent doctrine or at least a handful of settled principles'. On these points he found the notion wanting. Pointing out that it had no living doctrine or creed, he concluded that it was an imaginary system and pleaded that we should be absolved from having to reconcile the various ideas said to be part of it.

III

With the exception of Viner's point about Heckscher's treatment of the question of power,[26] this general body of criticism is not significantly reflected in the new edition. Had serious heed been taken of the more searching criticisms, then as Heckscher himself wrote, in the preface to the second edition, 'this would have meant an entirely new book. . . . So basic is this criticism that it might be said of the book as it has been said of the Jesuits: they must be as they are or not be at all'.[27] Apart from a number of modifications to the earlier text, particularly to meet Viner's criticisms, the main difference between the two editions is the presence of an additional chapter, in Vol. II, on 'Keynes and Mercantilism'. The content of this first appeared as an article in Swedish, in 1946;[28] it does not suggest any significant change in Heckscher's approach to the subject (see below, pp. 13 & 15). What, then, of mercantilism and *Mercantilism* today?

A question which readily comes to mind when examining the idea of mercantilism is simply: Is this about economic thought in the past or is it about economic policy?

The curiously hybrid parentage of the notion provides an important source of this confusion. It was, as Judges put it, 'conceived by economists for purposes of theoretical exposition and mishandled by historians in the service of their political ideals'.[29] One might add, moreover, that it was first mishandled by historians who were primarily *political* historians and then developed by an economist-cum-economic historian whose *economic ideals* had much in common with those of Adam Smith himself. This is one reason, perhaps, not only for the seeming unreality of the idea to the economic historian of today but also for its meaninglessness or irrelevance to the political historian. So the notion of mercantilism, as developed, is yet another of the wedges helping to keep open the gap between political and economic history. The gap is still wide today. It is not simply the product of an argument about the economic interpretation of history, though it has often been made to seem as though it were. Adam Smith had a low opinion of the wisdom of political action, but a great belief in the efficacy of certain economic principles. In speaking, for instance, about whether retaliation in a tariff dispute should be allowed, he described this as a difficult question of judgment belonging not so much to the science of the legislator whose deliberations should be governed by general principles which remain constant but 'to the skill of that insidious and crafty animal, vulgarly called a statesman or politician, whose councils are directed by the momentary fluctuations of affairs'.[30] Cunningham's emphasis fell upon the pre-eminence of politics; he believed in protectionism in his own time and in the merits of political action in other times: 'our national policy is *not* the direct outcome of our economic conditions . . . politics are more important than economics in English history'.[31] Schmoller's political orientation was even more striking. So engrossed was he with the idea of political achievement that he believed that the conception of national economic life, of national agriculture, industry, shipping, fisheries, of national currency and banking systems, of national division of labour and trade must have arisen before 'the need was felt of transforming old municipal and territorial institutions into national and state ones'.[32] To English history, this is largely irrelevant. Whatever its relevance elsewhere, it was in truth all part of the distasteful business by which history is pressed into the service of aggressive nationalism. His words in the 1880's found a sinister echo in the 1930's:

> The ideals of Mercantilism . . . meant, practically, nothing but the energetic struggle for the creation of a sound state and a sound national economy . . . they meant the belief of Germany in its own future, the shaking off of a commercial dependence on foreigners which was continually becoming more oppressive, and the education of the country in the direction of economic autarchy.[33]

Heckscher's approach resuscitated the Smithian ideas, though without Smith's concession to political realities, but also took over Cunningham's insistence on the secondary importance of economic conditions and Schmoller's interest in state-building. Consequently mercantilism in Heckscher's hands, is not, as he claims, 'a phase in the history of economic policy'[34] but is rather an explanatory term for the phase in economic thought which was roughly coincident with the early growth of state power in Europe. The price paid for the extension in range of the term and for the brilliant explanatory synthesis achieved was the severe damage done to its relationship with historical reality.

One of the bases of this divorce between ideas and reality was Heckscher's use of sources. Though he spoke of policy, in fact as already noted, he pressed into service all forms of economic pronouncement: statutes, edicts, pamphlets, tracts for the times. All sources thus become equal. Time and time again, Heckscher notes the possibility that a particular piece of economic writing may have born some relation to the circumstances of the time, only then to insist on the relative unimportance of this factor. Although, for instance, he admits that Thomas Mun and Sir Josiah Child had good practical reasons as East India merchants to hold the views on money that they expounded so skilfully, the events of the time 'played no essential motivating part in mercantilism as a monetary system though their influence was not altogether absent'.[35]

And this leads to the key assumption of Heckscher's whole approach—the insistence that economic policy is not to be seen as 'the outcome and result of the actual economic situation',[36] but that what matters is the power and continuity of economic ideas. This is not simply a viewpoint set out in the course of introductory remarks; it is reiterated insistently, hammered home in regard to all aspects of the subject. It will suffice to quote a few examples:[37]

> if economic realities sometimes made themselves felt, this did not divert the general tendency of economic policy. (i, 268)

> As used in this book [protectionism] does not refer to the presence or absence of governmental measures as such.... Protectionism is taken to be the outcome of a definite attitude towards goods. ... (ii, 58)

> Our concern here is not with economic realities but with the world of economic ideas. (ii, 151)

> We need no longer suppose that some peculiar state of affairs existed, corresponding to the mercantilists' theoretical outlook. (ii, 199)

This attitude secures its most extreme expression in the new chapter on 'Keynes and Mercantilism':

> There are no grounds whatsoever for supposing that the mercantilist writers constructed their system—with its frequent and marked theoretical orientation—out of any knowledge of reality however derived. (ii, 347)

In practice, it was impossible for Heckscher consistently to maintain this position. Sporadically he makes concessions to that real world in which meditation upon the complexity of economic forces is sometimes distressingly absent or often pursued in an atmosphere polluted by the baneful winds of interest and expediency. The result is a curiously capricious appeal to reality. Governmental need for revenue is the practical problem to which Heckscher is most willing to make concessions. It is hardly possible to avoid it. But Heckscher's approach means that his treatment of financial policy sits most awkwardly within the general framework which he constructed. Thus, as Heaton pointed out, he goes through 42 pages of description and discussion of French guild monopolies before admitting that financial needs were of paramount importance.[38] Though Colbert's efforts to create national trading companies in France may perhaps be made to fit into mercantilism under 'unification', the formation of similar English companies in the late sixteenth century fits very oddly into that category; and the rider that in fact these companies 'served as milch cows to the Government in its perpetual financial straits',[39] whatever its degree of truth, hardly makes their situation in Heckscher's work more convincing. And the treatment of English protectionism from the late seventeenth century onwards largely in terms of theoretical ideas and without significant reference to war finance and Anglo-French politico-economic relations[40] further emphasises the fact that this is really a work about economic thought and not about policy.

Again, whatever the truth of Heckscher's assertion that the Netherlands 'did not really follow mercantilist practice' and were 'less affected by mercantilist tendencies than most other countries',[41] it is arbitrary largely to ignore Dutch economic policy, save for some reference to trading companies. Heckscher indeed belittled the importance of regulation and control in Dutch trade and industry, and ignored changes and conflicts in Dutch policy which were clearly built not simply upon ideas but upon the changing economic circumstances of Holland.[42] Contemporaries had no doubts about the practical realities which underlay Dutch policy and success. Sir William Temple wrote of Holland in 1673:

> Thus the trade of this Country is discovered to be no effect of common contrivances, of natural dispositions or situations, or of trivial accidents; But of a great Concurrence of Circumstances, a long course of Time, force of Orders and Method, which never before met in the World to such a degree, or with so prodigious a Success and perhaps never will again.[43]

In this, was he not nearer to reality than Heckscher's appeal to 'the national characteristics of the people'?[44]

Heckscher's insistence upon the unimportance of actual circumstances in shaping policy reflected a strong distaste for anything which he regarded as smacking of economic determinism. It found him defending some indefensible positions, as in his dispute with Charles Wilson over the use of bullion in international trade in the seventeenth century.[45] Apparently what fired him to retort as vigorously as he did was that: 'Mr. Wilson starts from the attitude of Lord Keynes and Professor G. N. Clark and, like them, he wants to find an explanation of mercantilist tendencies in the actual economic conditions of the times.'[46] Similarly, he attacked Bruno Suviranta's effort to show that the balance of trade theory had its roots in the circumstances of the time.[47] Heckscher conceded that Misselden and Mun created 'the mercantilist monetary and commercial doctrine in its narrowest sense';[48] and recent research has shown that in fact much of Mun's formulation of the balance of trade doctrine sprang directly from his enquiries into the depression of 1622–3.[49]

The final irony in Heckscher's determination to stand by his principles, at whatever cost, is reached in his chapter on 'Keynes and Mercantilism'. Having vigorously denounced Keynes for supposing that the mercantilists, or indeed any other economic writers, ever reached their conclusions by their perceptions of actual experience, he then executed a complete volte-face in regard to Keynes' own work. The *General Theory* 'should be read in its historical context . . . its *specific* motivation is to be found in the persistent unemployment in England between the two World Wars'.[50]

Of more fundamental importance perhaps than any of these anomalous positions into which Heckscher thus led himself by insistence on this key assumption was that which arose from the problem inherent in the assumption itself. If at any given time, the approach to a problem is to be assessed not in terms of any contemporary awareness of reality, but in terms of the continuity of ideas, the question immediately arises: how did those ideas themselves arise in the first place? Did they spring fully-armed into the mind of man? Or was there some unregenerate past in which reality and mentality had some more positive relationship? Heckscher votes, though hardly enthusiastically, for the latter. The answer lies in that blurred historical distance where life was somehow different—the Middle Ages:

> town policy was also determined by certain ethical considerations . . . [which] arose from the general social ethic of the Middle Ages . . . these considerations also finding some support in the economic circumstances of the time. (i, 129)

> In the Middle Ages, the economic life and political outlook of the town had been largely a product of the conditions of the time. . . . (i, 135)

This enables Heckscher, in dealing with the regulation of economic life, consistently to appeal to the 'medieval heritage' as a determinant of action.

But it raises a pretty problem in the transition from the 'policy of provision' which he associates peculiarly with medieval towns, to the 'policy of protection' of the 'mercantilist' era. And here the *deus ex machina* which is invoked to explain the change is the transition from natural to money economy:

> the facts were seen much more clearly by medieval observers than by those of later times, because the conditions in precisely this connection were so much simpler.
>
> It was the condition of *natural economy* which brought out these facts. . . . (ii, 103)

The doubts which Heaton threw upon Heckscher's assumption of the prevalence of 'natural economy' in medieval Europe have been fully supported in the twenty years since Heaton wrote;[51] indeed the twin notions of 'natural economy' and 'money economy' now seem to be of rather dubious validity and limited application. In his concern with 'natural economy', Heckscher was heavily influenced by his work on sixteenth century Sweden,[52] and it would seem in retrospect that, valuable as that work is, it does not in all aspects provide a safe basis for generalizations about European economic life as a whole.

But if Heckscher wished to invoke this transition in order to explain one sort of change in economic policy, he was unwilling to use it to explain the 'mercantilist's' desire for bullion. This led him to further contradictions of his own position. Having correlated the rise of a money economy with protectionism and dated it from thirteenth-century Italy, extending to France and England in the fifteenth century,[53] when he comes to deal with monetary questions, he asserts that it was the sixteenth and seventeenth centuries which formed, 'at least in many countries . . . the period of transition from a predominantly natural to a predominantly money economy and at the same time from an insignificant to an extremely abundant silver production'.[54] It is perhaps scarcely surprising that he was later moved to observe that 'the transition to a money economy never occurs at once and can hardly be assigned to any definite period whatsoever'.[55] He demonstrated instead that the 'mercantilists' wanted bullion for a set of theoretical reasons, the exposition of which by contemporary writers was substantially later than the supposed transition from natural to money economy and the influx of precious metals from the West.[56] And so, again, 'the circumstances of the time were not decisive'.[57]

If the continued concern with natural economy makes the new edition of *Mercantilism* seem rather old-fashioned, so also does its invocation of 'medieval universalism'. The latter still has a tight hold on history, but its grip is slowly being loosened.[58] To Heckscher, however, it was real enough:

> the medieval combination of universalism and particularism.... (i, 22)
>
> the fundamental unity of medieval culture.... (i, 327)
>
> those universalist factors such as the Church and the empire which had fashioned medieval society.... (ii, 13)
>
> the Middle Ages which their universal static ideal.... (ii, 26)
>
> As for the general conception of society, a sharp division obtains between the Middle Ages and the following period.... (ii, 271)

Once again, because of his unwillingness to take into account the differing elements of continuity or of change in economic circumstances, he was led to adopt mutually confusing positions. Though he attributes to the medieval world and 'the medieval mind'[59] these especial and temporally limited qualities, he also endows them with remarkable staying powers in themselves and irrespective of that transition from natural to money economy which is otherwise supposed to have transformed medieval conceptions. Thus if middlemen in the trade in foodstuffs were attacked in Tudor and Stuart England, it was not because of special circumstances but because of a 'medieval conception';[60] and the general reason for the persistence or recurrence of elements of the 'policy of provision' was to be found not in any external conditions but because 'municipal economic principles stood out as almost the only clear principles of economic policy, and remained so for centuries, even after the political influence of the cities had ceased'.[61]

Heckscher emphasised the need to distinguish between economic conditions or economic reality and the attempts made by governments to influence or alter those conditions. This distinction is made briefly in *Mercantilism* and more clearly in the *Sveriges ekonomiska historia* where he further stresses the dangers of using information about policy as a means of getting to know about economic reality.[62] Acts of economic policy are statements of intention and not descriptions of reality. They will be a reflection of what is not to be found in the economy rather than what is. This is important and salutary advice when considering the development or structure of a country's economy, but it does leave policy as an entity in itself, exogenous, a determinant rather than in any way determinate. Heckscher admitted that the policy and conditions were 'inextricably bound up', but his approach is most clearly stated thus: 'economic policy is determined not so much by the economic facts as by people's conception of those facts'.[63] Now Heckscher had a low opinion of the economic perception of those who lived in the 'mercantilist' era. Consequently, because of his reluctance to concede that the ideas and policies of the time might owe something to contemporary awareness of economic reality, however crude or empirical, Heckscher did not bring out at all clearly certain fundamental distinctions both in ideas and in circumstances in the so-called 'mercantilist' period. He stressed the importance, for example, of the static conception of economic life, of economic resources and activity so evident at that time; he emphasised that this provided one reason for the many commercial wars; implicit in the 'tragedy of mercantilism' was the belief that what was one man's or country's gain was another's loss.[64] Yet, vital as this is, as he himself says, to an understanding of the attitudes of the time, he nowhere asks why men should have believed it to be true.

But is it in fact a surprising notion in the pre-industrialized economy? It was, after all, a world in which population remained remarkably static; in which trade and production usually grew only very gradually; in which the limits of the known world were expanded slowly and with great difficulty; in which economic horizons were narrowly limited; and in which man approximated more closely than today to Hobbes' vision of his natural state: for most men most of the time, life was 'poor, nasty, brutish and short'. The pervasive conception of a prevailingly inelastic demand, not readily capable of expansion, changeable not so much by economic forces as by the dictates of authority, is not unreasonable in a political world of absolute monarchs and an economic world in which population and trade did not move rapidly and in which the purchasing power of the overwhelming majority of men and women remained very low and changed very little. Nor were informed contemporaries unaware of such matters. When Botero commented on static population,[65] when Gustav Vasa or John Wheeler defended the merits of 'passive trade',[66] or when Colbert observed that the trade and shipping of Europe could not be increased 'since the number of people in all the States remains the same and consumption likewise remains the same'[67]—is it not reasonable to suppose that their conceptions of economic reality may have approximately coincided with the facts? Conversely, when Heckscher simply assumed that the demand for English cloth was necessarily elastic and chided the mercantilists for not being 'alive to the consequences of this elementary facts of everyday life'[68]—does this suggest a necessarily appropriate conception of economic reality?

These characteristics of the pre-industrialized economy, as well as others too numerous and complex to be considered here,[69] were true not simply of the 'mercantilist' times but of earlier centuries. The continuity of ideas which Heckscher was eager to stress was paralleled by a continuity of basic conditions which he ignored. It is upon these substrata of economic life that are built the general conceptions of economic life which men hold. These conceptions are not necessarily the same as what is commonly distinguished as the 'economic thought' of the age. They are the latent assumptions of belief and action, counterparts in the economic sphere to those which underlie philosophy or religion or art.[70] Contemporaries often did not bother to note them because they were too obvious to need noting. The historian has to dig for them. Sometimes, on the other hand, contemporaries did write down such things, and then the problem is to distinguish this from attempts at systematic, rational analysis of economic phenomena. Colbert was an administrator of genius but he had the ordinary man's view of economic life. Is his vision of reality the same as that of Petty or North or Davenant? This was a distinction which Heckscher did not make. And it is an important one, for he viewed the economic thought and policy of an age in which no systematized body of economic analysis existed, through the spectacles of an age in which it does. Consequently, apart from his unwillingness to take into account the special circumstances in which tracts were written or enactments made, he also failed to distinguish between: (a) limited descriptions of observed phenomena, (e.g. descriptions by contemporaries of exchange movements); (b) accounts or explanations drawing upon the long-held, deeply embedded economic pre-conceptions of the day (e.g. notions embodying the static view of economic activity, or the labour theory of value); and (c) attempts at rationalized analysis or calculation (e.g. some of the work of the 'Political Arithmetic' writers). By his methods, all were implicitly given the same weight and influence. Implicitly he identified a 'conception of economic reality' with the classical or neo-classical economists' conception. And he did not consider why they might be different.

At the same time as certain basic characteristics of economic life remained the same during these centuries, so also were forces of change gradually making themselves felt. Two main channels through which they made themselves felt were the great expansion of trade, to the East, to Africa and above all to the New World; and the growth of industry in many nations of Europe. As the economic implications of these new developments gradually became apparent, the old ideas of fixity and limited horizons became intolerable. In the course of the seventeenth century, for instance, imports from American sugar and tobacco plantations grew at rates unprecedented in the economic development of the era;[71] by the end of the century imports of Indian textiles were creating severe problems for existing European textile industries. Is it unreasonable to suppose that such developments left a mark on thought and policy? Much of the policy of the later seventeenth century is an attempt to deal with the new developments in terms of old conceptions: the so-called 'Old Colonial System' is one example. And the anticipation of 'Free Trade' ideas in late seventeenth-century England was partly a product of Indian textile imports.[72] But just as the old lingered with the new in economic circumstances, so it did in ideas. Faced with the decay of Dutch trade, the Amsterdam merchants who in 1751 drew up proposals for its rejuvenation still built on old and familiar conceptions: 'by these general amendments, we shall put ourselves in a condition to *reduce* the trade of Hamburgh, Bremen, Lübeck, Denmark, and other places; at least to prevent them doing us a further prejudice'[73] (my italics). Though they put forward the idea of a free port, the idea of mutual benefit from general expansion was not present; one port's loss was another's gain. And this in the country 'less affected by mercantilist ideas'.

Here, then, is another sort of distinction which Heckscher's treatment tends to obsure: the counterpoint of old and new conceptions. It developed particularly in the century from approximately 1650 to 1750, as the implications of European expansion made themselves felt. To compare the prolific 'mercantilist' writings of this period with their far fewer counterparts a century or more earlier, can be dangerous if it leads one to believe that because men in the earlier period were not attempting formal analysis of economic life, they did not know what was going on in the economic world. Colbert thought it 'in the natural order of things' that each nation should have its share of ships and commerce in proportion to its power, population and sea-coasts.[74] But the course of economic change was to show that this was an untenable concept, just as the birth of modern scientific ideas was to put an end to that other 'natural order' which was the inheritance of the natural philosophy of Aristotle.

The converse of Heckscher's unwillingness to grant much weight to current economic conditions in the formulation of policy was his insistence upon the importance of economic ideas, and their continuity in informing the actions of policy. How realistic is this for 'mercantilist' Europe? Today, faced with particular economic problems the governments of advanced societies draw upon the advice not only of businessmen or trade unionists, but also upon that of professional economists. Moreover, governments are increasingly coming to include men who have either had some formal training in economics or at least are acquainted with its teachings. Until comparatively recent times those teachings have been primarily those of classical economics, extended, modified, refined, but in essence the political economy of *laissez-faire* England. Eli Heckscher was peculiarly a product of this situation. An admirer of England and English economic institutions, an eminent theoretical economist, accustomed to handling problems of government economic policy, he had grown up in a rapidly industrializing Sweden in which various economic questions came more or less quickly to the forefront of discussion, and which threw up a number of economists of outstanding ability. It is perhaps hardly surprising that he should have exaggerated the role of economic thought in the formulation of policy.

It would be absurd to suggest that the ideas which men held about economic life had no influence on policy. But they are only one element in policy formulation, and their relative importance varies from place to place and time to time. The great value of Heckscher's work lies in its broad and searching presentation of the nature and complexity of those ideas, in spite of the fact that it is less successful in fitting them into the historical context of practical policy. George Unwin's dictum on policy in action, although going too far in the opposite direction, offers a useful antidote:

> Policy, as actually found in history, is a set of devices into which a government drifts under the pressure of practical problems, and which gradually acquire the conscious uniformity of a type, and begin, at last, to defend themselves as such.[75]

Heckscher's broad and synthesising approach to mercantilism left virtually no element of economic and social policy 'between the Middle Ages and the end of laissez-faire' that could not somehow be brought within its comprehensive embrace. Many acts of policy considered by him under the heading of 'unification' had little in common with each other and sometimes still less to do in practice with 'unification'. It is, for example, only by dint of this vast concept that Heckscher is enabled to write as he does, that 'The French tariff of 1664 ranks with Elizabeth's Statute of Artificers as one of the two unquestionable triumphs of mercantilism in the sphere of economic unification'.[76] But is this true in historical reality? Did the English Statute aim at or achieve unification in the same way as Colbert's enactment was concerned to unify and co-ordinate in matters peculiarly requiring unification and coordination? And what are the real links between these two, with a century separating them, and all the other edicts, be they about bullion, gilds, patents, cloth inspection, trading companies or catching herrings, which can, by Heckschers' definitions, be labelled as 'mercantilistic'?

Using a shorter historical focus, the Statute of Artificers can be seen as 'a classic example of the restrictive legislation which great depressions tend to produce'.[77] In this context, it was one of various measures taken after the collapse in the English boom in woollen cloth exports during the first half of the sixteenth century. It was part of the reaction to falling trade, increased unemployment and anxiety about home food supplies following upon much conversion of arable land to sheep pasturage; it was at once a naturally conservative reaction to the problem of public order and poverty as well as a move in the sharpening politico-economic conflict between Burleigh and Granvelle. Using a still shorter focus to examine the details of its enforcement, we find that in practice one of its important clauses—that demanding a seven-year apprenticeship—was enforced more by the pressure of private interests than by the force of public policy.[78] The trading jealousy of competition during periods of declining trade and the greed of the professional informer during the booms were the effective agents of such enforcement as there was of this particular item of 'mercantilism'. The government—central and local—showed itself to be more concerned with the pressing realities of an economy of widespread underemployment and periodic unemployment, with its poverty, vagrancy and inherent threats to public order. The 'really efficient central administration'[79] of the years of Charles I's personal government meant in practice, so far as the enforcement of apprenticeship was concerned, prosecutions by professional informers and trade rivals, most of which were inconclusive or ineffective in their results.

This was the reality of 'mercantilism'. It is a long way from simple *Staatsbildung*. And does it suggest the intention or achievement of unification in the Statute of Artificers?

It was by dint of his synthesising treatment that 'mercantilism' in Heckscher's hands became, as Professor C. W. Cole observed, 'a real entity ... which manifested itself through the centuries in various countries'.[80] Heckscher noted this criticism in the new edition, denied knowledge of what was meant by it, and observed that no specific quotation had been given.[81] It is not difficult to find such quotations:

> mercantilism in its struggle against the disintegration within the state ... (i, 137)
>
> the incapacity of French mercantilism to master even the particularisation of municipal policy ... (ii, 209)
>
> mercantilism had to leave much of its work of unification for its successors to complete. (i, 456)
>
> mercantilism would ... have had all economic activity subservient to the state's interest in power. (ii, 15)
>
> mercantilism often arrived at more erroneous conclusions on economic questions than the medieval mind had ever done. (ii, 112)
>
> we are concerned with the tasks which mercantilism imposed on itself ... (ii, 272)
>
> mercantilism was indeed a new religion. (ii, 155)

In the preface to the first edition, Heckscher voiced his disapproval of 'the method of treating all sorts of disconnected tendencies ... under the name of "modern capitalism"': he tended to put 'capitalism' in quotation marks; he spoke of it as a 'Protean conception'.[82] However true these strictures may be, they are equally applicable to his own treatment of mercantilism, though in truth there is little meaning in any comparison between 'mercantilism' and 'capitalism'. Capitalism has been written of and fought about in its own time, rightly or wrongly. It has come near to being a religion; Communism has come far nearer. But no man recognised and defended the cause of mercantilism during its supposed reign; no war was fought under its banner. Mercantilism was *not* 'a new religion'. So again we come back to asking what was this 'mercantilism'. Did it exist? As a description of a trend of economic thought, the term may well be useful, and worth retaining. As a label for economic policy, it is not simply misleading but actively confusing, a red-herring of historiography. It serves to give a false unity to disparate events, to conceal the close-up reality of particular times and particular circumstances, to blot out the vital intermixture of ideas and preconceptions, of interests and influences, political and economic, and of the personalities of men, which it is the historian's job to examine. It was in 1923 that G. N. Clark (Sir George Clark as he has since become) stressed the dangers of using the concept of the 'mercantile system' in dealing with the protagonists in international politico-economic conflict in the seventeenth century.[83] Heckscher's further inflation of the balloon of 'mercantilism' did much to obscure that admirable advice.

As a contribution to the history of economic thought, there can be no doubt whatsoever that Heckscher's work remains outstanding, still invaluable to the student of the period. Nor can the economic historian afford to ignore it. Nevertheless, for the economic historian, although packed with valuable information, it is curiously unrealistic. Taken as a whole, it is unquestionably a brilliant and stimulating study, a product of scholarship, immensely wide reading in several languages and intellectual ingenuity of a very high order. Yet at one and the same time as its range, subtlety and learning are formidable and impressive, so also is it misleading, a signpost built upon strangely unreal assumptions, pointing to an historical no-man's-land. In real life, policy is carried out by governments and governments are composed of men who, whatever their preconceived ideas and whatever their ultimate aims, deal in particular contexts with particular problems. In *Mercantilism*, Heckscher shunned particular contexts and particular problems: he ignored the composition of governments; and with the significant exception of Colbert, most of those mentioned in his pages were concerned less with governing than with writing economic tracts or with trading.

Notes

1 E. F. Heckscher, *Mercantilism* (Revised Edition, Ed. E. F. Söderlund, London, 1955). All page references given in the present article are to this edition.
   I would like to thank Professor Söderlund, as well as my colleagues Mr. J. Potter and Professor F. J. Fisher for advice and assistance in connection with this article, although no responsibility attaches to them for the opinions expressed therein.
2 Adam Smith, *An Inquiry into the Nature and Causes of the Wealth of Nations*, 1776 (Ed. E. Cannan. Modern Library Edition, New York, 1937), p. 397.
3 *Ibid.*, pp. 418–9.
4 *Ibid.*, p. 437.
5 *Ibid.*, pp. 429–31.
6 *Ibid.*, p. 549.
7 W. Cunningham, *The Growth of English Industry and Commerce* (Cambridge, 3rd Ed. 1903), ii, 16.
8 *Ibid.* (2nd Ed. 1892), ii, 16.
9 *Ibid.* (1892 Ed.) ii, 42; (1903 Ed.), ii, 403.
10 G. Schmoller, *The Mercantile System and Its Historical Significance* (translated from *Studien über die wirtschaftliche Politik Friedrichs des Grossen*, 1884), N.Y., 1931, p. 43.

11 *Ibid.*, pp. 50, 72.
12 *Ibid.*, pp. 50-1.
13 For some examples, see Heckscher, *Mercantilism*, ii, 262-6.
14 E. Lipson, *The Economic History of England* (4th Ed. London, 1947), iii, 1.
15 *Economic Journal*, ii (1892), 694-700.
16 G. Unwin, *Studies in Economic History* (London, 1927), p. 158.
17 J. Clapham, *A Concise Economic History of Britain from the Earliest Times to A.D. 1750* (Cambridge, 1949).
18 *Vierteljahrschrift für Sozial- und Wirtschaftsgeschichte*, xxv (1932), 68.
19 Viner in *Economic History Review*, vi, No. 1 (1935), 101.
20 Haley in *Quarterly Journal of Economics*, L (1936), 352; cf. also S. B. Clough in *Journal of Modern History*, VIII, No. 3 (1936), 357-8; and C. Brinkman in *Historische Zeitschrift*, 149 (1934), pp. 123-4.
21 M. Bloch, 'Le mercantilisme, un état d'ésprit', *Annales d'Histoire Économique et Sociale*, vi (1934), 162.
22 Marshall in *Economic Journal*, xlv (1935), 718-9.
23 H. Heaton, 'Heckscher on Mercantilism', *Journal of Political Economy*, xlv, No. 3 (1937), 370-93.
24 *Ibid.*, pp. 383-4.
25 A. V. Judges, 'The idea of a mercantile state', *Transactions of the Royal Historical Society*, 4th series, xxi (1939), 41-69.
26 *Mercantilism* ii, 13 and 359-63. This is perhaps a suitable place to point out that, owing to a publisher's error, an important footnote has been omitted. On p. 13 of Vol. II, there should be a footnote as follows:

> The present chapter has been largely re-written on the basis of a criticism of the original chapter by Professor Jacob Viner in his essay 'Power versus plenty as objectives of foreign policy in the seventeenth and eighteenth centuries' (*World Politics* I, 1948, 1-29). This article will be discussed in detail later. See below II, 359 ff. Addendum, para. 1.

The publishers, Messrs. Allen & Unwin, have asked me to state that an *erratum* notice has been issued, although this will not have been inserted in the earliest copies purchased.

27 *Ibid.*, i, 15.
28 'Något om Keynes "General Theory" ur ekonomisk-historisk synpunkt', *Ekonomisk Tidskrift*, xlviii (1946), 161-83.
29 Judges, *loc. cit.*, p. 68.
30 Smith, *op. cit.*, p. 435.
31 Cunningham, *op. cit.* (1890 Ed.) i, 9.
32 Schmoller, *op. cit.*, p. 59.
33 *Ibid.*, p. 76.
34 *Mercantilism*, i, 19.
35 *Ibid.*, ii. 224.
36 *Ibid.*, i, 20.
37 See also: i, 339, 384; ii, 30, 44, 54, 101-2, 121, 213 etc.
38 Heaton, *loc. cit.*, p. 377.
39 *Mercantilism*, i, 439.
40 *Ibid.*, ii, 112 ff.
41 *Ibid.*, i, 351-2.
42 See, e.g. C. Wilson, *Anglo-Dutch Commerce and Finance in the Eighteenth Century* (Cambridge, 1941); also P. D. Huet. *A View of the Dutch Trade* (translated from the French, 2nd Ed. London, 1722), Chap. III and *passim*.

43 W. Temple, *Observations upon the United Provinces* (2nd. Ed. London, 1673), p. 229.
44 *Mercantilism*, i, 353.
45 C. Wilson, 'Treasure and trade balances: the mercantilist problem', *Econ. Hist. Rev.*, 2nd series, ii (1949); E. F. Heckscher, 'Multilateralism, Baltic trade, and the Mercantilists', *Econ. Hist. Rev.*, 2nd series iii (1950); C. Wilson, 'Treasure and trade balances: further evidence', *Econ. Hist. Rev.*, 2nd Series, iv (1951).

In fact not only, as Wilson demonstrated, were Englishmen and Dutchmen aware of the need for bullion in 17th century Baltic trade, but so too were Frenchmen. If Colbert wanted to develop French trade with Sweden, then, as his emissary in Denmark wrote to him in 1669, it could be done, provided 'Monsieur Colbert were willing to allow a less constraint in the manner of business, and to approve, instead of that which is carried on by the exchange of goods, that which is done in cash'. Quoted, C. W. Cole, *Colbert and a Century of French Mercantilism* (N.Y., 1939), ii, 95.

46 *Econ. Hist. Rev.*, 2nd Series iii (1950), 219.
47 B. Suviranta, *The Theory of the Balance of Trade* (Helsinki, 1923); Heckscher, *Mercantilism*, ii, 266. This criticism appeared in the first edition, but is repeated twice in the new edition, ii, 266 and ii, 354.
48 *Mercantilism*, ii, 248.
49 B. E. Supple, 'Thomas Mun and the commercial crisis, 1623', *Bulletin of the Institute of Historical Research*, xxvii (1954); also R. W. K. Hinton, 'The mercantile system in the time of Thomas Mun', *Econ. Hist. Rev.* 2nd. Series vii, (1955).
50 *Mercantilism*, ii, 346, 357–8.
51 See, for example, Marc Bloch, 'Économie-nature ou économie-argent: un pseudo-dilemme', *Annales d'Histoire Sociale*, i (1939); M. M. Postan, 'The rise of a money economy', *Econ. Hist. Rev.* xiv (1944); M. Postan and E. Rich (Eds.), *Cambridge Economic History of Europe*, ii (Cambridge 1952); R. de Roover, *Money, Banking and Credit in Medieval Bruges* (Cambridge, Mass. 1948).
52 'Natural and money economy as illustrated from Swedish history in the sixteenth century', *Journal of Economic and Business History* iii (1930–1), reprinted in F. C. Lane and J. C. Riemersma (Eds.) *Enterprise and Secular Change* (London, 1953). The essence of this had already appeared in articles in Swedish and in German, and was subsequently embodied by Heckscher in his *Sveriges ekonomiska historia* (Stockholm, Part I, 1935–6, Part II, 1949), see especially I, i, Chap. 3.
53 *Mercantilism*, ii, 139, and ii, 145.
54 *Ibid.*, ii, 177.
55 *Ibid.*, ii, 219.
56 *Ibid.*, ii, 177, 219, 221.
57 *Ibid.*, ii, 177.
58 See, e.g. G. Barraclough, *History in a Changing World* (Oxford, 1955), esp. pp. 128–30.
59 *Mercantilism*, ii, 112.
60 *Ibid.*, i, 267.
61 *Ibid.*, ii, 102.
62 *Ibid.*, i, 20; *Sveriges ekonomiska historia I*, i, 12–13.
63 *Mercantilism*, ii, 59.
64 *Ibid.*, ii, 23–6.
65 G. Botero, *The Reason of State* (1589, translated from the Italian by P. J. & D. P. Waley, London, 1956), p. 155.
66 *Mercantilism*, ii, 61, 62 n; J. Wheeler, *Treatise of Commerce* (Ed. G. B. Hotchkiss N.Y. 1931), p. 69 *et seq.*

67 Quoted Cole, *op. cit.*, i, 343.
68 *Mercantilism*, ii, 241–2.
69 For an examination of some aspects of the 'mercantilist' attitude to labour, see D. C. Coleman, 'Labour in the English economy of the seventeenth century', *Econ. Hist. Rev.* 2nd series, viii (1956).
70 Cf. Basil Willey, *The Seventeenth Century Background* (London, 1934), p. 2 and *passim*.
71 See R. Davis, 'English foreign trade, 1660–1700', *Econ. Hist. Rev.*, 2nd series, vii (1954).
72 P. J. Thomas, *Mercantilism and the East India Trade* (London, 1926), p. 68 and *passim*.
73 Translated and printed as 'Proposals for Redressing and Amending the Trade of the Republic', 1751 in *A Select Collection of Scarce and Valuable Tracts on Commerce* (Ed. J. R. McCulloch, London, 1859).
74 Quoted Cole, *op. cit.*, i, 344.
75 Unwin, *op. cit.*, p. 184.
76 *Mercantilism*, i, 103.
77 F. J. Fisher, 'Commercial trends and policy in sixteenth century England', *Econ. Hist. Rev.* X (1940), 113 and *passim*.
78 M. G. Davies, *The Enforcement of English Apprenticeship, 1563–1642* (Havard, 1956), p. 258 and *passim*.
79 *Mercantilism*, i, 256, Davies, *op. cit.*, p. 239.
80 C. W. Cole, 'The heavy hand of Hegel', in *Nationalism and Internationalism* (Ed. E.M. Earle, N.Y., 1950), p. 74 ff.
81 *Mercantilism*, ii, 59n.
82 *Ibid.*, i, 14, 191n., 221.
83 G. N. Clark, *The Dutch Alliance and the War against French Trade, 1688–97* (Manchester, 1923), p. 7.

41

'IMPERIALISM'

An historiographical revision[1]

David K. Fieldhouse

Source: *Economic History Review* 14(2), 1961: 187–209.

It is now nearly sixty years since J. A. Hobson published *Imperialism: a Study*,[2] and thereby gave the word the connotation it still generally carries. His conception of the nature of 'imperialism'[3] has, indeed, been almost universally accepted and, partly through the expository literature it has generated, may be said to have exercised a significant historical influence. Yet, for all its success, Hobson's argument has always been extremely vulnerable to criticism: and it is therefore surprising that those historians and economists who have argued effectively that his analysis is basically unsound should have received so little attention. The aim of the present article is to draw together some of the more important arguments that have been put forward for and against his thesis, and to suggest that, on balance, the noes have it.

Hobson's own claim to importance and originality lies simply in his having induced British, and subsequently world, opinion to accept his own special definition of the word imperialism. Professor Koebner has already examined the various meanings given to the word before 1902.[4] He has suggested that, as used in England, it had two general connotations in the 1890's, both of which were morally neutral. In one sense, it was being used of those who wished to prevent the existing British settlement colonies from seceding and becoming independent states, and was therefore a conservative factor. In another, and increasingly common, sense, it was being used to indicate an expansionist and 'forward' attitude towards problems connected with the future control of the 'uncivilized' parts of the world, such as Africa, the Middle East and the Pacific. Salisbury was, in this sense, regarded as an imperialist in accepting the need for Britain to share in the partition of East Africa. Gladstone, in opposing the acquisition of Uganda, was emphatically anti-imperialist, even though he had acquiesced in the need to gain some control over Egypt in 1882. In the eyes of the anti-imperialists the sin of expansionism lay in the waste of money it entailed on armaments, in the cost of colonial governments, and in the danger of international conflicts over intrinsically unimportant territories which it would be wiser to leave alone. As a rule no worse motive was attributed to the imperialists than 'jingoism' or excessive concern with Britain's position as a great power.

But, between 1896 and 1902, imperialism, as a word, began to lose its innocence. Koebner has shown that events in South Africa, and particularly the Jameson Raid, gave rise to a suspicion that, here at least, the expansive urge was motivated by something other than a concern for national greatness, by what Harcourt called 'stock-jobbing imperialism' – based on the interests of financiers. This was, of course, a special case; and a distinction remained between an honest, even if misguided, imperialism, and the debased variety to be seen on the Rand. Yet the idea now gained ground that South Africa might not, after all, be a special case, but might exhibit in an extreme form a factor inherent in all expansionism. By 1900 radical opinion had moved so far in this direction that the Fifth International Socialist Congress, taught probably by its English delegation, could resolve

> ... que le développement du capitalisme mène fatalement à l'expansion coloniale ... : que la politique coloniale de la bourgeoisie n'a d'autre but que d'élargir les profits de la classe capitaliste et le maintien du système capitaliste ... .[5]

Here, in a nutshell, was Hobson's doctrine of 'imperialism'. But it remained to be seen whether such a dogmatic interpretation would ever command a wide support: and it was essentially his achievement to ensure that, in his own non-Marxist form, it should become the generally accepted theory.

Hobson's *Imperialism* therefore came out at a time when British public opinion, disillusioned by the Boer war, was already profoundly suspicious about the motives behind recent imperial expansion. It was, in fact, a pamphlet for the times, rather than a serious study of the subject; and, like all pamphlets that achieve influence, it owed much of its success to the fact that it expressed a current idea with peculiar clarity, force and conviction. It arose immediately out of Hobson's visit to South Africa during the war, and derived from reports he sent back to *The Speaker*, which were published as a book in 1900 as *The War in South Africa, Its Causes and Effects*. Yet, paradoxically, Hobson was not primarily concerned with imperial problems: and *Imperialism* can only be properly understood on the basis that his interest, then and throughout his life, was with the social and economic problems of Britain. In a sense, this book was primarily a vehicle for publicizing the theory of 'underconsumption', which he regarded as his main intellectual achievement, and which he expressed more fully in *The Evolution of Modern Capitalism*, and other works. In brief, the theory, which was an alternative to the Marxist concept of surplus value as an explanation of poverty, saw excessive investment by the capitalist, with its concomitant of underconsumption by the wage-earner, as the root cause of recurrent slumps, of low interest rates, and of permanent under-employment. Hobson thought there were only two answers to this problem. The correct one – which would also be the answer to the 'condition of England question' – was to increase the buying power of the workers by giving them a higher share of the profits of industry. The wrong one, which was no answer to the social question, was to invest the surplus capital overseas, where it could earn a high interest rate, and thus sustain domestic rates of interest, without benefiting the British worker. And this, he held, was what Britain had been doing since at least the middle of the nineteenth century.

To this point the economic theory, though highly vulnerable, has no apparent relevance to the phenomenon of overseas expansion, that is, to imperialism. The key to Hobson's theory of 'imperialism' lies in the connexion he makes between the two.

> Overproduction in the sense of an excessive manufacturing plant, and surplus capital which could not find sound investments within the country, forced Great Britain, Germany, Holland, France to place larger and larger portions of their economic resources outside the area of their present political domain, and then stimulate a policy of political expansion so as to take in the new areas.[6]

Thus 'imperialism', in the special sense used by Hobson, is an external symptom of a social malady in the metropolitan countries. Without this domestic pressure for investment overseas, there would be no effective impulse towards the acquisition of new colonies. Conversely, without colonies, capital would lack an outlet, and domestic rates of interest would sink. Thus the need to export capital and to make it politically secure overseas was what Mr John Strachey has recently called the 'prime mover for the modern imperialist process . . .'[7] And 'imperialism', on this assumption, is not variously 'sound' or 'stock-jobbing'; but, without exception, results from the special economic interests of the capitalist, and is therefore 'economic imperialism'.

It is not proposed at this stage to examine Hobson's theory in detail: but some comment must be made on the logical value of the argument he uses to demonstrate the historical truth of this hypothesis. Does he, in fact, supply any evidence to support the claim that colonies were the product of a demand either for new investment opportunities, or for security for existing investments? He begins with a straightforward account of the expansion of the European empires since 1870, printing a list of territories acquired by Britain, which Lenin, and later Mr Strachey, have reproduced. Then, in chapter two, he demonstrates that the expansion of the British empire had been of little apparent value to British trade; that trade with these recent acquisitions was the least valuable part of intra-imperial trade; and that British trade with all colonies was declining in relation to trade with the rest of the world.[8] Clearly, then, 'imperialism' was not good for trade. Nor was it good for emigration (which, in any case, he thought unnecessary), since these new tropical colonies were quite unsuited to white settlement.[9] And his conclusion was that

> The Imperialism of the last six decades is clearly condemned as a business policy, in that at enormous expense it has procured a small, bad, unsafe increase of markets, and has jeopardised the entire wealth of the nation in arousing the strong resentment of other nations . . .[10]

How then can a motive be found for this imperial expansion? The motive is to be seen if, alongside the list of territorial acquisitions, is placed a table showing the increase of British overseas investments in the same period.[11] It then becomes obvious that, during the period in which British possessions had increased by 4,754 m. square miles and by a population of 88 millions, British overseas investments had also increased enormously – from £144 m. to £1698 m. between 1862 and 1893 alone. Could there be any doubt that the two sets of figures were intimately connected as cause and effect? Hobson had no doubts about it: 'It is not too much to say that the modern foreign policy of Great Britain has been primarily a struggle for profitable markets of investment'.[12]

But it is immediately apparent that Hobson had in no sense proved that there was any connexion between the investments made overseas and the territory acquired contemporaneously. His table of investments[13] makes no differentiation between the areas in which investment had taken place, beyond such classifications as 'Foreign', 'Colonial', 'U.S.A.' and 'Various', and, in fact, he assumes quite arbitrarily that the new colonies had attracted a high proportion of the investment called 'Foreign' (i.e. before they were annexed) or 'Colonial' (subsequent to annexation). This, it will be suggested below, is a basic fault of his theory of 'imperialism'. Indeed, to put the case bluntly, Hobson performed an intellectual conjuring trick. Convinced of the essential truth of his economic theory, he deceived the eye by the speed of his hand, creating the illusion that, of the two sets of statistics he held up, one was the cause of the other.

It is not possible here to consider the rest of Hobson's *Imperialism*, interesting though it is in relation to related controversies over protection, tariff reform and imperial unity. But two additional points in his main argument must be mentioned because they were intrinsic to his definition of the origins and nature of 'imperialist' expansion.

The first of these concerns the relationship between the financial interest and other 'imperialists', and is therefore crucial to his theory. He was aware that, contrary to his argument, the obvious driving force of British expansion since 1870 appeared to lie in the explorers, missionaries, engineers, patriotic pressure groups, and empire-minded politicians, all of whom had evident influence, and had demonstrable interests, other than those of investment, in territorial acquisitions. And he was equally aware that if the impulse to expansion could be satisfactorily explained in the old-fashioned terms of their idealism, their ambition, or their concern with the status of Britain as a world power, rather than in terms of the self-interest of the capitalist, his own central thesis would collapse. It was therefore necessary that these men – the Lugards, the Milners, the Johnstons, and the Roseberys – should be shown to be mere puppets – the tools of 'imperialism' rather than its authors. Hobson did this by falling back on what may be called the 'faceless men' gambit:

> Finance manipulates the patriotic forces which politicians, soldiers, philanthropists, and traders generate; the enthusiasm for expansion which issues from these sources, though strong and genuine, is irregular and blind; the financial interest has those qualities of concentration and clear-sighted calculation which are needed to set Imperialism to work. An ambitious statesman, a frontier soldier, an overzealous missionary, a pushing trader, may suggest or even initiate a step of imperial expansion, may assist in educating patriotic public opinion to the urgent need of some fresh advance, but the final determination rests with the financial power.[14]

In this ingenious way Hobson inverted the apparent relationship between the obvious 'imperialists' and the investor. Instead of the financier being induced to invest in new possessions, with more or less enthusiasm, once political control had been imposed for other reasons, he becomes the essential influence in the take-over itself. Investment no longer follows the flag: it decides where it is profitable to plant it, and tells the government whether it is to follow the advice of men of action or of ideas in each particular case. Thus, 'imperialism' can never be interpreted as the spontaneous expression of the idealism, the chauvinism or the mere energy of a nation. In its practical form it is the expression of the special interests of the financier behind the scenes, who decides whether it is worth his while to allow a dream to become a reality, and who alone will reap the benefits.

This assumption, which has been adopted by most subsequent supporters of Hobson's thesis, will be examined later.

The other essential point in the theory of 'imperialism' is the suggestion that the possession of colonies by individual capitalist states results automatically in the exploitation of the indigenous peoples of Africa and Asia. In his long chapter 'Imperialism and the Lower Races',[15] which is in many ways one of the most undogmatic and constructive parts of the book, Hobson argued that exploitation, whether by appropriation of land, or by the use of cheap labour – forced or nominally free – in mines, farms and factories, had been a general feature of the colonies of all the European powers. Hobson, in the British humanitarian tradition, thought such exploitation to be both wrong and inexpedient. Economic development was good for undeveloped colonies and for the world as a whole. The danger lay in allowing the financiers to use the political power of the imperial authority for their own purposes; and the solution was for international control of colonies – the germ of the later mandate concept – and patience in allowing normal economic forces to give the natives an inducement to work freely in European enterprises. Sensible as his general attitude was, it is clear that Hobson had thus included in 'imperialism' the suggestion that countries possessing colonies were almost certain to exploit them in their own interests; and this argument was to become a staple of later critics of 'colonialism'.

II

The theory of 'imperialism' as it developed after the publication of Hobson's *Study* continued to be founded on the three main concepts outlined above. Yet, in examining its historiography, it is clear that it was Lenin, writing in 1916, rather than Hobson himself, who gave 'imperialism' its dogmatic coherence and much of its eventual influence. It is therefore necessary to consider briefly the extent to which Lenin modified Hobson's ideas.[16]

The greatest difference lies in the first and most important part of the argument; that is, in the nature of the internal pressure in the capitalist countries which forces them to expand their colonial possessions. Hobson had explained this pressure in terms of 'under-consumption': but Lenin naturally had a more orthodox theory to hand. Capitalism as a system was approaching the apocalypse Marx had foretold. Competitive capitalism had, in the late nineteenth century, been replaced by 'monopoly capitalism', with its characteristic agencies, the cartels, trusts and tariffs. It was no longer dynamic, but anxious only to maintain its profit margins by more intensive exploitation of limited and protected markets. Moreover, the 'finance-capitalists' – the banks and trusts – who now largely controlled capital itself, found that, under monopoly conditions, it was more profitable to employ surplus capital abroad than in domestic industry. At home, it could only increase production, lower prices, and raise wages. Abroad it could give a high interest return without any of these consequences. But, to gain the highest return from overseas investment it was desirable to have some political control over the territory in which the investment was made. This might be in the limited form of a 'semi-colony', such as the Argentine. But only in the colony proper could really comprehensive economic and political controls be imposed which would give investments their highest return. The result had been the competition between the great powers to acquire new colonies after 1870, which would continue until the whole uncivilized world had come under imperial rule. Then would follow the inter-imperial wars for the redivision of the empires, leading to proletarian revolutions in the 'imperialist' states, the creation of 'socialist' states, and so, automatically, to the end of 'imperialism'.

How much, then, does Lenin's explanation of the force behind 'imperialism' differ from that of Hobson? Fundamentally, only in this: that, whereas Hobson used his theory as evidence that social-democratic reform at home was necessary and possible to eliminate the evil of 'under-consumption' and therefore make 'imperialism' unnecessary, Lenin made 'imperialism' the definition of an inherent and unavoidable stage in the growth of capitalist society which could not be 'reformed'. Hobson was a doctor prescribing a remedy, Lenin a prophet forecasting catastrophe.[17] But, while they disagreed as to the precise causes, both maintained that there existed in the 'capitalist' countries a tremendous pressure for overseas investment, and that this was the main factor in producing 'imperialist' expansion after 1870.

On Hobson's second point – the control and influence exercised by 'finance' over government and over the men who actually carved out the new empires – there is little difference between them. Lenin, if anything, went further, ignoring the theory that in a democratic country like Britain Hobson's 'imperialists' found it necessary to corrupt public opinion through the press; and assuming, on the basis of Marxist theory and German experience, that the financial power of the banks and trusts was now so great that governments virtually did as they were told by the 'finance-capitalist'. Moreover, Lenin rejected entirely the possibility that the drive behind imperialism might have been the natural product of nationalism in international politics. To him as a Marxist such arguments were superficial. The only true explanation must lie in the fundamental economic environment which dictates political interests: and he castigates the unfortunate Kautsky on the grounds that he 'detaches the politics of imperialism from its economics...'[18] Economic factors are the root of all features of the 'imperialist' state; and even Franco-German competition for Alsace-Lorraine exists 'because an essential feature of imperialism is the rivalry between a number of great powers in the striving for hegemony, i.e. for the conquest of territory, not so much directly for themselves as to weaken the adversary and undermine *his* hegemony'.[19] There is no room here for explaining the actions of governments in any terms other than of the economics of 'imperialism'.

On Hobson's third point, Lenin had little explicit to say. As a Marxist he assumed it to be axiomatic that all workers were exploited by capital; so that a colony would differ from the metropolis only in the fact that the exploiting capitalist was an alien, and colonies merely added to the pool of labour from which he could extract 'surplus value'.

With the publication of Lenin's book it may be said that the concept of 'imperialism' had reached its mature form; for, on points on which they differed, Lenin's interpretation has generally been the dominant one. The subsequent historiography of the subject on the 'imperialist' side of the argument has tended to fall into two main categories – either glosses on the theory, or applications of it to the actual events of the period after 1870, and a few of the more important books in the English canon may be mentioned. First, in point of time, came Leonard Woolf's *Empire and Commerce in Africa* (1920) which was influential in British Labour Party thinking on the subject. P. T. Moon's *Imperialism and World Politics* (1928) used the theory to interpret the international politics of the age of 'imperialism'; and in 1942 P. M. Sweezey restated Lenin's theory in relation to the central Marxist argument with considerable clarity and some minor modifications in *The Theory of Capitalist Development*. Finally, in 1959, Mr John Strachey published *The End of Empire* which, as the most recent work of apologetics, deserves some comment as an honest and intelligent attempt to assess and defend the theory after the experience of half a century.

Like Professor Sweezey, Mr Strachey is aware that the theory, as stated by Hobson and Lenin, had important limitations, of which the most obvious was that it related only to the period after 1870, and therefore offered no explanation of earlier empires, or of developments since the First World War. It was Mr Strachey's main aim to demonstrate that at least one concept of 'imperialism' – that empire consists primarily in the exploitation of a dependent territory for the economic advantage of the metropolis – holds good for all empires at all times; and that it is the means, not the fact, of exploitation that varies. For the period after 1870 itself he thinks Hobson and Lenin were right in seeing 'imperialism' as the external expression of the surplus capital of the European states; preferring Lenin's theory of 'finance-capital' to Hobson's 'under-consumption' as the basic factor. But he recognizes also that Lenin was less successful as a prophet, for he ignored the reformative capacity of political democracy to modify the structure of a capitalist society to such an extent as to make both 'imperialism' and eventual revolution unnecessary. Much of the book consists of an attempt to apply the view that exploitation was the basic factor in the 'imperialism' of the period after 1870 to other empires; and to suggest that the characteristic feature of each empire has been its own peculiar method of exploiting its dependencies. In the modern empires this was, as Hobson had said, to make wage-slaves of indigenous peoples by exporting capital to their countries, and forcing them to work within the capitalist economy, and he instances copper-mining in Rhodesia as a typical example. But other empires had their own characteristic methods. In India, the British began in the eighteenth century with mere plunder, which they later rationalized into the system of revenues exacted from Bengal, and replaced in the nineteenth century by the enforcement of the open door to British exports at the cost of ruining indigenous industries. Further back in time, Mr Strachey suggests that the empires of the ancient world were based on the exploitation of slave labour – the original 'surplus value': 'Imperialism in its original form could almost be called enslavement applied externally . . .'[20] The medieval European empires he calls 'peasant empires'; and he thinks they were based on the 'invention of a way in which men could be exploited without the cumbrous and difficult business of directly enslaving them'.[21] After them came the mercantile empires, which ingeniously combined all known forms of exploitation – plunder (as in India or Mexico), enslavement for the silver mines and plantations, and trade on a one-sided basis with unsophisticated peoples.

Mr Strachey's book covers far more ground than can be suggested here, and deserves a place in the 'imperialist' canon both because of the ingenuity with which it attempts to give universality to the basic ideas of Hobson and Lenin, and because it shows the extent to which a confessed 'revisionist' can adapt these ideas to the circumstances of the mid-twentieth century. But, without following his arguments further, it is necessary to turn to a critical examination of the central theory of 'imperialism', and to alternative interpretations of the facts that first gave rise to it.

III

The central feature of the theory of 'imperialism', by which it must stand or fall, is the assertion that the empires built up after 1870 were not an option but a necessity for the economically advanced states of Europe and America: that these capitalist societies, because of their surplus of domestically produced capital, were forced to export capital to the under-developed regions of the world: and that it was only this investment – prospective or existing – that supplied a motive for the acquisition of new colonies.

Faced with this theory, the historian who does not take its truth for granted is likely to be sceptical on at least three main grounds. First, his instinct is to distrust all-embracing historical formulas which, like the concept of 'the rise of the middle class', seek to explain complex developments in terms of a single dominant influence. Again, he is likely to suspect an argument that isolates the imperial expansion of the period after 1870 from all earlier imperial developments if only because he is aware of so many elements of continuity in the history of overseas empires over the past few centuries. But, above all, he must be aware that the theory simply does not appear to fit the facts of the post-1870 period as he knows them. Looking, for example, at Hobson's list of territories acquired by Britain after 1870, it seems, at first sight at least, difficult to believe that any considerable part of them were annexed either because British capitalists had already invested much of their surplus capital there, or because they regarded them as fields for essential future investment. In some cases, perhaps, it seems that a *prima facie* case could be made out on these lines – for Egypt, the Transvaal and Rhodesia, to take Hobson's three main examples. But, even in these, further consideration must arouse doubts. Surely the strategic importance of the Suez Canal was as good a reason for controlling Egypt in 1882 as the preservation of the interests of the bond holders in the Canal Company. Was it really necessary, on purely economic grounds, to annex the Transvaal in 1899 when the British mine-owners were making vast fortunes under Kruger's government, and had shown themselves so divided over the question of the Jameson Raid and the independence of the Republic?[22] Again, granted that Rhodes and the British South Africa Company had excellent economic reasons for wanting British control over Rhodesia, was their anxiety really due to the pressure of British funds waiting for investment opportunity?

Doubts such as these concerning even the key examples chosen by Hobson inevitably stimulate further examination of his list: and this makes it clear that not even a *prima facie* case could be made out for most of the territories he includes. To take a random selection, it would surely be ludicrous to suggest that Fiji, British New Guinea or Upper Burma were annexed in order to protect large British investments, or even as a field for subsequent investment. In each case secular explanations seem fully to account for their annexation: the chaotic condition of a mixed society in the Pacific, the fears of Australia for her military security, and the frontier problems of India. And even where, as in Malaya, large capital investment did take place after annexation, the time factor must be considered. Were the British investor and the government really so alert to the possible future need for fields for investment? Or did annexation in fact take place for quite other reasons, being followed by investment when new conditions and new possibilities arose which were then totally unforeseen?

Yet, obvious though the weakness of the theory of 'imperialism' may seem when applied in specific cases, it is also clear that it would be extremely difficult to invalidate Hobson's model by a process of piecemeal examination. For the adherents of this, as of most comprehensive formulas, could counter, as Mr Strachey does, by asserting that an analytical explanation of the phenomenon merely supplied 'an unaccountable jumble of facts and dates ...'[23] or, as Professor Sweezey does, by calling all annexations that do not fit demonstrably into the pattern 'protective and anticipatory', or based on 'considerations of a strategic nature'.[24] That is, they could fight an indefinite rearguard action, retreating, as Mr Strachey does, on to the ultimate citadel of the historicist, with the assertion that 'After all, each of these things [capital exports and colonial annexation] undeniably existed. Only the intentionally blind will deny a connection between them'[25] Moreover, if the theory is false, it should be possible to demonstrate that its premises are false also. And, since the essential premise of 'imperialism' is the belief that the drive to acquire colonies after 1870 was the direct and necessary result of the need of the capitalists to export capital, this proposition demands careful examination.

It has been seen that this theory of surplus capital being forced out into the undeveloped world was expressed differently by Hobson and Lenin, and it will be convenient to consider Lenin's theory first. This was, it will be remembered, that the centrifugal force in the capitalist countries was the interest of the monopolistic 'finance-capitalists' who stood only to lose by investment at home.

In this the fallacy is immediately obvious. If it was true of any country, it was not true of Britain; for no one could maintain that British capital was then controlled by a few trusts or even cartels. These, of course, did exist in Britain, such as the Salt Union of 1888, the United Alkali Company of 1897, and others in textiles, shipping and steel. But, whatever the desires of their founders, they were in fact small, tentative and generally unsuccessful. British capital, whatever its tendencies, was still 'competitive' on Lenin's definition: and he in fact admitted that in Britain 'monopoly' must be taken to mean the reduction of the competing enterprises to 'a couple of dozen or so'.[26] This is hardly a satisfactory explanation of the need to export capital on a vast scale; so, presumably, Britain must have other reasons both for this and for territorial annexation. But, for different reasons, other countries also escape from the formula. Germany was Lenin's main example of the country dominated by trusts: but, as Professor Hancock has pointed out,[27] the age of German cartels came only after about 1900, while the main German grab for colonies had taken place during the previous twenty years. And America, which certainly had vast industrial and financial combinations, proved, in spite of Roosevelt's attempt to create an expansionist movement, to be the least 'imperialist' of all the capitalist states. It would therefore seem reasonable to conclude that Lenin's narrow explanation for the export of capital and the concurrent extension of European political control overseas is unacceptable.

Yet, whatever reasons are assigned to it, the fact of vast capital exports from the advanced countries in the period after 1870 remains. Sir G. Paish, in his much quoted article,[28] estimated that British overseas investment had increased between 1871 and 1911 from £785 m. to £3500 m., with a possible margin of error of 10 per cent either way. These figures are necessarily highly speculative; but there is no question that they were extremely large. And it is quite possible, even while rejecting Lenin's doctrinaire explanation, to see in the fact of this investment support for Hobson's theory that the urge to invest was the main cause of imperial expansion. Hence, the important questions must be faced. Was there in fact a vast reservoir of capital, generated (for example) in Britain, which was available for overseas investment? Why was it invested abroad rather than at home? And was it in fact invested in those areas which were annexed as colonies after 1871?

The publication in 1953 of Professor A. K. Cairncross's *Home and Foreign Investment 1870–1913*[29] has made it possible to approach these questions from a new and non-doctrinaire angle. The key to his interpretation lay in his rejection of Hobson's naive model of the British capitalist, embarrassed by an excess of capital, which could not be invested at home because of the 'under-consumption' factor, sending it abroad into undeveloped tropical territories where it would produce a high rate of interest. Instead, it is necessary to see that capital exports were not divorced from the economy of Great Britain but were in fact a necessary concomitant of the pattern of British trade and development. It can be shown that in fact the great majority of this capital went to the 'new' countries – to the United States, Canada, Argentine, Australasia and South Africa in particular – who were producing the primary materials that the British economy needed, and who had to have capital to expand their production for British consumption. To invest in these countries was therefore, in one sense, to invest in a primary sector of the British economy itself. And the return to Britain was not entirely, or even primarily, in a tribute of money, but in cheap and plentiful raw materials and food.

Moreover, far from weakening the British economy and reducing the living standards of the working class as both Hobson and Lenin thought they did, these capital exports were essential to both. Indeed, Cairncross argues convincingly that, by creating a demand for British products, these investments simultaneously kept up the level of profits at home, kept down the level of unemployment, and maintained wage levels. And, as the rate of overseas investment seems to have been greatest when the terms of trade were against Britain – the 1880's being an exceptional period when special factors in the United States offset the general tendency – Cairncross concludes that 'it was foreign investment that pulled Britain out of most depressions before 1914'.[30]

Seen, therefore, from the point of view of Britain's part in the world economy, rather than in purely domestic terms, capital exports no longer seem to have been forced out of the British economy by the selfish interests of the capitalists to maintain artificially high interest rates, and become, as Professor Nurkse has described them, 'a means whereby a vigorous process of economic growth came to be transmitted from the centre to the outlying areas of the world'.[31] That is to say that the force behind the export of capital was the pull exerted by urgent need for capital in the newly-developing countries, who, because of their higher potential productivity and because markets were available for their exports, could afford to pay higher rates of interest than were obtainable in Britain. Yet, important though it was in explaining why the British and European investor chose to send his capital abroad, this differential in rates of interest should not be overestimated. For the years 1905–9 Lehfeldt calculated the average interest on home, colonial and overseas investments to be 3.61 per cent, 3.94 per cent and 4.97 per cent respectively.[32] But even this to some extent obscures the real facts of the situation. The interest on British consols might be only 2.88 per cent: but rates of over 5 per cent were available on other British stocks, such as railway debentures and industrials. Equally, in railway loans, which were the most popular type of British overseas investment in the years before 1914, the interest rates varied from a mere 3.87 per cent on India railways to 4.7 per cent in foreign railways.[33] In fact it can be said that the British investor did not choose to invest abroad simply to get high interest rates, but, by and large, to get a slightly higher rate than on an equivalent type of stock at home. Above all, if he chose to invest in a British colony, it was not because he expected higher interest, but because he wanted greater security than he would get in an equivalent foreign investment. If he wanted a 'risk' investment – diamonds, copper, gold, nitrates, etc. – he went for it wherever the enterprise happened to be situated. But, in proportion to the whole, investments of this type were very small in 1911.[34]

But, for the present argument, the third and most important fact that emerges from the work of Paish, Cairncross and Nurkse is that Hobson was entirely wrong in assuming that any large proportion of British overseas investment went to those undeveloped parts of Africa and Asia which were annexed during the 'imperialist' grab after 1870. As Professor Nurkse has remarked of Hobson:

> Had he tried to do what he did for trade, that is, to show the geographical distribution of overseas investment, he would have found that British capital tended to bypass the primitive tropical economies and flowed mainly to the regions of recent settlement outside as well as inside the British Empire.[35]

And the figures published by Paish in 1911 demonstrate this conclusively.[36] The bulk of British investment then lay in the United States, £688 m., South America, £587 m., Canada, £372 m., Australasia, £380 m., India and Ceylon, £365 m., and South Africa, £351 m. By contrast, West Africa had received only £29 m., the Straits and Malay States, £22 m., and the remaining British possessions, £33 m. These last were, of course, by no means negligible amounts, and indicate clearly that in some at least of the tropical dependencies which had been recently acquired, British finance was finding scope for profit and investment. But this does not make Hobson's thesis any more valid. The sums invested in these tropical areas, whether newly annexed or not, were quite marginal to the total overseas investment, and continued to be relatively very small in the years immediately before 1911. Hence, to maintain that Britain had found it necessary to acquire these territories because of an urgent need for new fields for investment is simply unrealistic: and, with the rejection of this hypothesis, so ingeniously conjured up by Hobson, the whole basis of his theory that 'imperialism' was the product of economic necessity collapses.

IV

But to suggest that Hobson and Lenin were mistaken in thinking that the need to export capital from Europe after 1870 was so intense that it made the colonization of most of Africa and the Pacific necessary as fields for investment is merely to throw the question open again. The essential problem remains: on what other grounds is it possible to explain this sudden expansion of European possessions, whose motive force is called imperialism?

For the historian it is natural to look for an explanation of these developments which is not based on *a priori* reasoning, does not claim to be a comprehensive formula, and is not out of line with long-term historical developments. It would, of course, be unreasonable to expect to find in the late nineteenth century any precise repetition of earlier patterns of imperial expansion: at the same time it would seem reasonable to look carefully for evidence of continuity of motive and policy with earlier periods before falling back on the conclusion that events after 1870 were unique.

Looking broadly over the four centuries since the early Portuguese discoveries, it may be said that, although European motives for acquiring colonies were extremely complex, they fell into two general categories. First was the specifically economic motive, whose aim was to create a lucrative trade for the metropolitan country.[37] Its typical expression was the trading base or factory, secured by some form of agreement with the local ruler: but, where no commodities already existed for trade, it could result in territorial possessions, like the sugar islands of the Caribbean, or the spice islands of the East; the fur-producing parts of North America, and the silver mines of Peru. The export of capital played no significant part in this economic activity, for Europe had little surplus capital before the nineteenth century, and investment was restricted to the immediate needs of trade itself, of the mines, sugar estates, etc.

By contrast, it is clear that from the earliest days of European expansion the margin between economic and other motives was small, and that many colonies were rather the product of political and military rivalries than of the desire for profit. The mercantile practices followed by all European states were as much concerned with national power as with economic advantage, and tended, as Adam Smith pointed out, to subordinate opulence to the needs of security. Indeed, by the eighteenth century, imperial policies had come to be largely a reflection of European power politics: and the struggle for territorial supremacy in America, India and the strategic bases on the route to the East were the outcome of political rather than of strictly economic competition. Britain's decision to retain Canada rather than Guadaloupe in 1763 may perhaps stand as an example of preference given to a colony offering mainly military security and prestige over one whose value was purely economic.

FREE TRADE, MERCANTILISM, AND IMPERIALISM

If, then, a general view of pre-nineteenth century imperial policies shows the complexity of its aims – made still more complicated in the early nineteenth century by the important new element of humanitarianism – it must seem surprising that Hobson should have interpreted post-1870 imperialism in narrowly economic terms, and have ignored the possibility that strictly political impulses may once again have been of major importance. The reason would seem to be that the evolution of imperial practices since about 1815 appeared, at the end of the century, to have constituted a clear break with earlier methods; to have made both the economic and the political criteria of earlier times irrelevant; and thus to have made comparison pointless. With the independence of almost all the American colonies, and the subsequent adoption by Britain – the chief remaining colonial power – of the practices of free trade, the possession of colonies no longer offered any positive economic advantage. The colonial trades were now open to all; bullion-hunting became the function of the individual prospector; and emigration, although it led to new British colonies in Australasia, flowed more naturally into the existing states of the new world. On the political side also, colonies had ceased to play an important part in diplomacy. With the preponderance of Britain as a naval power, and the weakness of most European states, power politics were largely restricted to Britain, France and Russia. As between them competitive aggressiveness was recurrent: but, except briefly in the Pacific, and more frequently in the Near East and on the borders of India, their rivalry did not produce any major competition for new territory. And this seemed to imply that the end of mercantilism had been followed by the end also of political imperialism: which in turn suggested that the renewal of a general international desire for colonies after 1870 must have sprung from some new phenomenon – the unprecedented need to acquire openings for the safe investment of surplus capital.

It is mainly because Hobson's theory of 'imperialism' in his own time was based on this theory of discontinuity in nineteenth century history that it must be regarded as fallacious. For there had, in fact, been no break in the continuity of imperial development; merely a short-term variation in the methods used, corresponding with a temporary change in world conditions. In the first place, the extension of the territorial possessions of the three surviving great powers continued intermittently throughout: and the list of British acquisitions between 1840 and 1871 alone bears comparison with those of the following thirty years. On what grounds, in this period of so-called 'anti-imperialism', are these to be explained? Obviously no single explanation will serve. Hong Kong stood alone as a trading base with a specifically economic function. Queensland was the result of internal expansion in Australia, British Columbia of rivalry from the United States. But the rest – the Punjab, Sind, Berar, Oudh and Lower Burma on the frontiers of British India; Basutoland, Griqualand and (temporarily) the Transvaal on the Cape frontier; and small areas round existing trading bases in West Africa – stand as evidence that an existing empire will tend always to expand its boundaries. They were not the product of an expansive British policy, but of the need for military security, for administrative efficiency, or for the protection of indigenous peoples on the frontiers of existing colonies. Basically, they demonstrated the fact, familiar in earlier centuries, that colonies which exist in a power vacuum will tend always to expand slowly until they meet with some immovable political or geographical obstacle; and that a metropolitan government can do little more than slow down the speed of movement. For the purpose of the present argument this process may be said to indicate that Hobson needed no new explanation for the bulk of British acquisitions after 1870: for, as has already been pointed out, most of the new colonies on his list differed little in type or situation from those just mentioned – and were indeed mostly the extension of the same colonial frontiers. And, to this extent, late nineteenth century imperialism was merely the continuation of a process which had begun centuries earlier.

At the same time, it must be said that this 'contiguous area' theory does not fully cover certain of the new British possessions on Hobson's list. For some of them, like East Africa, were not strictly contiguous to an existing British colony; and others, such as Nigeria or Rhodesia, were clearly annexed too suddenly and on too large a scale to be seen as the product of the domestic needs of Lagos or the Cape. These therefore suggest that some other factor was at work – competition for new colonies on political grounds – which will be considered later.

Again, in the sphere of economic policy, the antithesis between different parts of the nineteenth century were greatly exaggerated and misunderstood by Hobson. The rejection of most of the mercantile devices for stimulating European trade had not meant that trade ceased to be a matter of national concern, or that governments ceased to use political means to support their men of business; the contrast with earlier centuries lay mainly in the methods now used. Hobson seemed to think that free trade had ended 'economic imperialism' of the mercantile variety simply because political control was no longer regarded as a prerequisite for economic exploitation of an undeveloped area. But, as Messrs. Gallacher and Robinson have pointed out,[38] 'formal' control, as in a colony, was not the only way in which 'economic imperialism' could operate; indeed, it now had two complementary features. On its specifically economic side it implied, as always, the control of the economic assets of some other country for the advantage of the metropolitan state. And the essential weapons of the European trader or financier were economic – the demand for his goods, his capital or his credit, and the effectiveness of the organization he built up in a country lacking business organization. The stranglehold he thus obtained differed only in detail from that held in the eighteenth century by British firms in the American colonies, transferred now to the similarly defenceless, though politically independent, states of South America, the Middle and Far East.

By the end of the nineteenth century most of the world had been thus brought under the economic control of European, and now also United States, business enterprise: their trade was organized and carried by foreign merchants, their revenues mortgaged to the loans they had received. This indeed was 'economic imperialism' in its purest form; cosmopolitan in outlook, unconcerned with political frontiers, showing no interest in the creation of 'formal' colonies except where, as in China, the formula of the open door proved otherwise unworkable. Only in the absolute volume of its activity, and in the increasing competition between rivals from newly industrialized countries, did the character of 'economic imperialism' change before 1914. And, while it remained thus strictly economic and cosmopolitan, the 'division of the world among the international trusts', which Lenin prophesied, remained a possibility.

Yet, even in its classical form, 'economic imperialism' required political support from governments at home: and, in view of developments after about 1870, it is important to define the nature of the support it received. Essentially the men of business needed only two things which their own enterprise could not supply: a minimum standard of political security at the periphery, and the solution of the quasi-political problems arising out of their relations with foreign rivals by diplomatic action at the centre. The first need was met by the network of treaties made for them with their client countries which secured equality of opportunity and reasonable tariffs, and was backed up, where necessary, by the use of threats and force. In the environment of the free world economy, these were the equivalents of the commercial monopolies of the mercantile period in that they supplied the political basis for successful business enterprise in undeveloped countries.

Second, and parallel with this, went the constant diplomatic work of the foreign offices of Europe in maintaining the balance between their nationals at the circumference. On the common assumption that it was to the general interest that competition should remain fair, that an artificial monopoly was to the advantage of none, and that such problems must not be allowed to harm international relations, diplomacy sought to settle these disputes without taking refuge in unilateral annexation of the area concerned. In this it was generally successful, where the will to succeed existed: and the Anglo-French condominium of 1906 in the New Hebrides stands as a late example of how such problems could be met.

It is now possible to place the imperialism of the period of Hobson's *Study* in its historical context, and to attempt a definition of the extent to which it differed from that of earlier years. The most obvious fact on which his theory was based was that, by contrast with the preceding half-century, vast areas of the world were quickly brought under European control for the first time: and it is now evident that this cannot be explained in terms of either of the two tendencies operating throughout the earlier nineteenth century. Although the break with the past was not as sharp as Hobson seemed to think, it remains true that many British annexations cannot be explained on the 'contiguous area' theory: and the new possessions of France, Italy and Germany were quite definitely in a different category. But neither can these facts be explained on Hobson's theory: for, as has been said, the places now to be taken over had hitherto attracted little capital, and did not attract it in any quantity subsequently. Nor, again, can an explanation be found in the more general theory of 'economic imperialism', for these places in the Pacific and in Africa for which the nations now competed were of marginal economic importance; and, on the assumptions of the past fifty years, governments might have been expected to reject demands by their nationals for annexation of territories whose administrative costs would be out of all proportion to their economic value to the nation. In sum, the most obvious facts of the new phase of imperialism cannot be explained as the logical continuation of the recent past, nor in Hobson's terms of a new economic factor. What, then, was the explanation?

An answer is not, of course, hard to find, and indeed emerges clearly from the vast literature now available.[39] With the exception of the supporters of the 'imperialism' thesis, the consensus of opinion is very marked. The new factor in imperialism was not something without precedent, certainly not anything uniquely economic, but essentially a throw-back to some of the characteristic attitudes and practices of the eighteenth century. Just as, in the early nineteenth century, the economic interests had demanded effectively that imperial questions should no longer be decided on political grounds, demanding opulence in place of security, so, at the end of the century, the balance was again reversed. The outstanding feature of the new situation was the subordination of economic to political considerations, the preoccupation with national security, military power and prestige.

Again, reasons are not hard to find. The significant fact about the years after 1870 was that Europe became once again an armed camp. The creation of a united Germany, the defeat of Austria and, above all, of France were to dominate European thinking until 1914. Between Germany and France there stood the question of Alsace-Lorraine: and for both the primary consideration was now a system of alliances which would, on the German side, prevent French counter-attack, on the French side, make revenge possible. Inevitably the rest of Europe was drawn into the politics of the balance of power between them; and for all statesmen military strength became once again the criterion of national greatness. Inevitably too this situation, with its similarities to the politics of the eighteenth century, brought in its train a return to many of the attitudes of mercantilism. Emigration to foreign states, instead of being regarded as an economic safety valve, became once again a loss of military or manufacturing manpower; and population statistics became a measure of relative national strength. Protective tariffs came back also, with the primary aim of building up national self-sufficiency and the power to make war.

Under such circumstances it was only to be expected that colonies would be regarded once again as assets in the struggle for power and status: but in fact the attitude of the powers to the imperial question was not at first a simple one. Indeed, it cannot be said that the attitudes characteristic of 'the imperialism of free trade' were seriously weakened until the mid-1880's; and until then it seemed possible that the colonial question might be kept clear of European politics. This is not in fact surprising. For most of the men who then ruled Europe retained a realistic appreciation of the potential value to their countries of those parts of the world that were available for annexation. Bismarck in particular recognized that, as sources of raw materials, as fields for emigration or as spheres for trade, the areas available in Africa and the Pacific had little to offer Germany, whatever national advantages those with private interests there might claim. At best they might offer naval bases, a strictly limited trade, and bargaining counters for use in diplomacy. It is improbable that Bismarck ever really changed this opinion: and, while he held off, it was unlikely that any other power would feel strong enough to precipitate a rush for new colonies. Even Belgian and French action in the Congo failed to do this; although their ambitions showed the probable trend of future events.

It was, therefore, Bismarck's action in 1884–5, in announcing the formal control by Germany over parts of West and South West Africa, and of New Guinea, that really began the new phase of political imperialism: and it is therefore important to consider his reasons for giving Germany a 'colonial policy'. Was it, as Miss Townsend has argued,[40] that the pressure of the commercial interest involved in these places, and the arguments of the new colonial party in politics convinced him that colonies were an economic necessity to Germany? The answer must be that it was not. In 1884 Bismarck seems to have decided that it was time for him to stop playing the honest broker in the disputes of other powers over their own possessions – such as Egypt and the Congo – and that, on two counts, both essentially diplomatic, Germany should now stake her own claims to colonies. The first was that it was politically desirable to show France that his recent support for Britain on the Egyptian question did not imply a general hostility towards her, since he was now prepared to take action resented by Britain: the second that Britain should be made to see that German support for her in the colonial field must be repaid by closer co-operation in Europe.[41]

In a narrow sense, then, the race for colonies was the product of diplomacy rather than of any more positive force. Germany set the example by claiming exclusive control over areas in which she had an arguable commercial stake, but no more, as a means of adding a new dimension to her international bargaining power, both in respect of what she had already taken, and of what she might claim in the future. Thereafter the process could not be checked; for, under conditions of political tension, the fear of being left out of the partition of the globe overrode all practical considerations.

Perhaps Britain was the only country which showed genuine reluctance to take a share; and this was due both to her immense stake in the continuance of the *status quo* for reasons of trade, and to her continued realism in assessing the substantive value of the lands under dispute. And the fact that she too joined in the competition demonstrated how contagious the new political forces were. Indeed, until the end of the century, imperialism may best be seen as the extension into the periphery of the political struggle in Europe. At the centre the balance was so nicely adjusted that no positive action, no major change in the status or territory of either side was possible. Colonies thus became a means out of the impasse; sources of diplomatic strength, prestige-giving accessions of territory, hope for future economic development. New worlds were being brought into existence in the vain hope that they would maintain or redress the balance of the old.

This analysis of the dynamic force of the new imperialism has been stated in purely political terms. What part was played in it by the many non-political interests with a stake in the new colonies: the traders, the investors, the missionaries, and the speculators? For these were the most vociferous exponents of a 'forward' policy in most countries: and to men like Hobson it seemed that their influence, if backed by that of the greater interest of the financier, was decisive in causing the politicians to act.

Again the problem is complex. In general terms the answer would seem to be that, while statesmen were very much aware of the pressure groups – conscious of the domestic political advantage of satisfying their demands, and often themselves sympathetic to the case they put up – they were not now, any more than earlier in the century, ready to undertake the burden of new colonies simply on their account. What made it seem as if these interests were now calling the tune was that the choice facing the statesman was no longer between annexation and the continued independence of the area in question: it was now between action and allowing a rival to step in. Salisbury and Rosebery may well have been convinced by the argument of men like Lugard that, on humanitarian grounds, it would be desirable for Britain to bring law and order to Uganda. But it was the threat of German or French occupation of the key to the Nile and Egypt that decided them to act. Yet if, in the last resort, the decision by Britain or any other country to annex was based on the highest reasons of state, it is also true that the very existence of these hitherto embarrassing pressure groups now became a diplomatic asset, since they were the obvious grounds on which valid claims could be made, an approximation to the principle of effective occupation.

Thus the relative importance of the concrete interests and demands of the various pressure groups, as compared with the political criteria of the statesmen, was the reverse of that assigned to them by Hobson; and, if the word 'investment' is taken to cover the whole range of these interests, the point has been well summarized by Professor E. Staley:

> Conflicts between the great powers over private investment matters have rarely, almost never, reached a state of dangerous international tension except in cases where the powers have been led into conflict by the pursuit of political policies extraneous to the investment affair itself. The best explanation of these facts runs in terms of the way in which those in charge of foreign policies interpret national advantage. Where investments can be regarded as economic aids to established lines of foreign policy, they are supported most vigorously; investments receive least vigorous political backing where they are not in any sense tools of national policy or where they run counter to national policy.[42]

Yet, if the first, and territorially decisive, factor in the imperialism of the post 1870 period was this unemotional, almost cynical, policy of the statesmen, it cannot be said that it was the only new feature, nor, in the long run, the most important one. For by the time Hobson wrote in 1902, those who supported a 'forward' policy were no longer the few diplomatic chess-players, nor even the relatively small pressure groups, but millions of people for whom an empire had become a matter of faith. Indeed, the rise of this imperialist ideology, this belief that colonies were an essential attribute of any great nation, is one of the most astonishing facts of the period. It was, moreover, an international creed, with beliefs that seemed to differ very little from one country to another. Its basic ideas had been clearly expressed as early as 1879 by a German, Treitschke:

> Every virile people has established colonial power . . . All great nations in the fulness of their strength have desired to set their mark upon barbarian lands and those who fail to participate in this great rivalry will play a pitiable role in time to come. The colonizing impulse has become a vital question for every great nation.[43]

By the end of the century, the 'imperial idea', as it has significantly been called,[44] after twenty years of propaganda by such groups of enthusiasts as the German *Kolonverein* and the British Imperial Federation League, had become dominant. The process of educating the public has now been examined in detail:[45] and it is interesting to see that in each case the historian has found it necessary to deal almost entirely in ideas, rather than in concrete facts. This is no accident. The imperialism of the early twentieth century, although ironically the product of the power politics of the previous two decades, bore little resemblance to the ideas of men like Bismarck and Salisbury. It was the generation of Kaiser Wilhelm II, of Theodore Roosevelt and of Chamberlain (in his later years) that came to adopt for the first time this mystical faith in the value of an empire. Chamberlain's tariff campaign of 1903–5 indicates that such tenuous links as the imperial movement had ever had with precise calculations of economic – and even of political – advantage had now ceased to be of primary importance.

For, by that time, imperialism had been shown to be a delusion. It was already the common experience of all the countries that had taken part in the partition of Africa and the Pacific that, except for the few windfalls, such as gold in West Africa, diamonds in South West Africa, and copper in the Congo and Rhodesia, the new colonies were white elephants: and that only small sectional interests in any country had obtained real benefits from them. Whether German, French, British or Italian, their trade was minute (German trade with her colonies was only $^1/_2$ per cent of her external trade); their attraction for investors, except in mines, etc., was negligible; they were unsuitable for large-scale emigration, and any economic development that had taken place was usually the result of determined efforts by the European state concerned to create an artificial asset. Moreover, in most cases, the cost of administration was a dead weight on the imperial power. By 1900 all these facts were apparent and undeniable. They were constantly pressed by opponents of colonial expansion in each country; and Hobson's book consisted primarily of an exposition of these defects. Yet public opinion was increasingly oblivious to such facts: the possession of colonies had become a sacred cow, a psychological necessity. While the financiers continued to invest their money, as they had done in the previous fifty years, in economically sound projects, such as the Baghdad railway, in the non-tropical settlement colonies and independent countries, and in places like India – remaining true to the criteria of true 'economic imperialism' – the politicians, pressed on now by a public demand they could not control, even if they had wanted to, continued, with increasing bellicosity, to scrape the bottom of the barrel for yet more colonial burdens for the white man to carry.

V

The reassessment of so abstract a concept as 'imperialism', particularly within the present limitations of space, cannot hope to prove or to disprove anything. At the most it may lead to the suggestion that an earlier synthesis does not appear to fit the facts. How far can it be said that the arguments put forward above make necessary a revision of the theory of 'imperialism' which derives from Hobson and Lenin?

The general conclusion would seem to emerge that, as an historical interpretation of the expansion of European empires between 1870 and 1914, it is unacceptable. As an economic theory it is unsatisfactory because detailed investigations have shown that the alleged need of the European investor, monopolist or individual capitalist, to find outlets for his surplus capital had little or nothing to do with the division of Africa and the Pacific between the European powers. Again, as a theory of historical development, which makes this expansion seem to be a unique phenomenon, capable of being understood only in terms of the special methodology used by Hobson and Lenin, it ignores both the continuity of nineteenth century developments, and also its similarity to earlier periods of European imperialism. In most respects, indeed, there was no break in continuity after 1870. On the political side, many of the new annexations of territory, particularly those made by Britain, resulted from the situation of existing possessions: and, on the economic side, the rapid expansion of European commercial and financial influence throughout the world – the true 'economic imperialism' – did not change its character after 1870; and was no more likely then than before to have resulted in significant acquisitions of land. The real break in the continuity of nineteenth century development – the rapid extension of 'formal' control over independent areas of Africa and the East – was a specifically political phenomenon in origin, the outcome of fears and rivalries within Europe. The competition for colonies, being as characteristic of economically weak countries like Italy as of others which had large resources of capital available for overseas deployment, was indeed more obviously a throw-back to the imperialism of the eighteenth century than the characteristic product of nineteenth century capitalism in an advanced phase. And the ideological fervour that became the dominant feature of the imperial movement after about 1890 was the natural outcome of this fevered nationalism, not the artifact of vested economic interests.

Yet, in conclusion, a paradox must be noted. Hobson's analysis of 'imperialism' was defective: but the fact that it was defective was probably the result of his having grasped one essential truth about the imperial movement – that it had become irrational. Seeing clearly that the new tropical colonies could not be justified in terms of their economic value to the metropolitan powers – the criterion a nineteenth century rationalist would naturally apply – he was forced back on the theory that they must have been of value to sectional interests at least; and that these had succeeded in hoodwinking a presumably sane public opinion. Seen in this light, Hobson's sinister capitalists and their 'parasites' were nothing more than a hypothesis, a *deus ex machina*, to balance an equation between the assumed rationality of mankind and the unreasonableness of imperial policies: and the book was a plea for a return to a sane standard of values.

His mistake, then, was to think that the equation needed such artificial adjustment. For, in the second half of the twentieth century, it can be seen that imperialism owed its popular appeal not to the sinister influence of the capitalists, but to its inherent attractions for the masses. In the new quasidemocratic Europe, the popularity of the imperial idea marked a rejection of the sane morality of the account-book, and the adoption of a creed based on such irrational concepts as racial superiority and the prestige of the nation. Whether we interpret it, as did J. R. Schumpeter in 1919,[46] as a castback to the ideas of the old autocratic monarchies of the *ancien régime*, or as something altogether new – the first of the irrational myths that have dominated the first half of the twentieth century – it is clear that imperialism cannot be explained in simple terms of economic theory and the nature of finance capitalism. In its mature form it can best be described as a sociological phenomenon with roots in political facts: and it can properly be understood only in terms of the same social hysteria that has since given birth to other and more disastrous forms of aggressive nationalism.[47]

Notes

1 This essay arose out of reading the following recently published books: John Strachey, *The End of Empire* (London: Victor Gollanz Ltd. 1959. Pp. 351. 30s.); W. M. Macmillan, *The Road to Self-rule* (London: Faber and Faber. 1959. Pp. 296. 2 maps. 35s.); A. P. Thornton, *The Imperial Idea and its Enemies* (London: Macmillan & Co. Ltd. 1959. Pp. xiv + 370. 30s.); B. Semmel, *Imperialism and Social Reform* (London: George Allen & Unwin Ltd. 1960. Pp. 283. 28s.); H. Brunschwig, *Mythes et Réalités de l'impérialisme colonial français* (Paris: Librairie Armand Colin. 1960. Pp. 205). The essay has benefited from being read by Miss M. Perham and A. F. McC. Madden.
2 Published in 1902. References are to the third edition (1954).
3 When used in Hobson's sense, the word will here be printed in inverted commas.
4 R. Koebner, 'The concept of Economic Imperialism', *Economic History Review*, 2nd ser. II, no. 1.
5 *Ibid.* p. 16.
6 Hobson, p. 80.
7 Strachey, *op. cit.* p. 123.
8 Hobson based this conclusion on figures taken from Cd. 1761, p. 407, which are quoted in Hobson, p. 33. These were inaccurate. A. K. Cairncross (*Home and Foreign Investment 1870–1913*, Cambridge University Press, 1953), p. 189, shows that British exports to the empire increased from 24 per cent to 33.6 per cent of total British trade between 1870–2 and 1890–2, and imports from 21.9 per cent to 22.9 per cent in the same period. Both percentages continued to increase to 1910–12. But Hobson was right in saying that the new colonies contributed little to the increased volume of intra-imperial trade.
9 Hobson, pp. 41–5.
10 Hobson, p. 46.
11 Hobson, p. 62.
12 Hobson, p. 53.
13 Hobson, p. 62.
14 Hobson, p. 59.
15 Hobson, pp. 223–84.
16 V. I. Lenin, *Imperialism, the Highest Stage of Capitalism* (1916). References are to the Moscow edition of 1947. For the genesis of Lenin's ideas on the Marxist side see W. K. Hancock, *Survey of British Commonwealth Affairs*, vol. II, part I (1940). Appendix I, by W. H. B. Court, pp. 293–305.
17 There are, of course, many other differences which cannot be considered here, e.g. Hobson ignored 'semi-colonies', and thought of 'finance' as operating in an essentially free-trade environment.
18 Lenin, p. 112.
19 Lenin, p. 111.
20 Strachey, p. 322.

21 Strachey, p. 327.
22 See J. S. Marais, *The Fall of Kruger's Republic* (Oxford, Clarendon Press, 1961), pp. 62–3, 138–40, 162 and n. 3, 228–9, 233–4, 247–56, 324–5.
23 Strachey, p. 123.
24 Sweezey, p. 303.
25 Strachey, p. 124.
26 Lenin, p. 26.
27 W. K. Hancock, *The Wealth of Colonies* (Cambridge, 1950), pp. 11–12.
28 G. Paish, 'Great Britain's foreign investments', *Journal of the Royal Statistical Society*, LXXIV, 187.
29 *Op. cit.* Since the present essay was written, an article has been published by M. Blaug, 'Economic Imperialism Revisited', *Yale Review*, L, no. 3 (1961), 335–49, which supports most of the arguments put forward in this section.
30 Cairncross, p. 188.
31 R. Nurkse, *Patterns of Trade and Development* (Stockholm, 1959), p. 14.
32 Quoted by Cairncross, p. 227.
33 *Ibid.*
34 Paish, *loc. cit.* tables on pp. 180, 182, 184.
35 Nurkse, p. 19.
36 Paish, *loc. cit.* p. 186.
37 R. Pares, 'The economic factors in the history of the Empire', *Economic History Review*, VII (1937), 2, for a fuller discussion of this. His interpretation of the period after 1870 differs from that of the present writer.
38 'The Imperialism of Free Trade', *Economic History Review*, 2nd ser. VI. no. 1 (1953).
39 It is impossible here to give an adequate list. On the British side a good bibliography, to about 1957, is available in the *Cambridge History of the British Empire*, vol. III. Later works include: M. Perham, *Lugard* (2 vols. London, 1956 and 1960); R. Oliver, *Sir Harry Johnston* (London, 1957); and W. M. Macmillan, *The Road to Self Rule* (London, 1959). For France there is a good bibliography in H. Brunschwig, *Mythes et Réalités de l'impérialisme colonial français* (Paris, 1960). For Germany see M. E. Townsend, *Origins of Modern German Colonization, 1871–1885* (New York, 1921), and *The Rise and Fall of the German Colonial Empire, 1884–1918* (New York, 1930).
40 *Origins of Modern German Colonization, 1871–1885* (New York, 1921).
41 A useful summary of the arguments and the evidence is in the *C.H.B.E.* III, 114–22. Mr A. J. P. Taylor described Bismarck's action as 'the accidental by-product of an abortive Franco-German entente'. Taylor, *Germany's first bid for colonies, 1884–1885* (London, 1938), p. 6.
42 E. Staley, *War and the private investor* (Chicago, 1935), pp. 387–8. It remains true, however, that in the aftermath the main, possibly the only, advantage of the new colonies went to these special interests – particularly the soldiers and administrators, to whom they offered careers; the missions, who gained security; and the wide range of concession-hunters and government contractors who swarmed in all the new colonies.
43 Quoted in M. E. Townsend, *Origins of Modern German Colonization, 1871–1885*, p. 27.
44 By A. P. Thornton, *The Imperial Idea and its enemies*.
45 For Britain, C. A. Bodelsen, *Mid Victorian Imperialism* (Copenhagen, 1924, reprinted 1960); B. Semmel, *op. cit.*; Thornton, *op. cit.* and J. E. Tyler, *The Struggle for Imperial Unity, 1868–95* (London, 1938), in particular. For France, H. Brunschwig, *op. cit.* For Germany, Townsend, *op. cit.*

46 *Imperialism and the Social Classes* (reprinted by Basil Blackwell, Oxford, 1951).
47 Since this essay went to press, *Africa and the Victorians*, by R. E. Robinson and J. Gallagher, with A. Denny (London: Macmillan & Co Ltd. 1961. Pp. xii + 491, 4 maps. 45*s*.) has become available: and it is hoped to print a review of it in the next issue of this journal. In relation to the present essay the book would appear to give strong support to the central argument on the political nature of the post-1870 imperialism. On the other hand it puts forward a specific motive for British participation in Africa – the security of the Suez Canal: and it makes British action there in 1882, rather than Bismarck's claims in 1884, the starting point of the general grab for African territory.

42

THE IMPERIALISM OF FREE TRADE

John Gallagher and Ronald Robinson

Source: *Economic History Review* 6(1), 1953: 1–15.

I

It ought to be a commonplace that Great Britain during the nineteenth century expanded overseas by means of 'informal empire'[1] as much as by acquiring dominion in the strict constitutional sense. For purposes of economic analysis it would clearly be unreal to define imperial history exclusively as the history of those colonies coloured red on the map. Nevertheless, almost all imperial history has been written on the assumption that the empire of formal dominion is historically comprehensible in itself and can be cut out of its context in British expansion and world politics. The conventional interpretation of the nineteenth-century empire continues to rest upon study of the formal empire alone, which is rather like judging the size and character of icebergs solely from the parts above the water-line.

The imperial historian, in fact, is very much at the mercy of his own particular concept of empire. By that, he decides what facts are of 'imperial' significance; his data are limited in the same way as his concept, and his final interpretation itself depends largely upon the scope of his hypothesis. Different hypotheses have led to conflicting conclusions. Since imperial historians are writing about different empires and since they are generalizing from eccentric or isolated aspects of them, it is hardly surprising that these historians sometimes contradict each other.

The orthodox view of nineteenth-century imperial history remains that laid down from the standpoint of the racial and legalistic concept which inspired the Imperial Federation movement. Historians such as Seeley and Egerton looked on events in the formal empire as the only test of imperial activity; and they regarded the empire of kinship and constitutional dependence as an organism with its own laws of growth. In this way the nineteenth century was divided into periods of imperialism and anti-imperialism, according to the extension or contraction of the formal empire and the degree of belief in the value of British rule overseas.

Ironically enough, the alternative interpretation of 'imperialism', which began as part of the radical polemic against the Federationists, has in effect only confirmed their analysis. Those who have seen imperialism as the high stage of capitalism and the inevitable result of foreign investment agree that it applied historically only to the period after 1880. As a result they have been led into a similar preoccupation with formal manifestations of imperialism because the late-Victorian age was one of spectacular extension of British rule. Consequently, Hobson and Lenin, Professor Moon and Mr Woolf[2] have confirmed from the opposite point of view their opponents' contention that late-Victorian imperialism was a qualitative change in the nature of British expansion and a sharp deviation from the innocent and static liberalism of the middle of the century. This alleged change, welcomed by one school, condemned by the other, was accepted by both.

For all their disagreement these two doctrines pointed to one interpretation; that mid-Victorian 'indifference' and late-Victorian 'enthusiasm' for empire were directly related to the rise and decline in free-trade beliefs. Thus Lenin wrote: 'When free competition in Great Britain was at its height, i.e. between 1840 and 1860, the leading British bourgeois politicians were ... of the opinion that the liberation of the colonies and their complete separation from Great Britain was inevitable and desirable.'[3] Professor Schuyler extends this to the decade from 1861 to 1870: '... for it was during those years that tendencies toward the disruption of the empire reached their climax. The doctrines of the Manchester school were at the height of their influence.'[4]

In the last quarter of the century, Professor Langer finds that 'there was an obvious danger that the British [export] market would be steadily restricted. Hence the emergence and sudden flowering of the movement for expansion.... Manchester doctrine had been belied by the facts. It was an outworn theory to be thrown into the discard.'[5] Their argument may be summarized in this way: the mid-Victorian formal empire did not expand, indeed it seemed to be disintegrating, therefore the period was anti-imperialist; the later-Victorian formal empire expanded rapidly, therefore this was an era of imperialism; the change was caused by the obsolescence of free trade.

The trouble with this argument is that it leaves out too many of the facts which it claims to explain. Consider the results of a decade of 'indifference' to empire. Between 1841 and 1851 Great Britain occupied or annexed New Zealand, the Gold Coast, Labuan, Natal, the Punjab, Sind and Hong Kong. In the next twenty years British control was asserted over Berar, Oudh, Lower Burma and Kowloon, over Lagos and the neighbourhood of Sierra Leone, over Basutoland, Griqualand and the Transvaal; and new colonies were established in Queensland and British Columbia. Unless this expansion can be explained by 'fits of absence of mind', we are faced with the paradox that it occurred despite the determination of the imperial authorities to avoid extending their rule.

This contradiction arises even if we confine our attention to the formal empire, as the orthodox viewpoint would force us to do. But if we look beyond into the regions of informal empire, then the difficulties become overwhelming. The normal account of South African policy in the middle of the century is that Britain abandoned any idea of controlling the interior. But in fact what looked like withdrawal from the Orange River Sovereignty and the Transvaal was based not on any *a priori* theories about the inconveniences of colonies but upon hard facts of strategy and commerce in a wider field. Great Britain was in South Africa primarily to safeguard the routes to the East, by preventing foreign powers from acquiring bases on the flank of those routes. In one way or another this imperial interest demanded some kind of hold upon Africa south of the Limpopo River, and although between 1852 and 1877 the Boer Republics were not controlled formally for this purpose by Britain, they were effectually dominated by informal paramountcy and by their dependence on British ports. If we refuse to narrow our view to that of formal empire, we can see how steadily and successfully the main imperial interest was pursued by maintaining supremacy over the whole region, and that it was pursued as steadily throughout the so-called anti-imperialist era as in the late-Victorian period. But it was done by shutting in the Boer Republics from the Indian Ocean: by the annexation of Natal in 1843, by keeping the Boers out of Delagoa Bay in 1860 and 1868, out of St Lucia Bay in 1861 and 1866, and by British intervention to block the union of the two Republics under Pretorius in 1860.[6] Strangely enough it was the first Gladstone Government which Schuyler regards as the climax of anti-imperialism, which annexed Basutoland in 1868 and Griqualand West in 1871 in order to ensure 'the safety of our South African Possessions'.[7] By informal means if possible, or by formal annexations when necessary, British paramountcy was steadily upheld.

Are these the actions of ministers anxious to preside over the liquidation of the British Empire? Do they look like 'indifference' to an empire rendered superfluous by free trade? On the contrary, here is a continuity of policy which the conventional interpretation misses because it takes account only of formal methods of control. It also misses the continuous grasp of the West African coast and of the South Pacific which British seapower was able to maintain. Refusals to annex are no proof of reluctance to control. As Lord Aberdeen put it in 1845: '... it is unnecessary to add that Her Majesty's Government will not view with indifference the assumption by another Power of a Protectorate which they, with due regard for the true interests of those [Pacific] islands, have refused.'[8]

Nor can the obvious continuity of imperial constitutional policy throughout the mid- and late-Victorian years be explained on the orthodox hypothesis. If the granting of responsible government to colonies was due to the mid-Victorian 'indifference' to empire and even a desire to be rid of it, then why was this policy continued in the late-Victorian period when Britain was interested above all in preserving imperial unity? The common assumption that British governments in the free-trade era considered empire superfluous arises from over-estimating the significance of changes in legalistic forms. In fact, throughout the Victorian period responsible government was withheld from colonies if it involved sacrificing or endangering British paramountcy or interests. Wherever there was fear of a foreign challenge to British supremacy in the continent or subcontinent concerned, wherever the colony could not provide financially for its own internal security, the imperial authorities retained full responsibility, or, if they had already devolved it, intervened directly to secure their interests once more. In other words, responsible government, far from being a separatist device, was simply a change from direct to indirect methods of maintaining British interests. By slackening the formal political bond at the appropriate time, it was possible to rely on economic dependence and mutual good-feeling to keep the colonies bound to Britain while still using them as agents for further British expansion.

The inconsistency between fact and the orthodox interpretation arises in yet another way. For all the extensive anthologies of opinion supposedly hostile to colonies, how many colonies were actually abandoned? For instance, the West Africa Committee of 1865 made a strong and much quoted case for giving up all but one of the West African settlements, but even as they sat these settlements were being extended. The Indian empire, however, is the most glaring gap in the traditional explanation. Its history in the 'period of indifference' is filled with wars and annexations.

Moreover, in this supposedly *laissez-faire* period India, far from being evacuated, was subjected to intensive development as an economic colony along the best mercantilist lines. In India it was possible, throughout most of the period of the British Raj, to use the governing power to extort in the form of taxes and monopolies such valuable primary products as opium and salt. Furthermore, the characteristics of so-called imperialist expansion at the end of the nineteenth century developed in India long before the date (1880) when Lenin believed the age of economic imperialism opened. Direct governmental promotion of products required by British industry, government manipulation of tariffs to help British exports, railway construction at high and guaranteed rates of interest to open the continental interior—all of these techniques of direct political control were employed in ways which seem alien to the so-called age of *laissez-faire*. Moreover, they had little to do, particularly in railway finance, with the folk-lore of rugged individualism. 'All the money came from the English capitalist' as a British official wrote, 'and, so long as he was guaranteed five per cent on the revenues of India, it was immaterial to him whether the funds which he lent were thrown into the Hooghly or converted into bricks and mortar.'[9]

To sum up: the conventional view of Victorian imperial history leaves us with a series of awkward questions. In the age of 'anti-imperialism' why were all colonies retained? Why were so many more obtained? Why were so many new spheres of influence set up? Or again, in the age of 'imperialism', as we shall see later, why was there such reluctance to annex further territory? Why did decentralization, begun under the impetus of anti-imperialism, continue? In the age of *laissez-faire* why was the Indian economy developed by the state?

These paradoxes are too radical to explain as merely exceptions which prove the rule or by concluding that imperial policy was largely irrational and inconsistent, the product of a series of accidents and chances. The contradictions, it may be suspected, arise not from the historical reality but from the historians' approach to it. A hypothesis which fits more of the facts might be that of a fundamental continuity in British expansion throughout the nineteenth century.

II

The hypothesis which is needed must include informal as well as formal expansion, and must allow for the continuity of the process. The most striking fact about British history in the nineteenth century, as Seeley pointed out, is that it is the history of an expanding society. The exports of capital and manufactures, the migration of citizens, the dissemination of the English language, ideas and constitutional forms, were all of them radiations of the social energies of the British peoples. Between 1812 and 1914 over twenty million persons emigrated from the British Isles, and nearly 70 per cent of them went outside the Empire.[10] Between 1815 and 1880, it is estimated, £1,187,000,000 in credit had accumulated abroad, but no more than one-sixth was placed in the formal empire. Even by 1913, something less than half of the £3,975,000,000 of foreign investment lay inside the Empire.[11] Similarly, in no year of the century did the Empire buy much more than one-third of Britain's exports. The basic fact is that British industrialization caused an ever-extending and intensifying development of overseas regions. Whether they were formally British or not, was a secondary consideration.

Imperialism, perhaps, may be defined as a sufficient political function of this process of integrating new regions into the expanding economy; its character is largely decided by the various and changing relationships between the political and economic elements of expansion in any particular region and time. Two qualifications must be made. First, imperialism may be only indirectly connected with economic integration in that it sometimes extends beyond areas of economic development, but acts for their strategic protection. Secondly, although imperialism is a function of economic expansion, it is not a necessary function. Whether imperialist phenomena show themselves or not, is determined not only by the factors of economic expansion, but equally by the political and social organization of the regions brought into the orbit of the expansive society, and also by the world situation in general.

It is only when the polities of these new regions fail to provide satisfactory conditions for commercial or strategic integration and when their relative weakness allows, that power is used imperialistically to adjust those conditions. Economic expansion, it is true, will tend to flow into the regions of maximum opportunity, but maximum opportunity depends as much upon political considerations of security as upon questions of profit. Consequently, in any particular region, if economic opportunity seems large but political security small, then full absorption into the extending economy tends to be frustrated until power is exerted upon the state in question. Conversely, in proportion as satisfactory political frameworks are brought into being in this way, the frequency of imperialist intervention lessens and imperialist control is correspondingly relaxed. It may be suggested that this willingness to limit the use of paramount power to establishing security for trade is the distinctive feature of the British imperialism of free trade in the nineteenth century, in contrast to the mercantilist use of power to obtain commercial supremacy and monopoly through political possession.

On this hypothesis the phasing of British expansion or imperialism is not likely to be chronological. Not all regions will reach the same level of economic integration at any one time; neither will all regions need the same type of political control at any one time. As the British industrial revolution grew, so new markets and sources of supply were linked to it at different times, and the degree of imperialist action accompanying that process varied accordingly. Thus mercantilist techniques of formal empire were being employed to develop India in the mid-Victorian age at the same time as informal techniques of free trade were being used in Latin America for the same purpose. It is for this reason that attempts to make phases of imperialism correspond directly to phases in the economic growth of the metropolitan economy are likely to prove in vain. The fundamental continuity of British expansion is only obscured by arguing that changes in the terms of trade or in the character of British exports necessitated a sharp change in the process.

From this vantage point the many-sided expansion of British industrial society can be viewed as a whole of which both the formal and informal empires are only parts. Both of them then appear as variable political functions of the extending pattern of overseas trade, investment, migration and culture. If this is accepted, it follows that formal and informal empire are essentially interconnected and to some extent interchangeable. Then not only is the old, legalistic, narrow idea of empire unsatisfactory, but so is the old idea of informal empire as a separate, non-political category of expansion. A concept of informal empire which fails to bring out the underlying unity between it and the formal empire is sterile. Only within the total framework of expansion is nineteenth-century empire intelligible. So we are faced with the task of re-fashioning the interpretations resulting from defective concepts of organic constitutional empire on the one hand and Hobsonian 'imperialism' on the other.

The economic importance—even the pre-eminence—of informal empire in this period has been stressed often enough. What was overlooked was the inter-relation of its economic and political arms; how political action aided the growth of commercial supremacy, and how this supremacy in turn strengthened political influence. In other words, it is the politics as well as the economics of the informal empire which we have to include in the account. Historically, the relationship between these two factors has been both subtle and complex. It has been by no means a simple case of the use of gunboats to demolish a recalcitrant state in the cause of British trade. The type of political lien between the expanding economy and its formal or informal dependencies, as might be expected, has been flexible. In practice it has tended to vary with the economic value of the territory, the strength of its political structure, the readiness of its rulers to collaborate with British commercial or strategic purposes, the ability of the native society to undergo economic change without external control, the extent to which domestic and foreign political situations permitted British intervention, and, finally, how far European rivals allowed British policy a free hand.

Accordingly, the political lien has ranged from a vague, informal paramountcy to outright political possession; and, consequently, some of these dependent territories have been formal colonies whereas others have not. The difference between formal and informal empire has not been one of fundamental nature but of degree. The ease with which a region has slipped from one status to the other helps to confirm this. Within the last two hundred years, for example, India has passed from informal to formal association with the United Kingdom and, since World War II, back to an informal connexion. Similarly, British West Africa has passed through the first two stages and seems to-day likely to follow India into the third.

III

Let us now attempt, tentatively, to use the concept of the totality of British expansion described above to restate the main themes of the history of modern British expansion. We have seen that interpretations of this process fall into contradictions when based upon formal political criteria alone. If expansion both formal and informal is examined as a single process, will these contradictions disappear?

The growth of British industry made new demands upon British policy. It necessitated linking undeveloped areas with British foreign trade and, in so doing, moved the political arm to force an entry into markets closed by the power of foreign monopolies.

British policy, as Professor Harlow has shown,[12] was active in this way before the American colonies had been lost, but its greatest opportunities came during the Napoleonic Wars. The seizure of the French and Spanish West Indies, the filibustering expedition to Buenos Aires in 1806, the taking of Java in 1811, were all efforts to break into new regions and to tap new resources by means of political action. But the policy went further than simple house-breaking, for once the door was opened and British imports with their political implications were pouring in, they might stop the door from being shut again. Raffles, for example, temporarily broke the Dutch monopoly of the spice trade in Java and opened the island to free trade. Later, he began the informal British paramountcy over the Malacca trade routes and the Malay peninsula by founding Singapore. In South America, at the same time, British policy was aiming at indirect political hegemony over new regions for the purposes of trade. The British navy carried the Portuguese royal family to Brazil after the breach with Napoleon, and the British representative there extorted from his grateful clients the trade treaty of 1810 which left British imports paying a lower tariff than the goods of the mother country. The thoughtful stipulation was added 'that the Present Treaty shall be unlimited in point of duration, and that the obligations and conditions expressed or implied in it shall be perpetual and immutable'.[13]

From 1810 onwards this policy had even better chances in Latin America, and they were taken. British governments sought to exploit the colonial revolutions to shatter the Spanish trade monopoly, and to gain informal supremacy and the good will which would all favour British commercial penetration. As Canning put it in 1824, when he had clinched the policy of recognition: 'Spanish America is free and if we do not mismanage our affairs sadly she is *English.*'[14] Canning's underlying object was to clear the way for a prodigious British expansion by creating a new and informal empire, not only to redress the Old World balance of power but to restore British influence in the New. He wrote triumphantly: 'The thing is done ... the Yankees will shout in triumph: but it is they who lose most by our decision ... the United States have gotten the start of us in vain; and we link once more America to Europe.'[15] It would be hard to imagine a more spectacular example of a policy of commercial hegemony in the interests of high politics, or of the use of informal political supremacy in the interests of commercial enterprise. Characteristically, the British recognition of Buenos Aires, Mexico and Colombia took the form of signing commercial treaties with them.

In both the formal and informal dependencies in the mid-Victorian age there was much effort to open the continental interiors and to extend the British influence inland from the ports and to develop the hinterlands. The general strategy of this development was to convert these areas into complementary satellite economies, which would provide raw materials and food for Great Britain, and also provide widening markets for its manufactures.

This was the period, the orthodox interpretation would have us believe, in which the political arm of expansion was dormant or even withered. In fact, that alleged inactivity is seen to be a delusion if we take into account the development in the informal aspect. Once entry had been forced into Latin America, China and the Balkans, the task was to encourage stable governments as good investment risks, just as in weaker or unsatisfactory states it was considered necessary to coerce them into more co-operative attitudes.

In Latin America, however, there were several false starts. The impact of British expansion in Argentina helped to wreck the constitution and throw the people into civil war, since British trade caused the sea-board to prosper while the back lands were exploited and lagged behind. The investment crash of 1827 and the successful revolt of the pampas people against Buenos Aires[16] blocked further British expansion, and the rise to power of General Rosas ruined the institutional framework which Canning's strategy had so brilliantly set up. The new regime was uncooperative and its designs on Montevideo caused chaos around the Rio de la Plata, which led to that great commercial artery being closed to enterprise. All this provoked a series of direct British interventions during the 1840's in efforts to get trade moving again on the river, but in fact it was the attractive force of British trade itself, more than the informal imperialist action of British governments, which in this case restored the situation by removing Rosas from power.

British policy in Brazil ran into peculiar troubles through its tactless attempt to browbeat the Government of Rio de Janeiro into abolishing slavery. British political effectiveness was weakened, in spite of economic predominance, by the interference of humanitarian pressure groups in England. Yet the economic control over Brazil was strengthened after 1856 by the building of the railways; these—begun, financed and operated by British companies—were encouraged by generous concessions from the government of Brazil.

With the development of railways and steamships, the economies of the leading Latin American states were at last geared successfully to the world economy. Once their exports had begun to climb and foreign investment had been attracted, a rapid rate of economic growth was feasible. Even in the 1880's Argentina could double her exports and increase sevenfold her foreign indebtedness while the world price of meat and wheat was falling.[17] By 1913, in Latin America as a whole, informal imperialism had become so important for the British economy that £999,000,000, over a quarter of the total investment abroad, was invested in that region.[18]

But this investment, as was natural, was concentrated in such countries as Argentina and Brazil whose governments (even after the Argentine default of 1891) had collaborated in the general task of British expansion. For this reason there was no need for brusque or peremptory interventions on behalf of British interests. For once their economies had become sufficiently dependent on foreign trade the classes whose prosperity was drawn from that trade normally worked themselves in local politics to preserve the local political conditions needed for it. British intervention, in any case, became more difficult once the United States could make other powers take the Monroe doctrine seriously. The slackening in active intervention in the affairs of the most reliable members of the commercial empire was matched by the abandonment of direct political control over those regions of formal empire which were successful enough to receive self-government. But in Latin America, British governments still intervened, when necessary, to protect British interests in the more backward states; there was intervention on behalf of the bond holders in Guatemala and Colombia in the 'seventies, as in Mexico and Honduras between 1910 and 1914.

The types of informal empire and the situations it attempted to exploit were as various as the success which it achieved. Although commercial and capital penetration tended to lead to political co-operation and hegemony, there are striking exceptions. In the United States, for example, British business turned the cotton South into a colonial economy, and the British investor hoped to do the same with the Mid-West. But the political strength of the country stood in his way. It was impossible to stop American industrialization, and the industrialized sections successfully campaigned for tariffs, despite the opposition of those sections which depended on the British trade connexion. In the same way, American political strength thwarted British attempts to establish Texas, Mexico and Central America as informal dependencies.

Conversely, British expansion sometimes failed, if it gained political supremacy without effecting a successful commercial penetration. There were spectacular exertions of British policy in China, but they did little to produce new customers. Britain's political hold upon China failed to break down Chinese economic self-sufficiency. The Opium War of 1840, the renewal of war in 1857, widened the inlets for British trade but they did not get Chinese exports moving. Their main effect was an unfortunate one from the British point of view, for such foreign pressures put Chinese society under great strains as the Taiping Rebellion unmistakably showed.[19] It is important to note that this weakness was regarded in London as an embarrassment, and not as a lever for extracting further concessions. In fact, the British worked to prop up the tottering Pekin regime, for as Lord Clarendon put it in 1870, 'British interests in China are strictly commercial, or at all events only so far political as they may be for the protection of commerce'.[20] The value of this self-denial became clear in the following decades when the Pekin government, threatened with a scramble for China, leaned more and more on the diplomatic support of the honest British broker.

The simple recital of these cases of economic expansion, aided and abetted by political action in one form or other, is enough to expose the inadequacy of the conventional theory that free trade could dispense with empire. We have seen that it did not do so. Economic expansion in the mid-Victorian age was matched by a corresponding political expansion which has been overlooked because it could not be seen by that study of maps which, it has been said, drives sane men mad. It is absurd to deduce from the harmony between London and the colonies of white settlement in the mid-Victorian age any British reluctance to intervene in the fields of British interests. The warships at Canton are as much a part of the period as responsible government for Canada; the battlefields of the Punjab are as real as the abolition of suttee.

Far from being an era of 'indifference', the mid-Victorian years were the decisive stage in the history of British expansion overseas, in that the combination of commercial penetration and political influence allowed the United Kingdom to command those economies which could be made to fit best into her own. A variety of techniques adapted to diverse conditions and beginning at different dates were employed to effect this domination. A paramountcy was set up in Malaya centred on Singapore; a suzerainty over much of West Africa reached out from the port of Lagos and was backed up by the African squadron. On the east coast of Africa British influence at Zanzibar, dominant thanks to the exertions of Consul Kirk, placed the heritage of Arab command on the mainland at British disposal.

But perhaps the most common political technique of British expansion was the treaty of free trade and friendship made with or imposed upon a weaker state. The treaties with Persia of 1836 and 1857, the Turkish treaties of 1838 and 1861, the Japanese treaty of 1858, the favours extracted from Zanzibar, Siam and Morocco, the hundreds of anti-slavery treaties signed with crosses by African chiefs—all these treaties enabled the British government to carry forward trade with these regions.

Even a valuable trade with one region might give place to a similar trade with another which could be more easily coerced politically. The Russian grain trade, for example, was extremely useful to Great Britain. But the Russians' refusal to hear of free trade, and the British inability to force them into it, caused efforts to develop the grain of the Ottoman empire instead, since British pressure at Constantinople had been able to hustle the Turk into a liberal trade policy.[21] The dependence of the commercial thrust upon the political arm resulted in a general tendency for British trade to follow the invisible flag of informal empire.

Since the mid-Victorian age now appears as a time of large-scale expansion, it is necessary to revise our estimate of the so-called 'imperialist' era as well. Those who accept the concept of 'economic imperialism' would have us believe that the annexations at the end of the century represented a sharp break in policy, due to the decline of free trade, the need to protect foreign investment, and the conversion of statesmen to the need for unlimited land-grabbing. All these explanations are questionable. In the first place, the tariff policy of Great Britain did not change. Again, British foreign investment was no new thing and most of it was still flowing into regions outside the formal empire. Finally the statesmens' conversion to the policy of extensive annexation was partial, to say the most of it. Until 1887, and only occasionally after that date, party leaders showed little more enthusiasm for extending British rule than the mid-Victorians. Salisbury was infuriated by the 'superficial philanthropy' and 'roguery' of the 'fanatics' who advocated expansion.[22] When pressed to aid the missions in Nyasaland in 1888, he retorted: 'It is not our duty to do it. We should be risking tremendous sacrifices for a very doubtful gain.'[23] After 1888, Salisbury, Rosebery and Chamberlain accepted the scramble for Africa as a painful but unavoidable necessity which arose from a threat of foreign expansion and the irrepressible tendency of trade to overflow the bounds of empire, dragging the government into new and irksome commitments. But it was not until 1898 that they were sufficiently confident to undertake the reconquest of so vital a region as the Sudan.

Faced with the prospect of foreign acquisitions of tropical territory hitherto opened to British merchants, the men in London resorted to one expedient after another to evade the need of formal expansion and still uphold British paramountcy in those regions. British policy in the late, as in the mid-Victorian period preferred informal means of extending imperial supremacy rather than direct rule. Throughout the two alleged periods the extension of British rule was a last resort—and it is this preference which has given rise to the many 'anti-expansionist' remarks made by Victorian ministers. What these much quoted expressions obscure, is that in practice mid-Victorian as well as late-Victorian policy makers did not refuse to extend the protection of formal rule over British interests when informal methods had failed to give security. The fact that informal techniques were more often sufficient for this purpose in the circumstances of the mid-century than in the later period when the foreign challenge to British supremacy intensified, should not be allowed to disguise the basic continuity of policy. Throughout, British governments worked to establish and maintain British paramountcy by whatever means best suited the circumstances of their diverse regions of interest. The aims of the mid-Victorians were no more 'anti-imperialist' than their successors', though they were more often able to achieve them informally; and the late-Victorians were no more 'imperialist' than their predecessors, even though they were driven to annex more often. British policy followed the principle of extending control informally if possible and formally if necessary. To label the one method 'anti-imperialist' and the other 'imperialist', is to ignore the fact that whatever the method British interests were steadily safeguarded and extended. The usual summing up of the policy of the free trade empire as ' trade not rule' should read 'trade with informal control if possible; trade with rule when necessary'. This statement of the continuity of policy disposes of the over-simplified explanation of involuntary expansion inherent in the orthodox interpretation based on the discontinuity between the two periods.

Thus Salisbury as well as Gladstone, Knutsford as well as Derby and Ripon, in the so-called age of 'imperialism', exhausted all informal expedients to secure regions of British trade in Africa before admitting that further annexations were unavoidable. One device was to obtain guarantees of free trade and access as a reward for recognizing foreign territorial claims, a device which had the advantage of saddling foreign governments with the liability of rule whilst allowing Britons the commercial advantage. This was done in the Anglo-Portuguese Treaty of 1884, the Congo Arrangement of 1885, and the Anglo-German Agreement over East Africa in 1886. Another device for evading the extension of rule was the exclusive sphere of influence or protectorate recognized by foreign powers. Although originally these imposed no liability for pacifying or administering such regions, with changes in international law they did so after 1885. The granting of charters to private companies between 1881 and 1889, authorizing them to administer and finance new regions under imperial licence, marked the transition from informal to formal methods of backing British commercial expansion. Despite these attempts at 'imperialism on the cheap', the foreign challenge to British paramountcy in tropical Africa and the comparative absence there of large-scale, strong, indigenous political organizations which had served informal expansion so well elsewhere, eventually dictated the switch to formal rule.

One principle then emerges plainly: it is only when and where informal political means failed to provide the framework of security for British enterprise (whether commercial, or philanthropic or simply strategic) that the question of establishing formal empire arose. In satellite regions peopled by European stock, in Latin America or Canada, for instance, strong governmental structures grew up; in totally non-European areas, on the other hand, expansion unleashed such disruptive forces upon the indigenous structures that they tended to wear out and even collapse with use. This tendency in many cases accounts for the extension of informal British responsibility and eventually for the change from indirect to direct control.

It was in Africa that this process of transition manifested itself most strikingly during the period after 1880. Foreign loans and predatory bankers by the 1870's had wrecked Egyptian finances and were tearing holes in the Egyptian political fabric. The Anglo-French dual financial control, designed to safeguard the foreign bondholders and to restore Egypt as a good risk, provoked anti-European feeling. With the revolt of Arabi Pasha in 1881, the Khedive's government could serve no longer to secure either the all-important Canal or the foreign investors' pound of flesh.

The motives for the British occupation of 1882 were confused and varied: the desire, evident long before Disraeli's purchase of shares, to dominate the Canal; the interests of the bondholders; and the over-anxiety to forestall any foreign power, especially France, from taking advantage of the prevailing anarchy in Egypt to interpose its power across the British road to India. Nearly all Gladstone's Cabinet admitted the necessity of British intervention, although for different reasons, and, in order to hold together his distracted ministry, the Prime Minister agreed.

The British expedition was intended to restore a stable Egyptian government under the ostensible rule of the Khedive and inside the orbit of informal British influence. When this was achieved, the army, it was intended, should be withdrawn. But the expedition had so crushed the structure of Egyptian rule that no power short of direct British force could make it a viable and trustworthy instrument of informal hegemony and development. Thus the Liberal Government following its plan, which had been hastily evolved out of little more than ministerial disagreements, drifted into the prolonged occupation of Egypt it was intent on avoiding. In fact, the occupying power became directly responsible for the defence, the debts and development of the country. The perverse effect of British policy was gloomily summed up by Gladstone: 'We have done our Egyptian business and we are an Egyptian government.'[24] Egypt, then, is a striking example of an informal strategy misfiring due to the undermining of the satellite state by investment and by pseudo-nationalist reaction against foreign influence.

The Egyptian question, in so far as it was closely bound with the routes to India and the defence of the Indian empire itself, was given the highest priority by British policy in the 'eighties and 'nineties. In order to defend the spinal cord of British trade and empire, tropical African and Pacific claims were repeatedly sacrificed as pawns in the higher game. In 1884, for example, the Foreign Office decided that British vulnerability in Egypt made it unwise to compete with foreign powers in the opening scramble for West Africa; and it was therefore proposed '... to confine ourselves to securing the utmost possible freedom of trade on that [west] coast, yielding to others the territorial responsibilities ... and seeking compensation on the east coast ... where the political future of the country is of real importance to Indian and imperial interests.'[25] British policy was not one of indiscriminate land-grabbing. And, indeed, the British penetration into Uganda and their securing of the rest of the Nile Valley was a highly selective programme, in so far as it surrendered some British West African claims to France and transferred part of East Africa to Germany.

IV

Thus the mid-Victorian period now appears as an era of large-scale expansion, and the late-Victorian age does not seem to introduce any significant novelty into that process of expansion. The annexations of vast undeveloped territories, which have been taken as proof that this period alone was the great age of expansion, now pale in significance, at least if our analysis is anywhere near the truth. That the area of direct imperial rule was extended is true, but is it the most important or characteristic development of expansion during this period? The simple historical fact that Africa was the last field of European penetration is not to say that it was the most important; this would be a truism were it not that the main case of the Hobson school is founded on African examples. On the other hand, it is our main contention that the process of expansion had reached its most valuable targets long before the exploitation of so peripheral and marginal a field as tropical Africa. Consequently arguments, founded on the technique adopted in scrambling for Africa, would seem to be of secondary importance.

Therefore, the historian who is seeking to find the deepest meaning of the expansion at the end of the nineteenth century should look not at the mere pegging out of claims in African jungles and bush, but at the successful exploitation of the empire, both formal and informal, which was then coming to fruition in India, in Latin America, in Canada and elsewhere. The main work of imperialism in the so-called expansionist era was in the more intensive development of areas already linked with the world economy, rather than in the extensive annexations of the remaining marginal regions of Africa. The best finds and prizes had already been made; in tropical Africa the imperialists were merely scraping the bottom of the barrel.

Notes

1. The term has been given authority by Dr C. R. Fay. See *Cambridge History of the British Empire* (Cambridge, 1940), 11, 399.
2. J. A. Hobson, *Imperialism* (1902); V. I. Lenin, *Imperialism, the Highest Stage of Capitalism* (Selected Works, (n.d.), v); P. T. Moon, *Imperialism and World Politics* (New York, 1926); L. Woolf, *Empire and Commerce in Africa* (n.d.).
3. Lenin, *op. cit.* v, 71.
4. R. L. Schuyler, *The Fall of the Old Colonial System* (New York, 1945), p. 45.
5. W. L. Langer, *The Diplomacy of Imperialism, 1890–1902* (New York, 1935), 1, 75–6.
6. C. J. Uys, *In the Era of Shepstone* (Lovedale, Cape Province, 1933); and C. W. de Kiewiet, *British Colonial Policy and the South African Republics* (1929), *passim*.
7. De Kiewiet, *op. cit.* p. 224.
8. Quoted in J. M. Ward, *British Policy in the South Pacific, 1786–1893* (Sydney, 1948), p. 138.
9. Quoted in L. H. Jenks, *The Migration of British Capital to 1875* (1938), pp. 221–2.
10. Sir W. K. Hancock, *Survey of British Commonwealth Affairs* (1940), 11, pt. 1, 28.
11. A. H. Imlah, 'British Balance of Payments and Export of Capital, 1816–1913', *Econ. Hist. Rev.* 2nd ser. v (1952), pp. 237, 239; Hancock, *op. cit.* p. 27.
12. V. T. Harlow, *The Founding of the Second British Empire, 1763–1793* (1952), pp. 62–145.
13. Quoted in A. K. Manchester, *British Pre-eminence in Brazil* (Chapel Hill, 1933), p. 90.
14. Quoted in W. W. Kaufmann, *British Policy and the Independence of Latin America, 1804–1828* (New Haven, 1951), p. 178.
15. Quoted in J. F. Rippy, *Historical Evolution of Hispanic America* (Oxford, 1946), p. 374.
16. M. Burgin, *Economic Aspects of Argentine Federalism* (Cambridge, Mass., 1946), pp. 55, 76–111.

17 J. H. Williams, *Argentine International Trade under Inconvertible Paper Money, 1880–1900* (Cambridge, Mass., 1920), pp. 43, 103, 183. Cf. W. W. Rostow, *The Process of Economic Growth* (Oxford, 1953), p. 104.
18 J. F. Rippy, 'British Investments in Latin America, end of 1913', *Inter-American Economic Affairs* (1951), v, 91.
19 J. Chesnaux, 'La Révolution Taiping d'après quelques travaux récents', *Revue Historique*, CCIX (1953), 39–40.
20 Quoted in N. A. Pelcovits, *Old China Hands and the Foreign Office* (New York, 1948), p. 85.
21 V. J. Puryear, *International Economics and Diplomacy in the Near East* (1935), pp. 216–17, 222–3.
22 Quoted in Cromer, *Modern Egypt* (1908), 1, 388.
23 Hansard, 3rd Series, CCCXXVIII, col. 550, 6 July 1888.
24 Quoted in S. Gwynn and G. M. Tuckwell, *Life of Sir Charles Wentworth Dilke* (1917), 11, 46.
25 F.O. Confidential Print (East Africa), 5037.

43

IMPERIALISM AND THE RISE AND DECLINE OF THE BRITISH ECONOMY, 1688–1989

Patrick O'Brien

Source: *New Left Review* 238, 1999: 48–80.

Historians seldom consider the metanarratives within which academic articles, monographs, models and analyses must eventually become embedded, if they are to inform public debate in modern societies.* Yet, however micro the problems they tackle, their findings can always be situated within some 'greater story'.[1] Since the Second World War, the central preoccupation of our national politics has been with the search for a post-imperial identity. After prolonged discussion, and at the very end of the twentieth century, the British seem to be on their way to recovering a cultural consciousness and reconstructing an economic system reconnected to active participation in intra-European trade, capital movements and labour markets.[2] To address the large problem concerned with the benefits and the costs that flowed from the realms, a move away from Europe into more than three centuries of engagement with Empire, seems opportune. Furthermore, the theme resonates beyond European into global history because a majority of intellectuals from Asia, Africa and Southern America continue to claim that the relative backwardness of their economies compared to the West can — to some degree — be imputed to the malign effects of imperialism. They suggest that economic relations with Britain — and with other European powers — operated to retard the development of their countries but, at the same time, promoted the progress of Europe's imperial and neo-imperial economies.[3]

Alas, my article will be 'repressively occidental', and 'Anglocentric' since it proposes to deal only with the long-term rise and relative decline of the British economy. In any case, for Europeans, it is not obvious that macroeconomic 'losses' suffered by the colonized from conquest and incorporation into empires led to commensurate material gains for the colonizers.[4] My aim is to construct a coherent, and convincing, metanarrative about the connections between imperialism and the long-term growth of the British economy. Historians do not write fiction, but they deploy methods and devices that provide them with advantages that are comparable to those enjoyed by novelists. For example, they 'impose order' on a plethora of otherwise disconnected sources, data and libraries of secondary literature. They exercise control over periodization by determining the beginning, the middle and end — as well as the outcomes — of their narratives in order to avoid the complexity and endless variation in detail across space and over time.[5] Thus, statistical averages and index numbers will appear as rhetorically persuasive evidence at various places in this text. I also opt to periodize my argument explicitly in two sections and implicitly in a narrative covering four stages of British imperialism. The first, from 1688 to 1846, will be associated with the First Industrial Revolution. The second, from 1846 to 1914, is that short period when Britain, as the world's hegemonic naval power, operated as guardian of the liberal international economic order and when the national economy achieved marked superiority over its European rivals. This 'golden age' was succeeded, from 1918 to 1948, by decades of neo-mercantilism, of armed struggle to maintain the balance of power in Europe, and intensified competition on world markets for shares of international trade that hardly changed in volume between 1913 and 1945. In our own times, the reluctant rediscovery of Europe occurred when Britain decolonized, submitted to American hegemony and suffered from relative economic decline upon almost all international indicators of income, wealth, productivity and comparative welfare.

1688–1846: Mercantilism and imperialism

Any serious analysis of discernible decline is inseparable from an appreciation of the major forces which promoted the rise of the national economy, simply because legacies of past success usually constrain possibilities for adjustment to changes in technology and opportunities for profit emerging in a rapidly evolving world economy. Where to begin the narrative is, however, a problem. British imperialism did not commence with the Glorious Revolution. Its origins can be traced to thrusts across the sea to Ireland as long ago as the High Middle Ages. Its antecedents included more than two centuries of 'piracy' against the Portuguese and Spanish empires followed by three wars in the seventeenth century fought to 'degrade' Dutch primacy in the international economy.[6]

Yet 1688 represents a discontinuity in British geopolitical history, and not merely the date of the replacement of the Stuart dynasty by Dutch and Hanoverian monarchies. Britain's Glorious Revolution led the state into playing a more aggressive role in great-power politics, which began with a very costly and successful effort to contain the ambitions of Louis xiv in

Europe from 1689 to 1713.[7] That conflict led to a permanent commitment to maintain a balance of power on the Continent, basically through the use of sea power but also by placing troops on the mainland — as and when that became necessary — for example, in the 1690s, the early 1700s and, again, during the conflict with Napoleon 1808–14. The Glorious Revolution also presaged the outbreak of a second 'Hundred Years' War' with France and her allies — particularly Spain — for the spoils of empire and the profits of global commerce. Engagement in six major and three minor wars occurred between 1689 and 1815 when the armed forces of the crown fought the navies and armies of the kingdom's enemies on every continent — Europe, of course, but also in the Americas (North and South) as well as in Asia and Africa.[8]

Eventually, the systematic deployment of power transformed a small realm off the mainland of Europe into the world's hegemonic commercial and imperial nation, but that required a sustained rise in the income and expenditure of the state. Taxes and loans (which, in real terms, had risen at an almost imperceptible rate since the beginning of the Tudor dynasty in 1485) went up by a series of jumps from plateau to plateau in wartime — to reach a peak at the time of Waterloo. For example, in real terms, taxes multiplied some fifteen times between 1688 and 1815 — when their share of national income amounted to 18 per cent, compared to around 3 per cent during the reign of James ii. At the same time, the royal or national debt rose from a tiny fraction to nearly three times the gross national product (gnp) for 1819. Servicing the debt absorbed only 12 per cent of the state's revenues in the 1680s. Immediately after the defeat of Napoleon, the government transferred nearly 60 per cent of taxes as interest and amortization payments to its creditors.[9]

Geopolitical might and profit

Something approximating 90 per cent of total governmental expenditure on goods, services and labour was for the navy and the army — principally the former — but the outcome turned out to be a decisive but profitable shift in the state's geopolitical position. After a century and a quarter of European and global warfare — punctuated by interludes of peace which occupied only a third of all the years between 1688 and 1815 — at the Treaty of Vienna, Britain emerged as the hegemonic naval power; as the ruler of the largest occidental empire since Rome; as the world's leading commercial economy (enjoying an extraordinary share of the profits obtained from servicing and financing global trade); and, finally, as the only European economy already half-way through an industrial revolution. At that conjuncture, the geopolitical might of the British state, the kingdom's supremacy in trade and the scale, diversity and technologically advanced status of the island's industries, were all recognized, envied and feared throughout Europe.[10]

Although contemporaries accepted the relationship between 'power and profit' as normal, modern economists — and historians — have analyzed connections between the conjoined and massive public and private investment in the complementary pursuits of national security and imperial expansion, on the one hand, and the rise of the British economy, on the other, in ways that expose their liberal, but anachronistic, antipathies to the use of violence in international economic relations even during this era of mercantilism and warfare.[11]

Alongside a discernible 'jack up' in public investment in naval and military force, increased private investment also occurred in the infrastructural facilities, the financial institutions, the labour of slaves and indentured servants, in the professional and artisanal skills that were required to promote and sustain ever higher levels of intercontinental and imperial commerce.[12] Correlations remain, however, less difficult to elaborate and to quantify than causal sequences. On this point, historians usually 'take cover' by pointing to a 'symbiotic relationship' which both the state and the mercantile sector of the economy found mutually profitable to maintain. Obviously, the government's top priorities remained with the preservation of the realm and its Hanoverian régime. Fortunately, Britain's aristocratic élite also perceived that its concerns with security and stability were not merely compatible with, but could be effectively achieved by, supporting the kingdom's investments overseas, protecting foreign trade and by using naval power, whenever necessary, to damage the commercial ambitions of rival powers — Portugal, Spain, Holland and, above all, France.[13] Running like a railroad track through any metanarrative of British imperial history is the growth of foreign trade, which was carried forward by an engine of consistently high and sustained investment by successive governments in naval power, maritime bases and the conquest of territories, populations and resources located on continents outside Europe.

As usual with trade and growth models, historians must try to specify connections, quantify their significance and, if possible, separate 'exogenous' from 'endogenous' forces behind the growth of commerce with the rest of the world.[14] Give or take acceptable margins of error, the trends in commodity exports and their evolving relationships to national income and industrial production are not, however, that contestable. Between the reigns of Elizabeth i and William of Orange, commodity exports grew at a mean annual rate of about 1 per cent per annum. From 1688 to 1815, that rate went up to around 1.5 per cent and the share of exports to gdp moved from around 8 per cent to around 15 per cent. More significantly, and over two long upswings in production (1700–1760 and 1783–1802), the shares of the increment to industrial output sold abroad came to around the 45 per cent mark. Mostly, that extra output ended up on imperial markets. Alas, no comprehensive data exists that tracks the growth of services — distribution, shipping, banking, insurance and credit — sold beyond the borders of the realm, but it seems safe to make two conjectures. First, that, in real terms, services increased faster than commodity exports and, second, that the servicing of imperial commerce probably expanded more rapidly than servicing global commerce in general.[15]

Growth

To sum up: the 'transition' (1688 to 1815) witnessed an accelerated growth of exports, an even faster growth of invisible trade and a marked shift in the sales of British manufactures and services away from Europe towards the Americas, Africa and Asia. Furthermore, a range of plausible spin-offs followed directly from this expanded involvement with intercontinental commerce. For example, merchants — as the key professional and entrepreneurial subgroup of the national workforce — became larger and more diversified in their economic activities. They set up networks, established new institutions, moved resources into manufacturing industry and supplied information for the formulation of commercial and imperial policy by Britain's élite of 'gentlemanly capitalists'.[16]

Exports also required increased inputs of raw materials from domestic agriculture (wool, flax, animal skins) as well as minerals (coal and ores). Exports demanded more shipping, shipbuilding, internal transportation and financial intermediation. Export industries stood amongst the first to demonstrate the advantages derived from regional concentration, factory organization and mechanization. Receipts from exports allowed for the import of tropical groceries (sugar, tobacco, coffee, tea, spices) and industrial raw materials (cotton fibres, dyestuffs, furs, hardwoods, fish and vegetable oils). At British ports, new forms of manufacturing developed to process imported foodstuffs and raw materials.[17] Finally, the success of the foreign trade sector in selling both domestic (and re-exported) goods and services to the rest of the world generated surpluses on the current account of Britain's balance of payments — manifested in the form of net imports of bullion — which provided the reserve asset required for the expansion of money and credit and the extension of financial intermediation.[18] For the state, bullion produced the reserves of hard currency required to purchase the strategic goods and mercenaries essential for waging war. No wonder ministers of the crown responsible for foreign and strategic policy lauded the 'power' of commerce and supported the activities of British merchants.[19]

A fairly robust set of data allows historians to say that the contribution of imperial and transoceanic trade to the industrialization of the British economy increased significantly over the long eighteenth century. That case can, moreover, be strengthened by citing business, commercial, and industrial histories that elaborate upon the range of spin-offs flowing from the integration of the British economy into networks of imperial and transcontinental trade. Paradoxically, this story, and, mutatis mutandis, the argument for the macro-economic significance of state-sponsored and subsidized imperialism, have been contested by a line of distinguished economic historians including Bairoch, Cole, Deane, Harley, McCloskey, Thomas and others.[20] They insist that global-cum-imperial commerce cannot be plausibly represented as really significant for the industrialization of the British economy because: (i) proportions of trade to national output are too low; (ii) the growth of commerce between Britain and its empire was endogenously and not exogenously determined; and (iii) although the gains from trade were positive, they were small.[21]

Banishing the state

As modern liberals, these economic historians remain reluctant to admit the state into their narratives of the First Industrial Revolution and 'represent' numbers in ways that minimize their rhetorical impact. For example, they insist on dividing Britain's foreign trade by gdp rather than by the far smaller denominator of 'tradeable output'. They marshal static cross-sectional ratios to support conclusions that exports formed a rising but 'smallish' share of gdp as conventionally measured. But how small is 15 per cent? Given that industry, not agriculture or services, was the 'leading' sector behind the rise of the British economy, is not the share of the increment to manufactured output sold to transcontinental, imperial and traditional European markets (also widening by way of commerce with the Americas, Asia and Africa) the more relevant ratio to contemplate? Finally, and in the context of a mercantilist international economic order, Britain can be 'distinguished' first as the national economy (moving to a dominant position on the European league tables, for productivity and outputs per capita) and, secondly, as the economy marked by increasingly divergent ratios — compared to its European rivals — of foreign and imperial commerce to domestic tradeable output.[22]

Nevertheless, the argument continues to founder upon the rocks of a seminal chapter written forty years ago in Deane and Cole's classic quantitative study of the long-run growth of the British economy.[23] They established an Anglocentric (and, by extension, neoliberal) case for the insignificance of trade and colonization by emphasizing 'endogenous forces' — in other words, rising real incomes within the home economy, flowing from domestic investment, internal and intersectoral trade, productivity growth in agriculture, the expansion of population and urbanization and the rise of a new consumer culture. All of these forces — defined by Deane and Cole as 'endogenous-internal' — shifted the British demand curve for colonial imports into the right sequence but with lags, that stimulated colonial and overseas demand for exports manufactured in Britain.

We can comprehend the dichotomous assumptions behind their view by considering bilateral trade between England and Jamaica. During the initial stages of colonization, settlement and the establishment of plantations — say, from the 1650s to the 1690s — the capacity of Jamaicans to buy English manufactures depended on capital inflows and sales of sugar to the metropolitan economy.[24] But this plantation model does not encompass imperial trade as a whole. For example, it does not include commerce with Asia or apply to trade between Britain and the thirteen colonies on the mainland of North America. Even for economies like Jamaica, other sources of colonial income soon emerged — from intersectoral trade, intra-imperial trade, sales to the French, Spanish, Dutch and Portuguese Empires, re-exports to European markets, productivity growth and diversification — that made such colonies steadily more autonomous and less dependent upon metropolitan markets and upon British capital and labour supplies.[25] For McCloskey, Thomas and Harley, adverse shifts in Britain's net barter terms provide an even stronger a priori case against the significance of exports — namely that productivity growth in British manufacturing industry allowed colonial consumers to buy a higher and growing volume of metropolitan commodities per unit of colonial produce exported to Britain.[26] Alas, the evidence for the volumes and prices of traded goods is simply not nearly comprehensive enough to allow for the construction of appropriate index numbers that would measure trends and cycles in Britain's net barter terms of trade with its colonies or the rest of the world. Meanwhile, a serious attempt at measurement by Esteban for the shorter period from 1772 to 1821 shows that, for commerce with the Americas, the net-barter terms of trade moved the other way — that is, in favour of Britain.[27]

Analysis

Unfavourable trends in the terms of trade could constitute 'presumptive' evidence that rising productivity and incomes within the British economy exercised a strong influence upon the evolution of imperial trade. Nevertheless, the timing, shifts and cycles in the terms of trade could be expected to vary by market and by commodity in response to the operation of both price and income effects. Once commerce between colonies and the United Kingdom had become established and proceeded on a routine basis decade after decade, to separate 'forces initiating' from 'forces sustaining' the shifts in colonial and metropolitan demand and supply curves — which lie behind the cyclical evolution and upward trend in trade over time — is probably impossible at a statistical level, and is irrelevant as a matter of logic.

'Irrelevant' is the right word, because, beyond some threshold stage of conquest and colonization (which presupposed the prior existence and sustained growth of a home market for colonial exports), to continue to dichotomize the development of the mother country as 'endogenous' — that is, as virtually disconnected from its possession, retention and expansion of its Empire overseas — could only have struck contemporaries as an unreal depiction of the range of inseparable forces promoting investment and productivity growth within the domestic economy during the long eighteenth century.[28]

Between 1688 and 1815, Britain became more integrated into a world economy and an international order that was anything but liberal. Very high proportions of transcontinental trade and of international capital and labour flows occurred within the boundaries of European empires — created, maintained and extended by force of arms.[29] If the territories, populations and resources under British control had been left undefended, they would have been incorporated into rival empires and their economic relations with the rest of the world regulated from Paris, Madrid, Lisbon or Amsterdam rather than London.[30] Colonies can be depicted as regions of an economic system connected by sea, integrating gradually into a lightly regulated network for commerce centred upon a metropolis.

Once such an imperial system matured into regular operation, and as its 'interregional' trade evolved over time, contemporaries found it ever more difficult to conceive of the pace and pattern of metropolitan economic development as something apart from an expanding empire into which the domestic economy was becoming increasingly embedded. That is why modern 'representations' of Britain's domestic industrialization as 'autonomous' and perceptions of developments within the colonies as reflexive responses to investment, productivity growth and the reallocation of resources within the home economy, seem anachronistic. After 1688, the metropolis and its regions, both within and beyond the boundaries of the Hanoverian kingdom, became inextricably interconnected.

Of course, an 'English' or home economy, with a favourable endowment of natural resources, a stock of capital, a skilled workforce, an efficient set of property rights and institutions for the conduct of internal and external trade, existed long before the Glorious Revolution. That economy had evolved over the centuries on a basis of intersectoral, interregional and intra-European trade. During the Tudor-Stuart period, a 'traditional' pattern of specialization and competition had carried the domestic economy and its workforce up to a plateau of efficiency from where it was poised to take full advantage of its position — as a latecomer and free rider — of opportunities for intercontinental trade and investment pioneered by Portuguese, Spanish and Dutch enterprise.[31]

In the absence of substantial discoveries of minerals on the British Isles or major breakthroughs in agrarian technology, at the time — and since — it has been difficult to conceive of *strategic* changes in the direction and composition of economic activities within the Hanoverian realm that might be meaningfully analyzed as 'disconnected' from transcontinental commerce, including the acquisition of a maritime and territorial empire overseas.

Naval power as Britain's leading comparative advantage

Growth occurs at the margins of national economies, and it has not proved difficult for British historians to uncover evidence of direct and circuitous linkages between commerce and empire at nearly every margin that mattered between 1688 and 1815. For example, in the public sphere, the sharp rise — after the Revolution of 1688 — of a successful fiscal-military state can be closely correlated to geopolitics and imperialism. That connection is manifested in the persistently high levels of public investment in the Royal Navy ordered by aristocratic ministers.[32] In government after government, the élite justified the money spent (on ships of the line, on naval cannon and on seamen) in terms of a range of spin-offs and complementarities between public investment in sea power, on the one hand, and the merchant navy, shipbuilding, the development of ports, dockyards, mercantile information and intelligence, the protection of the nation's commerce and the inflows of hard currency (which replenished the nation's war chest and provided a reserve asset for the extension of credit), on the other.[33] Aristocratic ministers of the crown also appreciated that the compliance they secured from a parliament of property owners, merchants and other men of business — confronted by ever mounting demands for taxes and a worrying accumulation of government debt — depended upon their success in delivering security for property rights within the realm and providing protected opportunities for trade and investment overseas. Only a handful of 'canonical' liberal intellectuals, and an even smaller minority of the ruling élite, entertained doubts about using the Royal Navy to damage and expropriate enemy ships, trade and assets overseas in times of war. And, long after Adam Smith, the consensus in favour of high tariffs and the Navigation Acts — which protected the kingdom's industry commerce and shipping during interludes of peace — remained solid.[34]

Men of property and business also appreciated how the Empire acted as a safety valve for the migration that was often enforced upon a potentially unruly minority of the underclass located in Britain's growing cities and towns. They also observed how opportunities for material gain helped to preserve political stability and order within a kingdom which included populations of potentially disaffected Celts from the internal peripheries of Scotland and Ireland.[35] At the same time as the upper and middle classes disliked the rise of public debt — and the taxes they paid to service it — they displayed no reluctance to purchase government bonds in order to diversify their portfolios into a prudent proportion of virtually riskless securities, as a base for more venturesome investments in agriculture, transportation, commerce and industry.[36] Although British governments of the period remained monarchical and aristocratic, their support for order and stability, for the protection of commerce and, whenever profitable, the acquisition of maritime bases and territories overseas are all policies that provided private investors with the incentives and security they needed to develop the kingdom's agriculture, transportation, commerce and industry.[37]

Thus, a return to the commentaries of mercantilists, writing before, after and against Adam Smith, will suggest that there should be no derogation of the significance of intercontinental commerce for the development of agriculture, as well as numerous industries within Britain's interconnected domestic and imperial economies.[38] Mercantilists certainly mentioned all the key connections. For example, they recognized that labour productivity rose in agriculture when a rising share of the nation's workforce found jobs in industries, services and towns, linked to exports and to imports. Landowners and farmers found it profitable to invest in urban housing, transportation and other forms of social overhead capital required to sustain economic progress, led by trade, because they expected to derive higher rents and royalties from their ownership rights to real property and minerals. Ambitious British workers found it paid to invest the time and money to upgrade the skills required to produce for expanding markets at home, within the Empire or for elsewhere in the world economy. Export industries tended to grow more rapidly than industries that sold their outputs within the borders of the realm. Such industries attracted the best entrepreneurial talent and skilled artisans, not merely from inside the kingdom but from neighbouring Protestant and Jewish communities resident on the European mainland. Export industries such as textiles, metals, pottery and shipbuilding mechanized and/or reorganized production ahead of the rest. Finally, and most obviously, the infrastructure of financial intermediation, required to support rising levels of industrial activity and the distribution of manufacturers across time and space, owed a lot to the experience, skills and investible funds acquired by merchants engaged in imperial and long distance trades.

The nexus of trade and imperialism

In short: at every 'margin' where accelerated commercial and industrial growth occurred between 1688 and 1815, economic and business historians have produced detailed evidence of links to transoceanic trade and to imperialism. Their scholarship may not, however, be persuasive enough to convince liberal economists — whose antipathies to making space in their metanarratives for state and for empire continues to generate opposed but essentially counterfactual arguments, which implicitly preserve conventional narratives of the British Industrial Revolution as a paradigm case of successful endogenous industrialization through laisser faire and competitive capitalism.[39]

To bolster that myth, liberals have used a standard Ricardian 'gains from trade' model. For example, Thomas and McCloskey observed that: 'The importance of trade can be measured by the potential it creates for extra income and consumption.' But, they add, since 'domestic demand or supply within limits could replace foreign demand or supply' and because 'all things are substitutes the actual division of British output between exports and domestic use is an interesting fact, but not significant for British economic growth.'[40]

Historians — who normally deal with what actually happened — will, nevertheless, recognize how the counterfactual preface at play in this argument implicitly supposes that, between 1688 and 1815, alternative strategies for development were available to the British economy that could conceivably have led to a similar outcome to that actually achieved through the pursuit of trade and empire.

Such a counterfactual (or Jacobite) strategy could only have been based upon a delinking of the economy from global and imperial trade and involved the reallocation of the resources — that is, the capital, labour, land and raw materials — used for transcontinental trades into production for home or European markets. Since merchants, businessmen and statesmen never expected increasingly protected markets on the mainland to be opened up to manufactured exports made in Britain, the core of this counterfactual 'scenario' must be that the rate of British industrialization from 1688 to 1815 could have been sustained by way of intersectoral and interregional trade within the boundaries of a home market that roughly doubled in size from 5 to 10 million consumers over this period.

Liberal arguments claiming that the net gains from trade could have been a small and potentially dispensable component behind the longrun growth of the British economy also rest upon several other 'Ricardian' assumptions that need to be undermined. They are: that British resources were given and fully employed; that foreign trade functioned to reallocate labour, capital and other inputs more efficiently between domestic production and exports; and that British consumers made gains in the form of extra consumption from shifting resources to superior positions on a 'production possibility boundary' by exchanging exports for imports. Liberals maintain that the use of domestic resources to produce exports led to higher levels of consumption, but insist that the internal transformation ratios underlying such choices meant that their employment in the production of substitutes for imports could have been only marginally less efficient. They also suppose that the higher rates of investment and technical progress, human capital formation, institutional innovation, political stability, and security from invasion that accrued to British society from the allocation of resources to transcontinental trade and its corollary set of activities — in other words, exporting and importing and supplying services for the global economy — would not have been significantly diminished if those same resources had been engaged in production for the home market. Finally, and to wind up the liberal case, its advocates must argue that British investment in the sea power and maritime bases required to protect, stabilize and service intercontinental commerce can be regarded as dispensable elements in the growth of international trade and the integration of a global economy.

Vent for surplus

On reflection, historians of both British and global economic growth are unlikely to accept such highly theoretical and implausible arguments, made in order to denigrate gains from commerce. They will point out that, by the mid-eighteenth century, only 14 per cent of retained imports took the form of manufactured goods and provided only limited opportunities for import substitution in the manufacturing sector. By that time, the bulk of Britain's imports consisted of raw materials and tropical groceries from the Empire or included such 'strategic necessities' as timber, copper, pitch, tar, hemp and bar iron from the Baltic — which Britain paid for by reexporting sugar, tea, coffee, spices, tobacco and Indian textiles to that region. Only a small share of the imports carried into British ports could have been produced within the kingdom at other than prohibitively high costs.[41]

Historians will reach for Adam Smith's view that the international commerce of his era offered Britain — and other the European economies — a 'vent for surplus'. 'Foreign trade', Smith wrote,

> carries out that surplus part of the produce of their land and labour for which there is no demand among them and brings back, in return, something else for which there is a demand. By means of it, the narrowness of the home market does not hinder the division of labour in any particular branch of art or manufacture from being carried to the highest perfection. By opening a more extensive market for whatever part of the produce of their labour may exceed the home consumption, it encourages them to improve its productive powers and to augment its annual produce to the utmost, and thereby to increase the real revenues and wealth of society.[42]

Both Smith and his mercantilist contemporaries regarded the opportunity costs of the labour and capital employed in transoceanic commerce as being rather low. During the eighteenth century, something like 40 to 50 per cent of Britain's non-agricultural workforce produced directly — or indirectly — for markets overseas. There is no evidence that more than a fraction of these workers could have been absorbed into alternative employment for the home market at other than sharply reduced levels of productivity. That is why mercantilist and Malthusian commentators rarely envisioned the eighteenth-century labour market as being in a state of full employment.[43]

Transcontinental trade — in close association with British imperialism created jobs, social overheads, capital and industrial capacity outside agriculture. Commerce beyond the realm supported by state power reinforced a more productive division of labour both within the kingdom and between the kingdom and its empire overseas. Adam Smith also saw trade as promoting outward shifts of Britain's 'production possibility boundary'. Neither liberals nor their more mercantilistic contemporaries engaged in anything resembling a debate about alternative scenarios for the long-term development that could conceivably have carried the British economy and the British state to the hegemonic position the country occupied when Castlereagh signed the Treaty of Vienna in 1815.[44]

Other than peace and free trade — which, pending divine intervention, were still decades away — there were no viable alternative strategies on offer between 1688 to 1815. Furthermore, the more harmonious and liberal international economic order that emerged after the final victory at sea at Trafalgar and on the mainland at Waterloo could not have evolved without that massive investment by government and British merchants in the security of the realm conjoined with transcontinental commerce and empire. The vigorous pursuit of a mercantilist and imperialist strategy decade after decade, war after war, represented the most significant and enduring economic outcome of the Glorious Revolution of 1688. As persuasive rhetoric, imperialism — and everything that this emotive label connotes — must be ranked as a major factor pushing British industrialization and the British economy ahead of its European rivals between 1688 and 1846. Power, as mercantilists long insisted, really mattered!

But, a final word of qualification: my argument for the significance of empire and trade has been positioned to countervail a liberal historiography that has become dominant in recent decades. That Anglo-American perspective has been predisposed to ignore the state and to denigrate the role played by power, the aristocracy, London and imperialism for the industrialization of the British economy. My attempt to restore some balance does not imply that transoceanic commerce and imperialism can be reified — as it has been in the writings of the world-systems school of historical sociology — into the 'engine' of the First Industrial Revolution.[45] Such views are hyperbolic simply because a base of structural and institutional preconditions for industrialization had been built up long before 1688. Endogenous forces and intra-European trade continued, moreover, to be important throughout the transition from the Glorious Revolution to the Treaty of Vienna.[46]

Liberal imperialism 1846–1914

After 1815 — when Britain emerged as Europe's hegemonic imperial and commercial power and matured into the guardian of peaceable international economic order — dissent over the retention and expansion of the Empire reappeared on the political agenda. Antipathy to imperialism can be traced back to the Jacobites and to Adam Smith, but, after the war, the economic case for withdrawal from empire was cogently analyzed by a distinguished line of nineteenth-century radicals — including Bentham, Mill, Cairnes, Bright, Goldwyn Smith, Thorold Rogers and, famously, by Cobden and Hobson.

Thorold Rogers was forced out of his chair in political economy at Oxford for including, among his attacks on aristocracy, statements to the effect that, '[t]he presumed political benefits of the present colonial system are an exploded fiction', because '[t]he Empire adds nothing to the economic and military strength of the home country but rather diminishes it'.[47] Since the growth of the economy and the security and stability of the realm had, for more than a century, owed so much to transcontinental commerce, how could Rogers and other critics insist that the continued retention, expansion and support for the British Empire could no longer be defended on economic grounds? Although they never used such modern terminology, nineteenth-century radicals in effect sought to persuade Parliament and public opinion that, once Britain had secured a balance of power in Europe, enjoyed dominion at sea and had industrialized to become the workshop of the world, the 'macro-economic' costs of imperial rule and the persistence of imperial culture began to exceed its social benefits by wide and growing margins.

In recent decades, historians have revisited nineteenth-century debates between radicals and imperialists and have used hindsight, economic analysis and statistics to argue that the critics of empire now seem percipient and that a retrospective assessment of the Empire as an economic burden and a significant component behind the long-run decline of the British economy is a tenable position to hold.

That position which is focused upon the material costs and benefit of empire *for society* as a whole, gives no weight to the psychic, sexual or spiritual gains that considerable sections of the British population undoubtedly derived from the fact that Queen Victoria's government ruled over the largest occidental empire since Rome. Revisionists also conceded that subgroups among the middle and upper classes obtained rather substantial material gains from their direct and indirect involvement with empire. Modern discussions have been more concerned, however, to construct a plausible and persuasive metanarrative of just how the growth of the domestic economy and the welfare of the British population could be connected over time with empire; via trade, capital and labour flows and through taxation — allocated for its defence and support. Logically, and consistently, that metanarrative has elaborated upon an alternative path or strategy for development that might conceivably have been pursued by a society committed to a policy of 'delinking' its economy from imperial commercial connections and costly political responsibilities for empire. Without some explicit specification of a counterfactual strategy, the analysis would be 'merely theoretical' and about as persuasive as the modern neoliberal critique of the imperial strategy pursued by the Hanoverian régime from 1688 to 1815. A counterfactual argument for the long nineteenth century involves an analysis of the flows of commodities, capital, labour and taxes between Britain and its empire from 1846–1913.[48]

Although the economy of the United Kingdom became steadily more involved in transcontinental trade, and the ratio of exports to gdp doubled to reach 33 per cent over the century before 1913, the share of Britishmade exports sold on imperial markets just about halved between 1790 and 1860 and showed no tendency to rise above the 25 per cent mark for several decades thereafter. Imports from the Empire also declined from a peak during the French Wars, but rose again from 20 per cent in 1860 up to 36 per cent by 1914.[49] Almost everything purchased from imperial sources of supply could have been obtained, however, from other primary producers outside the British Empire. Finally, there is no reason to suppose that the highly competitive shipping, banking, insurance, distribution and other commercial services supplied by British firms for the world economy depended on the maintenance of imperial preferences. Indeed, it seems likely that the share of such services sold to the Empire declined over the nineteenth century.

The delinking hypothesis

On balance, the data suggests that, despite the relentless extension of territories and populations included within the British empire, the domestic economy became less interconnected with the colonies and dominions than it had been during Hanoverian times. Nevertheless, the key question remains: what might have happened to domestic exports if the British government had relinquished political responsibilities for its colonies and dominions and allowed them to operate as independent political units within the nineteenth-century international order of trading nations? Several conjectures have been formulated as responses to this question. The most pessimistic follow 'self-serving' predictions, made by imperialists during the Victorian era, namely that India would have relapsed into anarchy and disrupted the system of multilateral payments upon which the evolution of global trade depended between 1846 and 1914.[50] Other Anglo- and Eurocentric scenarios assume that the construction of the social overhead, capital and institutions required for the integration of various regions, resources and workforces outside Europe into global networks of trade and commerce continued to be predicated upon the imposition and/or maintenance of colonial rule.[51] That could have been the case for some parts of Africa and Asia, pushed by force of arms into international trade over the nineteenth century. But the problem is to gauge how long the tutelage and institutions of colonialism were needed in order to integrate the regional and local economies of other continents into world trade. Did the threshold costs and investments required for integration have to be funded from British savings and taxes? Why did Victorian governments not leave these 'opportunities' to their European rivals to pursue? Furthermore, as post-colonial historians of India — and other parts of Asia — now point out, the British assertion that alien rule was necessary to preserve good order and the institutions necessary for foreign trade betrays ignorance about the history of intra-Asian trade and commercial civilization that operated for centuries before Europeans sailed into Indian oceans and China seas.[52]

Michael Edelstein has pursued more plausible counterfactual scenarios with commendable rigour. He assumes that, if India and other parts of the British empire had recovered full independence, their governments might well have imposed tariffs on British exports — say, at the high levels favoured by the government of the United States. Official and reasonably secure data is available, which he uses to express exports to the Empire as proportions of Britain's gdp for years around 1870 and 1913. Edelstein then made a plausible conjecture for the price elasticity of demand for British goods purchased by the colonies and dominions. On the assumption that the labour, capital and other imports used to produce exports for the Empire enjoyed no alternate economic uses, his *outer-bound* estimates of the macro-economic losses incurred by an early withdrawal from empire amount to only 1.1 per cent of gdp for 1870 and some 2.6 per cent for 1913.[53]

Edelstein's exercise is interesting to contemplate. His estimates of potential losses from early withdrawal from empire are not 'small' numbers, but they do represent upper-bound conjectures. Given the diverse ranges of manufacturing activity carried on within the British economy by the second half of the nineteenth century, there could no longer be any case for accepting traditional mercantilist perceptions — formulated with plausibility for the Hanoverian period — that the labour and capital employed in industries exporting to the Empire possessed low opportunity costs. Rather, these estimates suggest that a post-1846 adjustment to decolonization would not have been anything like as costly as any serious shift away from the geopolitical and imperial strategy pursued during the long eighteenth century, 1688–1815.

A culture of imperialism with free trade

After the mid-nineteenth century, the maintenance of rule from London and the strengthening of imperial culture provided Victorian and Edwardian industrialists with the confidence to persist with product mixes, technologies, organizational forms, institutions and patterns of investment that had served them and the economy well during the Industrial Revolution and when Britain ranked as the workshop of the world. Thereafter, British businessmen anticipated that, as and when competition from rival European economies and the United States intensified, imperial preferences could be reinstated to protect their markets and to provide a cushion against the expensive and unwelcome adjustments required to cope with the Second Industrial Revolution. Meanwhile, long-established networks of commerce — as well as linguistic and cultural ties — could be used to hold onto market shares in the dominions, India and the colonies to 'prop up' the old staples of the First Industrial Revolution as they came under growing pressure on home and foreign as well as imperial markets.[54]

Ironically, between 1873 and 1914, and as British industry lost market share on all three markets, the Empire continued to function as little more than an insurance policy for which British taxpayers and their domestic economy paid a rather high premium. Legally, the markets and resources of this vast and developing Victorian empire remained virtually open to foreign commerce, investment and labour flows. Liberal and Conservative governments resisted organized pressure from the Fair Trade League and from Joseph Chamberlain's more serious campaign for imperial preference to disengage from an ideological commitment to the unilateralist version of free trade. As the promoter and guardian of a liberal international economic order, for something like five decades before 1914, the British state pursued a laisser-passer stance, while the governments of their European rivals and the United States erected tariffs and placed other impediments in the way of British manufactured exports to third markets.[55]

Before the Great War of 1914–18, Britain's supposedly 'hegemonic' state conspicuously failed to use its geopolitical power or the markets and resources of an economically rich and expanding domestic economy and its empire overseas to maintain a level playing field in international economic relations. Neither the tariff, nor — as the controversy over bimetallism reveals — international monetary polices were used as 'weapons' by liberal governments to preserve the country's position, within the world economy, won at high cost, by their Hanoverian predecessors.[56]

Meanwhile, there appears to be little substance to the 'Leninist' argument that rates of return accruing to capital accumulating within the United Kingdom was declining, and that the 'exploitative' profits earned on the reallocation of capital to the Empire helped Victorian capitalists stave off some iron law of diminishing returns.[57] Yet British investors did indeed place their savings outside the realm on an unprecedented and internationally remarkable degree over the nineteenth century. For example, in the 1830s, something like 12 per cent of the nation's investible funds flowed beyond its borders. By the 1870s, that proportion had reached 30 per cent. Between 1905–13 — when nearly a third of the kingdom's wealth consisted of foreign and imperial assets — an astonishing 46 per cent of British savings went abroad.[58] What seems more extraordinary — and this stands out in sharp contrast to the mercantilist era — is the fact that only a limited share of total capital outflow (just 36 per cent from 1865–1914) ended up as investments placed within the Empire. Nearly two-thirds of that flow funded capital formation, consumption and governmental expenditures elsewhere in the world economy, particularly in the United States. Furthermore, from the not inconsiderable flows of British savings into the Empire, about 65 per cent were placed in white, quasi-autonomous dominions rather than in India — or in other colonies of ex-slaves or indigenous peoples — where opportunities for exploitation should, presumably, have been far higher. Something like two-thirds of all imperial assets and purchases by British investors in the period 1856–1914 consisted of government bonds and other securities that provided their holders with low risk and rather stable rates of return.[59]

After the Napoleonic Wars, political and institutional conditions for a liberal international capital market evolved and made it possible for British — and other European — investors to place funds outside national frontiers and empires with far greater guarantees of security than had ever existed during the previous epoch of mercantilism and European warfare. By the second half of the nineteenth century, the location and patterns of British investment overseas displayed no particular preference — and, ipso facto, no obvious economic need — for the maintenance of a formal empire.

Imperialism and exploitation

Nevertheless, a *marxisant* question remains: did the persistence of dominions and colonies — dependent upon and, to very different degrees, 'ruled' from London — help to guarantee higher (or even exploitative) rates of return on capital invested in the Empire? Alas, this question is sometimes conflated and confused with a wider question concerned with the 'rationality' displayed by British capitalists in opting to invest overseas compared with opportunities of comparable risk available in the home economy. Edelstein's research demonstrates their 'rationality' by analyzing a sample of shares, debentures and other securities quoted on the London stock exchange. His results indicate that *foreign* assets yielded a positive differential rate of return 1.12 per cent per annum between 1870 and 1914.[60]

Edelstein's sample of imperial assets is too small to be definitive, but it does suggest a positive differential, which was, however — and so much for exploitation through colonization — discernibly lower than the rate obtained on foreign securities over the same decades. For reasons well elaborated in economic theory, it is only over the long run, in a perfectly competitive market generating full information about returns — that is, capital gains and dividends reported on paper claims quoted on the stock exchange — that the real flows of profits accruing to companies and dividends paid to their share-holders actually converge. To answer the central question which is about *realized relative rates of return*, historians will need to study and compare the annual balance sheets and reports from representative samples of firms, partnerships and enterprises which operated in all three locations: the home economy, the Empire, and overseas.[61]

Unfortunately, primary data from the only available sample covering 42 firms — as constructed and analyzed by Davis and Huttenback — is not yet in the public domain and may turn out to be too small and unrepresentative for the decades before 1885. It displays considerable variations in returns by cycle and by sector and the reported unweighted average rates of profit relate to firms of very different sizes. Here are their figures:[62]

Annual Average Rates of Return on Investments

	Located in UK	Located in the Empire	In Foreign Locations
1860–84	5.8 per cent	9.7 per cent	5.8 per cent
1885–1912	5.5 per cent	3.3 per cent	5.3 per cent

Highly profitable imperial enterprises show up not only in archetypal sectors like mining and land speculation, but also in public utilities and brewing. This is an insecure sample, but the estimates do not display any trends towards diminishing returns for investments in the home economy and suggest that high rates of return obtained on investment in the Empire plummeted during the wave of European imperialism that followed Britain's occupation of Egypt in 1882. Until more data are available, agnosticism would seem to be the sensible position to adopt towards Marxists, imperialists and third-world intellectuals who claim that the Empire provided above normal profits for private investors and for British society as a whole.

The export of British savings

If such scepticism is valid, then the long-standing, and unresolved, debate connecting the performance of the economy to the high tide of capital exports from Britain 1873–1914, becomes central for the discussion about the profitability of liberal imperialism. For the purposes of that discussion, there seems to be no need to engage with current attempts to date and to measure the degree to which the British economy had entered into relative and discernible decline before the outbreak of the First World War.[63] It will be sufficient to refer to several indicators that are deployed by British economic historians to suggest that the *overall performance* of the economy between 1873 and 1914 does not look impressive and that it could and should have done better. Many of us remain unconvinced that the opportunities presented for the introduction of advanced technologies, more efficient forms of organization and improved legal and institutional frameworks for investment, production and distribution were diffused at optimum rates for several decades before the First World War.[64] After all, it is now clear that even if the long-established gaps across advanced economies in terms of gdp per worker were sufficient to keep the British economy near to the top of familiar league tables — constructed post hoc to compare the status of developed market economies — the several decades of relatively slow growth after 1873 did eventually lead to convergence, overtaking and to unequivocal relative decline.[65]

For example, on the indicators currently available for industrial and agricultural production, labour and total factor productivities for industry agriculture and for gdp as a whole, there is, first of all, evidence of a discontinuity when trend rates of growth for the years 1873–1913 are compared with 1831–73; and, secondly, some data suggests several rival economies in Europe and North America experienced faster growth in commodity outputs and factor productivities than Britain. Finally — but not unexpectedly — more conjectural sets of data suggest that uk shares in world industrial output declined from 23 per cent (circa 1880), down to 14 per cent (circa 1913). In world trade in manufactured goods, relevant shares fell from roughly 46 per cent in 1870 to 30 per cent by 1913. For some four decades after 1873, imports of manufactures into the kingdom grew far more rapidly than exports, so that, by 1910, about 25 per cent of all manufactured goods sold on the home market were made abroad, compared with a mere 6 per cent in the 1860s.[66]

Of course, there is nothing surprising, necessarily deplorable or remediable about slower growth and declining shares in global industrial output and trade. These numbers simply provide relevant statistical evidence about convergence or catch-up towards the levels of productivity and structures of output and employment enjoyed during 'golden ages' by leading economies. In a world of competitive economies and predictable shifts in comparative advantage, the problem remains one of performance rather than positions in international league tables that reveal little about the *potential* of different national economies for slower or more rapid rates of growth.

Disputes on the speed of growth

On the issue of Britain's performance from 1873–1914, some historians remain resolutely Panglossian. They are committed to their perceptions that the legal rules, institutional frameworks, structure of incentives and cultural values within which late-Victorian and Edwardian capitalism operated could only have worked to push the British economy pretty close to its production possibility boundary. Others, looking at the same sets of data, are convinced that the speed and extent of the overall response to a discernible slowdown in the rate of growth and intensified international competition creates a prima facie case for historical investigation into the political, legal, institutional and cultural heritage of a national economy destined for relative decline, but capable — as so many informed contemporaries suggested — of reform and more efficient adjustments to the challenges of the Second Industrial Revolution.[67]

A key macro indicator for historians who prefer to trace 'the origins' of Britain's economic decline back to the period 1873–1914 is the rate of investment in the domestic economy. That rate — gross fixed domestic capital formation — peaked between 1821–51 and displayed no tendency to rise above 10 per cent for the next six decades. Meanwhile, the share of investment placed overseas rose from 3.3 per cent of gnp around mid-century to reach 8.0 per cent by 1905-14, when Britain's leading rivals Germany and the United States invested about 20 per cent of their national incomes within their borders.[68] Critics 'play' with counterfactual models and hypothesize that if the savings exported overseas had been invested within the kingdom, then British per capita incomes might have been considerably higher by 1911.[69]

Decisions about how much to save and where to place investible funds were made in the first instance by Victorian and Edwardian households. When they opted to purchase foreign and/or imperial assets, they looked for security, constrained risk, low variance and yields somewhat greater than returns available from comparable domestic investments. For example, in 1910, 38 per cent of foreign assets held by uk nationals made 3 per cent to 4 per cent for their owners; 42 per cent made 4 per cent to 5 per cent and only 20 per cent returned more than 5 per cent.[70]

The absence of 'listening and action' banks

Given the risk-averse preferences of the classes with savings to allocate, the glare of post hoc historical inspection has turned latterly upon the institutions and personnel who garnered and invested funds and constructed portfolios of assets to offer their wealthy and prudential clients. The body of research into the histories of merchants, stockbrokers, merchant banks, joint stock banks and discount houses is now accumulating and British historians begin to elaborate upon an interlocked network of institutions and cultures that has been memorably labelled as 'gentlemanly capitalism'.[71] Unfavourable contrasts are drawn between Britain's financial institutions and their counterparts in Germany and the United States — which are perceived to have exercised more positive policies towards the long-term development of their domestic industrial sectors and to have been less concerned with supplying the credit and loans required to sustain global commerce.[72] British banks and other financial intermediaries, managed by the best educated, prudent and talented of Victorian businessmen, are, however, no longer represented as being obdurately antipathetic to industries, trades and construction firms in the North and Midlands. Nevertheless, their 'detachment' from the domestic economy can still be criticized as unhelpful. Foresight and vision — rather than short-term rationality — seems, in retrospect, to be the missing quality in the decisions taken by a cosmopolitan élite who exercised responsibility for investing such a large proportion of the nation's savings. As directors of long established and reasonably profitable concerns, they displayed almost no propensity to innovate by providing their cautious clients with the range of assets they demanded in order to obtain stable and secure returns — while offering British manufacturers the type of financial support that might have persuaded smaller entrepreneurial firms in new industries to invest more in expansion and diversification. While it is, obviously, well-nigh impossible to document examples of financial intermediaries who refused requests from businessmen whose plans eventually matured into profitable investments and enterprises over the long run, it is clear that historical counterparts of today's 'action', 'listening' and 'promotional' banks; or British analogues of German *Kreditbanken* did not emerge. Finally, there seems to be no evidence that the 'gentlemanly' managers and directors from this prestigious and successful sector of the economy took any interest in promoting the changes in company law required to further the pace of change towards larger scale and professionally managed joint stock companies.[73]

Economic historians who are not sanguine about the 'comfortable' pace and pattern of Britain's economic performance from 1873–1914 now search for possible institutional and cultural constraints that inhibited an earlier and innovatory adjustment of a mature and successful economy to the challenges of the Second Industrial Revolution.[74] Business historians are beginning to uncover evidence that exposes the prudential and rational responses of Britain's banks and other financial intermediaries as unimaginative and excessively conservative.[75]

As historians looked into the origins of Britain's financial institutions, analyzed their routine practices for the allocation of loans, enquired into how well they managed their cosmopolitan and imperial as well as domestic concerns, they rediscovered a 'British tradition' of mercantile banking. That tradition can be traced back to the eighteenth century, when financial intermediation in the metropolis and other towns consisted of funding exchanges across the regions of the kingdom, trade between Britain and Europe and commerce with the realm's expanding empire in the Americas and Asia. Industrial banks — that is, banks involved with lending longterm to promote fixed investment, innovation and the rationalization of manufacturing activity — hardly existed beyond some scattered examples of country banks.[76] The historical development of banks and other financial institutions in Britain has been represented as a significant factor behind the expansion of internal and external trade, and important for integration of regions and enterprises within and beyond the realm into a single market. In short, the dominant concern of the financial sector was to supply the credit and short-term loans required to fund and facilitate the distribution of raw materials, intermediate goods and finished outputs through time and across the territory of a world empire.

Initially, that space for the operation of financial intermediation included regional, national and intra-European networks of trade. Between 1688 and 1815, British financial intermediation became more imperial. Thereafter, the sector broadened out to offer its highly professional skills and services to provide credit for commerce and loans and to fund the overhead capital required to facilitate trade for the global economy as a whole. British financial institutions evolved into firms with clearly defined concerns, cultures and rules for the management of credit and longer-term loans. That evolution included ever more refined and efficient modes of specialization. Banks proceeded geographically from regional to national through imperial to embrace cosmopolitan clients and their demands for funds.[77] The financial sector had never accorded any particular interest or displayed any 'patriotic' concern for manufacturing industry, for capital formation, innovation or for the organization of production within the domestic economy.[78] By the late nineteenth century, when its very success and recognized prudence was attracting an ever-increasing share of the nation's savings, the legacy of mercantile, imperial and cosmopolitan practices, routines and cultures embedded in British financial institutions encouraged a truly massive export of capital that a minority of contemporary critics with foresight — and historians with hindsight — represent as malign for the long-term vitality of the domestic economy.[79] No one is to blame! There could be no culprits to arraign at the bar of history for the pursuit of business as usual.[80] Nevertheless, Britain's powerful financial sector did not diversify to take on new responsibilities for the domestic economy but continued to play its traditional part in maintaining Britain's imperial and hegemonic role in global commerce.

Missed opportunities for the reduction of taxation

That role also depended on the state's capacity and willingness to continue to allocate considerable shares of its tax revenues to imperial defence and to borrow money whenever necessary to support naval and military actions for the seemingly irresistible extension of the frontiers of the Empire. Two debates are currently in play about the state's continued commitment to empire.[81] The easiest to pursue is concerned with the economic burdens of taxes collected to defend and maintain possessions overseas. In terms of national costs and benefits, the second — and, alas, non-resolvable — discussion about the mal-formation of strategic thought and policy conducted in the context of imperial security can only be regarded ex-post as exercising a far more serious impact on the long-term growth of the economy than all the extra taxes appropriated from British families in order to sustain the pretensions of the élite (and the populace) for 'grandeur' between 1846 and the outbreak of an extremely costly and avoidable European war in 1914.

Let us begin, however, by reviewing several salient points that have emerged from recently clarified evidence about the burden of taxes collected to defend and to extend the empire. First, it is now clear that taxpayers resident in the United Kingdom carried a grossly disproportionate share of the taxes spent upon the defence of the Empire. Between 1865 and 1914, in per capita terms, the taxes they paid for defence amounted to nine times the comparable burden carried by the citizens of the dominions, and was about fifty times larger than expenditures for armies and navies funded by the populations of India and other colonies. For several decades before 1914, the Treasury perceived the skewed and anomalous distribution of such theoretically hypothecated taxes as 'free riding'. Protracted negotiations with dominion governments and pressure on the colonies did almost nothing, however, to redistribute the burden amongst different parts of the Empire.[82] Surely, the British electorate would have been more aroused if they had been appraised of revealing estimates — only recently constructed by Davis and Huttenback — which show that, if the residents of each of the dominions and colonies had somehow been compelled to pay taxes for imperial defence in proportion to the potential taxable capacity of each territory, (that is, in relation to its wealth and income), then the taxes collected from British taxpayers in order to fund the forces of the crown could have been halved and their overall tax bills reduced by at least a quarter.

If radical critics of empire had been able to conceptualize and to publicize the 'tax burdens' in this way, then the popularity of the Empire might have waned. At the time, statesmen and informed commentators on fiscal policy certainly knew that British expenditures on defence per head seemed discernibly higher then the levels reported for Germany and France and stood well above the levels recorded for Russia, Austria and the United States. Davis and Huttenback have confirmed contemporary impressions. Their recent calculations show that, over the decades 1870–1913, naval and military spending per capita by France amounted to 80 per cent of overall British levels; by Germany to 63 per cent; by Russia 49 per cent; by Austria 38 per cent and by the United States 36 per cent, compared to 11 per cent by Canada, Australia and the other affluent white dominions.[83] Contemporaries also recognized that an advanced economy and a wealthy society like Britain could afford to carry heavier tax burdens for the defence of its empire. They did not know that the proportions of the national income that the United Kingdom 'used up' for these purposes were probably around the 3 per cent mark and on a par with German, Austrian and Italian shares but below the French and Russian proportions of 4 per cent and 5 per cent respectively.

The ratios recently and carefully calculated by John Hobson have undermined any strong case for 'imperial overstretch'.[84] Nevertheless, it cannot be concluded that the British state ran 'its huge empire on the cheap'. Withdrawal from empire leading to potential tax cuts of around 25 per cent which would have been welcomed by all British families and could have widened the home market for electricity, gas and a diverse range of domestically manufactured consumer durables that only came on stream in Britain after the Great War.[85] Alternatively, a 'defence dividend' could have been reallocated by successive governments to satisfy the aspirations of an expanding electorate for social security, better health and education and other 'missing' supplies of public goods now perceived to be among the factors constraining the growth of the domestic economy before 1914.[86]

Instead, the political élite regarded themselves as fiscally constrained. After the long roll-back of the fiscal military state from 1815–70, taxes began to rise again and, in per capita terms, multiplied by a factor of three between 1870 and 1914.[87] 'Imprisoned' within a liberal rhetoric advocating free trade, laisser faire and a small state, Victorian politicians began to confront all the familiar conflicts of twentieth-century democracies: the demands of mass electorates, widespread antipathy to taxation — especially to direct taxes from voters with surpluses to spare — and the dichotomized claims for public expenditures perceived to promote the growth of national wealth on the one hand and social welfare and national security on the other.[88]

Imperial responsibilities and the rise of Germany

Against this tight fiscal and increasingly complex array of political demands, successive British cabinets formulated policies for the security of the realm and for defence of imperial frontiers that lengthened almost willy-nilly year after year. By the early 1900s, the imperial responsibilities of her majesty's ministers included: India, a territory of 2 million square miles inhabited by 322 million people; 5 dominions covering 24 million square miles of territory; countless smaller colonies, islands and maritime bases all over the globe, adding up to another 3.2 million square miles of territory and occupied by around 500 million people.[89] Britannia ruled the waves but also shared imperial frontiers with all major European powers — France, Germany, Russia, Turkey — as well as the United States. As railways diffused around the world, the troops of Britain's rivals and enemies could be transported to within 'striking distances' of indefensible imperial borders in a matter of hours. Enemy forces could no longer be interdicted by the Royal Navy, operating out of strategically placed bases on nearly all the world's seas and oceans. To statesmen who contemplated it at all seriously, the problem of imperial defence appeared awesome, untenable and unaffordable, against anything other than a limited range of threats posed by rival powers. How to contain, manage and if necessary mobilize sufficient force to countervail potential attacks against an indefensible empire matured into nothing less than the central preoccupation of late Victorian and Edwardian cabinets, and the admirals, generals and strategic planners offered ministers advice as to how to cope with an impossible task and to do so 'on the cheap'.[90]

That task became enormously more complex with the emergence of Germany as a great power after 1871. German unification had been consolidated by force of arms under Prussian leadership and through a series of decisive military victories against Denmark in 1864, Austria 1866 and France in 1871, as well as Bismarck's diplomatic triumph over Russian ambitions in the Balkans in 1878.

As early as the formation of the *Zollverein*, it became clear — at least to Palmerston — that Britain might have to restrain German ambitions on the

Continent by forming alliances and understandings with other European states. As time went on, the need to revitalize traditional Hanoverian priorities, concerned with the balance of power on the mainland, became apparent to several commentators on international affairs as Prussia achieved military pre-eminence within Germany and Europe between 1864–78.[91] Unfortunately, nearly all available and viable options could only be discussed within an overall strategic context that conflated the security of the realm with the defence of an expanding empire. Given the widely perceived fiscal constraint (accepted by both parties) on raising more revenue in the unpopular form of direct taxes and their ideological antipathy to the erosion of free trade — which seriously constrained policy initiatives designed to raise more money in the form of customs and excise duties — the appropriation of higher shares of the national income to fund increased expenditures on the army and navy could not appear to be a politically viable agenda for either liberal or conservative parties to pursue in peacetime.[92]

Efforts by the Treasury to persuade the dominions and to pressure colonies to pay more for their own defence largely failed.[93] Proposals to build up a large conscript army in order to deter potential German aggression on the mainland foundered against democratic and traditional British antipathies to standing armies.[94] Suggestions that higher proportions of public expenditure might be diverted from the navy to a larger and more effective professional army ran up against similar powerful traditions and cultures. The navy could always count upon popular, liberal and imperial support when it came to conflicts over shares of the budget allocated for defence.[95]

Finally, and most significant of all, the construction of understandings, ententes and alliances with the only states capable of deterring German threats to the balance of power in Europe — France and Russia — turned out to be extremely difficult. For decades, France continued to be perceived as Britain's traditional enemy. Liberals also disliked the whole notion of accords with the autocratic Romanov régime. In British eyes, both powers represented potential enemies because they possessed large empires and their ambitions in central Asia, the Far East and Africa appeared to threaten Britain's imperial interests around the world. Thus, following the formation of the Franco-Russian Alliance of 1892, the Admiralty's main anxiety was how the Royal Navy might cope with the combined fleets of these two rival navies.[96]

The wary Titan and the vacillation of diplomacy

After the turn of the century, British diplomacy proceeded with reluctance and equivocation to build up ententes — not alliances — first with France (1904) and then with Russia (1908) which came too late in the day to seriously confront and contain the long-standing German problem.[97] Alas, and at the same time, several British statesmen and the Foreign Office continued to adopt an ambiguous and conciliatory stance towards the Kaiser and his Triple Alliance — Germany, Austria and Italy. Admiral Fisher pulled back part of the Royal Navy to home waters, but plans to conscript a large army to support allies on the mainland remained on paper. For more than a decade — indeed, right up to the very declaration of war in August 1914 — British policy towards the maintenance of a balance of power in Europe appeared, to its allies and foes alike, to be one of vacillation, and indecision.[98] No wonder the Kaiser and his High Command became, in turn, surprised and furious in August 1914, when Britain mobilized for war in concert with France and Russia. They, and the German foreign office, had anticipated that, provided the security of the kingdom and the integrity of its empire — particularly India — could be assured, then Britain would probably remain aloof from any military conflict between European powers.[99] To have mobilized and committed such a pathetically small force of troops to Europe after so much equivocation at that point in time — rather then sooner and more decisively — turned out, by 1918, to have been an enormously costly but (except to Panglossian historians) not an unavoidable error of judgement.[100]

That huge mistake can only be comprehended in the context of British strategic policy which had for decades remained too 'imperial' in scope, scale and focus. The Hanoverians had neither neglected nor derogated the significance of Europe in their pursuit of trade and empire. Unless the outbreak of the Great War is regarded as the inevitable outcome of 'Prussian' culture and *Weltpolitik*, or, more simply, as an unfortunate accident flowing from the assassination of an Austrian Archduke, then the failure of British statesmen to pursue a more consistent and purposeful strategy to preserve the balance of power in Europe must now be represented as a massive indictment of the liberal imperial imagination.[101]

In economic terms, 'massive' can be the only appropriate adjective because both the immediate and the longer term costs that flowed from the Great War remain incalculable, particularly if that tragic conflict is perceived to be the starting point for something like four decades of global warfare, revolution, neo-mercantilism and disruption to the liberal international economic order.[102]

A metanarrative of success leading to failure: mercantilism, 1688–1815 and liberal imperialism, 1846–1914

Implicit in the writings of historians are metanarratives that embody a plot that carry such narratives forward from one episode to the next and on, ultimately, to some outcome or story. My story began as one of combined political and economic achievement for Britain from 1688 to 1815, which led to naval, commercial and industrial hegemony as the workshop of the world, 1846–73. That heritage of geopolitical and economic success reordered and permeated British culture to include an almost unquestioned acceptance of an imperial role for the state, the navy, the army and for its political élite.

Even during the high-water years of the liberal international economic order (1846–1914), British statesmen, popular opinion and the widening electorate, that provided them with their constitutional power and authority, remained culturally immune to the entirely plausible arguments from radicals, citing hard evidence that economic benefits from the Empire were falling below its costs, to society as a whole, by a large and increasing margin.

Meanwhile, the continued preoccupation of successive governments with empire throughout the late Victorian and Edwardian period obfuscated and delayed a more realistic and efficient response to the German problem that appeared with the formation of the *Zollverein* and emerged menacingly onto the stage of great-power politics after the defeat of France in 1871.

Historians normally construct their metanarratives about the rise and decline of the British economy in terms that bring to the foreground the loss of entrepreneurial vigour, the waning of the industrial spirit, the malign heritage of an early start, failures to invest in education, science and technology and even that theoretically fashionable but spurious inevitability of convergence and overtaking — which is now perceived to be the fate of all hegemons in a world economy of competing nations. My metanarrative reincorporates power into British economic history. It is emplotted around the heritage of private and public investment which, for more than a century (1688–1815), did so much to carry the economy to a peak of success. Thereafter, that distinguished radical and economic historian Thorold Rogers was surely percipient to point out that the retention and extension of empire within a liberal international order contributed next to nothing to the security of the realm and operated to restrain the long-run growth of the economy. Rogers did not live long enough to observe that responsibilities for empire led a succession of conservative and liberal cabinets towards the most costly strategic error in British history. The Great War and the unfurling of its consequences — including neo-mercantilism, the Great Depression, the reintegration of empires 1919–39, followed by a Second World War and the protracted and costly disengagement from empire and from geopolitical pretensions from 1945–89 — have surely contributed far more to the relative decline of the British economy than even he imagined. Economies that rise by the sword also decline by the sword.

Notes

* Many friends participated in the construction of this metanarrative, if only by way of illuminating disagreement with several parts of the story. I thank and apologize to Andrew Adonis, Daniel Baugh, Nicholas Crafts, Francois Crouzet, John Davis, Martin Daunton, David Eastwood, Stanley Engerman, Lawrence Goldman, Anthony Howe, Paul Kennedy, Andrew Lambert, Colin Matthew, Roland Quinault, Patricia Thane, Barry Supple, Frank Trentman and Donald Winch for prolonging a conversation opened by Adam Smith when Britain was losing thirteen colonies in North America.

1. R. F. Berkhoffer, *Beyond the Great Story: History as Text and Discourse*, Cambridge, ma 1995.
2. P. Clarke and C. Trebilcock, eds, *Understanding Decline: Perceptions and Realities of British Economic Performance*, Cambridge 1997.
3. J. M. Blaut, *The Colonizers' Model of the World*, London 1993.
4. P. K. O'Brien and L. Prados De La Escosura, 'The Costs and Benefits of European Imperialism from the Conquest of Cueta, 1415 to the Treaty of Lusaka, 1974', in *Debates and Controversies in Economic History*, edited by C-E. Nunez, Madrid 1998, pp. 9–69
5. M. Bunzl, *Real History: Reflections on Historical Practice*, London 1997.
6. *Oxford History of the British Empire*, vol. 1, 'The Origins of Empire', edited by N. Canny, Oxford 1998.
7. W. A. Speck, *Reluctant Revolutionaries: Englishmen and the Revolution of 1688*, Oxford 1989.
8. J. Black, *A System of Ambition: British Foreign Policy, 1660–1793*, London 1991.
9. P. K. O'Brien, 'Political Preconditions for the Industrial Revolution', in *The Industrial Revolution and British Society*, edited by P.K. O'Brien and R. Quinault, Cambridge 1993.
10. P. Kennedy, *The Rise and Fall of the Great Powers*, New York 1987.
11. E. Silberner, *The Problem of War in 19th Century Economic Thought*, New York 1972.
12. P. K. O'Brien, 'The Political Economy of British Taxation, 1688–1815', *Economic History Review*, 41, 1988, pp. 1–32.
13. D. Baugh, 'Great Britain's Blue Water Policy, 1689–1815', *International History Review*, 10, 1988, pp. 1–58.
14. J. Mokyr, 'Editor's Introduction' in *The British Industrial Revolution: An Economic Perspective*, edited by J. Mokyr, Boulder 1993, pp. 69–78.
15. P. K. O'Brien and S. L. Engerman, 'Exports and the Growth of the British Economy from the Glorious Revolution to the Peace of Amiens', in *Slavery and the Rise of the Atlantic System*, edited by R. Solow, Cambridge 1991, pp. 177–209.
16. P. J. Cain and A. G. Hopkins, *British Imperialism: Innovation and Expansion, 1688–1914*, London 1993.
17. K. Morgan, 'Atlantic Trade and British Economic Growth', in *The Nature of Industrialization: International Trade and British Economic Growth*, edited by P. Mathias and J. Davis, Oxford 1996, pp. 66–75.
18. M. Collins, *Money and Banking in the UK: A History*, London 1988.
19. L. Gomes, *Foreign Trade and the National Economy*, London 1987.
20. This debate is judiciously surveyed by Mokyr, 'Editor's Introduction'.
21. K. Harley, 'Foreign Trade: Comparative Advantage and Performance', in *The Economic History of Britain since 1700*, vol. 1: 1700–1860, edited by R. Floud and D. McCloskey, Cambridge, 1994, pp. 300–31.
22. P. K. O'Brien, 'The Britishness of the First Industrial Revolution and the British Contribution to the Industrialization of 'Follower Countries' on the Mainland', *Diplomacy and Statecraft*, 8, 1997, pp. 48–67.
23. P. Deane and W. A. Cole, *British Economic Growth, 1688–1959*, Cambridge 1962.
24. N. Zahedieh, 'Overseas Expansion and Trade in the Seventeenth Century', in *The Oxford History of the British Empire*, vol. 1, 'The Origins of Empire', edited by N. Canny, Oxford 1998, pp. 398–422.
25. N. Zahedieh, 'Trade, Plunder and Economic Development in Early English Jamaica', *Economic History Review*, 38, 1986, pp. 570–93.

26 R. P. Thomas and D. McCloskey, 'Overseas Trade and Empire 1700–1860' in *The Economic History of Britain since 1700*, vol. 1, pp. 87–102 but see T. J. Hatton, *et al*, Eighteenth Century British Trade: Homespun or Empire Made', *Explorations in Economic History*, 20, 1983, pp. 163–82.
27 J. Cuenca Esteban, 'The Rising Share of Industrial Exports in Industrial Output', *Journal of Economic History*, 57, 1997, pp. 879–906.
28 K. E. Knorr, *British Colonial Theories, 1570–1850*, Toronto 1944. This is the position taken by R. Blackburn in *The Making of New World Slavery*, Verso, London 1997, Chapters 9 and 12.
29 A. K. Smith, *Creating a World Economy. Merchant Capital, Colonialism and World Trade, 1400–1825*, Boulder 1991.
30 C. P. Kindleberger, *World Economic Primacy, 1500–1990*, Oxford 1996.
31 P. K. O'Brien, 'Inseparable Connections: Trade, Economy, Fiscal State and the Expansion of Empire, 1688–1815', in *Oxford History of the British Empire*, vol. 2, 'The Eighteenth Century', edited by P.J. Marshall, Oxford 1998, pp. 53–77.
32 J. Brewer, *The Sinews of Power. War, Money and the English State, 1688–1783*, London 1989.
33 H. Bowen, *Élites, Enterprise and the Making of the British Empire Overseas*, London 1996.
34 L. Colley, *Britons. Forging the Nation 1707–1837*, London 1992.
35 J. Horn, 'British Diaspora. Emigration from Britain, 1680–1815', in *Oxford History of the British Empire*, vol. 2, 'The Eighteenth Century', edited by P.J. Marshall, Oxford 1998, pp. 28–52.
36 L. Stone, ed., *An Imperial State at War from 1689 to 1815*, London 1994.
37 O'Brien, 'Political Preconditions for the Industrial Revolution'.
38 T. Hutchinson, *Before Adam Smith: The Emergence of Political Economy 1662–1776*, Oxford 1988.
39 A. Gunder Frank, *Re Orient: Global Economy in the Asian Age*, Berkeley 1998.
40 Thomas and McCloskey, 'Overseas Trade and Empire'.
41 S. L. Engerman, 'British Imperialism in a Mercantilist Age, 1492–1849', *Revista de Historia Economica*, 1, 1998, pp. 195–225.
42 A. Smith, *The Wealth of Nations*, New York 1937.
43 O'Brien and Engerman, 'Exports and the Growth of the British Economy'.
44 J. Viner, *Studies in the Theory of International Trade*, London 1937.
45 Gunder Frank, *Re Orient*.
46 P. K. O'Brien, 'From the Voyages of Discovery to the Industrial Revolution', in *The European Discovery of the World and its Economic Effects on Pre-Industrial Society*, edited by H. Pohl, Stuttgart 1990, pp. 154–77.
47 J. C. Ward, *British Economists and the Empire*, London 1983, pp. 60–3.
48 P. K. O'Brien, 'The Costs and Benefits of British Imperialism, 1846–1914', *Past and Present*, 120, 1988, pp. 163–200, and, for the other view, see A. Offer, 'The British Empire 1870–1914: A Waste of Money', *Economic History Review*, 46, 1993, pp. 215–38.
49 F. Crouzet, 'Trade and Empire: the British Experience from the Establishment of Free Trade until the First World War', in *Great Britain and her World*, edited by B.M. Radliffe, Manchester 1975, pp. 209–35.
50 S. B. Saul, *Studies in British Overseas Trade*, Liverpool 1960.
51 P. M. Kennedy, 'The Costs and Benefits of British Imperialism', *Past and Present*, 125, 1989, pp. 186–92.
52 A. K. Banerji, *Aspects of Indo-British Relations*, Oxford 1982, and K. N. Chaudhuri, *Asia Before Europe: Economy and Civilization of the Indian Ocean from the Rise of Islam to 1750*, Cambridge 1990.

53 M. Edelstein, 'Imperialism: Cost and Benefit' in *The Economic History of Britain Since 1700*, vol. 2: 1860–1939, edited by R. Floud and D. McCloskey, Cambridge 1994, pp. 173–96.
54 E. Hobsbawm, *Industry and Empire*, New York 1968.
55 P. K. O'Brien and G. Pigman, 'Free Trade, British Hegemony and the International Order in the Nineteenth Century', *Review of International Studies*, 18, 1992, pp. 89–113.
56 A. Friedberg, *The Weary Titan: Britain and the Experience of Relative Decline*, Princeton 1988.
57 M. Barratt-Brown, *The Economics of Imperialism*, London 1974.
58 M. Edelstein, 'Foreign Investment and Accumulation', in *The Economic History of Britain since 1700*, vol. 2: 1860–1939, edited by R. Floud and D. McCloskey, Cambridge 1994, pp. 197–216.
59 L. Davis and R. Huttenback, *Mammon and the Pursuit of Empire 1860–1912*, Cambridge 1986.
60 M. Edelstein, *Overseas Investment in the Age of High Imperialism: The United Kingdom 1850–1914*, London 1982.
61 J. H. Lorie and M. Hamilton, *The Stock Market: Theories and Evidence*, Horewood 1973.
62 Davis and Huttenback, *Mammon and the Pursuit of Empire*.
63 P. Temin, 'Measuring Economic Decline', in *Understanding Decline. Perceptions and Realities of British Economic Performance*, edited by P. Clarke and C. Trebilcock, Cambridge 1997, pp. 285–301.
64 W. P. Kennedy, *Industrial Structure, Capital Markets and the Origins of British Economic Decline*, Cambridge 1987.
65 A. Maddison, *Dynamic Forces in Capitalist Development*, Oxford 1991.
66 An up-to-date bibliography and review of the data has been published by N. F. Crafts, 'Forging Ahead and Falling Behind: The Rise and Relative Decline of the First Industrial Nation', *Journal of Economic Perspectives*, 12, 1998, pp. 193–210.
67 Modern surveys of the key debates on the origins of British decline with extensive bibliographies are included as essays in *The Economic History of Britain Since 1700*, vol. 2: 1860–1939, edited by R. Floud and D. McCloskey, Cambridge 1994.
68 Edelstein, 'Foreign investment and accumulation'.
69 The debate about overseas (foreign plus imperial) investment is surveyed by S. Pollard, *Britain's Prime and Britain's Decline, The British Economy 1870–1914*, London 1989.
70 W. P. Kennedy, 'Foreign Investment, Trade and Growth in the UK, 1870–1914', *Explorations in Economic History*, 2, 1974, pp. 422–39.
71 P. Cain and A. G. Hopkins, *British Imperialism: Innovation and Expansion, 1688–1914*, London, 1993.
72 B. Elbaum and W. Lazonick, eds, *The Decline of the British Economy*, Oxford 1987.
73 This thesis is associated with the writings of Kennedy, *Industrial Structure*.
74 A. Gamble, *Britain in Decline: Economic Policy, Political Strategy and the British State*, London 1990.
75 J. J. Van Helten and Y. Cassis, eds, *Capitalism in a Mature Economy*, London 1990.
76 M. Collins, *Banks and Industrial Finance in Britain*, London 1991.
77 Collins, *Money and Banking*.
78 P. L. Cottrell, *Industrial Finance 1830–1914*, London 1980.

79 G. Ingham, *Capitalism Divided: The City and Industry in British Social Development*, London 1984.
80 F. Capie and W. Webber, *A Monetary History of the United Kingdom, 1870–1982*.
81 They are very well surveyed in a forthcoming essay by A. Offer, 'Costs and Benefits, Prosperity and Security', in *Oxford History of the British Empire*, vol. 3: 'The Nineteenth Century', edited by A. Porter, Oxford 1999.
82 The debate is appraised by P. Cain, 'Was it Worth Having?, The British Empire 1850–1950', *Revista de Historia Economica*, 1, 1998, pp. 351–76.
83 Davis and Huttenback, *Mammon and the Pursuit of Empire*.
84 J. Hobson, *The Wealth of States*, Cambridge 1997.
85 J. Foreman-Peck, ed., *New Perspectives on the Victorian Economy*, Cambridge 1991.
86 S. Sretzer, 'British Economic Decline and Human Resources', in *Understanding Decline: Perceptions and Realities of British Economic Performance*, edited by P. Clarke and C. Trebilcock, Cambridge 1997, pp. 73–102.
87 P. K. O'Brien, 'The Rise, Roll Back and Return of the Fiscal State', forthcoming 2000.
88 N. Ferguson, *The Pity of War*, London 1998, ch. 5.
89 A. Porter, *An Atlas of Overseas Expansion*, London 1991.
90 B. Porter, *Britain, Europe and the World: Delusions of Grandeur 1850–1982*, London 1993.
91 P. Kennedy, *The Rise of Anglo-German Antagonism 1860–1914*, London 1982.
92 E. H. Green, *The Politics, Economics and Ideology of the Conservative Party*, London 1994 and Ferguson, *The Pity of War*.
93 J. Eddy and D. Schreuder, eds, *The Rise of Colonial Nationalism*, Sydney 1988.
94 R. J. C. Adams and P. Poirer, *The Conscription Controversy in Britain*, Basingstoke 1987.
95 B. Semmel, *Liberalism and Naval Strategy*, London 1986.
96 I. Beckett and J. Gooch, eds, *Politicians and Defence Studies in the Formulation of British Defence Policy*, Manchester 1981.
97 K. M. Wilson, *The Policy of Entente*, London 1985.
98 M. Howard, *Continental Commitment*, London 1972 and Ferguson, *The Pity of War*, Chs 2 and 3.
99 V. R. Berghahn, *Imperial Germany, 1871–1914. Economy, Society, Culture and Politics*, Oxford 1994.
100 A. D. Harvey, *Collision of Empires: Britain in Three World Wars 1793–1945*, London 1992.
101 K. Robbins, *The Eclipse of a Great Power. Modern Britain 1870–1945*, London 1983.
102 Ferguson, *The Pity of War*, 'Conclusion: Alternatives to Armageddon'.

Part 7

THE GREAT DEPRESSION

44

A NEW INTERPRETATION OF THE ONSET OF THE GREAT DEPRESSION

Alexander J. Field

Source: *Journal of Economic History* 44(2), 1984: 489–98.

Summary

Over the 1919–1929 period, fluctuations in the value of stock trading on the New York Stock Exchange exercised statistically significant and economically important impacts on the demand to hold cash balances. The marked post-1925 rise in the volume and value of stock trading led to a measurable increase in the transactions demand to hold cash balances, an increase in demand not recognized or seriously discussed by individuals inside or outside of the system. Had it been recognized, it is unlikely that the Fed would have persisted in its antispeculative policies in 1928–1929, policies associated with rises in interest rates and the beginnings of a downturn in real activity in the second quarter of 1929.

The proposition that exchanges of assets in secondary markets might influence the transactions demand for money was debated extensively in the 1920s among English, German, and American monetary theorists. But in the late 1920s and early 1930s a consensus was reached: Although such effects were theoretically possible, they were empirically unimportant because of the very high and inexpensively flexible velocity in the financial circulation. This conclusion was reached on the basis of casual empiricism; the early investigators did not have access to inexpensive multiple regression analysis.

I have recently tested the proposition by including a measure of transactions on the New York Stock Exchange in a regression explaining the monthly demand for a variety of monetary aggregates during the 1919–1929 period (131 observations), and I obtain statistically significant and economically important estimates of the influence of stock market trading on the transactions demand for money.[1] Six monetary aggregates were used as dependent variables, ranging from demand deposits in New York City to the Friedman/Schwartz M3 series. Right-hand variables included, in addition to the lagged endogenous variable, seasonally adjusted industrial production times a wholesale price index (a GNP proxy), the prime commercial paper rate (4- to 6-month maturity), or the call loan rate on new securities, and the value of trading on the New York Stock Exchange. The econometric issues associated with the interpretation of these results are discussed extensively in a paper in the *American Economic Review*.[2]

I wish here to consider in more detail the implications of these results for our understanding of the onset of the central macroeconomic cataclysm of our century, the Great Depression. There are four propositions, some but not all of them new, that make up what I consider to be, in the aggregate, a novel interpretation of the onset of the Depression. Note that I am concerned here with why the downturn in real activity began in 1929, not primarily with why it was so long or so deep:

(1) The marked post-1925 rise in the volume and value of transactions on the New York Stock Exchange led to a measurable increase in the transactions demand for money at given (Y,r) combinations.
(2) The dimensions and nature of the additional source of transactions demand were not seriously discussed or recognized by individuals within or outside of the System.
(3) Had that demand been recognized, it is unlikely that the Fed would have persisted in its antispeculative policy in 1928–1929, a policy whose theoretical underpinnings were, in any case, weak.
(4) The high real interest rates prevailing in 1928–1929, the result of the Fed's antispeculative policies, were the proximate cause of the downturn in real activity that later mushroomed—because of a confluence of other developments (including the collapse of the international economic order)—into the Great Depression.[3]

Stock trading and the transactions demand for money

Almost all commentaries on the stock market boom of the 1920s have focused on the rise in asset prices. That rise was indeed remarkable: from an August 1921 trough to a September 1929 peak, asset prices increased 334 percent, more than quadrupling in nominal value.[4] In contrast to subsequent stock market booms, this occurred over a period during which commodity prices were declining at a rate of about 1 percent a year. What is less often emphasized, however, is that the rise in trading volume was even more dramatic than the rise in asset prices. Although there is no theoretically necessary relationship between trading volume and asset prices, their monthly values were closely correlated over the 1919–1929 period (r = .93). From a July 1921 trough to an October 1929 peak, trading volume grew 1478 percent.[5] The upward trend in both series meant that their product (trading value) experienced unprecedented growth. From a July 1921 trough of $1.6 billion (at an annualized rate), trading value rose to an October 1929 peak of $97.8 billion, almost the rate of annualized GNP in that month. This more than 6000 percent rise is to be compared with a 46 percent growth in nominal income between 1921 and 1929.

This astronomical increase is to some extent misleading because trading volume was at a very low level in July 1921. Perhaps a fairer comparison is between average levels in 1925 and peak level in 1929. This comparison shows volume rising 272 percent and asset prices rising 146 percent, which together imply that trading value's 1929 peak was more than nine times its 1925 average.

Whereas more modest fluctuations in trading value had minor influences on the transactions demand for money, because of the use of clearance mechanisms by brokers and the general efficiency and flexibility of the financial circulation, rises in trading value of the magnitude that took place during the second half of the 1920s did have economically important impacts on the system-wide demand to hold cash balances—not only by brokers, but also by their customers. Had such increases been fully accommodated, there would have been no necessary impact of the rise in the volume of asset trading on real activity through monetary (interest rate) channels. But for reasons discussed below, that transactions demand was not accommodated.

Failure to recognize a new source of transactions demand

There were many individuals, both inside and outside of the System, who complained that stock exchange speculation "absorbed" cash balances.[6] But the explanations of absorption they offered were almost uniformly illogical. Some argued as if cash balances used to purchase already existing securities vanished into a bottomless pit, ignoring the fundamental truism that for every buyer there must be a seller. "Speculation" (broadly definable as the holding of a nonmonetary asset in anticipation of its future rise in terms of money) can "absorb" cash balances only if such activity is associated with an increased desire to hold such balances.[7] Yet a speculative fever of the sort that apparently gripped the stock market in the late 1920s represented in a sense "illiquidity" preference, and should have reduced the desire to hold balances that could pay no dividends or interest and definitionally could not exhibit nominal capital gains. On the other hand, if such speculative activity were associated with a rising volume of transactions, giving rise to a systemic increase in the demand to hold cash balances for transactions purposes at any given interest rate and output level, then one can speak of speculation "absorbing" cash balances. In the absence of monetary accommodation, such an increase shifts an economy's LM schedule to the left. Although this possibility was recognized by some monetary theorists in the 1920s, a consensus emerged toward the end of the decade that such effects were empirically insignificant. No one, either inside or outside of the System, argued in the 1920s that the economy was experiencing an unprecedented increase in non-GNP-related transactions demand as a result of the explosion of trading volume and value on the stock exchange.[8] Concern was almost uniformly focused on the causes and possible consequences of the rise in asset prices.

Consequences of this failure: persistence of tight money

The third proposition advanced above rests on a series of dynamic simulations conducted using the regression results referred to earlier. Most of the rise in trading value that occurred between the trough in trading value in July of 1921 and its peak in October 1929 occurred in the post-1925 period. The scenario simulated imagines that trading value remained constant at its average 1919–1924 value throughout the period but that interest rates and output followed their historical course. Under these assumptions, the monthly average of demand deposits in New York City over the last 24 months of the 1920s would have been 20.3 percent lower than in fact it was. For Friedman/Schwartz M1, the corresponding figure is 17 percent. As it happened, the rise in interest rates in 1928–1929 had little discernible effect on monetary growth rates.

Absent the rise in the value of stock trading (but adopting its antispeculative policies), the Fed would have been confronted already in 1928 with a fairly precipitous decline in the money stock. Although the Board of Governors in the 1920s did not exhibit the modern obsession with money stock growth rates, at least over the short run, members were concerned with trends in the banking system's supply (stock) of bank credit, the reflection on the asset side of bank balance sheets of changes in the stock of bank liabilities, the major component of the money stock. There is reason to believe that a precipitous downturn in bank liabilities (and assets) would have strengthened the hand of those who opposed the antispeculative policy, and led to its moderation. In any event, the reduction in high-powered money resulting from the open market sales in the first part of 1928 was approximately neutralized by a rise in discounts; the monetary base and M1 hardly changed, in spite of the Fed's contractionary policies.[9] Interest rates, however, rose substantially in the last two years of the decade: it is here, rather than in the money stock figures, that the impact of contractionary policy can be seen.

The unrecognized impact of stock trading on the transactions demand for money can thereby be indirectly linked to the onset of the Great Depression.

Table 1 Money Stock Simulations, 1919–1929, Assuming Constancy of Trading Value at 1919–1924 Average.

A. Regression Equations[a]

Dependent Variable and Statistics	Log of Lagged Endogenous Variables	Log of Trading Value, NYSE[b]	Log of Nominal Income Proxy[c]	Log of Call Loan Rate	Seasonal Dummies Jan.	Seasonal Dummies Aug.	Constant
Demand Deposits, NYC R^2 = .980 D.W. = 1.87 ρ = .200 (2.20)	.754 (17.61)	.020 (5.16)	.040 (2.67)	−0.39 (−4.81)	.011 (1.70)	−0.20 (−3.28)	1.80 (5.61)
M1 R^2 = .994 D.W. = 2.19 ρ = −.512 (−6.52)	.874 (50.32)	.0073 (5.44)	.031 (5.96)	−.015 (−5.80)			1.09 (6.94)

B. Simulation Results

Variable	1927 Peak (December) (million $)	Actual 1928–1929 Monthly Average (million $)	Simulated 1928–1929 Monthly Average[d] (million $)	Percent Difference 1928–1929, Simulated vs. Actual
Demand Deposits, NYC	5,570	5,379	4,286	−20.3
M1	26,436	26,300	21,824	−17.0

[a] 131 observations. The method of estimation was ordinary least squares with first-order autocorrelation coefficient selected by a maximum likelihood procedure. Dependent variables are logs. t-statistics are in parentheses. For a full discussion of the economic and econometric issues associated with the interpretation of these and other results, see A. J. Field, "Asset Exchanges and the Transactions Demand for Money, 1919–1929," *American Economic Review*, 74 (Mar. 1984), 43–59.
[b] Trading volume, millions of shares x asset price index.
[c] Industrial production index, seasonally adjusted x WPI, other than farm products x a scaling factor (.0518) to make estimates comparable to other GNP estimates.
[d] Logged values (the output of the simulation) converted to dollars and then averaged.

Sources: Federal Reserve System, Board of Governors, *Banking and Monetary Statistics, 1919–1941* (Washington, D.C., 1976), Tables 49, 120, 133 and 135.
Federal Reserve System, Board of Governors, *Industrial Production, 1976 Revision* (Washington, D.C., 1976), p. S-27.
U.S. Department of Commerce, *Survey of Current Business*, 20 (Sept. 1940), 18.
Milton Friedman and Anna J. Schwartz, *A Monetary History of the United States, 1867–1960* (Princeton, 1963), Appendix A.

This chain of reasoning is based on the propositions that this additional source of transactions demand was economically important and that it was unrecognized. Suppose the effect had not been empirically important. Then, according to these simulations, the rise in interest rates in 1928–1929 would have led to a measurable decrease in monetary growth rates, a decrease that would likely have alarmed policy makers sufficiently to cause them to moderate what was in fact a very contractionary policy. Suppose, on the other hand, that the effect had been empirically important but had been recognized as such. Then, in all probability, the System would have viewed the fact that the increase in interest rates had virtually no effect on monetary growth not with complacency, but rather with alarm, given what that implied about the trend in GNP-related transactions demand. Although one cannot predict exactly how the System would have responded to these hypothetical situations, there is reason to believe that under either of these alternate scenarios, monetary policy would have been looser than in fact it was.

In the first half of 1928, the Fed conducted massive contractionary open market purchases, practically emptying the System Investment Account of government securities. Early in 1928 when these policies were begun, some members of the committee and the Board expressed concern about what this would do to interest rates, and therefore real activity, particularly in construction and small manufacturing. But as tight money/higher interest rates persisted into late 1928 and 1929, these concerns became subtly deflected by the conflict between the New York Fed and the Board, with the Board repeatedly rejecting New York's request to raise its discount rate. The dispute over whether (for example) a divergence between a discount rate of 4.5 percent and market rates of 6 percent was untenable (the New York position) or could be dealt with through selective credit rationing (the Board of Governors' position) diverted attention from the more fundamental question: Was tight money adversely affecting the real side of the economy?[10] An understanding of the transactions demand emanating from the stock market might have prevented that diversion and refocused attention on the fundamental issue.

The theoretical underpinnings of the antispeculative policy were, in any case, weak. It is argued by Friedman/Schwartz, and not disputed by Temin, that a policy of high interest rates, if applied earlier—could have been an effective antispeculative policy.[11] Extreme monetary restriction possibly would have driven stock prices down before October 1929. A shortage of cash balances would have induced individuals to try to liquidate some of their nonmoney assets, forcing down their prices. On the other hand, assets aside from stocks might first have felt the selling pressure. Expectations of even higher stock prices, not necessarily easy money, were what fueled speculation. In 1929 Andrew Mellon believed that raising the discount rate as high as 9 percent would not necessarily break the speculative fever unless and until it had run its course.[12]

The systemic effect of the expansion of bank loans—whatever their security—was to increase the stock of transactions balances available to facilitate the rapidly growing volume of security transactions, along with GNP-related transactions. Refusal to accommodate that transactions demand (which was, in retrospect, the essence of the Fed's antispeculative policies), could not be expected to do other than adversely affect real activity.

High interest rates and their impact on real activity

Most commentators agree that short-term interest rates were pushed to relatively high levels in 1928–1929. The prime commercial paper rate, 4 to 6 month maturity began 1928 at 4 percent, rose steadily through September to 5.63 percent, declined briefly to 5.38 (December 1928/January 1929) and then rose steadily to 6.25 percent in September/October 1929.[13]

Investments in the call money market were extremely liquid and well collateralized—an appealing alternative to holding cash for those who did not believe—and there apparently were many—that stock prices could only go up. The call money rate on loans on new securities rose from 4.15 in January 1928 to 9.8 in March 1929, declined for 3 months, and then hit a new peak in July of 1929 (9.41).[14] Although call loan rates are on the face of it less relevant than commercial paper or long-term rates in measuring the impact of tight money on real activity, they do testify dramatically to the effects of monetary stringency in the last two years of the decade. Both Friedman and Schwartz (1963) and Temin (1976) agree that interest rates were high in 1928–1929, and agree on the reasons: in Temin's words, "The Federal Reserve tried to dampen the stock market boom."[15] Nancy Dorfman, in her unpublished dissertation (1967), questioned the relative height of interest rates, arguing that the peak in the prime commercial paper rate in 1929 was about two points below the previous peak in 1920.[16] The difficulty with her argument is that the earlier peak occurred in the context of substantial inflation, and presumably contained at least some inflation premium, whereas the peak in 1929 occurred in the context of a persistent decline in the WPI of approximately 1 percent a year since 1922. It is difficult to conclude other than that short-term interest rates were at higher levels in 1928–1929 than they would be at any time again before the early 1980s.

These high interest rates were associated with a downturn in real activity in the second and third quarters of 1928/29, well before the stock market crash. The downturn is particularly noticeable in one component of investment (construction) and one component of consumption (automobiles). Both of these sectors historically have been sensitive to interest rates and credit availability.

Construction activity generally is perceived as having peaked in 1926, but it was making a strong recovery in 1928. The Commerce Department index of building contracts, for example, began the year at 96, yet in April/June occupied the high ground of 142.2/143.5. A year later, in April 1929, the index stood at 128, in May, 122.4 and June, 109.7. The index was lower in every month of 1929 than in the corresponding month in 1928.[17] Although Dorfman was unable to pick up any effect of credit tightness on long-term mortgage rates, yields on four grades of corporate bonds, high grade municipals and U.S. government bonds all rose between 1928 and 1929.[18] There is reason to believe that an apparent recovery in the construction sector, evident in the second quarter of 1928, was choked off by the monetary tightness associated with the Fed's antispeculative policy.

Automobile production turned down in April of 1929, although seasonal adjustment pushes the downturn to June.[19] Again, there is reason to believe that the high interest rate environment was partially responsible for triggering the initial stages in the downturn of a record production year of 1929—a level of production not reached again until 1953.

The evidence of the beginnings of the downturn is somewhat disguised in annual aggregate data.[20] One would expect investment to be hardest hit by a tight money policy, yet annual data show gross private domestic investment actually rising from $14.1 billion in 1928 to $16.2 billion in 1929. Almost all of the increase in investment can be accounted for by a swing from a 1928 net inventory decumulation of $-.38 billion to a 1929 net accumulation of inventories of $1.71 billion. The vast bulk of the change in inventories represented involuntary holdings on December 31, 1929, not voluntary investment, which we expect to respond negatively to higher interest rates. The aggregate data are further complicated by the peculiar disjuncture between the costs of debt and equity financing prevailing in 1928/29 until the stock market crash. Even though the cost of debt finance was rising, equity finance remained cheap because of the inflated price of securities. The willingness of investors to borrow money at high call loan rates and "lend" it to corporations at rates of return that *ex post* were negative, permitted corporations with access to the stock market to invest more cheaply than credit conditions suggested. The result was that producer durables investment in 1929 actually rose by about the same amount as gross private new construction fell.

Recent economic history (that is, 1981–1983) has reinforced the proposition that, except in rare circumstances, monetary policy is not neutral in the short run with respect to the real side of the economy. The history of the early 1980s reminds us that a negative demand shock induced by contractionary or slower monetary growth, even when announced (but possibly not believed) in advance, can have a serious effect on output and employment: There can be a significant output loss from disinflation. There is reason to believe that the sectors most sensitive to high interest rates in the 1980s—automobiles and construction—were also hardest hit in 1928/29. Construction and automobiles traditionally rely more heavily on debt as opposed to equity financing.

The evidence suggests that tight money, the result of the Fed's antispeculative policies, started the Depression. The stock market crash may have reinforced it by drastically raising the cost of equity finance, and through its effect on household wealth, depressing less interest-sensitive components of consumption (that is, components less vulnerable than automobiles to high pre-crash interest rates).[21] But it was tight money that triggered the downturn. As Keynes wrote in the *Treatise on Money*, "I attribute the slump [of 1929–1930] primarily to the deterrent effects on investment of the long period of dear money which preceeded the stock market collapse."[22] The argument was heard widely in the business press of the time, and to the extent that Temin and Friedman/Schwartz have an analysis of events in 1929, they are in agreement with respect to the causes of the initial downturn.

This research has built on that foundation but questions the Friedman/Schwartz position that the antispeculative policy—even if applied earlier—was feasible. Moreover, it argues that the unrecognized source of transactions demand coming from the stock exchange was, in an indirect sense, responsible for the continuation of the antispeculative policy and the associated high interest rates. The unrecognized transactions demand arising from asset exchanges short-circuited a feedback mechanism that otherwise would have alerted policy makers to the damage they were inflicting on the real side of the economy.

Notes

The author thanks Anna Schwartz and Robert Zevin for comments on an earlier version of this paper.

1 Similar results are obtained running the regressions on the 1919–1927 subsample (107 observations) and a 1921–1927 subsample (84 observations). In other words, the results are not an artifact of developments during the last two years of the 1920s.
2 A. J. Field, "Asset Exchanges and the Transactions Demand for Money," *American Economic Review*, 74 (March 1984), 43–59.
3 Charles P. Kindleberger, *The World in Depression, 1929–1939* (Berkeley, 1973).
4 Federal Reserve System, Board of Governors, *Banking and Monetary Statistics, 1919–1941* (Washington, D.C., 1976), Table 133, pp. 480–81.
5 Ibid., Table 135, p. 485.
6 For a critical review of these debates, see Fritz Machlup, *The Stock Market, Credit and Capital Formation*, trans. Vera C. Smith (New York, 1940, translation of *Borsenkredit, Industriekredit und Kapitalbildung*, 1931), especially Chs. 2–4.
7 Burton Malkiel prefers a narrower definition of speculation, distinguishing it from investment, which he defines as the buying and holding of assets in anticipation of "reasonably predictable income . . . and/or appreciation *over the long term*" (his italics). Speculation is defined in contrast as the holding of assets over the short term in anticipation of unpredictable gains. The emphasis on the short-term orientation of speculation does suggest that speculation might be associated with higher trading volume, but Malkiel does not develop this point. Malkiel has a strong normative preference for a buy and hold strategy (also reflected in our income tax treatment of short- and long-run capital gains), believing it

beneficial for the individual (and presumably the economy, aside from the brokerage industry). See *A Random Walk Down Wall Street*, Second College Ed. (New York, 1981), p. 20.

8 In fact, the opposite was maintained. A "Preliminary Memorandum for the Open Market Investment Committee" distributed before the meeting of May 24, 1928 asserted that "the movement of stock prices . . . rather than the volume of trading has caused the expansion of security loans." George Leslie Harrison papers, Columbia University Library, file labeled "Open Market Investment Committee, 1928." I argue that this analysis is basically incorrect. The increased demand for bank credit, regardless of how collateralized, was a reflection of an increased demand to hold cash balances for transactions purposes. The expansion of the asset side of bank portfolios reflected the increased desire to hold bank liabilities in an environment in which, over the short run, interest rates, not money stock figures, were being targeted.

9 Total U.S. government security holdings of Federal Reserve Banks fell from $617 million at the end of 1927 to $228 at the end of 1928. Total bills discounted, however, jumped from $581 million at the end of 1927 to $1056 million at the end of 1928. (Board of Governors, *Banking and Monetary Statistics*, p. 331.) Rough stability in the monetary base and M1 disguises a contractionary policy that manifested itself in rising market interest (and eventually discount) rates. M1 remained virtually unchanged from September 1925 to September 1929.

10 This section is based on a reading of the folders labelled "Open Market Investment Committee" for 1927–1929 in the Harrison papers, and the entries organized under "Discount Rate" in the typewritten summary of the Hamlin diary. Charles Sumner Hamlin diary, Library of Congress manuscript division.

11 Milton Friedman and Anna J. Schwartz, *A Monetary History of the United States, 1867–1960* (Princeton, 1963), p. 291; Peter Temin, *Did Monetary Forces Cause the Great Depression?* (New York, 1976).

12 On April 18, 1929 "Mellon said he wished rates had been increased long ago, but he felt sure that even if they had been increased conditions could not have been essentially different from what they are now, that increased discount rates would not have decreased speculation." On April 25, according to Hamlin, Mellon reiterated the proposition that "you cannot break [the] stock market by increasing discount rates," and on May 16, 1929, "Secretary Mellon said 6 percent rate would not cure the situation in New York stock market, nor would even 9 percent—that the stock market was beyond control through discount rates; that what he wanted to do was to restore the proper relation between Federal Reserve rates and market rates." These quotes are from the typewritten guide to the Hamlin diary, all entries under "Discount Rates."

13 Board of Governors, *Banking and Monetary Statistics*, Table 120, p. 450.

14 Ibid.

15 Temin, *Monetary Forces*, pp. 1, 123, 137, 170.

16 Nancy Dorfman, "The Role of Money in the Investment Boom of the Twenties and the 1929 Turning Point," unpublished Ph.D. dissertation, University of California, Berkeley, 1967, p. 61.

17 U.S. Department of Commerce, *Survey of Current Business*, 10 (Feb. 1930), 2, 3, 7, 15.

18 Board of Governors, *Banking and Monetary Statistics*, Table 128, pp. 468–69.

19 *Survey of Current Business*, 10 (Feb. 1930), 12, 17, 49.

20 J. A. Swanson and S. H. Williamson, "Estimates of National Product and Income for the United States Economy, 1919–1941," *Explorations in Economic History*, 10 (Spring 1973), 235–51.

21 Frederic S. Mishkin, "The Household Balance Sheet and the Great Depression," this JOURNAL, 38 (Dec. 1978), 918–37.
22 J. M. Keynes, *A Treatise on Money*, 2 vols. (New York, 1930), Vol. 2, p. 196. In this quote Keynes refers to the slump of 1930, but it is clear he means the slump that began in 1929, since two pages earlier he attributes the "slump of 1929–1930 ... to a deficiency of investment" (p. 194).

45

WHAT ENDED THE GREAT DEPRESSION?

Christina D. Romer

Source: *Journal of Economic History* 52(4), 1992: 757–84.

Summary

> This paper examines the role of aggregate-demand stimulus in ending the Great Depression. Plausible estimates of the effects of fiscal and monetary changes indicate that nearly all the observed recovery of the U.S. economy prior to 1942 was due to monetary expansion. A huge gold inflow in the mid- and late 1930s swelled the money stock and stimulated the economy by lowering real interest rates and encouraging investment spending and purchases of durable goods. That monetary developments were crucial to the recovery implies that self-correction played little role in the growth of real output between 1933 and 1942.

Between 1933 and 1937 real GNP in the United States grew at an average rate of over 8 percent per year; between 1938 and, 1941 it grew over 10 percent per year. These rates of growth are spectacular, even for an economy pulling out of a severe depression. Yet the recovery from the collapse of 1929 to 1933 has received little of the attention that economists have lavished on the Great Depression. Perhaps because the cataclysm of the early 1930s was so severe, modern economists have focused on the causes of the downturn and of the turning point in 1933. Once the end of the precipitous decline in output has been explained, there has been a tendency to let the story drop.[1] The eventual return to full employment is simply characterized as slow and incomplete until the outbreak of World War II.

In this article I examine in detail the source of the recovery from the Great Depression. I argue that the rapid rates of growth of real output in the mid- and late 1930s were largely due to conventional aggregate-demand stimulus, primarily in the form of monetary expansion. My calculations suggest that in the absence of these stimuli the economy would have remained depressed far longer and far more deeply than it actually did. This in turn suggests that any self-correcting response of the U.S. economy to low output was weak or nonexistent in the 1930s.

The possibility that aggregate-demand stimulus was the source of the recovery from the Depression has been considered and discounted by many studies. E. Cary Brown, for example, used a conventional Keynesian multiplier model and the concept of discretionary government spending to argue that fiscal policy was unimportant. His often-cited conclusion was that "fiscal policy . . . seems to have been an unsuccessful recovery device in the 'thirties—not because it did not work, but because it was not tried."[2] Milton Friedman and Anna Schwartz stressed that Federal Reserve policy was not the source of the recovery either: "In the period under consideration [1933–1941], the Federal Reserve System made essentially no attempt to alter the quantity of high-powered money."[3] While they were clearly aware that other developments led to a rise in the money supply during the mid-1930s, Friedman and Schwartz appear to have been more interested in the role that Federal Reserve inaction played in causing and prolonging the Great Depression than they were in quantifying the importance of monetary expansion in generating recovery.

The emphasis that these early studies placed on policy inaction and ineffectiveness may have led the authors of more recent studies to assume that conventional aggregate-demand stimulus could not have influenced the recovery from the Great Depression. Ben Bernanke and Martin Parkinson, for example, analyzed the apparent reversion of employment toward its trend level in the 1930s and were struck by the strength of the recovery. They believed, however, that "the New Deal is better characterized as having 'cleared the way' for a natural recovery . . . rather than as being the engine of recovery itself."[4] As a result, they argued that the trend reversion of the interwar economy is evidence of a strong self-corrective force. J. Bradford De Long and Lawrence Summers sounded a similar theme: "the substantial degree of mean reversion by 1941 is evidence that shocks to output are transitory." The only aggregate-demand stimulus that they thought might have contributed to the recovery was World War II, and they concluded that "it is hard to attribute any of the pre-1942 catch-up of the economy to the war."[5]

Despite this conventional wisdom, there is cause to believe that aggregate-demand developments, particularly monetary changes, were important in fostering the recovery from the Great Depression. That cause is the simple but often neglected fact that the money supply (measured as M1) grew at an average rate of nearly 10 percent per year between 1933 and 1937, and at an even higher rate in the early 1940s. Such large and persistent rates of money growth were unprecedented in U.S. economic history. The simulations I present in this paper using policy multipliers based on the experiences of 1921 and 1938, as well as multipliers derived from macroeconometric models, suggest that these monetary changes were crucially important to the recovery. According to my calculations, real GNP would have been approximately 25 percent lower in 1937 and nearly 50 percent lower in 1942 than it actually was if the money supply had continued to grow at its historical average rate. Similar simulations for fiscal policy suggest that changes in the government budget surplus played little role in generating the recovery.

In addition to estimating the effects of the tremendous monetary expansion during the mid- and late 1930s, I also examine the source of this expansion and the transmission mechanism that operated between the monetary changes and the real economy. The increase in the money supply was primarily due to a gold inflow, which was in turn due to devaluation in 1933 and to capital flight from Europe because of political instability after 1934. My estimates of the ex ante real interest rate suggest that, coincident with this gold inflow, real interest rates fell precipitously in 1933 and remained low or negative throughout most of the second half of the 1930s. These low real interest rates are closely correlated with a strong rebound in interest-sensitive spending. Thus, it is plausible that expansionary monetary developments were working through a conventional interest-rate transmission mechanism.

The strength of the recovery

My concern in this article with finding the source of the high rates of real growth during the recovery from the Great Depression may seem strange to those accustomed to thinking of that recovery as slow. The conventional wisdom is that the U.S. economy remained depressed for all of the 1930s and only returned to full employment following the outbreak of World War II. The reconciliation of these two seemingly disparate views lies in the fact that the declines in real output in the early 1930s, and again in 1938, were so large that it took many years of unprecedented growth to undo them and return real output to normal levels.

For most of my analysis I examined annual estimates of real GNP from the U.S. Bureau of Economic Analysis.[6] Because this series begins at 1929, I extended it backward in time, when necessary, with my revised version of the Kendrick-Kuznets GNP series.[7] The percentage changes in real GNP shown in Figure 1 clearly demonstrate both the severity of the collapse of real output between 1929 and 1933 and the strength of the subsequent recovery. Between 1929 and 1933, real GNP declined 35 percent; between 1933 and 1937, it rose 33 percent. In 1938 the economy suffered another 5 percent decrease in real GNP, but this was followed by an even more spectacular

WHAT ENDED THE GREAT DEPRESSION?

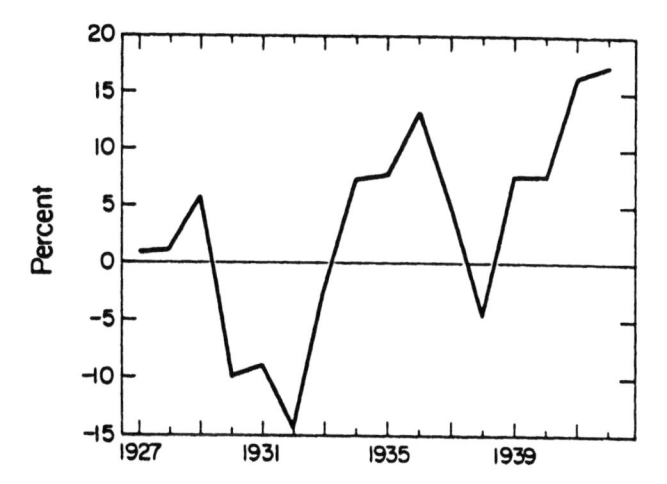

Figure 1 Percentage Changes in Real Gross National Product, 1927–1942.
Sources: The data for 1929–1942 are from the U.S. Bureau of Economic Analysis, National Income and Product Accounts, table 1.2, p. 6. The data for 1927–1928 are from Romer, "World War I," table 5, p. 104.

increase of 49 percent between 1938 and 1942. By almost any standard, the growth of real GNP in the four-year periods before and after 1938 was spectacular.

It is certainly the case, however, that despite this rapid growth, output remained substantially below normal until about 1942. A simple way to estimate trend output for the 1930s is to extrapolate the average annual growth rate of real GNP between 1923 and 1927 forward from 1927. The years 1923 through 1927 were chosen for estimating normal growth because they are the four most normal years of the 1920s; this period excludes the recession and recovery of the early 1920s and the boom in 1928 and 1929. This was also a period of price stability, suggesting that output was neither abnormally high nor abnormally low. The resulting figure for normal annual real GNP growth is 3.15 percent. Figure 2 shows the log value of actual real GNP and trend GNP based on this definition of normal growth. The graph shows that GNP was about 38 percent below its trend level in 1935 and 26 percent below it in 1937. Only in 1942 did GNP return to trend.

The behavior of unemployment during the recovery from the Great Depression is roughly consistent with the behavior of real GNP. Although many scholars have rightly emphasized that the unemployment rate was still nearly 10 percent as late as 1941, it had fallen quite rapidly from its high of 25 percent in 1933.[8] It declined, for example, by more than three percentage points in both 1934 and 1936. That full employment was not reached again until 1942 is consistent with the fact that real output remained significantly below trend until that year.

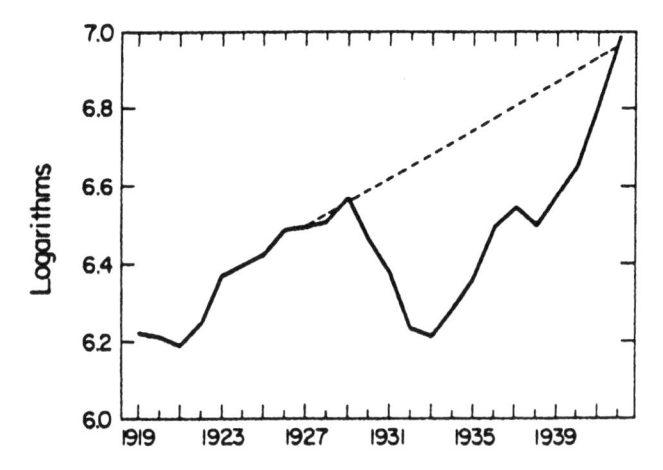

Figure 2 Actual and Trend Real Gross National Product, 1919–1942.
Note: Trend GNP, which is shown by the dashed line, is calculated by extrapolating the growth rate of real GNP between 1923 and 1927 forward from 1927. Therefore, this series does not start until 1927.
Source: The source for real GNP is the same as in Figure 1.

The effects of aggregate-demand stimulus in the recovery

To examine whether aggregate-demand stimulus can explain the high rates of real growth during the recovery phase of the Great Depression, I performed an illustrative calculation. Consider decomposing the deviation of output growth from normal into the effect of lagged deviations of monetary and fiscal changes from normal and the effect of all other factors that might influence real growth, so that

$$\text{output change}_t = \beta_m(\text{monetary change})_{t-1} + \beta_f(\text{fiscal change})_{t-1} + \varepsilon_t \quad (1)$$

where β_m and β_f are the multipliers for monetary and fiscal policy and ε_t is a residual term that includes such things as supply shocks and changes in animal spirits. This residual term also includes any tendency that the economy might have to right itself following a recession. Using annual data, this decomposition is most likely to hold with a one-year lag between policy changes and output changes because policy changes do not immediately affect real output.

Within this framework, if one measures β_m, β_f, output deviations, and policy changes, it is possible to calculate what the residual term must be in any given year. Since these yearly residual terms reflect all the factors affecting growth other than policy, they show how fast the economy would have grown (relative to normal) had monetary and fiscal changes not occurred. A comparison of the actual path of real output with what output would have been in the absence of policy changes provides a way of quantifying the importance of policy.

To apply this decomposition to the recovery phase of the Great Depression, I used as the measure of output change the deviation of the growth rate of real GNP from its average annual growth rate during the years 1923 through 1927. For the monetary policy variable I used the deviation of the annual (December to December) growth rate of M1 from its normal growth rate, where normal is again defined as the average annual growth rate between 1923 and 1927.[9] The average annual growth rate of M1 over this period was 2.88 percent. For the fiscal policy variable I used the annual change in the ratio of the real federal surplus to real GNP.[10] This measure of fiscal policy assumes that the normal change in the real federal surplus is zero.[11]

Estimates of the policy multipliers

Deriving the policy multipliers to use in the decomposition is a far more difficult task than measuring the deviation of monetary and fiscal policy from normal. One way of deriving the multipliers is to take estimates from a large postwar macroeconomic model. Another strategy is to simply posit reasonable values for these multipliers. In my later discussion of robustness, I show the results of both of these approaches. However, an alternative procedure that is more in the spirit of the exercise is to use historical evidence to identify certain years when the residual term in equation 1 was small and when the changes in monetary and fiscal policy were independent of movements in real output. If there were two such episodes, one can simply infer estimates of β_m and β_f from the decomposition itself.[12]

The recessions of 1921 and 1938 are arguably two such crucial episodes. In both cases there were large movements in real output that have been almost universally ascribed to monetary and fiscal policy decisions. Friedman and Schwartz, for example, stated that "in both cases, the subsequent decline in the money stock was associated with a severe economic decline."[13] This emphasis on monetary factors in 1921 and 1938 was echoed by W. Arthur Lewis and by Kenneth Roose.[14] Other authors assigned a much more important role to fiscal policy as the source of these two interwar downturns. Alvin Hansen, Arthur Smithies, Leonard Ayres, and Robert A. Gordon all attributed the recession of 1938 to the decline in government spending.[15] Gordon also argued that the decline in government spending after World War I and the increase in the discount rate were the two factors that helped to tip a vulnerable economy into a severe recession in 1920.[16]

Furthermore, most alternative explanations that have been advanced for these two recessions are easily disproved; there is little evidence that other factors (the ε_t in equation 1) were important in determining the behavior of real output in 1921 and 1938. For example, one explanation for the downturn in 1938 is that increases in wages due to increased unionization decreased output and investment; in short, that there was an adverse supply shock in 1937.[17] An adverse supply shock, however, should have been accompanied by rising prices. This did not occur: between 1937 and 1938 producer prices fell 9.4 percent. On the other hand, the policy hypotheses that stress a fall in aggregate demand are consistent with the observed fall in prices. The monetary explanation is also consistent with the fact that interest rates rose sharply in early 1937 and interest-sensitive spending such as construction expenditures plummeted in late 1937.

The main alternative explanation advanced for the recession of 1921 is that the tremendous pent-up demand for consumer goods that developed during and after World War I was satisfied by 1920 and firms faced a dramatic decline in sales.[18] The problem with this story is that real consumer expenditures rose 4.8 percent between 1919 and 1920 and 6.2 percent between 1920 and 1921.[19] Any spending story also conflicts with the fact that interest rates rose substantially in 1920.

One partial explanation for the behavior of real output in 1921 that is hard to dismiss is the occurrence of a positive supply shock. In a previous article I argued that the recovery of agricultural production in Europe caused prices of agricultural goods in the United States to plummet in 1920.[20] This, in turn, stimulated the production of industries that used agricultural commodities as inputs. The presence of a favorable supply shock in this episode implies that the ε_t in equation 1 for 1921 could be positive. In the discussion of robustness that follows the simple calculation of the multiplier, I show that even the inclusion of a substantial positive residual in 1921 does not change the qualitative results.

The nature of the policy changes in the years preceding the recessions of 1921 and 1938 indicates that these changes were independent of movements in the real economy: the money supply and the government surplus changed in 1920 and 1937 because of active policy decisions, not because of endogenous responses of money growth or government spending to a fall in real output. Most obviously, in 1920 it was the end of World War I that led to an enormous drop in real government spending. The magnitude of this change can be seen in the fact that the surplus-to-GNP ratio rose from −8.3 percent in 1919 to 0.5 percent in 1920.

Monetary policy changes in this episode were also quite pronounced and largely independent. According to Friedman and Schwartz, the Federal Reserve in 1919 became concerned about the lingering inflation from World War I and the postwar boom.[21] In response, the Federal Reserve raised the discount rate three-quarters of a percentage point in December. The diaries and papers of members of the Board of Governors of the Federal Reserve System that Friedman and Schwartz analyzed suggest that the Federal Reserve did not understand the lags with which monetary policy affected the economy. As a result, when the economy failed to respond immediately to the increase in interest rates, the Federal Reserve raised the discount rate another 1 1/4 percentage points in January 1920 and an additional percentage point in June 1920. Because these large increases in interest rates appear to be mainly the result of Federal Reserve inexperience, they represent independent monetary developments rather than conscious responses to the current state of the real economy.

In 1937 the tightening of fiscal policy was less dramatic, but still quite severe. In 1936 a large bonus had been paid to veterans of World War I. In 1937, not only was there no payment of this kind, but social security taxes also were collected for the first time. This increase in revenues was clearly unrelated to developments in the real economy; it reflected a conscious decision to permanently raise taxes to finance a pension system. The result of these two changes was that the surplus-to-GNP ratio rose from −4.4 percent in 1936 to −2.2 percent in 1937.

Monetary changes in 1937 were less straightforward than those in 1920, but still largely independent. Friedman and Schwartz viewed the main monetary shock as the doubling of reserve requirements in three steps between July 1936 and May 1937.[22] The Federal Reserve raised reserve requirements because it was concerned about the high level of excess reserves in 1936 and wanted to turn them into required reserves. According to Friedman and Schwartz, this action greatly decreased the money supply because banks wanted to hold excess reserves. As a result, they decreased lending so that reserves were still higher than the new required levels.[23] Friedman and Schwartz viewed the resulting change in the money supply as independent because the Federal Reserve was not responding to the real economy: it inadvertently contracted the money supply because it misunderstood the motivation of bankers.[24]

The independence of policy movements in 1920 and 1937 and the absence of additional causes of the recessions of 1921 and 1938 suggest that these two episodes can be used to estimate multipliers for monetary and fiscal policy. To do this calculation, I merely substituted the relevant data for 1921 and 1938 into equation 1 and then solved the two equation system for β_f and β_m. Table 1 shows the calculation.

Using this approach, the estimated multiplier for monetary policy is 0.823 and the estimated multiplier for fiscal policy is −0.233. The signs of the two multipliers are what would be expected. β_f is negative because the fiscal policy variable is based on the federal surplus; an increase in the fiscal policy measure is contractionary. The magnitude of the monetary policy multiplier is quite reasonable. It implies that a growth rate of M1 that is one percentage point lower than normal results in real output growth that is 0.82 percentage points lower than normal. As I describe in more detail later, this result is consistent with the effects of monetary factors found in large macromodels. The magnitude of the fiscal policy multiplier is quite small. It implies that a rise in the surplus-to-GNP ratio of one percentage point lowers the growth rate of real output relative to normal by 0.23 percentage points. The reason for this small multiplier is the fact that the deviation of

Table 1 Calculation of the Policy Multipliers.

Substituting data into equation 1 and setting ε_t equal to zero yields:

1921: $-0.0554 = \beta_m (-0.0424) + \beta_f (0.0878)$
1938: $-0.0772 = \beta_m (-0.0877) + \beta_f (0.0218)$

Solving two equations for two unknowns yields:

$$\beta_m = \frac{(-0.0554)(0.0218) - (0.0878)(-0.0772)}{(-0.0424)(0.0218) - (-0.0877)(0.0878)} = 0.823$$

$$\beta_f = \frac{-0.0772 - \beta_m(-0.0877)}{0.0218} = -0.233$$

Note: The intermediate calculations presented differ slightly from the final multipliers because of rounding.
Source: See the text.

real output growth from normal was slightly smaller in 1921 than in 1938, but the fiscal policy shock was nearly four times as large in 1920 as in 1937. Consequently, it would be very difficult to attribute most of the declines in output in 1921 and 1938 to fiscal policy.

Simulations

Armed with these multipliers, it is possible to calculate the likely effects of monetary and fiscal developments during the mid- and late 1930s. As I have set up the analysis, the multiplier times the policy measure lagged one year shows the effect of policy on the deviation of output growth from normal in a given year. If one subtracts this effect of unusual policy from the actual growth rate of real output, one is left with estimates of what the growth rate of output would have been under normal policy. Accumulating these growth rates of real output under normal policy and then adding them to the level of output in a base year yields a series of the levels of output under normal policy.

The difference between the path of actual output and the path of output under normal policy shows how much slower the recovery would have been in the absence of expansionary policy. In calculating the path of real output under normal policy I used 1933 as the base year. This path shows what output would have been under normal policy after 1933, without taking into account the fact that the Depression was probably caused to a large extent by serious policy mistakes. This procedure is appropriate because the purpose of this article is not to argue that policy did not contribute to the downturn of the early 1930s, but rather that policy was central to the recovery in the mid- and late 1930s. In calculating the effects of unusual policy, I did the analysis separately for monetary and fiscal policy. In one experiment I asked what output would have been if fiscal policy had been

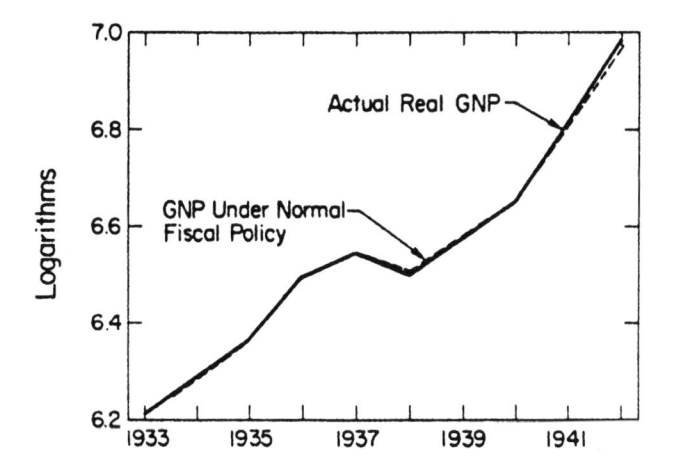

Figure 3 Actual Output and Output Under Normal Fiscal Policy, 1933–1942.
Note: The dashed line shows the path of the log-value of real GNP under the assumption that fiscal policy was at its normal level throughout the mid- and late 1930s; the solid line shows the path of actual real GNP.
Sources: The calculation of output under normal fiscal policy is described in the text. The source for real GNP is the same as in Figure 1.

normal but monetary policy had followed its actual historical path. In a second, I held monetary policy to its normal level and let fiscal policy follow its actual path.

Figure 3 shows the experiment for fiscal policy. The great similarity of actual real GNP and GNP under normal fiscal policy indicates that unusual fiscal policy contributed almost nothing to the recovery from the Great Depression. Only in 1942 is there a noticeable difference between actual and hypothetical output, and even in this year the difference is small.

The small estimated effect of fiscal policy stems in part from the fact that the multiplier based on 1921 and 1938 is small, but it is more fundamentally due to the fact that the deviations of fiscal policy from normal were not large during the 1930s. This fact can be seen in Figure 4, which shows the change in the surplus-to-GNP ratio (lagged one year). The change in this ratio in the mid-1930s was typically less than one percentage point and was actually positive in some years, indicating that fiscal policy was sometimes contractionary during the recovery. Even in 1941, the first year of a substantial wartime increase in spending, the surplus-to-GNP ratio only fell by six percentage points.

Figure 5 shows the experiment for monetary policy.[25] This time the paths for actual GNP and GNP under normal monetary policy are tremendously different. The difference in the two paths indicates that had the money growth rate been held to its usual level in the mid-1930s, real GNP in 1937 would have been nearly 25 percent lower than it actually was. By 1942 the difference between GNP under normal and actual monetary policy grows to nearly

THE GREAT DEPRESSION

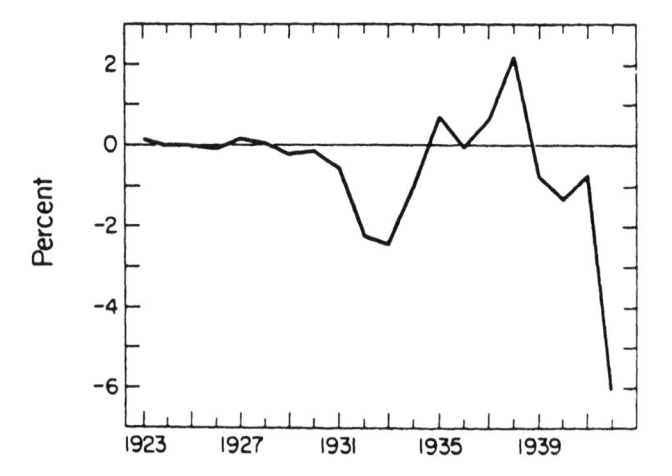

Figure 4 Changes in Surplus-to-Gross National Product Ratio, 1923–1942.
Note: The changes are shown lagged one year because this is the form in which they enter my calculation.
Sources: The surplus data are from the U.S. Department of the Treasury, Statistical Appendix, table 2, pp. 4–11. The text describes adjustments that I made to the base data. The source for real GNP is the same as in Figure 1.

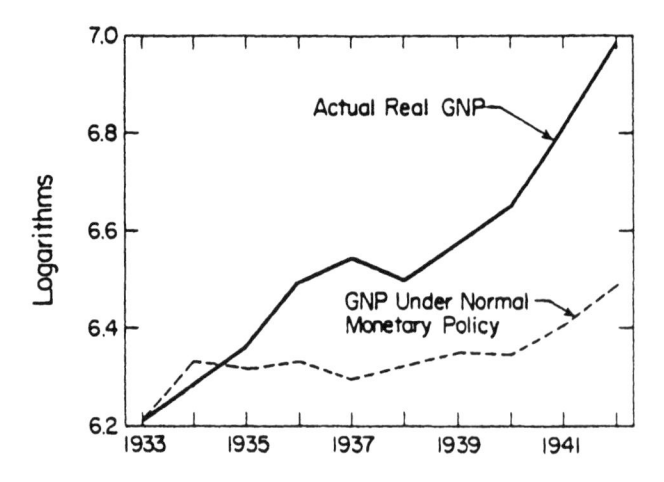

Figure 5 Actual Output and Output Under Normal Monetary Policy, 1933–1942.
Note: The dashed line shows the path of real GNP under the assumption that the money growth rate was held to its normal pre-Depression level throughout the mid- and late 1930s; the solid line shows the path of actual real GNP.
Sources: The calculation of output under normal monetary policy is described in the text. The source for real GNP is the same as in Figure 1.

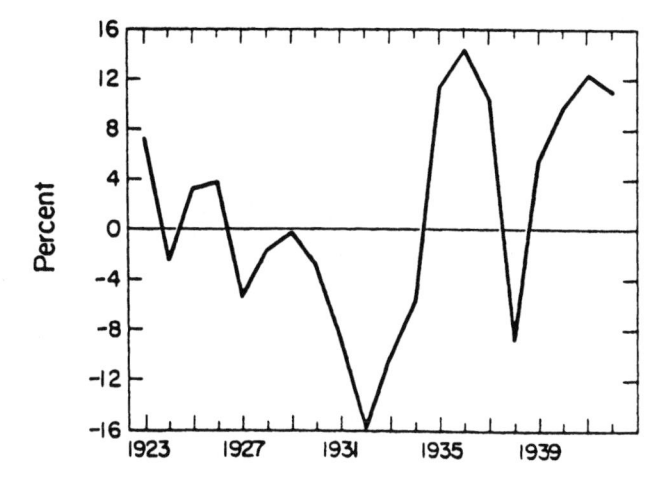

Figure 6 Deviations of Money Growth Rate from Normal, 1923–1942.
Notes: The normal money growth rate is defined as the average growth rate of M1 between 1923 and 1927. The deviations are shown lagged one year because this is the form in which they enter my calculation.
Source: The data on M1 are from Friedman and Schwartz, Monetary History, table A-1, column 7, pp. 704–34.

50 percent. These calculations suggest that monetary developments were crucial to the recovery. If money growth had been held to its normal level, the U.S. economy in 1942 would have been 50 percent below its pre-Depression trend path, rather than back to its normal level.[26]

The source of this large estimated effect of monetary developments is not hard to find. As I point out in greater detail in the following discussion, the monetary policy multiplier estimated from 1921 and 1938 is not implausibly large: it is roughly of the magnitude found in postwar macromodels. The large estimated effects of monetary developments are due to the extraordinarily high rates of money growth in the mid- and late 1930s. The monetary policy variable (lagged one year) is graphed in Figure 6. As can be seen, the deviations of the money growth rate from normal were enormous in the mid- and late 1930s. For most years these deviations were over 10 percent. It is not at all surprising, therefore, to find that had this deviation from normal been held at zero, the recovery from the Depression would have been dramatically slower.

Robustness

The results of these simulations are quite robust. Monetary policy was so expansionary during the recovery, and fiscal policy so non-expansionary, that changing the multipliers substantially would not make monetary policy unimportant and fiscal policy crucial. For example, assuming that there was a substantial positive supply shock in 1921 decreases the monetary policy multiplier and increases the fiscal policy multiplier.[27] Even with an extreme change, however, such as cutting the monetary policy multiplier in half and quadrupling the fiscal policy multiplier, real GNP in 1942 would have been roughly 25 percent lower than it actually was had monetary policy been held to its normal level during the mid- and late 1930s. This result still suggests that the aggregate-demand stimulus of monetary policy was crucial to the recovery. In the case of fiscal policy, quadrupling the multiplier leads to the conclusion that real GNP would have been 6 percent lower in 1942 than it actually was had the change in the surplus-to-GNP ratio been held to zero. This increases the apparent role of fiscal policy, but not dramatically.

Another way to evaluate the robustness of the calculations is to use policy multipliers derived from the estimation of a postwar macromodel. The Massachusetts Institute of Technology–University of Pennsylvania–Social Science Research Council (MPS) model is the main forecasting model currently used by the Federal Reserve Board. In this model, the short-run multiplier for monetary policy is 1.2, slightly larger than the multiplier derived from the 1921 and 1938 episodes; the multiplier for fiscal policy is −2.13, roughly ten times larger than that derived from the 1921 and 1938 episodes.[28]

Using the multipliers from the MPS model in place of those derived from my calculation increases the apparent importance of monetary policy—real GNP in 1942 would have been roughly 70 percent lower than it actually was had monetary policy been held to its normal course—and increases the role for fiscal policy—real GNP in 1942 would have been 14 percent lower than it actually was had fiscal policy been held to its normal level. Essentially all of this effect of fiscal policy, however, comes from the last year of the simulation; real GNP in 1941 would have been only 1 percent lower than it actually was if fiscal policy had been held to its normal level. Thus, using policy multipliers derived from a much different procedure than I used in my illustrative calculation leads to the same conclusion that monetary policy was crucial to the recovery from the Great Depression and fiscal policy was of little importance.[29]

One characteristic of most multipliers derived from large macromodels is that the effects of aggregate-demand policy on the level of real output are forced to become zero in the long run. This is certainly the case in the MPS model in which the long-run behavior of the economy is assumed to follow the predictions of a Solow growth model. In my simulations, both with my own multipliers and with those from the MPS model, I only considered the short-run multipliers and did not require that the positive effects of an expansionary aggregate-demand shock on the level of real output be eventually undone. I did this because the constraint that the long-run effects of policy are zero is simply imposed a priori in most models; available evidence indicates that the real effects of policy shifts are in fact highly persistent.[30]

Provided that we do not assume that the positive effects of expansionary policy are quickly reversed (that is, within a year or two), allowing for negative feedback effects from a policy stimulus would not substantially diminish the role of policy in generating the high real growth rates observed in the mid- and late 1930s. This is true for two reasons: in the first few years of the expansion there would have been no negative feedback effects from previous policy expansions, and there were progressively larger monetary growth rates toward the end of the recovery. Furthermore, there is no support for the view that the effects of policy shifts are counteracted rapidly. In the MPS model, for example, the effects of both fiscal and monetary shocks do not start to be counteracted substantially until twelve quarters after the shocks. Thus, even under the assumption that policy does not matter in the long run, we would still find that policy was important for the eight to ten years that encompassed the recovery phase of the Great Depression.

The source of the monetary expansion

That economic developments would have been very different in the mid- and late 1930s had money growth been held to its normal level is evident from the calculations above. But to go further and argue that aggregate-demand stimulus actually caused the recovery, it must be shown that the rapid rates of monetary growth were due to policy actions and historical accidents, and were not the result of higher output bringing forth money creation. This is easy to do.

The main way that the money supply might grow endogenously is through demand-induced changes in the money multiplier. If, in response to a boom, banks raise the deposit-to-reserve ratio and customers accept a higher deposit-to-currency ratio, a given supply of high-powered money can support a larger stock of M1. Neither of these changes, however, occurred during the recovery from the Great Depression. The deposit-to-reserve ratio fell steadily in the mid- and late 1930s, from 8.86 in January 1933 to 4.67 in December 1942. The deposit-to-currency ratio rose initially in the recovery as the banking system regained credibility, but remained fairly constant from 1935 until 1941, and then fell sharply in late 1941 and 1942.[31]

Since the behavior of both these ratios suggests that the money multiplier fell during the recovery from the Great Depression, the observed rise in M1 must have been due to even larger increases in the stock of high-powered money during this period. This increase in the stock of high-powered money was also not endogenous. There is no evidence that the Federal Reserve increased the stock of high-powered money to accommodate the higher transactions demand for money caused by increased output. Instead, the Federal Reserve maintained a policy of caution throughout the recovery and even stopped increasing Federal Reserve credit to meet seasonal demands in the mid- and late 1930s.[32]

The source of the huge increases in the U.S. money supply during the recovery was a tremendous gold inflow that began in 1933. Friedman and Schwartz stated that the "rapid rate [of growth of the money stock] in the three successive years from June 1933 to June 1936 . . . was a consequence of the gold inflow produced by the revaluation of gold plus the flight of capital to the United States. It was in no way a consequence of the contemporaneous business expansion."[33] The monetary gold stock nearly doubled between December 1933 and July 1934 and then increased at an average annual rate of nearly 15 percent between December 1934 and December 1941.[34] Arthur Bloomfield agrees with Friedman and Schwartz that "the devaluation of the dollar, for technical reasons, was . . . the direct cause of much of the heavy net gold imports of $758 million in February–March, 1934."[35] Thus, the initial gold inflow was the result of an active policy decision on the part of the Roosevelt administration.

Both these studies, however, attributed most of the continuing increases in the U.S. monetary gold stock throughout the later 1930s to political developments in Europe. Bloomfield pointed out that the continued gold inflow was caused primarily by huge net imports of foreign capital into the United States; the United States ran persistent and large capital account surpluses in the mid- and late 1930s.[36] He then argued that "probably the most important single cause of the massive movement of funds to the United States in 1934–39 as a whole was the rapid deterioration in the international political situation. The growing threat of a European war created fears of seizure or destruction of wealth by the enemy, imposition of exchange restrictions, oppressive war taxation. . . . Huge volumes of funds were consequently transferred in panic to the United States from Western European countries likely to be involved in such a conflict."[37] Friedman and Schwartz were more succinct when they concluded: "Munich and the outbreak of war in Europe were the main factors determining the U.S. money stock in those years [1938–1941], as Hitler and the gold miners had been in 1934 to 1936."[38]

Finally, the Roosevelt Administration's decisions to devalue and not to sterilize the gold inflow were clearly not endogenous. Barrie Wigmore showed that Roosevelt spoke favorably of devaluation in January 1933.[39] Since this was many months before recovery commenced, Roosevelt could not have been responding to real growth. Indeed, G. Griffith Johnson's analysis of the Roosevelt administration's gold policy suggested that, if anything, the Treasury was trying to counteract the Depression through easy money, rather than trying to accommodate the recovery.[40] Johnson and Wigmore also showed that Roosevelt's desire to encourage a gold inflow was not based on a conventional view of the monetary transmission mechanism, but rather on the view that devaluation would directly raise prices and reflation would directly stimulate recovery.[41]

The fact that the continuing gold inflow of the mid-1930s was not sterilized appears to be partly the result of technical problems with the sterilization process. The Gold Reserve Act of 1934 set up a stabilization fund and made explicit the role of the Treasury in intervening in the foreign exchange market. However, because the stabilization fund was endowed only with gold, it was technically able only to counteract a gold outflow, not a gold inflow.[42] As a result, sterilization would have required an active decision to change the new operating procedures. Such a decision was not made because Roosevelt believed that an unsterilized gold inflow would stimulate the economy through reflation.

The devaluation and the absence of sterilization thus appear to have been the result of active policy decisions and a lack of understanding about the process of exchange market intervention. To the degree that active policy was involved, it was clearly aimed at encouraging recovery, not simply at responding to a recovery that was already under way. Combined with the fact that political instability caused much of the gold inflow in the late 1930s, these findings indicate that the increase in the money supply in the recovery phase of the Great Depression was not endogenous. Since the simulation results showed that the large deviations of money growth rates from normal account for much of the recovery of real output between 1933 and 1937 and between 1938 and 1942, it is possible to conclude that independent monetary developments account for the bulk of the recovery from the Great Depression in the United States.

The transmission mechanism

The argument that monetary developments were the source of the recovery can be made more plausible by identifying the transmission mechanism. It is generally assumed that the usual way an increase in the money supply stimulates the economy is through a decline in interest rates. An increase in the money stock lowers nominal interest rates; with fixed or increasing expected inflation, this decline in nominal rates implies a decline in real interest rates. A fall in real interest rates stimulates purchases of plant and equipment and durable consumer goods by lowering the cost of borrowing and by reducing the opportunity cost of spending.

For this mechanism to have been operating in the mid- and late 1930s, the rapid money growth could not have been immediately and fully offset by increases in wages and prices. If wages and prices increased as rapidly or more rapidly than the money supply, real balances would not have increased and there would have been no pressure on nominal interest rates. The real money supply did in fact rise at a very rapid rate during the second half of the 1930s: M1 deflated by the wholesale price index increased by 27 percent between December 1933 and December 1936 and by 56 percent between December 1937 and December 1942.[43] This suggests that prices and wages did not fully adjust to the rapid rates of money growth. The fact that nominal interest rates fell during the recovery is consistent with this increase in real balances. The commercial paper rate, for example, fell from an average value of 2.73 in 1932 to 0.75 in 1936.[44]

For the interest-rate transmission mechanism to have been operating in the mid- and late 1930s, it would also have to have been the case that the rapid money growth rates generated expectations of inflation. By 1933 nominal interest rates were already so low that there was little scope for a monetary expansion to lower nominal rates further. Therefore, the main way that the monetary expansion could stimulate the economy was by generating expectations of inflation and thus causing a reduction in real interest rates. Such expectations of inflation are not inconsistent with the existence of the wage and price inertia. Indeed, a very plausible explanation is that the rapid money growth rates did not immediately increase wages and prices by an equivalent amount because of internal labor markets, government regulations, or managerial inertia.[45] However, consumers and investors realized that prices would have to rise eventually and therefore expected inflation over the not-too-distant horizon.

Regression estimates of the ex ante real interest rate suggest that this condition is met in the recovery phase of the Great Depression. Frederic Mishkin showed using the Fisher identity that the difference between the ex ante real rate that we want to know and the ex post real rate that we observe is unanticipated inflation.[46] Under the assumption of rational expectations, the expectation of unanticipated inflation using information available at the time the forecast is made is zero. Therefore, if one regresses the ex post real rate on current and lagged information, the fitted values provide estimates of the ex ante real rate.

To apply this procedure I first calculated ex post real rates by subtracting the change in the producer price index over the following quarter (at an annual rate) from the four-to-six month commercial paper rate.[47] These ex post real rates, along with the nominal commercial paper rate, are shown in Figure 7. I then regressed the ex post real rates on the current value and four quarterly lags of the monetary policy variable described in the multiplier calculations (but disaggregated to quarterly values), the percentage change in industrial production, inflation, and the level of the nominal commercial paper rate. To account for possible seasonal variation I also included a constant term and three quarterly dummy variables. I ran this regression over the sample period 1923:1 to 1942:2.[48]

The results are shown in Table 2. The explanatory variables I included in the regression explain a substantial fraction of the total variation in the ex post real interest rate: the R^2 of the regression is .52. Of the individual explanatory variables, the one of most interest is the monetary policy variable. If the conventional transmission mechanism was operating, the monetary policy variable should be negatively correlated with the ex post real rate. As can be seen, this is clearly the case: the first lag of the monetary policy variable enters the regression with a coefficient of −0.463 and has a t-statistic of −3.02.

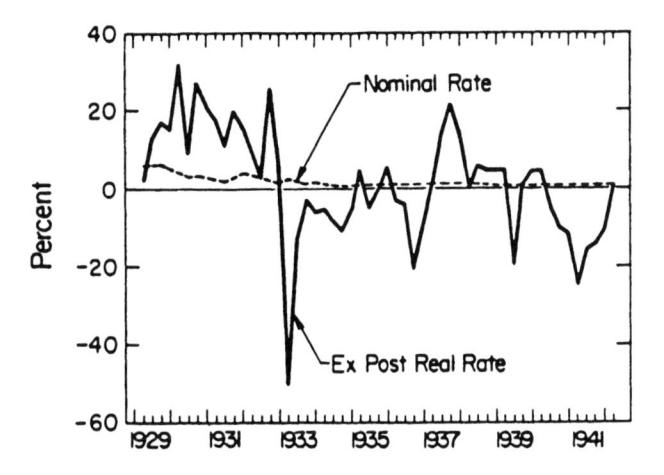

Figure 7 Nominal and Ex Post Real Commercial Paper Rates, 1929–1942.
Note: The data are quarterly observations.
Sources: The commercial paper rate data are from the U.S. Board of Governors of the Federal Reserve System, Banking and Monetary Statistics, 1943, pp. 448–51, and 1976, p. 674. The calculation of the ex post real rate is described in the text.

The fitted values of the regression, which provide an estimate of the ex ante real rate, are graphed in Figure 8. These estimates suggest that ex ante real rates dropped precipitously at the start of the monetary expansion in 1933 and remained low or negative for the rest of the decade (except for the rise during the monetary contraction of 1937/38).[49] Indeed, the drop in real rates between the contractionary and expansionary phases of the Great Depression is remarkable: ex ante real rates fell from values often over 15 percent in the early 1930s to values typically between −5 and −10 percent in the mid-1930s and early 1940s. While one cannot be sure that actual ex ante real rates dropped the same amount as these estimates or that the drop was caused by monetary developments, the regression results certainly suggest that the expansionary monetary developments of the mid- and late 1930s did have a substantial impact on real interest rates.[50] Thus, this aspect of the conventional monetary transmission mechanism appears to have been operating in the recovery phase of the Great Depression.

For expansionary monetary developments to have stimulated the economy in the mid- and late 1930s, real interest rates not only had to fall, but investment and other types of interest-sensitive spending had to respond positively to this drop. Figure 9 shows the annual percentage changes in real total fixed investment and Figure 10 shows the changes in real consumer expenditures on durable goods.[51] In both figures the annual averages of the estimates of the ex ante real interest rate are also shown. These graphs suggest that there was a very strong negative relationship between real interest rates and the percentage change in spending in the mid- and late 1930s. Fixed investment

Table 2 Regression Used to Estimate Ex Ante Real Interest Rates.

Explanatory Variable	Coefficient	T-Statistic
Monetary Policy Variable		
Lag 0	0.044	0.29
Lag 1	−0.463	−3.02
Lag 2	0.182	1.09
Lag 3	−0.196	−1.20
Lag 4	0.352	2.30
Nominal Commercial Paper Rate		
Lag 0	0.834	0.25
Lag 1	0.191	0.04
Lag 2	1.181	0.22
Lag 3	0.954	0.18
Lag 4	−1.079	−0.32
Inflation Rate		
Lag 0	−0.396	−2.54
Lag 1	0.129	0.81
Lag 2	−0.014	−0.09
Lag 3	0.111	0.72
Lag 4	−0.031	−0.21
Change in Industrial Production		
Lag 0	−0.026	−0.47
Lag 1	0.045	0.78
Lag 2	−0.120	−2.00
Lag 3	0.012	0.22
Lag 4	−0.036	−0.67
Quarterly Dummy Variables		
Quarter 2	1.497	0.27
Quarter 3	−6.961	−1.76
Quarter 4	5.271	0.97
Constant	−1.804	−0.44

Notes: The dependent variable is the quarterly ex post real interest rate. The sample period used in the estimation is 1923:1 to 1942:2. The R^2 of the regression is .52.
Source: See the text.

and the consumption of durable goods both turned upward soon after the plunge in real rates in 1933. Over the next four years, real rates remained negative and spending grew rapidly. In 1938 the recovery was interrupted, as real rates turned substantially positive and spending fell sharply. Starting in 1939 real rates fell again, and the rapid growth of spending resumed.

The relationship between spending and interest rates can be quantified by computing the correlations between the percentage change in fixed investment or consumer spending on durables and the level of the ex ante real rate. Table 3 shows these correlations estimated over the period 1934 to 1941. The table shows that there is a strong negative contemporaneous correlation between interest rates and the growth rates of investment and consumer spending on durable goods during the recovery phase of the Great Depression.

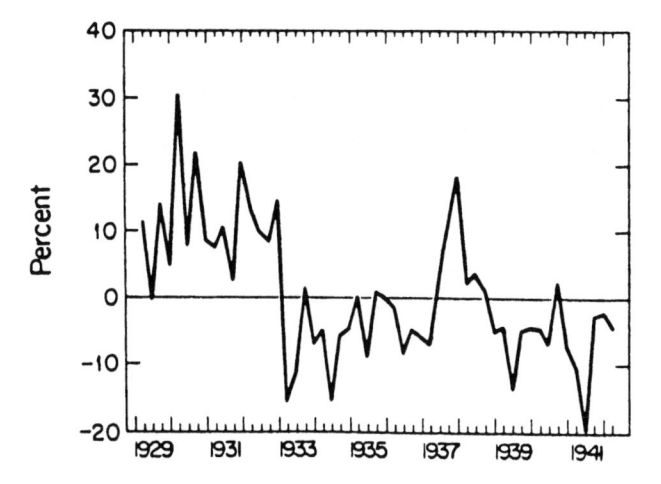

Figure 8 Ex Ante Real Commercial Paper Rates, 1929–1942.
Note: The data are quarterly observations.
Source: The regression used to estimate ex ante real rates is given in Table 2 and described in the text.

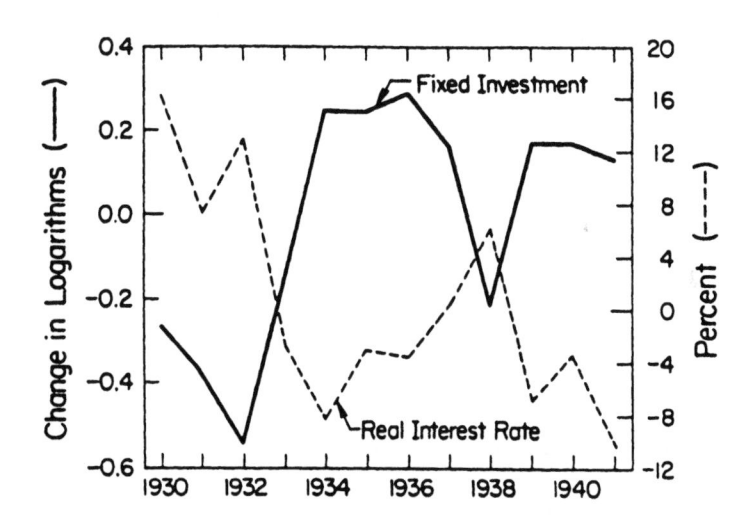

Figure 9 Real Fixed Investment and Ex Ante Real Rates, 1930–1941.
Sources: Data on real fixed investment are from the U.S. Bureau of Economic Analysis, National Income and Product Accounts, table 1.2, p. 6. The estimation of ex ante real rates is described in the text.

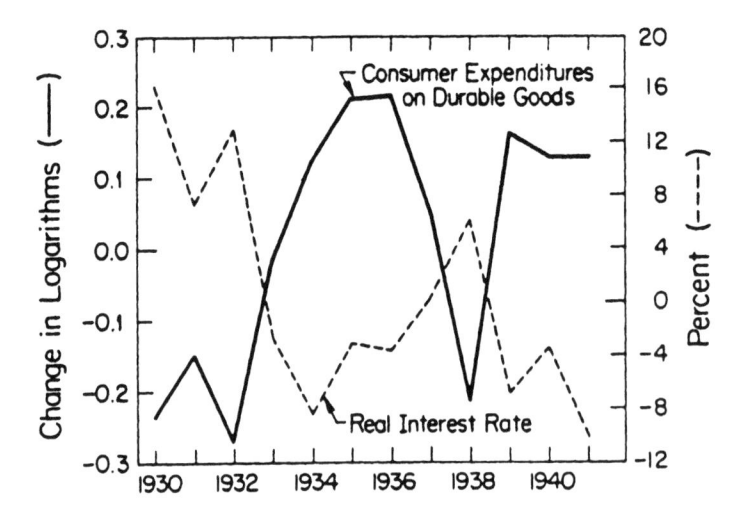

Figure 10 Real Consumer Expenditures on Durable Goods and Ex Ante Real Rates, 1930–1941.
Sources: Data on real consumer expenditures on durable goods are from the U.S. Bureau of Economic Analysis, National Income and Product Accounts, table 1.2, p. 6. The estimation of ex ante real rates is described in the text.

Table 3 Correlation Between Spending and Real Interest Rates, 1934–1941.

	Percentage Change in Real Fixed Investment	*Percentage Change in Real Consumer Expenditures on Durable Goods*
Ex Ante Real Rate		
Lag 0	−0.687	−0.746
Lag 1	−0.292	−0.238
Lag 2	−0.052	−0.030

Sources: The sources are the same as for Figures 9 and 10.

There is also a moderately strong negative correlation between the percentage change in spending and interest rates lagged one year.

A negative relationship also exists between quarterly data on construction contracts and real interest rates. The contracts data show the floor space of new buildings for which contracts were drawn up during the quarter.[52] One might reasonably expect the volume of such contracts to respond quickly to movements in interest rates because they involved planned rather than actual expenditures. And indeed, over the period 1933:2 to 1942:2 the contemporaneous correlation between the percentage change in construction contracts and the ex ante real rate is −0.4.[53] The low interest rates of the mid-1930s and the early 1940s correspond to periods of rapid increase in construction contracts.

These correlations cannot prove that the fall in interest rates caused the surge in investment, durable goods expenditures, and construction. They do, however, suggest that there is no obvious evidence that the conventional transmission mechanism for monetary developments failed to operate during the mid- and late 1930s. One piece of evidence that suggests a more causal link between the fall in interest rates and the recovery is the lag in the rebound of consumer expenditures on services compared with those on durables. Expenditures on durables increased between 1933 and 1934, but real consumer expenditures on services did not turn around until 1935. This suggests that it was not a surge of optimism that was pulling up all types of consumer expenditures in 1934, but rather some force, such as a fall in interest rates, that was operating primarily on durable goods.[54]

Conclusions

Monetary developments were a crucial source of the recovery of the U.S. economy from the Great Depression. Fiscal policy, in contrast, contributed almost nothing to the recovery before 1942. The very rapid growth of the money supply beginning in 1933 appears to have lowered real interest rates and stimulated investment spending just as a conventional model of the transmission mechanism would predict. The money supply grew rapidly in the mid- and late 1930s because of a huge unsterilized gold inflow to the United States. Although the later gold inflow was mainly due to political developments in Europe, the largest inflow occurred immediately following the revaluation of gold mandated by the Roosevelt administration in 1934. Thus, the gold inflow was due partly to historical accident and partly to policy. The decision to let the gold inflow swell the U.S. money supply was also, at least in part, an independent policy choice. The Roosevelt administration chose not to sterilize the gold inflow because it hoped that an increase in the monetary gold stock would stimulate the depressed economy.

That monetary developments were very important, whereas fiscal policy was of little consequence even as late as 1942, suggests an interesting twist on the usual view that World War II caused, or at least accelerated, the recovery from the Great Depression. Since the economy was essentially back to its trend level before the fiscal stimulus started in earnest, it would be difficult to argue that the changes in government spending caused by the war were a major factor in the recovery. However, Bloomfield's and Friedman and Schwartz's analyses suggested that the U.S. money supply rose dramatically after war was declared in Europe because capital flight from countries involved in the conflict swelled the U.S. gold inflow. In this way, the war may have aided the recovery after 1938 by causing the U.S. money supply to grow rapidly. Thus, World War II may indeed have helped to end the

Great Depression in the United States, but its expansionary benefits worked initially through monetary developments rather than through fiscal policy.

The finding that monetary developments were crucial to the recovery confirms or complements a number of analyses of the end of the Great Depression. Most obviously, it supports Friedman and Schwartz's view that monetary developments were very important during the 1930s. It suggests, however, that Friedman and Schwartz's emphasis on the inaction of the Federal Reserve after 1933 is somewhat misplaced. What mattered is that the money supply grew rapidly; the fact that this rise was orchestrated by the Treasury rather than the Federal Reserve is of secondary importance. The finding that fiscal policy contributed little to the recovery echoes Brown's finding that fiscal policy was not obviously expansionary during the mid-1930s.

My analysis also supports studies that emphasize the devaluation of 1933/34 as the engine of recovery. Peter Temin and Wigmore argued that the devaluation signalled the end of a deflationary monetary regime and that this change in regime was crucial to improving expectations.[55] In this explanation it was the change in expectations that brought about the turning point in the spring of 1933. My work bolsters Temin and Wigmore's conclusion by showing that the deflationary regime was indeed replaced by a very inflationary monetary policy. This may explain why the regime shift was viewed as credible. More importantly, it can explain why the initial recovery was followed by continued rapid expansion. Without actual inflation and actual declines in real interest rates, the recovery stimulated by a change in expectations would almost surely have been short-lived. In the same way, this article also bolsters the argument of Barry Eichengreen and Jeffrey Sachs that devaluation can stimulate recovery by allowing expansionary monetary policy.[56] It shows that in the case of the United States, devaluation was indeed followed by salutary increases in the money supply.

On the other hand, my findings appear to dispute studies that suggest that the recovery from the Great Depression was due to the self-corrective powers of the U.S. economy in the 1930s. I find that aggregate-demand stimulus was the main source of the recovery from the Great Depression. Thus, the Great Depression does not provide evidence that large shocks are rapidly undone by the forces of mean reversion. Rather, it suggests that large falls in aggregate demand are sometimes followed by large rises, the combination of which leaves the economy back on trend.

Notes

Michael Bernstein, Barry Eichengreen, Robert Gordon, Richard Grossman, Frederic Mishkin, David Romer, Peter Temin, Thomas Weiss, David Wilcox, and two anonymous referees provided extremely helpful comments and suggestions. The research was supported by the National Science Foundation and the Alfred P. Sloan Foundation.

WHAT ENDED THE GREAT DEPRESSION?

1. Temin and Wigmore, "End of One Big Deflation," for example, provided a convincing explanation for the turning point in 1933 but did not analyze the process of recovery after 1934. A notable exception to this usual pattern is Bernstein, *Great Depression*, which analyzed the importance of structural changes throughout the recovery period.
2. Brown, "Fiscal Policy," pp. 863–66.
3. Friedman and Schwartz, *Monetary History*, p. 511.
4. Bernanke and Parkinson, "Unemployment, Inflation, and Wages," p. 212.
5. De Long and Summers, "How Does Macroeconomic Policy?" p. 467.
6. U.S. Bureau of Economic Analysis, *National Income and Product Accounts*, table 1.2, p. 6.
7. Romer, "World War I," table 5, p. 104.
8. The unemployment statistics are from Lebergott, *Manpower*, table A-3, p. 512. Darby, "Three-and-a-Half Million," argued that the return of unemployment to its full employment level was significantly more rapid if one counts workers on public works jobs as employed. Margo, "Interwar Unemployment," concluded from an analysis of the 1940 census data that at least some of Darby's correction was warranted.
9. The data on M1 are from Friedman and Schwartz, *Monetary History*, table A-1, column 7, pp. 704–34. An alternative measure of monetary policy that might be considered is the deviation of real money growth from normal. However, changes in nominal money are what shift the aggregate-demand function; changes in real money result from the interaction of aggregate-demand and aggregate-supply movements. Since the purpose of this paper is to isolate the effects of aggregate-demand stimulus, it is appropriate to use a measure of monetary policy that only reflects changes in demand.
10. The surplus data are from the U.S. Department of the Treasury, *Statistical Appendix*, table 2, pp. 4–11, and are based on the administrative budget. Because these data are for fiscal years, I converted them to a calendar-year basis by averaging the observations for a given year and the subsequent year. The data were deflated using the implicit price deflator for GNP. The deflator series and the real GNP series for 1929 to 1942 are from the U.S. Bureau of Economic Analysis, *National Income and Product Accounts*; data for 1919 to 1928 are from Romer, "World War I." I used the administrative budget data instead of the NIPA surplus data because they are available on a consistent basis for the entire interwar era. While the two surplus series differ substantially in some years, the gross movements in the series are generally similar. I divided the surplus by GNP to scale the variable relative to the economy.
11. In place of the actual surplus-to-GNP ratio, the full-employment surplus-to-GNP ratio could be used. I did not use this variable because it treats a decline in revenues caused by a decline in income as normal rather than as an activist policy. This is inappropriate for the prewar and interwar eras, when raising taxes in recessions was usually preferred to letting the budget slip seriously into deficit. However, the differences between the full-employment surplus and the actual surplus were so small even in the worst years of the Depression that the two measures yield similar results. Another possible measure of fiscal policy is the weighted surplus, which takes into account the fact that a surplus caused by changes in taxes and transfers will have a different impact than a surplus caused by a change in government purchases. Blinder and Solow, "Analytical Foundations," showed that the practical effects of such weighting are typically small and sensitive to model specification and the time horizon considered.

THE GREAT DEPRESSION

12 This method of deriving rough estimates of the effects of policy is an example of the narrative approach described in Romer and Romer, "Does Monetary Policy Matter?"
13 Friedman and Schwartz, *Monetary History*, p. 678.
14 Lewis, *Economic Survey*, pp. 19–20; and Roose, *Economics of Recession*, p. 239.
15 Hansen, *Full Recovery*; Smithies, "American Economy"; Ayres, *Turning Points*; and Gordon, *Economic Instability*.
16 Gordon, *Economic Instability*, p. 20.
17 See, for example, Roose, *Economics of Recession*, p. 239.
18 See, for example, Lewis, *Economic Survey*, p. 19.
19 The consumption data are from Kendrick, *Productivity Trends*, table A-IIa, p. 294.
20 Romer, "World War I."
21 Friedman and Schwartz, *Monetary History*, pp. 221–39.
22 Ibid., pp. 543–45.
23 The fact that interest rates rose substantially in 1937 adds credence to the view that lending fell because banks restricted loans and not because the demand for loans declined.
24 In addition to the change in reserve requirements, the Treasury in 1936 began sterilizing the gold inflow. This resulted in a substantial slowing in the growth rate, though not an actual decline, of the stock of high-powered money. This switch to sterilization appears to be part of the same policy mistake that led to the increase in reserve requirements. According to Chandler, *America's Greatest Depression*, pp. 177–181, the Treasury undertook the sterilization at the behest of the Federal Reserve, which feared that an unsterilized gold inflow would exacerbate the excess reserves problem. Chandler cited as evidence that the Treasury did not mean to affect the money supply the fact that they were greatly concerned by the resulting rise in interest rates in 1937.
25 McCallum, "Could a Monetary Base Rule?" also used a simulation approach to analyze the effects of monetary factors in the 1930s. McCallum's focus, however, was on whether a monetary base rule could have prevented the Great Depression, rather than on whether actual money growth fueled the recovery.
26 One could start the simulations in 1929 to estimate the role of monetary developments in causing the Depression. While this procedure is not strictly correct, because some of the monetary developments in the early 1930s were clearly endogenous, the results confirm the conventional wisdom: monetary forces had little effect during the onset of the Great Depression in 1929 and 1930, but were the crucial cause of the deepening of the Depression in 1931 and 1932.
27 The assumption that ε_t in equation 1 is large and positive can be included in the calculation shown in Table 1 by simply subtracting the residual from the change in output in 1921. This reflects the fact that in the absence of the supply shock, the effect of the monetary and fiscal contraction would have been larger. An increase in the effective contraction of GNP in 1921 would decrease the estimate of β_m and increase the estimate of β_f. For example, if ε_t in 1921 were 0.0554, then the change in real GNP less the supply shock would be -0.1108, double the actual change in real GNP. Redoing the calculation with this change results in a monetary policy multiplier of 0.644 and a fiscal policy multiplier of -0.951.
28 These multipliers are reported in the U.S. Board of Governors of the Federal Reserve System, "Structure and Uses of the MPS Quarterly Econometric Model," tables 1 and 2. The monetary policy shock used in the MPS simulation is a permanent increase in the level of M1 of 1 percent over the projected baseline. This is equivalent to the shock I considered in my simulations, which is a one-time deviation

in the growth rate of M1 from its normal growth rate. I used the MPS multiplier derived from the full-model response (case 3 of table 2). The fiscal shock used in the MPS simulation is a permanent increase in the purchases of the federal government by 1 percent of real GNP over the baseline projection. This differs from the shock I considered, which is a change in the surplus-to-GNP ratio, because tax revenues will rise in response to the induced increase in GNP. To make the MPS multiplier consistent with my measure of fiscal policy, I assumed the marginal tax rate to be 0.3 and then calculated the change in the surplus-to-GNP ratio that corresponded to a 1 percent increase in federal purchases. The MPS multiplier that I adjusted in this way is based on the full-model response, with M1 fixed (case 4 of table 1).

29. Weinstein, "Some Macroeconomic Impacts," performed a similar calculation for monetary policy using multipliers derived from the Hickman-Cohen model and found a large potential effect of the monetary expansion in 1934 and 1935. However, he emphasized that the National Industrial Recovery Act acted as a negative supply shock and counteracted the monetary expansion. While the NIRA may indeed have stunted the recovery somewhat, it does not follow from this that monetary policy was unimportant to the recovery. In the absence of the monetary expansion, the supply shock could have led to continued decline rather than to the rapid growth of real output that actually occurred.
30. See, for example, Romer and Romer, "Does Monetary Policy Matter?"
31. The data are from Friedman and Schwartz, *Monetary History*, table B-3, pp. 799–808.
32. Ibid., pp. 511–14.
33. Ibid., p. 544.
34. The data are from Chandler, *America's Greatest Depression*, p. 162.
35. Bloomfield, *Capital Imports*, p. 142.
36. According to Bloomfield, *Capital Imports*, p. 269, the United States also ran a small current account surplus in every year except 1936.
37. Ibid., pp. 24–25.
38. Friedman and Schwartz, *Monetary History*, p. 545.
39. Wigmore, "Was the Bank Holiday of 1933?" p. 743.
40. Johnson, *Treasury and Monetary Policy*, pp. 9–28.
41. Johnson, *Treasury and Monetary Policy*, pp. 14–16; and Wigmore, "Was the Bank Holiday of 1933?" p. 743.
42. Johnson, *Treasury and Monetary Policy*, pp. 92–114.
43. To calculate real money I subtracted the logarithm of the producer price index (PPI) from the logarithm of M1. The data on the PPI are from the U.S. Bureau of Labor Statistics, *Historical Data*. Because M1 is only available seasonally adjusted, I also seasonally adjusted the PPI by regressing it on monthly dummy variables and a trend.
44. The commercial paper rate data are from the U.S. Board of Governors of the Federal Reserve System, *Banking and Monetary Statistics*, 1943, pp. 448–51, and 1976, p. 674. They cover four- to six-month prime commercial paper and are not seasonally adjusted.
45. O'Brien, "A Behavioral Explanation," provided one such explanation for wage rigidity during the 1930s.
46. Mishkin, "The Real Interest Rate."
47. In this calculation neither series was seasonally adjusted.
48. The monetary policy variable was disaggregated by converting the quarterly growth rates of M1 during the recovery to annual rates and then subtracting off the average annual growth rate of M1 in the mid-1920s. The industrial production

series is from the U.S. Board of Governors of the Federal Reserve System, *Industrial Production*, table A. 11, p. 303.
49 The estimates are strikingly robust to variations in the specification of the regression. I tried many variants of the basic regression, such as excluding contemporaneous values of the explanatory variables, extending the sample period to include 1921, and leaving out the seasonal dummy variables. None of these changes noticeably altered the estimates of the ex ante real rate.
50 Some of the inflation in 1933 and 1934 could have been due to the NIRA, which encouraged collusion aimed at raising prices, rather than to monetary policy. However, the NIRA was declared unconstitutional in 1935 and its policies were ones that would tend to cause a one-time jump in the price level rather than continued inflation. Thus, though some of the initial fall in real interest rates could have been due to the NIRA, the continued negative real rates in the mid- and late 1930s must have been due to other causes.
51 These data are from the U.S. Bureau of Economic Analysis, *National Income and Product Accounts*, table 1.2, p. 6.
52 The Dodge construction contract series for residential, commercial, and industrial structures is available in Lipsey and Preston, *Source Book*, series A8, p. 73; series A17, pp. 95–96; and series A19, pp. 100–101. I used the version that shows the floor space of each type of building without seasonal adjustment. The data for 27 states was spliced onto data for 37 states in 1925. I seasonally adjusted the series by regressing the logarithm of contracts on a trend, a constant, and three quarterly dummy variables.
53 For this calculation, I seasonally adjusted the ex ante real interest rate series by regressing it on a constant and three quarterly dummy variables.
54 The conventional monetary transmission mechanism need not have been the only way that expansionary monetary developments stimulated real growth during the mid- and late 1930s. Recent studies, such as Bernanke, "Nonmonetary Effects," have emphasized that debt-deflation could have been an important source of weakness in the banking sector, and that banking failures could have hurt real output by reducing the amount of credit intermediation. If this was indeed the case, then the inflation generated by the tremendous increase in the money supply starting in 1933 could have had a beneficial effect on the financial system. By reducing the real value of outstanding debts, the inflation may have strengthened the solvency of banks and businesses and hastened the recovery of the financial system.
55 Temin and Wigmore, "End of One Big Deflation." The importance of devaluation is also discussed in Temin, *Lessons from the Great Depression*.
56 Eichengreen and Sachs, "Exchange Rates."

References

Ayres, Leonard P., *Turning Points in Business Cycles* (New York, 1939).
Bernanke, Ben S., "Nonmonetary Effects of the Financial Crisis in the Propagation of the Great Depression," *American Economic Review*, 73 (June 1983), pp. 257–76.
Bernanke, Ben S., and Martin S. Parkinson, "Unemployment, Inflation, and Wages in the American Depression: Are There Lessons for Europe?" *American Economic Review*, 79 (May 1989), pp. 210–14.
Bernstein, Michael A., *The Great Depression* (New York, 1987).
Blinder, Alan S., and Robert M. Solow, "Analytical Foundations of Fiscal Policy," in *The Economics of Public Finance*, Brookings Institution Studies in Government Finance (Washington, DC, 1974), pp. 3–115.

Bloomfield, Arthur I., *Capital Imports and the American Balance of Payments, 1934–39* (Chicago, 1950).

Brown, E. Cary, "Fiscal Policy in the 'Thirties: A Reappraisal," *American Economic Review*, 46 (Dec. 1956), pp. 857–79.

Chandler, Lester V., *America's Greatest Depression, 1929–1941* (New York, 1970).

Darby, Michael, "Three-and-a-Half Million U.S. Employees Have Been Mislaid: Or, an Explanation of Unemployment 1934–1941," *Journal of Political Economy*, 84 (Feb. 1976), pp. 1–16.

De Long, J. Bradford, and Lawrence H. Summers, "How Does Macroeconomic Policy Affect Output?" *Brookings Papers on Economic Activity* (1988:2), pp. 433–80.

Eichengreen, Barry, and Jeffrey Sachs, "Exchange Rates and Economic Recovery in the 1930s," this JOURNAL, 45 (Dec. 1985), pp. 925–46.

Friedman, Milton, and Anna J. Schwartz, *A Monetary History of the United States, 1867–1960* (Princeton, 1963).

Gordon, Robert Aaron, *Economic Instability and Growth: The American Record* (New York, 1974).

Hansen, Alvin, *Full Recovery or Stagnation?* (New York, 1938).

Johnson, G. Griffith, *The Treasury and Monetary Policy, 1933–1938* (Cambridge, MA, 1939).

Kendrick, John W., *Productivity Trends in the United States* (Princeton, 1961).

Lebergott, Stanley, *Manpower in Economic Growth: The Record Since 1800* (New York, 1964).

Lewis, W. Arthur, *Economic Survey, 1919–1939* (London, 1949).

Lipsey, Robert E., and Doris Preston, *Source Book of Statistics Related to Construction* (New York, 1966).

Margo, Robert, "Interwar Unemployment in the United States: Evidence from the 1940 Census Sample," in Barry Eichengreen and T. J. Hatton, eds., *Interwar Unemployment in International Perspective* (Dordrecht, 1988), pp. 325–52.

McCallum, Bennett T., "Could A Monetary Base Rule Have Prevented the Great Depression?" *Journal of Monetary Economics*, 26 (Aug. 1990), pp. 3–26.

Mishkin, Frederic, "The Real Interest Rate: An Empirical Investigation," in Karl Brunner and Alan Meltzer, eds., *The Costs and Consequences of Inflation*, Carnegie-Rochester Conference Series on Public Policy, vol. 15 (Amsterdam, 1981), pp. 151–200.

O'Brien, Anthony Patrick, "A Behavioral Explanation for Nominal Wage Rigidity During the Great Depression," *Quarterly Journal of Economics*, 104 (Nov. 1989), pp. 719–35.

Romer, Christina D., "World War I and the Postwar Depression: A Reinterpretation Based on Alternative Estimates of GNP," *Journal of Monetary Economics*, 22 (July 1988), pp. 91–115.

Romer, Christina D., and David H. Romer, "Does Monetary Policy Matter? A New Test in the Spirit of Friedman and Schwartz," *NBER Macroeconomics Annual*, 4 (1989), pp. 121–70.

Roose, Kenneth D., *The Economics of Recession and Revival* (New Haven, 1954).

Smithies, Arthur, "The American Economy in the Thirties," *American Economic Review*, 36 (May 1946), pp. 11–27.

Temin, Peter, *Lessons from the Great Depression* (Cambridge, MA, 1989).

Temin, Peter, and Barrie Wigmore, "The End of One Big Deflation," *Explorations in Economic History*, 27 (Oct. 1990), pp. 483–502.
U.S. Board of Governors of the Federal Reserve System, *Banking and Monetary Statistics* (Washington, DC, 1943 and 1976).
U.S. Board of Governors of the Federal Reserve System, *Industrial Production* (Washington, DC, 1986).
U.S. Board of Governors of the Federal Reserve System, "Structure and Uses of the MPS Quarterly Econometric Model of the United States," *Federal Reserve Bulletin*, 73 (Feb. 1987), pp. 93–109.
U.S. Bureau of Economic Analysis, *The National Income and Product Accounts, 1929–1982* (Washington, DC, 1986).
U.S. Bureau of Labor Statistics, *Historical Data on the Producer Price Index* (Microfiche, Washington, DC, 1986).
U.S. Department of the Treasury, *Statistical Appendix to the Annual Report of the Secretary of the Treasury on the State of the Finances* (Washington, DC, 1979).
Weinstein, Michael, "Some Macroeconomic Impacts of the National Industrial Recovery Act, 1933–1935," in Karl Brunner, ed., *The Great Depression Revisited* (Boston, 1981), pp. 262–81.
Wigmore, Barrie A., "Was the Bank Holiday of 1933 Caused by a Run on the Dollar?" this JOURNAL, 47 (Sept. 1987), pp. 739–55.